TERM PAPER
RESOURCE GUIDE
TO LATINO HISTORY

**Recent Titles in
Term Paper Resource Guides**

TERM PAPER RESOURCE GUIDE TO LATINO HISTORY

Michael P. Moreno and Kristin C. Brunnemer

Term Paper Resource Guides

GREENWOOD

AN IMPRINT OF ABC-CLIO, LLC
Santa Barbara, California • Denver, Colorado • Oxford, England

Library of Congress Cataloging-in-Publication Data

Moreno, Michael P.
  Term paper resource guide to Latino history / Michael P. Moreno and Kristin C. Brunnemer.
    p. cm. — (Term paper resource guides)
  Includes bibliographical references and index.
  ISBN 978-0-313-37932-1 (hard copy : alk. paper)—ISBN 978-0-313-37933-8 (ebook)
1. Hispanic Americans—History. 2. Hispanic Americans—History—Sources. 3. Academic writing—Handbooks, manuals, etc. 4. Report writing—Handbooks, manuals, etc. I. Brunnemer, Kristin C. II. Title.
  E184.S75M668   2010
  973'.0468—dc22   2010022998

ISBN: 978-0-313-37932-1
EISBN: 978-0-313-37933-8

14 13 12 11 10   1 2 3 4 5

This book is also available on the World Wide Web as an eBook.
Visit www.abc-clio.com for details.

Greenwood
An Imprint of ABC-CLIO, LLC

ABC-CLIO, LLC
130 Cremona Drive, P.O. Box 1911
Santa Barbara, California 93116-1911

This book is printed on acid-free paper ∞

Manufactured in the United States of America

To *La Familia*, both the families into which we were born and those friends who became family along life's path. *Se lo agradacemos a todos.*

Contents

Acknowledgments

We thank the librarians at Green River Community College, Pierce College, and Evergreen State College for their assistance with research for this project. We also thank our editor, Wendi Schnaufer, for initiating this project and for her patience.

Introduction

Since the 1960s, the U.S. media have, at one time or another, predicted that forthcoming years would be remembered as "the Decade of the Hispanic," "the Latino Decade," or even "the Decade of the Latino Boom." Citing the United States' growing population of Latinos and the rising prominence of individual Latinos in positions of government and leadership, arts and entertainment, and law and medicine, the media declared then and maintain now that the years ahead would be remembered as those when Latino influence would hold its rightful place at the forefront of U.S. history and culture.

In reviewing the 100 entries listed in *Term Paper Resource Guide to Latino History*, however, it is clear that most years of every decade have belonged to Latinos. Indeed, Latino presence and influence can be seen from the formation of the California Mission Program in 1789 to the confirmation of Sonia Maria Sotomayor as the first Latina U.S. Supreme Court Justice in 2009. During that time, Latino history and culture have been at the forefront of U.S. foreign policy and domestic legislation; Latino influence can be seen in the arenas of education, arts, and social change, in formative events as disparate as the ratification of the Bilingual Education Act, the formation of the Nuyorican Poets Café, or the United Farm Workers Grape Boycott. Taken together, these 100 events clearly showcase that Latino history is U.S. history. Our goal with this guide is to shed light on the immeasurable contributions of Latino thought and culture to U.S. history. Too often, these contributions are silenced, elided, or forgotten.

In choosing topics for *Term Paper Resource Guide to Latino History*, we faced the difficult process of selecting merely 100 events that encapsulate these contributions. As such, the guiding philosophy has been to include both those events where Latino input plays a critical role in history and those events that impacted the lives and character of Latinos in the United States. Special attention has also been paid to offering an array of political, cultural, and social events to illustrate that history is more than wars fought and court cases won. While this guide offers critical attention to the instrumental role Latinos have played in the U.S. legal system, it also profiles the artistic and social expressions that have influenced and continue to influence U.S. history. As the second decade of the 21st century begins, the project of remembering and of seeing these contributions in relationship to one another becomes increasingly important. Within the next several years, Latinos will become the majority population in many states, and a new term, "minjority" has come into being to describe the "minority-majority" status held by Latinos in the United States today. Yet, little attention has been paid to illustrating the undeniable links between Latino history and historical transformations that have changed the United States.

Accordingly, the intended audience for *Term Paper Resource Guide to Latino History* will include three types of readers. This book is primarily designed for high school and college students seeking to generate both ideas for history assignments and a starting place for 21st century research where the plethora of Internet sources can be daunting and relevance and credibility of some Internet sources can be questionable. This guide will help students to find and focus on credible sources for their work. Librarians and faculty members working to assist students with the complex process of selecting a relevant topic and finding germane support is a second, equally important audience for this guide. As professors, we are familiar with the predicaments faced by faculty and librarians alike who seek to help students find their own topics of interest while still providing quality instruction on the selection and research process. We hope this guide generates both ideas for scholarly assignments and a starting point for research that is not reliant on questionable, nonvetted, "wiki-sources." An additional audience will be those students, faculty, and librarians seeking a chronological overview of Latino history and the crucial historical events impacting and impacted by Latino social, political, cultural, and literary thought. In developing term paper suggestions and alternative assignments, we have attempted to demonstrate the many concurrent interactions between these events and other historical situations so that the entries demonstrate greater continuity with each other.

USING THE GUIDE

A brief description of each historical event is given to provide students with general background information that will initiate further study and investigation. A series of essay prompts follows to direct students toward specific research and writing topics. As such, the Term Paper Suggestions function as a scholarly catalyst to initiate a starting point for the student-historian. At least two Alternative Term Paper Suggestions complement these suggestions to permit students to take a creative and original approach to historical inquiries. Many of these suggestions allow students to design unique history projects in the form of iMovies, Web sites, podcasts, literary analysis, interactive timelines, PowerPoint presentations, or newspaper articles. What follows then is an annotated bibliography that enables a researcher to begin the investigative process employing a variety of sources. These include the following:

Primary Sources, which span from eyewitness accounts, ratified laws, and letters to books authored by those associated with the event, or newspaper articles from the period.

Secondary Sources, which consist of peer-reviewed material that may provide specific details or generalized views of the event.

World Wide Web sources, which include significant Internet links to printed materials that are overviews or are connected to one of the Term Paper Suggestions.

Multimedia Sources, which comprise audio clips, streaming videos from DVDs or Internet sites.

Taken together, each entry provides students and scholars with a gateway into a key moment in Latino history and a starting point for their own discoveries, research, and knowledge of this rich, increasingly important, American community.

1. California Mission Program (1769–1834)

Under the direction of the Franciscan priest Junípero Serra (1713–1784) and the Spanish (Alta) California governor Gaspar de Portolá, Spain established both an official religious and military presence along the California coast. Mission San Diego de Alcalá (1769) was the first to be created. Between 1769 and 1823 a total of 21 missions were founded along *El Camino Real* (The King's Highway), a 650-mile stretch of road that ensured a traveler no more than a day's journey between San Diego and Mission San Francisco de Solano in Sonoma. The Mission Program would serve as the instrument for religious indoctrination and cultural assimilation of Native American tribes throughout California while securing social and military colonization over Alta California. Although mission land size varied and the labor-based economy depended on the local region and climate—ranging from farmlands, vineyards, ranches, and orchards—the system used the native local population as a source of cheap labor. The mission fathers viewed the tribes as potential converts to Catholicism and workers who could construct the mission buildings, farm the lands, and produce textiles that the mission would then sell to Spanish settlers and the local garrisons. The system was favorable to the Spanish crown since the empire was already stretched quite thinly; moreover, the Catholic Church approved of the arrangement because it guaranteed an ecclesiastical presence in the New World. Daily life, however, for the Native Americans was not ideal, for the Mission Program broke down the social, economic, political, and religious systems of the California tribes and decimated thousands through disease, malnutrition, and mistreatment. After Mexican independence in 1821, Mexico eventually decided to end the costly Mission Program and secularize the mission lands in 1834.

TERM PAPER SUGGESTIONS

1. Select two separate Native American uprisings that occurred at the missions and discuss what led up to them and how they were resolved. Draw relevant parallels and distinctions between the confrontations.

2. Despite Franciscan efforts to acculturate the local tribes, much of the tribal hierarchies remained intact. Discuss how traditional chiefs

and shamans maintained influence over their communities and how they served as a counter-system to catholic indoctrination during the Mission Program.

3. When Native Americans were brought into the mission lands to be assimilated to Spanish colonial life and service, the traditional roles and duties of gender were often compromised. Explain how these gender expectations were different between the local tribes and mission life and what consequences were created as a result of this shift in social norms.

4. After the Mexican Revolution in 1821, the leadership within the Mission Program changed with some priests choosing to remain loyal to Spain while others loosely acknowledged the new government in Mexico City. On the mission lands, how did the revolution change the way business was conducted, especially the way mission Indians were being used? Who were key players in the post-revolutionary missions?

ALTERNATIVE TERM PAPER SUGGESTIONS

1. During the Mission Program, countless visitors from around the world made their way to the various Franciscan missions throughout California. Using photographs, maps, and texts, create an iMovie or a PowerPoint presentation that summarizes the significance of these structures to California's colonial history.

2. Mission Indians were constantly exposed to unsanitary living conditions, malnutrition, inadequate medicine, and a high infant mortality rate. Imagine you are a modern-day physician sent to the various California missions by a neutral party to investigate the daily life of mission Indians and their health conditions during the early 19th century. Through first-hand testimonials, letters, memoirs, interviews, and articles, produce a comprehensive report outlining why the demographics at key missions have been in decline. What recommendations would you make to the medical board that sent you?

SUGGESTED SOURCES

Primary Sources

Bancroft, Hubert Howe. *California Pastoral: 1869–u 1848*. San Francisco, CA: The History Company, 1888. A staunch critic of the Mission Program, Bancroft exposed the difficult life of mission Indians in this early collection of Spanish colonization in the New World. http:// books.google.com/books?id=zu80AAAAIAAJ.

Castillo, Edward, trans. and ed. "An Indian Account of the Decline and Collapse of Mexico's Hegemony over the Missionized Indians of California," *American Indian Quarterly* 13 (1989): 391–408. Includes the 1877 oral testimony of Lorenzo Asisara, a Santa Cruz Mission Indian born there in 1820, concerning the role that mission-controlled Indian leaders (*alcaldes*) had among the tribes.

Costello, Julia G. *Documentary Evidence for the Spanish Missions of Alta California*. New York: Garland, 1991. Includes a collection of memoirs, testimonies, articles, journal excerpts, and letters of various first-hand accounts of life in the California missions.

De la Pérouse, Jean Francois. *Life in a California Mission: Monterey in 1786: The Journals of Jean Francois de la Pérouse*. Berkeley, CA: Heyday Books, 1989. Commissioned by King Louis XVI to lead a global expedition, de la Pérouse provides a critical account of the treatment of mission Indians at the famous Carmel Mission in the late 18th century.

Farnsworth, Paul. "The Economics of Acculturation in the Alta California Missions: A Historical and Archaeological Study of Mission Nuestra Señora de la Soledad." PhD diss. University of California, Berkeley, 1987. This study incorporates first-account responses from Franciscan missionaries to a questionnaire conducted between 1813 and 1815 by Cádiz Cortes, the Spanish legislative body during French occupation of Spain. It also provides details regarding California tribal culture and religious beliefs at the time of the Mission Program.

Secondary Sources

Cook, Sherburne F. *The Conflict between the California Indian and White Civilization*. Berkeley: University of California Press, 1976. Highlights the quality of life for mission Indians and the causes of their decreased demographics.

Couve de Murville, M.N.L. *The Man Who Founded California: The Life of Blessed Junípero Serra*. San Francisco: Ignatius Press, 2000. Couve de Murville, the Archbishop Emeritus of Birmingham, England, reverently explores Fr. Serra's world and his impact on California culture and history, leading up to the Franciscan's controversial beatification by Pope John Paul II.

Engelhardt, Zephyrin. *Missions and Missionaries of California*. 4 vols. Santa Barbara, CA: Mission Santa Barbara, 1930. A Franciscan priest provides a comprehensive work with an in-depth examination of the political and social worlds of the missions. Written in response to critical publications of the Mission Program, especially H. H. Bancroft's *California Pastoral* (1888), this scholarship views the endeavors of the missionaries in highly favorable light.

Jackson, Robert H., and Edward Castillo. *Indians, Franciscans, and Spanish Colonization: The Impact of the Mission System on California Indians.* Albuquerque: University of New Mexico Press, 1995. Examines the social and ideological framework of the Franciscan Mission Program in California during Spanish Colonization that attempted to assimilate and acculturate the Native American tribes.

Leffingwall, Randy, and Alastair Worden. *California Missions and Presidios.* Osceola, WI: Voyageur Press, 2005. A balance between historical text and contemporary photography, this resource provides more of a visual aide to the background of the missions.

Sandos, James A. *Converting California: Indians and Franciscans in the Missions.* New Haven, CT: Yale University Press, 2004. Contains a critical account of the mission Indian lifestyle, the specific tactics used by the Franciscans to maintain control over indigenous populations and address uprisings, and the political role the missions played between loyalty to Spain or Mexico after the Mexican independence.

World Wide Web

"California Mission History." http://www.californiamissions.com/cahistory/index.html. Includes a broad historical overview, photographs, and drawings of all 21 missions.

"California Mission Studies Association." http://www.ca-missions.org/. Contains an extensive collection of annotated links, photographs, illustrated glossary section, California Mission Studies Association books, articles, bibliographies, and current archeological excavations devoted to the continued study of the California missions.

"The Lewis and Clark Journey of Discovery: California Missions." http://www.nps.gov/archive/jeff/LewisClark2/Circa1804/WestwardExpansion/EarlyExplorers/CaliforniaMissions.htm. Provides a comprehensive overview of mission history by organizing it in an easy to follow Frequently Asked Question (FAQ) format.

"Santa Barbara Mission Archive Library." http://www.sbmal.org/. This research institution maintains relevant maps, texts, photographs, and documents concerning the California missions and the influence of Spain and Mexico in California. The institution also sponsors educational, professional, and community lectures and events.

"The Spanish Colonial Mission System in the United States and Northern Mexico." http://www.statemuseum.arizona.edu/oer/missionsini/english/

spanish.shtml. This section provides a brief overview of how extensive the Mission Program was throughout New Spain.

Multimedia Sources

California Missions. Los Angeles: Huell Howser Productions, 2000. 10 VHS videos. 300 minutes. Emphasizing the aesthetics of the missions and journeys between them, this 10-part mini-series provides a general account of the missions' history and their function today.

Landmarks of Faith: The California Missions: A Travelogue of American Spirituality. Portland, OR: Odyssey Productions, 1998. VHS. 48 minutes. Examines the history of the founding of the missions and their eventual abandonment. Underscores the role religion and spirituality have in architectural and aesthetic design.

The Missions of California. Laguna Hills, CA: Shannon and Company Productions, 2007. DVD. 60 minutes. This is the first documentary to capture both the interior and exterior of all 21 missions. In addition to underscoring the religious impact the missions had, the documentary examines the architectural and social influences on California history.

2. Santa Fe Trail and Railroad Are Established (1821, 1880)

For nearly 60 years, the Santa Fe Trail served to ferry commercial items from the Missouri Valley, across the Great Plains, and into the desert city of Santa Fe, New Mexico, during the 19th century. Although later-established westbound American trade routes such as the Oregon and California Trails principally functioned as conduits for emigration and large freight, the Santa Fe Trail was intended to move a wide variety of domestic goods and luxuries such as tea, rice, construction metals, whiskey, clothing, mirrors, and kitchen stoves. After a successful expedition to Santa Fe in 1821, William Becknell, a freight-operator, was eventually christened "Father of the Santa Fe Trail" when in 1822 he led the first group of farm wagons and pack animals from Franklin, Missouri, down to New Mexico. This prompted the U.S. Congress in 1824 to declare the Trail to be the first official international trade route between the United States and the newly established Republic of Mexico. Despite the eventual presence of over 5,000 wagons annually on the Santa Fe Trail, the rough terrain and constant change in weather patterns constantly posed serious difficulties in permanently marking the route. In fact, the actual Trail was often 100 yards wide in many places since wagon trains would have to improvise when crossing streams and rivers, avoiding skirmishes in Native American territories, or taking refuge from frequent rain and sand storms. Like many entrepreneurial Americans, Mexican citizens also participated in the trade route. As early as 1826, they could be found moving along the Trail, actively bartering goods. Wagon-freighters such as Manuel Escudero, Felipe Chávez, and Francisco Elguea of Chihuahua helped place 50 percent control over the trade into the hands of Mexicans during the first half of the 1840s. However, the U.S.-Mexican War (1846–1848) further militarized the Santa Fe Trail and served to attract Anglo-American settlers into the newly acquired Southwest. With the ambition of connecting Topeka, Kansas, with Santa Fe, New Mexico, the Atchison, Topeka, and Santa Fe Railroad fought bitterly beginning in the 1860s with competing railroad companies to lay track across the open plains and replace wagon-freight as a means for moving goods to the growing settlements of the American Southwest. In 1880, the Santa Fe Railroad finally reached the city of Santa Fe, thus closing the Trail.

TERM PAPER SUGGESTIONS

1. Despite a commerce treaty that had been signed between the United States and Mexico in 1831, there was still an enormous amount of bureaucratic tape to cut through in the form of taxes, banned goods, and discriminatory practices that slowed down the trading of goods along the Santa Fe Trail. Describe what some of these difficulties were, who the principal characters involved were, and what resolutions were made to address the day-to-day complications of these early stages of international trade between these two nations.

2. Prior to Mexican independence from Spain in 1821, the Spanish forbade commercial trade between U.S. cities and the city of Santa Fe. However, the newly installed government of Mexico reversed this sanction. Explain why Spain initially imposed this trade embargo against the United States and why Mexico chose to end this. What does it suggest about the U.S.-Spanish relations versus U.S.-Mexican relations?

3. Up until the start of the U.S.-Mexican War in 1846, Mexican citizens controlled 50 percent of the trade along the Santa Fe Trail. Investigate some of the difficulties Mexicans had selling their goods

to the United States and what transformations in commerce took place once the United States invaded Mexico.

4. While railroad companies such as the Santa Fe, Southern Pacific, and Denver and Rio Grande Western struggled politically and financially to gain the upper hand in dominating the commerce markets, physical and legal battles often occurred among them. Identify some of the key battles such as the Royal Gorge Railroad War, which hastened the closure of freight trails like the Santa Fe in favor of rail lines as a means for moving people and products in the late 19th century.

ALTERNATIVE TERM PAPER SUGGESTIONS

1. Write a detailed advertisement for potential wagon masters and teamsters for the wagon freight you want to move along the Santa Fe Trail. Consider realistic situations such as weather and trail conditions, regional issues like access through Native American territories, checkpoints, and trading posts. Use accounts of life along the Trail from American pioneers like William Becknell, Charles Bent, or "Uncle Dick" Wootton to assist you with these details.

2. Although the city of Santa Fe served as a pivotal hub for cultural and commercial trade between the United States and Mexico, between 1822 and 1848 40 percent of the goods that ended up in Santa Fe actually went 550 miles farther south to the city of Chihuahua since Santa Fe did not have the infrastructure to absorb them. Imagine you are a prosperous businessperson in Chihuahua during the height of the Santa Fe Trail trade and are being interviewed by the local newspaper. Discuss how the commercial "run-off" from the Trail has made not only your business successful, but the city as well.

SUGGESTED SOURCES

Primary Sources

Field, Matt. *Matt Field on the Santa Fe Trail.* Collected by Clyde and Mae Reed Porter. Ed. John E. Sunder. Norman: Oklahoma University Press, 1995. Highlights the journal entries and articles of Matt Field, an actor, poet, and reporter whose travels along the Santa Fe Trail in 1839 depict his experiences during this period.

Magoffin, Susan Shelby. *Down the Santa Fe Trail: The Diary of Susan Shelby Magoffin 1845–1847,* edited by Stella M. Drumm. New Haven, CT:

Yale University Press, 1962. Magoffin's 15-month account of life on the Trail with her trader husband charts her daily encounters as a young woman enduring the transformations of the U.S.-Mexico region at the start of the war.

Segale, Sister Blandina. *At the End of the Santa Fe Trail.* Whitefish, MT: Kessinger Publishing, 2005. Follows the eyewitness account of Sister Blandina, a member of the Sisters of Charity in Cincinnati, who served throughout southern Colorado and northern New Mexico between 1872 and 1894 and was a critic of settling the West and the denial of land rights to Native Americans.

Webb, James Josiah. *Adventures in the Santa Fe Trade, 1844–1847.* Ed. Ralph P. Bieber. Lincoln: University of Nebraska Press, 1995. Provides Webb's first hand profiles of domestic and commercial life in Santa Fe during the 1840s as well as descriptions of trade methods and encounters with Mexican customs officials.

Secondary Sources

Boyle, Susan Calafate. *Los Capitalistas: Hispano Merchants and the Santa Fe Trade.* Albuquerque: University of New Mexico Press, 1997. Investigates commercial enterprises of prominent Spanish/Mexican businessmen such as Felipe Chávez and others and how they established their own networks along the Santa Fe Trail in competition with Anglo-American freighters.

Chalfant, William F. *Dangerous Passage: The Santa Fe Trail and the Mexican War.* Norman: University of Oklahoma Press, 1994. Explores the Trail's increased importance in the U.S.-Mexican political theater during the war and provides detailed insights of significant personalities involved during the late 1840s.

Hill, William E. *The Santa Fe Trail, Yesterday and Today.* Caldwell, ID: Caxton Printers, 1992. Captures the struggles of the Trail's month-long journey and is divided into various sections including maps, historical and biographical accounts, and illustrations.

Hyslop, Stephan G. *Bound for Santa Fe: The Road to New Mexico and the American Conquest, 1806–1848.* Norman: University of Oklahoma Press, 2002. Explores the rich lives of those who lived along the trade route between the Missouri Valley and Santa Fe while underscoring the social and cultural variations between Anglo Missourians and Hispanic New Mexicans.

Inman, Henry. *The Old Santa Fé Trail: The Story of a Great Highway.* Topeka, KS: Crane and Company, 1899. This comprehensive early account by a U.S. Army colonel outlines the history of the Trail from the dawning days of the Spanish Conquistadors in the Southwest to the arrival of the railroad in Santa Fe, New Mexico.

Marshall, James. *Santa Fe: The Railroad That Built an Empire.* New York: Random House, 1945. Details the waning days of the Santa Fe Trail as the major railroad companies began to dominate trade in the Southwest.

Walker, Henry Pickering. *The Wagonmaster: High Plains Fighting from the Earliest Days of the Santa Fe Trail to 1880.* Norman: University of Oklahoma Press, 1966. Profiles the diversity of men and women who traversed the Santa Fe Trail during its period of commerce, outlining the details of personalities and encounters they would have.

World Wide Web

"The Interactive Santa Fe Trail." http://www.kansasheritage.org/research/sft. This Kansas Heritage site includes relevant links to the Trail's history, detailed timelines, a listing of current print and electronic books, images and interactive maps of various parts of the Trail.

"New Mexico Office of the State Historian." http://www.newmexicohistory. org/filedetails.php?fileID=502. William H. Wroth provides a comprehensive overview of the Santa Fe Trail's history and includes a useful bibliography for further research.

"Santa Fe Trail Association." http://www.santafetrail.org/index.php. The association's official Web site includes links to each participating state chapter, news and information on Trail related lectures and events, and the quarterly journal *Wagon Tracks* devoted to Trail scholarship.

Multimedia Sources

Cab Ride along the Santa Fe Trail. Indianapolis, IN: Railway Productions, 2005. 6 DVDs. 425 minutes. Captures the modern train journey from La Junta, CO, to Albuquerque, NM, while providing insightful commentary by crew members of the old Santa Fe Trail and railroad line's respective histories.

With Each Turn of the Wheel: The Santa Fe Trail, 1821–1996. Albuquerque, NM: NMPBS Home Video, 2007. DVD. 58 minutes. Features history of the Trail as told from the perspective of Latinos and Native Americans.

3. Monroe Doctrine (December 2, 1823)

Fearing European and Russian colonial expansion in the Western Hemisphere, President James Monroe and his Secretary of State John Quincy

Adams outlined a new foreign policy that announced the United States would not interfere in the political activities in Europe and it would not tolerate influence or intervention from European nations or Russia within Latin American countries. Delivering this speech to the U.S. Congress in 1823, Monroe captured popular sentiment with U.S. citizens who desired separate realms of power between Europe and the United States. Monroe saw this as an opportunity to increase the nation's own influence among like-minded democratic nations. With the backing of a powerful military by the early 20th century, President Theodore Roosevelt invoked the Monroe Doctrine to expand U.S. territories and assert control over neighboring countries in Latin America. This unilateral policy has always been negatively received by Latin American nations who believed the United States merely desired to establish its own imperial control over the American continents despite its claims to democratic principles of liberty and self-governance. Throughout the Cold War era, the United States had been involved in numerous overt and covert military interventions in the Caribbean, Central America, and South America in an effort to curtail the spread of communism. President John F. Kennedy invoked the Monroe Doctrine in the 1960s to justify interventions in Cuba, while Presidents Ronald Reagan and George H. W. Bush used this policy to intervene in Central American nations during the 1980s and 1990s.

TERM PAPER SUGGESTIONS

1. Discuss how the Monroe Doctrine has been invoked to justify U.S. intervention in Latin American nations during the 20th century. Read the December 2, 1823, speech Monroe delivered to Congress to become familiar with the language used in this new foreign policy. Argue how these interventions have impacted diplomatic relations between the United States and the respective countries involved.

2. Theodore Roosevelt's Roosevelt Corollary of 1904 and Franklin D. Roosevelt's Good Neighbor Policy of 1933 are contrasting interpretations of the Monroe Doctrine. Describe the background and historical context for these two policies, and articulate how each one was received and interpreted by Latin American countries during the 20th century.

3. Argue whether the 1989 U.S. invasion of Panama to protect the Panama Canal Zone and to oust General Manuel Noriega was part

of the invocation of the Monroe Doctrine and whether it was justified in your opinion. Consider how the Roosevelt Corollary, the Good Neighbor Policy, and the Torrijos-Carter Treaties of 1977 play a role in supporting or opposing the Monroe Doctrine.

ALTERNATIVE TERM PAPER SUGGESTIONS

1. In October 1962, the Kennedy administration was involved in a political showdown with the Soviet Union. President Kennedy invoked the Monroe Doctrine in part to justify his actions against the presence of nuclear missile sites being constructed in Cuba. Prepare a PowerPoint presentation that will be shown to the U.S. Congress that includes news footage, maps, images, and citations from the Monroe Doctrine to demonstrate how the United States was invoking this policy in its response to the Soviet Union.

2. As a Latin American political activist from a vocal organization, create a series of podcasts that accuses the United States of employing the Monroe Doctrine to influence and control political and economic structures throughout the Western Hemisphere. Cite historical interventions to justify your claims.

SUGGESTED SOURCES

Primary Sources

"The Essential Monroe Doctrine Primary Documents." http://edsitement. neh.gov/lesson_images/lesson578/PrimaryDocs.pdf. Contains a compilation of Web sites that includes primary sources associated with the research and instruction of the Monroe Doctrine gleaned from the Library of Congress and several academic institutions.

Finkleman, Paul, and Bruce A. Lesh. *Milestone Documents in American History: Exploring the Primary Sources That Shaped America*. Dallas, TX: Schlager Group, 2008. Includes 32 documents from 1763 to 1823 that transformed U.S. politics. Includes the complete address to Congress by President Monroe, in which the Monroe Doctrine was established.

Secondary Sources

Collin, Richard H. *Theodore Roosevelt's Caribbean: The Panama Canal, the Monroe Doctrine, and the Latin American Context*. Baton Rouge: Louisiana State

University Press, 1990. Investigates the role the Roosevelt Corollary played in redefining the Monroe Doctrine in Latin America at the beginning of the 20th century.

Dent, David W. *The Legacy of the Monroe Doctrine: A Reference Guide to U.S. Involvement in Latin America and the Caribbean.* Westport, CT: Greenwood Press, 1999. Geared toward upper-level high school and undergraduate audience, this work is divided into country chapters and analyzes pivotal events involving U.S. intervention since 1823.

Dietz, James L. "Destabilization and Intervention in Latin America and the Caribbean." *Latin American Perspectives* 11.3 (Spring 1984): 3–14. Discusses U.S. involvement throughout the Western Hemisphere from the perspective of Latin American nations.

Livingstone, Grace. *America's Backyard: The United States and Latin America from the Monroe Doctrine to the War on Terror.* London: Zed Books, 2009. Through the lenses of culture, drugs, and economics, this text argues how the United States has been involved in coups, revolutions, and death squads throughout Latin America and how the 21st century War on Terror continues the legacy of the Monroe Doctrine.

Murphy, Gretchen. *Hemispheric Imaginings: The Monroe Doctrine and Narrative History of U.S. Empire.* Durham, NC: Duke University Press, 2005. Introduces how popular journalism and works of fiction have been used to create alternative narratives and perceptions of the United States' position throughout Latin America.

Smith, Gaddis. *The Last Years of the Monroe Doctrine, 1945–1993.* New York: Hill and Wang, 1995. Critically articulates how this U.S. foreign policy has impacted diplomatic relations with Latin American nations since the end of World War II.

World Wide Web

"James Monroe: 5th President of the United States." http://www.monroedoctrine. net/. Features overview of the Monroe presidency and policies. Includes link to excerpts of Monroe's address to Congress in 1823 establishing the Monroe Doctrine.

"Monroe Doctrine, 1823." http://www.state.gov/r/pa/ho/time/jd/16321.htm. Provides the U.S. State Department's official summary of the Monroe Doctrine.

"Monroe Doctrine; December 2, 1823." http://avalon.law.yale.edu/19th_ century/monroe.asp. Provides the Yale University Avalon Project's reprinting of Monroe's speech to Congress that concerns the section of U.S. sovereignty to intervene in Latin American nations.

Multimedia Sources

The American President, Executive Vision. Alexandria, VA: PBS Home Video, 2004. DVD. Disc 3. 120 minutes. Episode 6 includes the presidency of James Monroe and the role the Monroe Doctrine played in establishing U.S. sovereignty in the Western Hemisphere.

In An Era of Good Feeling: The Monroe Doctrine. Peoria, IL: Thomas S. Klise Company, 2007. DVD-ROM. 15 minutes. Includes a PDF of a teacher guide and covers the 1823 U.S. congressional address and its implications.

4. Secularization of Alta California Mission Lands (1833)

During Napoleonic occupation of Spain in the early 19th century, sweeping legislative reforms were passed, including an anticlerical decree in 1813 by the liberal courts to secularize the missions throughout the colonies. After going back and forth politically with the pro-clerical King Ferdinand VII, this decree was officially reinstated in 1820; however, pro-clerical conservatives in Mexico declared independence from Spain in 1821. They maintained control and prevented secularization of the missions until Gen. Antonio López de Santa Anna and liberal leaders overthrew the Mexican regime in 1832 and ratified the Secularization Act in November 1833. However, pro-cleric conservatives, supported by the Catholic Church and the military, dismantled the liberal regime in Mexico and ended secularization rules in 1835. Because of its loose political autonomy and distance from Mexico City, Alta California, nevertheless, had moved forward with implementing secularization among the Franciscan-controlled missions and set about emancipating the mission Indians. Originally, the secularization laws acknowledged that the Mission Program was a temporary structure that would establish a colonial system in California, and educate and train Native Americans to support themselves. Eventually, the Franciscans would turn cultivated mission buildings, farms, and ranches over to converted Native Americans, while encouraging the development of free tribal settlements that sustained a balanced socioeconomic system. From the start, Franciscan padres were unwilling to relinquish their authority, believing that the mission Indians were unprepared to take over. Nevertheless, the provincial government in California slowly installed their own administrators to replace the Franciscans. This led to a breakdown in the Mission Program since the secularization was not executed equally. Many missions lost their lands, livestock, and goods to local ranchers and opportunists. In most cases, mission property was not turned over to the converted Native Americans; rather, the government installed its own administrators to oversee the Mission Program. This inevitably led to a mass exodus of many of the mission Indians who were denied full rights of emancipation. Eventually, the missions fell into disrepair and were abandoned by the 1840s.

TERM PAPER SUGGESTIONS

1. After the decree was made in 1833 to secularize the missions, many Native Americans began to flee the missions and relocate to other missions, colonial settlements, and ranches. What impact did this diaspora have on local economies, and what new policies were established to address the mass migration of the Native American tribes to these new locations?

2. In 1833, Gov. José Figueroa emancipated Native Americans living at Mission San Juan Capistrano, thus creating a *pueblo de indios*, a settlement made up of converted mission Indians with a municipal government. However, this social experiment only lasted a year. Discuss the design of this social experiment and what made it eventually collapse during this early period of secularization.

3. During the period of mission secularization, many governors ruled Alta California. Discuss what the political relationship was between Alta California and Mexico City during this time and how this impacted the manner in which the Secularization Act of 1833 was carried out in and around the 21 missions.

4. Historians and critics alike have compared the Franciscan Mission Program to everything from the plantation system of the American South, to indentured servitude, to an awkward socioeconomic interdependency between tribal communities and mission padres. Drawing on evidence and arguments made by scholars, develop an argument that characterizes the role of labor in the pre- and post-secularized Mission Program.

ALTERNATIVE TERM PAPER SUGGESTIONS

1. Assume the role of an ethnographer who is recording the social, political, and economic upheaval the Secularization Act is having on the California missions beginning in 1833. Who are some of the key players among the Church, tribes, military, provincial administration, or local landowners? Prepare a PowerPoint presentation and a written account of what is taking place at key mission properties.

2. Design an interactive map showing landholdings of the California missions at the time of the Secularization Act. Demonstrate how and where large tracts of land were divided up by ranchers and other California leaders.

SUGGESTED SOURCES

Primary Sources

Beebe, Rose-Marie, and Robert M. Senkewicz. *Land of Promise: Chronicles of Early California, 1535–1846.* Berkeley, CA: Heyday Books, 2001. Includes selections from journals, personal and official correspondence, interviews, reports, and decrees with extensive commentary, particularly on the waning days of the Mission Program and the period of mission secularization and land redistribution.

Hartnell, William E. P. *The Diary and Copybook of William E. P. Hartnell: Visitador General of the Missions of Alta California in 1839 and 1840.* Trans. Starr P. Gurcke. Ed. Glenn J. Farris. Spokane, WA: Arthur H. Clark, 2004. This is the collected correspondence, journal entries, and mission property inventory lists of the Visitador General appointed by Gov. Juan Bautista Alvarado to survey the secularization process throughout the mission system.

Secondary Sources

Gutiérrez, Ramón A., and Robert J. Orsi, eds. *Contested Eden: California Before the Gold Rush.* Berkeley: University of California, 1998. While this anthology covers a broad spectrum of early California history, there are many detailed sections on each of the missions and the repercussions of the Secularization Act.

Jackson, Robert H., and Edward Castillo. *Indians, Franciscans, and Spanish Colonization: The Impact of the Mission System on California Indians.* Albuquerque: University of New Mexico Press, 1995. Chapter 5, "Mission Secularization and the Development of Alta California in the

1830s and 1840s," provides a detailed discussion of this process and includes tables for the missions illustrating the demographic and economic transformations occurring during secularization.

Johnson, John R. *The Chumash Indians after Secularization.* Santa Barbara, CA: California Mission Studies Association, 1995. Explores how the Chumash people in the Santa Barbara region were denied the return of their traditional lands, despite the secularization laws that ensured this; instead, the Mission lands were sold and distributed to Mexican loyalists and other settlers.

Robinson, W. W. *Land in California: The Story of Mission Lands, Ranchos, Squatters, Mining Claims, Railroad Grants, Land Scrip, Homesteads.* Berkeley: University of California Press, 1979. This work makes the countless legal claims and battles over colonial, indigenous, and mission lands that redesigned California interesting and accessible to a broad audience. It also includes a chapter on California Native American land ownership.

Servín, Manuel P. "The Secularization of the California Missions: A Reappraisal." *Southern California Quarterly* 47 (1965): 133–149. Servín's article provides a comprehensive discussion and assessment of the legal background on mission secularization.

Weber, David J. *The Mexican Frontier, 1821–1846: The American Southwest under Mexico.* Albuquerque: University of New Mexico Press, 1982. Establishes both a balanced and detailed analysis of the collapse of the Mission Program under secularization and the land grab that follows.

World Wide Web

"But What about Faith? Catholicism and Liberalism in Nineteenth-Century Spain." http://www.ewtn.com/library/HUMANITY/FR90402.TXT. Patrick Foley's detailed article from *Faith and Reason* (1990) outlines the process of the liberal political movement to counteract the Church's authority and provides background on the liberal legislative reforms of secularization spearheaded by the Cádiz Cortes, the liberal courts headquartered in Cádiz, Spain, during French occupation of Madrid.

"California Missions—Secularization of the Missions." http://www.oldandsold .com/articles17/california-missions-5.shtml. This site provides a concise account of the history of mission secularization and the events that led up to it.

"Mexican American Voices: Secularization of the Missions." http://www .digitalhistory.uh.edu/mexican_voices/voices_display.cfm?id=42. The excerpt includes general background information on the Secularization

Act of 1833 and its impact on the California Mission Program. It also includes a first-hand testimony from Narciso Dúran, O.F.M, the last Father-President of the Franciscan California missions.

"Native Americans in the Mission Economy." http://www.shapingsf.org/ezine/labor/native/main.html. A brief discussion details and explains the role mission Indians played in establishing the economic system that sustained the California missions.

Multimedia Source

The Missions of California. Laguna Hills, CA: Shannon and Company Productions, 2007. DVD. 60 minutes. This is the first documentary to capture both the interior and exterior of all 21 missions. In addition to underscoring the religious impact the missions had, it examines the architectural and social influences on California history.

5. Texas Revolution (1835–1836)

After gaining independence from Spain in 1821, the new Republic of Mexico faced the reality that it was not only bankrupt, but also sparsely militarized, especially in northern states, such as newly conjoined Coahuila y Tejas. To address this, the Mexican government encouraged the settlement of some of its less-populated regions through land grants to Mexican citizens and new immigrants. Foremost among these immigrant "empresarios," or land agents, was Stephan F. Austin who secured the first and largest of these land grants for his American community in 1822. Initially, Mexican officials anticipated that settlers would establish their own local militia divisions to curtail the growing American Indian raids while acting as substitutes for an otherwise thin military presence. However, the Anglos quickly began to outnumber the Tejanos, the ethnic Mexicans living in Texas, and were dismissive of Mexican laws and cultural expectations. This prompted Mexican President Anastacio Bustamante to issue a series of policies in April 1830 aimed at slowing down immigration from the United States specifically into Coahuila y Tejas. These political resolutions also provided for increased tariffs on American imports and reiterated the ban on slave trade in which the American Texans were deeply involved. Despite Bustamante's efforts, by 1834 the state of Coahuila y Tejas comprised nearly 30,000 Anglos, 7,800 Tejanos, and 500 slaves. More and more, the Anglo immigrants felt Mexico City alienated them by dismissing their desire to become a separate Mexican state within the Republic. Moreover, the political and cultural differences between the Anglos and the Mexican government regarding the definition of basic liberties like religious freedom or legal processes only further divided these groups from each other. When General Antonio López de Santa Anna became president of Mexico in 1833, he suspended the constitution and dissolved congress. Furthermore, he set about centralizing his power by disarming the militias and eradicating the independence movement in Coahuila y Tejas. The growing animosity and altercations between Mexican soldiers and Anglo Texans eventually led to the Declaration of Causes in 1835 that ignited Texas's revolt from Mexico and the seizure of Mexican garrisons. Leading the counter-revolution, Santa Anna and his legions fought and killed the 182 revolutionaries at the Alamo in San Antonio in 1836 and executed 342 of the prisoners. Eventually, the Texans won their independence at the decisive Battle of San Jacinto on April 21, 1836, where Santa Anna surrendered to Sam Houston, the Texan Commander-in-Chief.

TERM PAPER SUGGESTIONS

1. In 1829, President Vicente Guerrero signed Mexico's own emancipation proclamation to end the slave trade system within its borders. Many critics have suggested that Mexico's unfair hacienda peonage system was nothing short of a form of slavery. What similarities and/or differences exist between the United States' slave trade in the South and Mexico's peonage system during the time of Texas independence?

2. After Santa Anna's surrender at San Jacinto in 1836, the defeated Mexican leader is sent to Washington, D.C., to sign the Treaty of Velasco with President Andrew Jackson, thus acknowledging Texas' independence. However, the Mexican congress deposes Santa Anna while he is gone and refuses to accept Texas as a republic. Discuss what exactly led to the divisive nature between the former leader and statesmen in Mexico City, and explain what political associations can be drawn with the U.S.-Mexican War that follows a decade later.

3. Although in the early 1820s immigrants were encouraged to settle land in the more sparsely populated areas of Mexico, their presence

soon became a complicated issue for Mexico City. Explain what cultural and legal actions were taken by the host government to address Anglo-Texans' refusal to assimilate. In your analysis, determine how the Anglos viewed their own treatment in comparison with how the Mexican government perceived or acknowledged their actions.

4. Created in 1836, the Republic of Texas enjoyed its independence until it was eventually admitted into the union of American states in December 1845. Report on how Texas fared as a sovereign nation. Discuss how its presidential administrations dealt with the continued land disputes along its borders. What was its relationship with Washington, D.C.; Mexico City; and the American Indian tribes?

ALTERNATIVE TERM PAPER SUGGESTIONS

1. When General Antonio López de Santa Anna became President of Mexico in 1833, he surprised and angered many by dissolving the constitution and congress and by promising to control rebellion growing throughout the republic. Imagine you are Santa Anna himself during this pivotal time in Mexican history, and create a detailed PowerPoint presentation with maps, diagrams, and statements that justify your escalated takeover and the need to quiet the resistance emerging in the Mexican state of Coahuila y Tejas.

2. Use clips and selections from DVD documentaries, online maps, Google-image photographs, and eyewitness accounts to create a brief iMovie of the revolt in the Mexican state of Coahuila y Tejas from the perspective of the Mexican citizens, military officers, and political governing body. In your depiction, pay attention to the arguments made by Mexico regarding the activities and attitudes of the Anglo immigrants that led to the altercations.

SUGGESTED SOURCES

Primary Sources

De la Pena, Jose Enrique. *With Santa Anna in Texas: A Personal Narrative of the Revolution.* Trans. Carmen Perry. College Station: Texas A & M University, 1997. Provides an eyewitness account from one of Santa Anna's officers of the Mexican perspective of the Alamo, including the capture and execution of Davy Crockett.

Dimmick, Gregg J., ed. *General Vicente Filisola's Analysis of Jose Urrea's Military Diary: A Forgotten 1838 Publication by an Eyewitness to the Texas Revolution.* Trans. John R. Wheat. Austin: Texas State Historical Association, 2007. Second in command during the Texas Revolution, Filisola takes command of the remaining army after Santa Anna's defeat in 1836. This diary of the general was a critical response to rival General Urrea and debunks the praises often given to Urrea by historians at the expense of Filisola.

Jackson, Jack, ed. *Almonte's Texas: Juan N. Almonte's 1834 Inspection, Secret Report, and Role in the 1836 Campaign.* Austin: Texas State Historical Association, 2005. Contains accounts of the last inspection by this Mexican colonel of the Tejas region on the eve of the revolution, and includes among other critical observations Colonel Almonte's recommendations for avoiding Texan cessation from Mexico.

Secondary Sources

Brands, H.W. *Lone Star Nation: The Epic Story of the Battle for Texas Independence.* New York: Anchor Books, 2005. Articulates a strong defense for Texas leaders such as Austin and Houston and their justification for revolution.

Crimm, Ana Carolina Castillo. *De Leon, a Tejano Family History.* Austin: University of Texas Press, 2004. Follows the life experiences of three generations of the de Leon family, whose members first arrived in Tejas in 1801, and whose relatives later endured the Mexican and Texan revolutions and the legal aftermath concerning rights to their lands and holdings.

Huffines, Alan. *The Texas War of Independence 1835–1836: From Outbreak to the Alamo to San Jacinto.* New York: Osprey Publishing, 2005. Part of a larger series entitled *Essential Histories*, this work provides a comprehensive overview of the revolution with a unique emphasis on military life during the campaigns.

Reichstein, Andreas. *Rise of the Lone Star: The Making of Texas.* Trans. Jeanne R. Wilson. College Station: Texas A & M University, 1989. Includes a close examination of events and circumstances leading up to the Texas Revolution, the military and political altercations during the war, and the policies and actions taken by the newly formed Republic of Texas.

Stout, Jay A. *Slaughter at Goliad: The Mexican Massacre of 400 Texas Volunteers.* Annapolis, MD: Naval Institute Press, 2008. Print. Provides detailed descriptions and analysis of the mass execution of over 400 Texan soldiers ordered by Gen. Santa Anna in March 1836.

World Wide Web

"The Alamo." http://www.thealamo.org/main.html. Provides historical information on the battle and the revolution, photographs, letters from garrison members, a photo tour of the complex with a written narrative and links, and educational links on conducting further research on the Alamo and the Texas Revolution.

"Albert and Ethel Herzstein Library." http://www.sanjacinto-museum.org/Herzstein_Library/. Part of the San Jacinto Museum of History, this site includes an on-line collection of biographies of those who fought in the Battle of San Jacinto.

"Daughters of the Republic of Texas Library." http://www.drtl.org/index.asp. Located at the Alamo Complex, this on-line feature has assembled an annotated list of relevant links to Texas museums, special collections, online journals, and historical Web sites.

"The Hispanic Experience: Tejano History." http://houstonculture.org/hispanic/alamo.html. Includes a discussion of Tejano patriots who defended the Alamo as well as links to other sites that highlight contributions by pro-revolutionary Tejanos. There is a Works Cited page for further research on this topic.

"The Sam Houston Memorial Museum." http://www.shsu.edu/~smm_www/index.html. Operated by the Sam Houston State University, this living museum dedicated to Sam Houston includes a timeline of his life and a virtual tour of the museum complex, which houses original buildings.

"Texas Revolution Maps." http://www.latinamericanstudies.org/texas-maps.htm. Illustrates military campaigns of the revolution and detailed plans of attack used at the Alamo and San Jacinto battles.

"Westward Expansion—The Texas Revolution." http://digitalhistory.uh.edu/database/article_display.cfm?HHID=312. Provides comprehensive biographies of important Mexican and Texan military leaders and includes general historical facts and events of the revolution itself.

Multimedia Sources

The Texas Revolution from Anahuac to San Jacinto 1832–1836. Austin, TX: Forest Glen Productions, 2005. DVD. 65 minutes. Underscores the pivotal events in the Texas Revolution through still photography and live interviews.

The U.S.-Mexican War 1846–1848. Alexandria, VA: PBS Home Video, 2000. 2 DVDs. 240 minutes. Disc one focuses on what led up to the war and provides an examination of the Texas Revolution through interviews with American and Mexican historians, re-enactments, and archived photos.

6. Bear Flag Revolt (June 14, 1846)

With the United States' annexation of Texas in 1845 and Mexico's refusal to accept this decree, California inevitably became the next theater of political and military action. Concern over British interest in California and Oregon also made the immediate acquisition of this Mexican state an important goal of the Polk administration. While U.S. ground troops and naval ships were surrounding strategic Mexican military and political outposts throughout California by 1846, Anglo Americans, who had been illegally entering and settling in Northern California for quite some time, were preparing their own revolt. One of the leaders of the Anglo California rebels was Capt. John C. Frémont, whose passion for exploration and high-level connections with the U.S. Senate encouraged him to pave the road toward the United States' annexation of California. Despite war against Mexico not being officially declared in Washington, D.C., American settlers in the Napa and Sacramento river valleys feared their illegal status would soon become grounds for expulsion from California. Therefore, the settlers opted for a pre-emptive strike. On June 14, 1846, a small group of armed settlers, led by Ezekiel Merritt, arrested the northern California commander Gen. Mariano Guadalupe Vallejo at his Sonoma home and seized a supply of weapons. Since no official announcement of war had been made, the settlers, also known as the Bear Flaggers, proclaimed the sovereignty of the Bear Flag Republic on July 4, 1846, and raised a crude, hand-painted flag that bore a grizzly bear and the inscription "California Republic." Despite efforts made by Gen. José María Castro to suppress the revolt, Frémont's association with the civilian rebels staved off further counter-attacks while lending the revolt greater military legitimacy. While the Bear Flag Revolt was occurring in the regions of Sonoma and Sutter's Fort, U.S. Commodore John D. Sloat peacefully captured Monterey and San Francisco in early July. Likewise, Commodore Robert F. Stockton took Los Angeles a month later and assumed the title of California's governor in the name of the United States. By July 9, 1846, control over Sonoma and Sutter's Fort was transferred to the U.S. military. The replacement of the Bear Flag with the U.S. flag officially dissolved the Bear Flag Republic and absorbed Capt. Frémont's California Battalion of civilians into the U.S. military. Eventually, California became a territory in 1848 as a provision of the Treaty of Guadalupe Hidalgo that ended the U.S.-Mexican War and was annexed officially by the U.S. Congress in 1850.

TERM PAPER SUGGESTIONS

1. As the son-in-law of Thomas H. Benton, one of the most powerful and influential American senators in the mid-19th century, Frémont could count on legislative support for his plans with California. Explain why Frémont chose to ignore his initial orders to survey the Arkansas and Red rivers and what he did instead. Also, discuss how these actions correlated with the agenda Sen. Benton had for wresting control over California from Mexico.

2. The strong, visible presence of Anglo settlers in California aided in the state's eventual social and political transformation. Indeed, events such as the Bear Flag Revolt, the military take-over of key California cities, and the acquisition of this former Mexican state at the end of the U.S.-Mexican War set the stage for the massive waves of opportunists who came to California at the start of the Gold Rush in 1849 and during the state's annexation the following year. Discuss what long-term changes and social, cultural, and political impact this chain of events had on the Californios (the citizens of the Republic of Mexico), who remained in the former Mexican state.

3. Gen. Vallejo has been noted for being sympathetic to the American presence in California. Nevertheless, his dishonor and loss of vast tracts of lands illustrated how Californios, regardless of their social station or extent of their cooperation, were denied basic rights afforded to them by the 1848 Treaty of Guadalupe Hidalgo. Describe the nature of Vallejo's sympathy toward Anglo Americans and how he still was not protected by articles VIII and IX of the Treaty.

4. Critique the political and military leadership of significant Californios such as Gen. José María Castro, Capt. Joaquín de la Torre, Capt. José María Flores, and Gov. Pio Pico. Consider what assistance, in terms of supplies and directions, they were receiving in 1846 from Mexico City and argue how their respective decisions as leaders shaped the outcome of the Bear Flag Revolt and U.S. military seizures of key California cities.

ALTERNATIVE TERM PAPER SUGGESTIONS

1. Although Commodore Stockton seized Los Angeles in July 1846, he lost control over this important military center and its surrounding towns to Capt. José María Flores two months later. Eventually, Gen. Stephan W. Kearny arrived on the scene to supplement Stockton's forces and recapture Southern California by January 1847. Design a

PowerPoint presentation using maps, original timelines and captions, period photographs, and images outlining this pivotal struggle over California that had been set in motion by the Bear Flag Revolt only a few months earlier.

2. Sloat and Stockton had very different military approaches to the American presence in California at the dawn of the U.S.-Mexican War. Both were praised and criticized for overstepping their roles in decisions they made. Prepare a detailed report to Congress either defending or condemning the military campaign in California. Use official period correspondence as well as the U.S. Constitution and international law at the time to prove your case.

SELECTED SOURCES

Primary Sources

Bayard, Samuel J. *A Sketch of the Life of Com. Robert F. Stockton with an Appendix, Comprising His Correspondence with the Navy Department Respecting His Conquest of California: and Extracts from the Defence of Col. J.C. Frémont, in Relation to the Same Subject: Together with His Speeches in the Senate of the United States, and His Political Letters.* New York: Derby and Jackson, 1856. Comprises important letters and documents written by the top U.S. naval commander in the California military theater who assumed the title of governor on behalf of the United States.

Beebe, Rose Marie, and Robert M. Senkewicz, eds. *Lands of Promise and Despair: Chronicles of Early California, 1535–1846.* Berkeley, CA: Heyday Books, 2001. Accompanied by maps, illustrations, and portraits, this work assembles over 60 selections of first-hand accounts from Californios, including the immigration of Anglo Americans and seizure of California.

Beebe, Rose Marie, and Robert M. Senkewicz, eds. *Testimonios: Early California through the Eyes of Women, 1815–1848.* Berkeley, CA: Heyday Books, 2006. Presents original interviews with 13 Californio women during the pivotal transformations of California from its Spanish and Mexican origins to the annexation in the mid-19th century by the United States.

Bidwell, John. "Frémont in the Conquest of California." http://www.sfmuseum. com/hist6/fremont.html. Presents a first-hand account of Frémont, the Bear Flaggers, and U.S. Armed Forces and their military takeover of California. Also includes links to other significant events in early California history.

Hulaniski, Frederick J., ed. *The History of Contra Costa County, California.* Berkeley, CA: The Elms Publishing Company, 1917. Includes general overviews of the East Bay region during the 19th century with a detailed account of key participants in the Bear Flag Revolt.

Secondary Sources

Chaffin, Tom. *Pathfinder: John Charles Frémont and the Course of American Empire.* New York: Hill and Wang, 2002. Explores how Frémont embodied the United States' vision of Manifest Destiny and articulates his participation in the Bear Flag Revolt.

Harlow, Neal. *California Conquered: The Annexation of a Mexican Province, 1846–1850.* Berkeley: University of California Press, 1982. Provides detailed attention to primary sources from key figures during the conquest of California.

Pitt, Leonard, and Ramón A. Gutiérrez. *Decline of the Californios: A Social History of the Spanish-Speaking Californians, 1846–1890.* Berkeley: University of California Press, 1998. Charts how the native-born Californios fell from their positions of social and economic power to a state of disenfranchisement.

Rosenus, Alan. *General Vallejo and the Advent of the Americans.* Berkeley, CA: Heyday Books/Urion Press, 1999. This rich biography examines how Vallejo maintained that a policy of open immigration for Anglo Americans was the only way to settle California.

Walker, Dale L. *Bear Flag Rising: The Conquest of California, 1846.* New York: Forge Books, 2000. Focuses on the rivaling personalities of Commodore Robert F. Stockton and General Stephan W. Kearny and how Capt. John C. Frémont is caught between these military luminaries.

World Wide Web

"The Bear Flag Museum." http://www.bearflagmuseum.org/index.html. Comprehensive collection of images, documents, and analytical resources on the evolution of California's flag. Incorporates links to graphics, statutes pertaining to the flag, and a chronology of the flag.

"The Bear Flag Revolt and the Anglo-American Conquest of California." http://www.militarymuseum.org/BFR.html. Includes detailed historical account of the 1846 revolt with interactive maps and links for more information on early California history.

"Captain John Charles Fremont and the Bear Flag Revolt." http://www.militarymuseum.org/fremont.html. Contains brief overview of Frémont's role in the revolt with images of Frémont and Anglo-American flags used during the conflict.

"General Vallejo practiced the art of living well." http://www.berkeleyheritage. com/essays/lachryma_montis.html. This is Daniella Thompson's article reprinted by the Berkeley Architectural Heritage Association that contains architectural history and contemporary pictures of Gen. Vallejo's home on his 200-acre ranch called Lachryma Montis and was one of the dramatic scenes during the Bear Flag Revolt.

Multimedia Source

Frémont, the Conqueror of California. New York: History Channel, 2005. DVD. 50 minutes. Through period portraits and historical reenactments, this documentary explores the complicated relationship Frémont had with other U.S. military leaders in the seizing of California from Mexico.

7. Treaty of Guadalupe Hidalgo (1848)

Manifest Destiny, which was the belief that European Americans were divinely destined to inherit the whole of the North American continent, had been the driving force behind President James K. Polk's ambitious plan to colonize all westward lands that stretched to the Pacific Ocean. As such, events like Mexico's refusal to recognize the Republic of Texas (1836) after the revolution, the eventual annexation of Texas by the United States (1845), and the short-lived Bear Flag Republic revolt in California (1845) were all contributing factors that had ignited the larger conflict between the United States and Mexico (1846 to 1848), and had allowed the United States to reach the Pacific Ocean. The U.S.-Mexico War itself made national American heroes out of men like Zachary Taylor, who fought successfully along the Rio Grande and later became the 12th American president, or Generals Stephan Kearney and Winfield Scott, who were successful in invading the rest of Mexico and defeating Santa Anna in Mexico's capital in 1847. However, once the war closed militarily, it soon became a political one. Refusing to return to Washington, D.C., from Mexico despite angering President Polk, Chief Clerk of the State Department Nicholas P. Trist remained at his post and eventually negotiated and signed a treaty with Mexican officials in Guadalupe Hidalgo, a suburb of the Mexican capital, on

February 2, 1848, a week after gold was discovered in California. Growing opposition in the American Congress between Whigs, who loathed Polk's imperialist ambitions for westward expansion, and Democrats, who advocated taking all of the Mexican Republic rather than just its northern territories, necessitated the immediate ratification of the treaty. In the end, the U.S. Senate passed the treaty on March 10, 1848, with a vote of 38 to 14. Likewise, Mexico's Congress ratified the treaty and its alterations made by the United States two months later on May 25. For the United States, the Treaty of Guadalupe Hidalgo included the purchase of New Mexico and Alta California (the present-day states of New Mexico, western sections of Wyoming and Colorado, Arizona, Utah, Nevada, and California) for the sum of $15 million and American land claims of $3,250,000. For the people of Mexico, the treaty signified not only the loss of strategic military and economic sites such as San Francisco and San Diego bays; the fertile California Central Valley; the vast systems of the rancheros; or Santa Fe, New Mexico, but also the loss of thousands of its citizens who remained in the northern states and no longer belonged to the Republic of Mexico or fully welcomed into European American society politically, economically, or culturally.

TERM PAPER SUGGESTIONS

1. To push the Treaty of Guadalupe Hidalgo through Congress, President Polk removed Article X. Discuss what was provided for in this repealed article, and speculate why it was removed. How did its removal underscore Polk's vision of a postwar United States in terms of land grants and legal ownership of property?

2. The cultural and psychological legacy of losing the American Southwest and California during the Mexican-American War has long impacted Mexican Americans and their relationship between their American citizenship and Mexican identity. Discuss how Chicanos have used Aztlan as a way to re-establish Mexican-American identity and bring a sense of unity and pride to the community politically and artistically.

3. The Gadsden Purchase in 1853 signaled the final phase of Mexican-American postwar negotiations. Describe what this transaction was and what economic, political, and cultural impact it had on Mexico and the United States.

4. The approaching U.S. presidential election of 1848 politicized the ratification process of the Treaty of Guadalupe Hidalgo. Who were the primary voices in the debate over the treaty and its provisions? Which key issues were on the table for discussion? How did they impact the manner in which the treaty was interpreted? What effect did the treaty have on Congress' vision of a postwar America?

ALTERNATIVE TERM PAPER SUGGESTIONS

1. In March 1947, Harry S. Truman becomes the first American president to visit Mexico. As a Mexican journalist, create an iMovie of news clips and photographs, accompanied by an article describing the significance of where Truman went and how the 100-year anniversary of the Mexican-American War served as backdrop for his diplomatic visit and the impact it had on Mexican leaders and citizens.

2. Chief Clerk of the State Department Nicholas P. Trist, who negotiated the Treaty of Guadalupe Hidalgo for the Americans, was renown for his detailed and extensive correspondences. Write an open letter as Trist justifying your defiance of President Polk's order to quit the diplomatic team and immediately return to Washington, D.C.

SUGGESTED SOURCES

Primary Sources

Libura, Krystyna M., Luis Gerardo Morales Moreno, Jesús Velasco Márquez, eds. *Echoes of the Mexican-American War.* Trans. Mark Fried. Toronto, Canada: Groundwood Books, 2005. Contains an extensive collection of eyewitness accounts and documents, photographs, and period illustrations that represents both perspectives from the United States and Mexico.

"The Treaty of Guadalupe Hidalgo." http://www.loc.gov/rr/hispanic/ghtreaty/. This Library of Congress site includes a basic overview of the treaty, maps of negotiated areas, and the treaty itself article by article.

Secondary Sources

Chávez, Ernesto. *The War with Mexico: A Brief History with Documents.* Boston: Bedford/St. Martin's, 2007. Part of the Bedford Series in History and Culture, this text articulates the buildup and aftermath of the war in terms of how military conflict racializes an enemy and underscores the position and privilege of white male citizenship in contrast to Mexican men and women, American Indians, and slaves. Includes detailed maps and a bibliography for further research in this area.

Francaviqlia, Richard V., and Douglas W. Richmond, eds. *Dueling Eagles: Reinterpreting the U.S.-Mexican War, 1846–1848.* Fort Worth: Texas Christian University Press, 2000. Incorporates critical essays from American and Mexican scholars concerning the role of Great Britain in the war and the impact of the first war correspondents in the press. Also explores some of the collaboration that took place between American and Mexican troops during the conflict.

Griswold Del Castillo, Richard. *The Treaty of Guadalupe Hidalgo: A Legacy of Conflict.* Norman: University of Oklahoma Press, 1990. Provides a comprehensive study and analysis of the treaty including a copy of the treaty itself, with maps, appendixes, and detailed notes on published and unpublished material.

Henderson, Timothy J. *A Glorious Defeat: Mexico and Its War with the United States.* New York: Hill and Wang, 2007. Offers a unique perspective of the war from Mexico's point of view and highlights the complex ideological debates and discussions concerning 19th-century U.S. aggression and Mexican politics.

Ohrt, Wallace. *Defiant Peacemaker: Nicholas Trist in the Mexican War.* College Station, TX: Texas A & M University Press, 1997. Analyzes the Chief Clerk of the State Department's defiance of President Polk's recall to Washington, D.C., to secure a treaty with Mexico that would ensure that nation's full surrender.

Singletary, Otis A. *The Mexican War.* Chicago: University of Chicago Press, 1960. Part of the Chicago History of American Civilization series, this work focuses on how the Mexican-American War embodied the rhetoric of America's Manifest Destiny through a comprehensive examination of the conflict's military campaigns and diplomatic actions.

Wheelan, Joseph. *Invading Mexico: America's Continental Dream and the Mexican War, 1846–1848.* New York: Carroll & Graf Publishers, 2007. Describes engaging battles and thought-provoking analyses of the war while exploring the political identity crisis the United States was experiencing as an emerging superpower in the Western Hemisphere. Also examines the public opposition to the war by Americans such as Henry David Thoreau, Ralph Waldo Emerson, and Abraham Lincoln.

World Wide Web

"The Mexican War." http://www.sonofthesouth.net/mexican-war/war.htm. This inclusive site offers countless links to specific battles, key players in the war, historical overviews, and original maps of the Mexican-American War.

"War Message of President Polk, May 11, 1846." http://historicaltextarchive. com/sections.php?op=viewarticle&artid=219. Presents President James K. Polk's complete declaration of war with Mexico to Congress.

Multimedia Sources

The Mexican-American War. New York: A & E Home Video, 2008. DVD. 100 minutes. Explores the entirety of the war from both sides of the conflict featuring in-depth analysis and discussion from eminent Mexican and American historians.

The U.S.-Mexican War 1846–1848. Alexandria, VA: PBS Home Video, 2000. 2 DVDs. 240 minutes. Disc two focuses on the closure to the war and the detailed features of the Treaty of Guadalupe Hidalgo through interviews with American and Mexican historians, re-enactments, and archived photos and illustrations.

8. José Martí Exiled in New York (1880–1895)

Born in Havana, Cuba, on January 8, 1853, José Martí is regarded as Cuba's premier national hero for his political, philosophical, and literary contributions in creating the identity of a post-colonial Cuban republic. By the late 19th century, Cuba and Puerto Rico were the last Spanish colonies in the New World. Long-standing inequalities in civil liberties and political representation between Cuban-born Spanish subjects (called the Creoles) and Spanish-born subjects living in the New World (called the *peninsulares*) eventually led to the Ten Years' War (1868–1878). However, this initial struggle to gain independence from Spain failed. The following decade, severe economic depression, unchecked social disenfranchisement, and continued political oppression forced many into exile. Chief among these Cuban émigrés was José Martí, an early patriot of Cuban independence and an outspoken political journalist who was convicted of treason and banished from the island in 1871. Over the next several decades of his life, Martí became more politically involved in the liberation of Cuba, and by 1880, Martí traveled to New York City and throughout Florida to rally the support of exiled Cubans and others in his cause to liberate Cuba. While residing in the United States, he wrote for a variety of U.S. and South American newspapers as an expert on Latin American and

Caribbean politics; served as a consul for Argentina, Paraguay, and Uruguay; published original poetry and essays; and translated many works into Spanish including Helen Hunt Jackson's 1884 epic *Ramona*. Martí's and other Cuban émigrés' in New York and Florida concern over splinter Cuban political groups liberating the island and the U.S. growing interest in acquiring Cuba as a colony led them to form the Cuban Revolutionary Party in 1892. As party leader, Martí continued to travel throughout the United States and Latin America speaking on behalf of Cuban liberation and democracy. He believed that Cuba should be independent from Spain while being free from internal racism and exploitation. Eventually, he organized and participated in invading Cuba with the aid of former Cuban generals exiled after the Ten Years' War. However, during the first invasion in 1896, he was killed, thus ensuring his prominent place in post-colonial Cuban history.

TERM PAPER SUGGESTIONS

1. Among his many significant roles in the struggle for basic human rights and Cuba's liberation, José Martí was also a respected poet. Select two of his prolific poems and provide an interpretive analysis of them that underscores Martí's social and political philosophies.

2. Often called the Latin American Alexis de Tocqueville, José Martí had a unique perspective on the changing dynamics of the late-19th century United States. Discuss what qualities in U.S. culture he admired and which practices he criticized. For Martí, how was the United States both an embodiment of the democratic ideal and paradoxically a paragon of new imperialism in the West?

3. While there were a number of exiled figures and political action groups who disagreed over what a post-Spanish Cuba would look like, José Martí did his best to bring these disparate voices together. Compare some of the other important liberators such as Generals Máximo Gómez and Antonio Maceo and analyze how their strategies differed from Martí's in framing a Cuban republic.

4. Along with José Martí, there were a few thousand Cuban exiles residing along the Eastern seaboard by the late 19th century. Identify some of these key émigré communities, and articulate their connection with Martí and the idea of a liberated Cuba.

ALTERNATIVE TERM PAPER SUGGESTIONS

1. Despite the various leaders and governments that have ruled Cuba since the end of the Spanish-American War in 1898, most of them have claimed to rule in accordance with the philosophies and dictates of Cuba's national hero: José Martí. However, in the 21st century there continues to be a wide ideological chasm between those groups who say they uphold the tenets of Martí. The Castro regime and the anti-Castro Cuban American National Foundation are examples of this. Write a speech as Martí himself that will be delivered to the United Nations General Assembly addressing the manner in which these groups argue they have Cuba's interests at heart. As a modern-day Martí, how do you perceive their respective actions and rhetoric? How would a modern-day José Martí interpret a 21st-century Cuba?

2. Using online documents, images, maps, photographs, and timetables, generate an iMovie of José Martí's life of exile and travels through Europe, the United States, Latin America, and the Caribbean. Highlight his important political philosophies and his continued significance to Cuban nationals and Cuban Americans today.

SUGGESTED SOURCES

Primary Sources

Martí, José. *Selected Writings.* Trans. Esther Allen. New York: Penguin Classics, 2002. Includes Martí's major works with the first English translation of his final achievement: "War Diaries."

———. *Versos Sencillos: Simple Verses.* Trans. Manuel A. Tellechea. Houston, TX: Arte Público Press, 1997. This is a bilingual edition of Martí's complete work of poetry.

"Old Poetry." http://oldpoetry.com/oauthor/show/Jose_Marti. Reproduces a number of José Martí's translated poems.

Schulman, Ivan A., ed. *José Martí Reader: Writings on the Americas,* 2nd ed. New York: Ocean Press, 2006. Provides one of the most comprehensive collections of Martí's essays, letters, and poetry.

Secondary Sources

Abel, Christopher, and Nissa Torrents, eds. *José Martí: Revolutionary Democrat.* Durham, NC: Duke University Press, 1986. Features a collection of lectures on the patriot presented at London's Institute of Latin American Studies in 1986.

Belnap, Jeffrey, and Raúl Fernández, eds. *José Martí's "Our America": From National to Hemispheric Cultural Studies.* Durham, NC: Duke University Press, 1998. Features a comprehensive collection of essays analyzing Martí's political writings, fiction and poetry, essays, speeches, and a choice of his works he translated in his lifetime.

Gray, Richard Butler. *José Martí, Cuban Patriot.* Gainesville: University of Florida Press, 1962. Charts the biographical and philosophical image of Martí through a careful study of his personal life and symbolic life in Cuban culture.

Guerra, Lillian. *The Myth of José Martí: Conflicting Nationalisms in Early Twentieth-Century Cuba.* Chapel Hill: University of North Carolina Press, 2005. Examines how the varying and often conflicting interpretations of Cuba's early democratic identity are rooted in Martí's speeches and writings.

Montero, Oscar. *José Martí: An Introduction.* New York: Palgrave Macmillan, 2004. Provides an excellent overview of Martí's life and philosophies that is easily accessible and relevant to a 21st-century audience.

Ronning, C. Neale. *José Martí and the Émigré Colony in Key West: Leadership and State Formation.* Westport, CT: Praeger, 1990. This detailed explication of José Martí's style and manners as a community organizer and political activist centers on his involvement with the Cuban émigré colony situated in Key West, Florida.

Schwarzmann, Georg M. *The Influence of Emerson and Whitman on the Cuban Poet José Martí: Themes of Immigration, Colonialism, and Independence.* Lewiston, NY: Edwin Mellen Press, 2009. Articulates some of the most significant parallels and divergences on social and political issues of American poets that Martí translated and wrote about.

Turton, Peter. *José Martí: Architect of Cuba's Freedom.* Totowa, NJ: Zed Books, 1986. Explores how Martí's life of exile in New York and travel to places such as Spain, the United States, the Caribbean, and Latin America exposed him to numerous classes of people and to political ideologies such as imperialism, capitalism, and socialism, all of which influenced his writing and activism.

World Wide Web

"History of Cuba." http://www.historyofcuba.com/history/havana/Marti.htm. Contains a brief biography of José Martí and includes relevant links to his translated letters and articles. Also provides historical timelines and period photographs and portraits of the Cuban revolutionary.

"José Martí: A Letter to the Board of Advisors for Key West." http://cnx.org/content/m23122/latest/. This brief article discusses one of Martí's unpublished letters, which asks for funds to keep a Cuban émigré newspaper in operation. The article analyzes the letter in the context of Martí's political activism.

"The Limits of Analogy: José Martí and the Haymarket Martyrs." http://www.ncsu.edu/project/acontracorriente/fall_04/Conway.pdf. Christopher Conway's article focuses on the 1886 Haymarket Square Riot in Chicago and the sensationalized trial and executions that followed. He presents Martí's perspective on the event and its aftermath since Martí believed that the labor movement was an integral aspect of how the working class and developing nations in Latin America would engineer new and liberating forms of governance.

"The Spanish American War Centennial Web site." http://www.spanamwar.com/Marti.htm. Offers biographical information on Martí's life and ideologies and includes a short bibliography of online sources pertaining to Martí.

Multimedia Sources

Destino de imperios 1898: la guerra de España-Cuba-USA. Princeton, NJ: Films for the Humanities and Sciences, 2001. DVD. 54 minutes. Focuses on the life and accomplishments of Cuba's greatest patriot: José Martí. English version.

Politicians and Revolutionaries. Princeton, NJ: Films for the Humanities and Sciences, 2008. DVD. 49 minutes. Documents the cultural independence Latin America experienced from the Old World during the 19th and 20th centuries by highlighting pivotal writers and revolutionaries including José Martí.

9. Ybor City, Florida, Established (1886)

One of the major centers for cigar production in the world, Ybor City was founded in the northeast corner of Tampa, Florida, in the spring of 1886 as a company town by Vicente Martínez Ybor. Ybor, who immigrated to Cuba from Spain in 1832, established a cigar factory in Havana, Cuba, in 1856 and began producing the famous Prince of Wales brand of cigars. Because of his support of Cuban insurgents during the Ten Years' War (1868–1878), he fled the island along with a number of Cuban cigar workers, to Key West, Florida, in 1869 to resume cigar operations. Finding Key West to be a difficult location because of few expansion opportunities and growing labor unrest among Spanish and Cuban workers, Ybor again relocated to Tampa, Florida, and purchased an initial 40 acres with the assistance of the Tampa Board of Trade in 1885. His Ybor City, which was officially established in 1886, was an ideal location because of a new railroad line that moved in, the humid climate, and a growing port. To ensure that workers would not have to migrate back and forth from Florida to Cuba to be with family, Ybor constructed homes he called "casitas" that workers could purchase at cost. He also encouraged small businesses to move in, which attracted Italian and Jewish immigrants to cater to workers' needs. In 1887, Tampa officially annexed Ybor City, which allowed it to grow, develop, and prosper well into the first decades of the 20th century. From this growth and permanence, a number of fraternal organizations and social clubs emerged in Ybor City that provided services to Cubans and Spaniards including free medical attention and libraries, educational programs, and social and sports functions. However, most significantly, the "clubs" created a stronger sense of community and extended family. Just before the Stock Market Crash in 1929, Ybor City had produced nearly 500 million cigars. However, during the Great Depression, many factories were closed and workers were replaced with cigar-rolling machines. Ybor City never fully recovered after World War II. Indeed, it was not until the 1980s and 1990s that Ybor City came back to life not as a cigar capital, but a tourist site. Today, many of the formerly abandoned cigar factory structures and buildings have been converted into hotels, nightclubs, and restaurants, and the city continues to make a social and economic comeback as one of the first Cuban American cities in the United States.

TERM PAPER SUGGESTIONS

1. Cuban exile José Martí would frequently make trips to Ybor City, Florida, to speak with cigar workers and industry leaders to gain their support for Cuban independence. Explain what Martí's relationship to Ybor City was in the late 19th century and describe how the cigar factories remained politically informed, organized, and active. What was their commitment to Cuba's revolutionary cause?

2. What was life like for the average immigrant working in a cigar factory? Discuss the living conditions and social-political atmosphere of

Ybor City in the late 19th century and early 20th century. Draw from primary sources to maintain a stronger sense of how events and circumstances impacted the neighborhoods of this vibrant immigrant enclave.

3. Ybor City was often revered historically as an integrated community. However, argue how integrated people were. Consider the various social clubs that were created and the kinds of groups who came to Ybor City at the end of the 19th century: the Spanish, Cuban, Afro-Carribean, Italian, and Jewish communities. How did these immigrants interact with one another and what were the challenges of assimilation?

4. After the Great Depression and World War II, Ybor City never fully recovered socially or economically. However, by the 1980s and 1990s, the city enjoyed a kind of renaissance. Discuss how this came about, and describe how the city survives today in the 21st century. How does Ybor City attempt to recapture its past while projecting a new image for the future?

ALTERNATIVE TERM PAPER SUGGESTIONS

1. As a late-19th century newspaper reporter, conduct an interview with the founder and benefactor of Ybor City, Vicente Martínez Ybor. Create a Web site that discusses the visions Ybor has for his new town and the role he plays in a booming industry.

2. You are a member of the Ybor City Chamber of Commerce and have been appointed to design an online pamphlet, which includes graphic illustrations that encourage tourists or businesses to visit/ invest in your city. Draw on the city's historical and cultural significance, but project your ideas for how Ybor City is now a 21st-century city and worthy of attention.

SUGGESTED SOURCES

Primary Sources

Espinosa, Jack. *Cuban Bread Crumbs.* Philadelphia: Xlibris Corporation, 2008. A memoir from a child of Spanish immigrants recounts the events from his life and the Spanish, Cuban, and Italian communities before and after World War II.

Ingalls, Robert P., and Louis A. Perez. *Tampa Cigar Workers: A Pictorial History.* Gainesville: University Press of Florida, 2003. Contains over 200 photographs of Cuban, Spanish, and Italian workers and their families, and provides detailed captions for the images, which are drawn from newspaper articles, archives, and oral accounts.

Pacheco, Ferdie. *Ybor City Chronicles: A Memoir.* Gainesville: University Press of Florida, 1994. Pacheco, who was boxer legend Muhammad Ali's personal physician in the 1960s and 1970s, recaptures his life growing up in Ybor City during the Great Depression and following World War II. His memoir includes photographs of the events and personalities that made this immigrant enclave a vital one for fostering cultural identity and community.

Secondary Sources

Lastra, Frank Trebín. *Ybor City: The Making of a Landmark Town.* Tampa, FL: University of Tampa Press, 2006. Provides details of the lives and everyday experiences of Cuban, Spanish, and Italian immigrants and the city's transformation throughout the early 20th century.

Mormino, Gary R., and George E. Pozzetta. *The Immigrant World of Ybor City: Italians and Their Latin Neighbors in Tampa, 1885–1985.* Gainesville: University Press of Florida, 1998. Focuses on the Italian community and experience in Ybor City using a broad range of oral testimony and official documents.

Pacheco, Ferdie. *Pacheco's Art of Ybor City.* Gainesville: University of Florida Press, 1997. Includes 33 original paintings of this celebrated artist's childhood city.

Westfall, L. Glenn. *Don Vicente Martínez Ybor, the Man and His Empire: Development of the Clear Havana Industry in Cuba and Florida in the Nineteenth Century.* New York: Garland Publishing, 1987. Provides an in-depth examination of how Ybor himself built his cigar industry first in Cuba and then in Florida, becoming the world leader in cigar production.

Ybor Redevelopment Agency (Ybor City, FL). *Ybor City Historic District Revitalization Plan.* Los Angeles, CA: Economic Research Associates, 1983. Official city report highlights the gentrification plans and process that reanimated Ybor City in the early 1980s.

Yglesias, Jose. *A Wake in Ybor City.* Houston, TX: Arte Publíco Press, 1988. Features a fictional account of three Cuban immigrant sisters who work in one of the cigar factories in Ybor City. It is a provocative examination of assimilation into U.S. culture.

World Wide Web

"The Afro-Cuban Community in Ybor City and Tampa, 1886–1910." http://www.oah.org/pubs/magazine/africanamerican/mirabel.html. Nancy Raquel Mirabel's 1993 article published by the Organization of

American Histories discusses how the Afro-Cuban population created a separate community in the shadow of the cigar industry as a result of Jim Crow laws of discrimination.

"Ybor City Chamber of Commerce." http://www.ybor.org. Official Web site for Ybor City, Florida, provides general information for visitors and businesses.

"Ybor City: Cigar Capital of the World." http://www.nps.gov/history/nr/twhp/wwwlps/lessons/51ybor/51ybor.htm. Details lesson plans on teaching about Ybor City as a historical site and features links to historical reading and visual material.

"Ybor City Historical Site." http://www.lcweb2.loc.gov/diglib/legacies/FL200 002851.html. Presents a brief overview of the city's history and cultural significance.

"Ybor City Museum Society." http://www.ybormuseum.org. Incorporates general information about the history of Ybor City and includes links to classroom learning activities for students, educational packets for history instructors, and relevant Web sites for historical societies and social clubs of Ybor City.

Multimedia Sources

The Fabulous Story of the Cuban Cigar. New York: Palm Pictures, 1999. DVD. 60 minutes. Contains an intriguing look at the production of the cigar industry and culture as told by historical experts and connoisseurs of cigars.

Living in America: One Hundred Years of Ybor City. New York: Filmakers Library, 1987. DVD. 53 minutes. Focuses on the Spanish, Cuban, and Italian communities and their contributions to the culture emerging from the cigar industry during pivotal challenges and changes such as the Great Depression and World War II.

10. Destruction of the USS *Maine* (February 15, 1898)

Tensions between the United States and Spain's continued colonial rule in the Caribbean had been escalating during the second half of the 19th century. Cuban guerilla conflicts such as the Ten Years' War (1868–1878), the Guerra Chiquita or "Little War" (1879–1880), and the cruel violations of civil liberties by the Spanish military governor Valeriano Weyler in 1896 were widely sensationalized by the "yellow" American press and drew great public sentiment from the American people. In response to volatile conditions in Cuba, the U.S. government sent the USS *Maine* to Havana principally to ensure that American sugar corporations, business investments, and its own citizens were being protected. On the evening of February 15, 1898, the front section of the USS *Maine* suddenly exploded, sinking the entire battleship and killing over 260 crew members. Media moguls like William R. Hearst used this event to fuel the flames of war sentiment with Spain, which was slowly escalating. "Remember the Maine! To hell with Spain!" was the headline of the *New York Journal* on February 18 and quickly became a national rallying cry for revenge. Even Theodore Roosevelt, who was serving as Assistant Secretary of the Navy at the time, publicly accused Spain of orchestrating the plot. Theories rapidly surfaced over the following weeks as to the cause of the explosion and its potential architects. Some claimed it was Spain, while others implied it had been Cuban rebels trying to draw the United States into a war with Spain and gain their own independence. Still, some argued that the United States itself staged the explosion to justify going to war with Spain since it had long made overtures of possessing the island colony since Thomas Jefferson's administration at the beginning of the 19th century. However, despite President William McKinley's desire not to rush into a war with Spain, a U.S. naval Court of Inquiry established by the president determined that a mine in Havana's harbor had caused the USS *Maine* to explode. Although it was never clearly determined who was responsible for this, Congress was quickly influenced by the pro-war sentiment that had swept the country and declared war on April 25, 1898. The war was swift and decisive, lasting only until the end of that year and with few U.S. casualties. In compliance with the Treaty of Paris, which was signed on December 10, 1898, the United States gained control over Spain's remaining empire, which included Cuba, Puerto Rico, Guam, and the Philippines, and emerged on the world stage as a viable colonial power.

TERM PAPER SUGGESTIONS

1. The Teller Amendment was a provision authored by U.S. Senator Henry Teller and became a part of Congress' recognition of Cuban independence on April 19, 1898. It clearly stated that the United States did not seek to govern Cuba and promised it would "leave the government and control of the island to its people" once war with Spain ended. Argue whether the United States kept its promise after the Spanish American War ended in December 1898.

2. For over a century, the truth behind the destruction of the USS *Maine* has initiated countless investigations and inquiries because it was a seminal event that drew Americans into a war with Spain. Describe the various reports that have been presented and determine their validity. Do you believe the Spanish American War was inevitable whether the USS *Maine* event occurred?

3. Theodore Roosevelt, who later became president of the United States in 1901, quit his position as Assistant Secretary of the Navy in June 1898 to create the First Volunteer Cavalry Regiment, commonly referred to as the "Rough Riders." Roosevelt gained notoriety for his military campaigns in Cuba and Puerto Rico during the Spanish American War and set the political stage for continued colonial expansion and involvement in the early 20th century. Discuss how U.S. statesmen like McKinley and Roosevelt viewed Latin America and what the role was for the United States at the turn of the 20th century.

4. In what ways did "yellow" newspapers in the United States sensationalize not only the insurrections in Cuba, but also the destruction of the USS *Maine* on February 15, 1898? What responsibility did the media and businessmen like William R. Hearst have in igniting a war between the United States and Spain over Cuban independence?

ALTERNATIVE TERM PAPER SUGGESTIONS

1. Read several first-hand accounts of the destruction of the USS *Maine* from key publications at the time. As a journalist writing for a "yellow" newspaper such as the *New York World*, the *New York Journal*, or many others by the end of the 19th century, create a "yellow" iMovie of this momentous event with text and period political cartoons and photographs that mimic the kind of sensational journalism being generated on the eve of the Spanish American War. Write a short analysis of the role the media can play in generating pro-war or antiwar sentiments among the public.

2. Create a series of interactive maps of key locations during the Spanish American War including the site of the USS *Maine,* the U.S. naval blockade under Admiral William T. Sampson, the movement of the Spanish naval force under Admiral Pascual Cervera y Topete, and pivotal battles in Cuba, Puerto Rico, and the Philippines. Include a brief timeline of these collective events.

SELECTED SOURCES
Primary Sources

Post, Charles Johnson. *The Little War of Private Post: The Spanish-American War Seen Up Close*. Lincoln, NE: Bison Books, 1999. Features a personal account of a private enlisted in the 71st New York Infantry during key battles in Cuba.

United States Army. *Correspondence Relating to the War with Spain Including the Insurrection in the Philippine Islands and the China Relief Expedition: April 15, 1898, to July 30, 1902*. Vols. 1 and 2. Washington, DC: Center of Military History, 1993. Provides full and comprehensive compilation of first-hand military correspondence through the war and its aftermath.

United States House Committee on Naval Affairs. *Hearings on the Disposition of the Wreck of the U.S.S. Maine in Habana Harbor, Cuba*. Washington, DC: GPO, 1910. This government publication continues the in-depth investigation on the cause of the USS *Maine*'s destruction, which initiates the war.

Secondary Sources

Crampton, Samuel Willard. *The Sinking of the U.S.S. Maine: Declaring War against Spain*. New York: Chelsea House Publications, 2008. Part of the Milestones in American History series, this source provides a comprehensive overview of the event itself and the immediate aftermath.

Hamilton, Richard F. *President McKinley, War and Empire. Volume 1: President McKinley and the Coming War, 1898*. New Brunswick, NJ: Transaction Publishers, 2006. This first volume investigates McKinley's dealings with the U.S. press, Cuban affairs, and the American public in the moments leading up to the war and the destruction of the USS *Maine*.

Offner, John L. *An Unwanted War: The Diplomacy of the United States and Spain over Cuba, 1895–1898*. Chapel Hill: University of North Carolina Press, 1992. Focuses on the diplomatic circumstances between the United States, Cuba, and Spain during the war and scrutinizes key decisions made in Washington, D.C., and Madrid.

O'Toole, G.J.A. *The Spanish War: An American Epic 1898*. W.W. Norton, 1984. Explores how the sinking of the USS *Maine* immediately launched a war with Spain and examines how political alliances were created by the United States during key moments of the military campaign.

Rickover, Hyman G. *How the Battleship Maine Was Destroyed*. Annapolis, MD: Naval Institute Press, 1995. Provides provocative 1976 investigation by a Navy admiral who challenges the 1911 Court of Inquiry and comes to a different conclusion as to how the USS *Maine* was sunk.

Stallman, R.W., and E.R. Hagemann, eds. *The War Dispatches of Stephen Crane.* New York: New York University Press, 1964. Includes the unique accounts of this American writer during his observations of war. The second half of the text examines Crane's work from the Spanish American War.

Trask, David F. *The War with Spain in 1898.* Lincoln: University of Nebraska Press, 1996. Well- researched and detailed analysis of the war from a chief historian at the U.S. Army Center for Military History, this work offers a cross-over discussion including American, Spanish, Cuban, and Filipino perspectives on the conflict.

World Wide Web

"Events—Spanish-American War." http://www.history.navy.mil/photos/events/ spanam/eve-pge.htm. The Naval Historical Center's collection of period images and photographs of U.S. actions, ships, and people involved during the conflict includes a link to images and information related to the sinking of the USS *Maine.*

"The Spanish-American War." http://www/smplanet.com/imperialism/remem-ber.html. Breaks down historical sections of the war including the controversy surrounding the USS *Maine*'s bombing. Incorporates links to photographs, maps, and background information of the entire conflict. Of particular interest are the period photographs of the USS *Maine*'s wreckage.

"The World of 1898: The Spanish-American War." http://www.loc.gov/rr/ hispanic/1898/. The Hispanic Division of the Library of Congress presents an inclusive examination of the history of the war through links to chronologies, bibliographies, maps, and period images covering Cuba, Puerto Rico, Spain, and Philippines.

Multimedia Sources

Crucible of Empire: The Spanish-American War. New York: Great Projects Film Company, 2007. DVD. 120 minutes. Investigates the role race and the media played in igniting this war. PBS.org additionally features background information on the film with links to a timeline, popular war songs of the time, teacher/student activities, and a discussion of yellow journalism. http://www.pbs.org/crucible/frames/_film.html.

The Spanish American War. New York: History Channel, 2007. DVD. 141 minutes. Presents a full and engaging analysis from the sinking of the USS *Maine* to the Battle of Manila Bay.

The Spanish-American War: A Conflict in Progress. Princeton, NJ: Films for the Humanities and Sciences, 2003. DVD. 52 minutes. Contains archival images, documents, and newspaper reports of the period highlighting the roles of Roosevelt's Rough Riders, Cuba's generals, and Spain's naval commanders.

11. Guantánamo Bay Naval Base Established (1898)

As the oldest operating U.S. naval base overseas, Guantánamo Bay was established in 1898 as a strategic naval location by the United States during the Spanish American War on the southeast corner of Cuba. As part of the Platt Amendment in 1903, the Cuban-American Treaty provided the indefinite lease of 45 square miles of Guantánamo Bay for coaling and U.S. naval operations. In 1934, another treaty between the United States and Cuba included the annual payment of just over $3,000 to lease the territory. Furthermore, the lease could only be dissolved if both parties agreed. After Fidel Castro came to power in Cuba in 1959, he objected to the U.S. presence and the lease agreement; however, one of the rent checks had been cashed, and according to then U.S. President Dwight D. Eisenhower, that act confirmed that the U.S. Navy had a right to continue leasing Guantánamo Bay indefinitely. Part of the naval base was transformed after the September 11, 2001, U.S. terrorist attacks as a detention center to house "enemy combatants" arrested during the 2001 U.S. invasion of Afghanistan. Since 2002, the three camps that make up the detention center have housed them. Despite international outcry, President George W. Bush maintained that the detainees were not protected under the 1948 Geneva Convention; however, in 2004 and 2006 the U.S. Supreme Court ruled both times that the Bush administration was in partial violation of the Geneva Convention. One of President Barack Obama's first executive orders was to sign a January 2009 declaration closing the detention center at Guantánamo Bay within a year.

TERM PAPER SUGGESTIONS

1. Discuss how the presence of Guantánamo Bay Naval Base impacts the daily life of not only the U.S. military personnel but also the

Cuban nationals. As the only U.S. naval base in a nation with no diplomatic ties to the United States, how are relations carried out? What difficulties are created on both sides of the base walls?

2. Examine the U.S. Supreme Court cases *Hamdan v. Rumsfeld* in 2004 and *Rasul v. Bush* in 2006, and provide an overview of the respective positions regarding interpretation of the provisions of protection under the 1948 Geneva Convention. What were the differences between these cases? Also include your own argument as to whether the Bush administration or the U.S. Supreme Court was complying with appropriate jurisprudence in both legal proceedings.

3. Profile what daily life was like for the detainees at the three camps in the detention center. Who exactly were the detainees and what charges brought them to Guantánamo Bay?

ALTERNATIVE TERM PAPER SUGGESTIONS

1. Using digital images of relevant photographs, streaming videos, maps, charts, and text, create an interactive timeline of Guantánamo Bay Naval Base and its historical transformations from 1898 to the 21st century.

2. Put together a legal case with well-researched and documented primary and secondary sources arguing for the continuation or suspension of Guantánamo Bay Detention Center. Create a PowerPoint presentation in addition to showcase the most vital features of this project. Consider the arguments that have been made already and offer new insight to whichever position you choose to take, taking into account potential consequences for this decision.

SUGGESTED SOURCES

Primary Sources

"CNIC: Naval Station Guantanamo Bay." http://www.cnic.navy.mil/guantanamo/index.htm. Official Web site contains links to departments, programs, family life information, facilities, and history of the base complex.

Kurnaz, Murat. *Five Years of My Life: An Innocent Man in Guantanamo.* New York: Palgrave Macmillan, 2008. Provides a first-hand account of a Turkish German Muslim caught up in the 2001 U.S. invasion of Afghanistan and sentenced to the detention center, only to be released with no formal charges after five years.

"Obama Signs Executive Order to Close Guantánamo Bay." http://www. huffingtonpost.com/2009/01/22/obama-and-guantanamo-unde_n_ 159849.html. Assembles live footage of U.S. President Barack Obama signing the Executive Order on January 22, 2009. Also incorporates a lengthy article discussing the presidential decision and reactions from prominent Republican senators.

"Would Sell Cuban Estate." *New York Times,* April 4, 1909: 3. Discusses the offer to sell 40,000 acres of land beside the naval base for military use, thus increasing the Cuban territory controlled by the U.S. Navy.

Secondary Sources

Lipman, Jana K. *Guantánamo: A Working-Class History between Empire and Revolution.* Berkeley: University of California, Press, 2009. Documents the narratives of pivotal persons and everyday interaction between U.S. and Cuban officials and approaches the problematic existence of a U.S.-leased territory on sovereign Cuban soil from a unique perspective.

Schwab, Stephen Irving Max. *Guantánamo, USA: The Untold History of America's Cuban Outpost.* Lawrence: University Press of Kansas, 2009. Concentrates on the 1898 establishment of the naval base and the territory's function, role, and operation during World War I and II and the Cold War. Balances both U.S. and Cuban perspectives on the base's presence.

Strauss, Michael J. *The Leasing of Guantanamo Bay.* Westport, CT: Praeger Security International, 2009. Covers the complex leasing arrangement and history of the territory between the United States and Cuba, and articulates new definitions of sovereignty and legality.

World Wide Web

"Guantanamo." http://jurist.law.pitt.edu/currentawareness/guantanamo.php. Provides background information on the base's establishment, but focuses on the various legal discussions surrounding the presence of detention camps on base property. Provides links to useful Web sites, editorials, and documents pertaining to the detention camps are also included.

"Guantanamo Bay Naval Base." http://www.associatedcontent.com/article/ 1503793/guantanamo_bay_naval_base.html. Presents a general overview of the base's history with links to related articles for further research.

"Rasul v. Bush." http://www.oyez.org/cases/2000-2009/2003/2003_03_334/. Contains a brief overview of the U.S. Supreme Court case that reversed the Bush administration policy to deny Guantánamo detainees civil liberties and rights provided for by the 1948 Geneva Convention.

Multimedia Sources

Inside Guantánamo. Washington, D.C.: National Geographic Channel, 2009. DVD. 90 minutes. Examines the daily routines and perspectives of both the prisoners in the detention camps and the guards.

The Road to Guantántamo. Culver City, CA: Sony Pictures, 2006. DVD. 95 minutes. Focuses on three British Muslims who were arrested in Afghanistan during the 2001 U.S. invasion and sent to Guantánamo Bay in Cuba. Uses dramatic reenactments, news footage, and in-depth interviews to provide an inside view into the prison.

12. Platt Amendment (1901)

At the close of the Spanish American War in December 1898, the United States had acquired Cuba along with the remaining oceanic colonies of Spain. However, despite the U.S. Congress' promise to leave Cuba independent according to the provisions of the Teller Amendment, the United States maintained that the newly freed colony was too volatile economically and politically and too geographically strategic to let go. Therefore, Congress ratified Republican Senator Orville Platt's proposal to ensure a long-term U.S. naval presence and influence over Cuban affairs. The Platt Amendment of 1901 was explicit in the specific role the United States would play in the 20th century. Its principal articles stated that Cuba could not freely sign treaties with other nations nor allow them to occupy any section of the island. Moreover, Cuba would have to allow the United States to intervene in its political affairs and approve of any action the occupying forces decided to take. This was especially significant to the United States since it wanted to protect U.S. companies and citizens residing in Cuba. Establishing a permanent treaty with the United States also ensured that Cubans would have to forfeit, through sale or lease, any land to be used for coal mining or construction of naval stations. Congress maintained that these provisions were necessary in preserving Cuban independence. Unless Cuba adopted the requirements outlined in the Platt Amendment, U.S. forces would not leave the island. Indeed, the amendment had to be part of Cuba's new constitution. It was clear to the Cubans that the United States did not favor Cuban home rule, and many Cuban liberators such as Gen. Máximo Gómez were rendered powerless on the island. Despite Cuban opposition to the amendment, the Cuban Parliament ratified it and incorporated it into their constitution at the start of 1903 only after President Theodore Roosevelt withdrew troops from the island in late 1902. With the acquisition of the neighboring island of Puerto Rico, the United States was a powerful force in the Caribbean at the start of the 20th century, and the Platt Amendment guaranteed this domination. Eventually, as part of his Good Neighbor Policy toward the republics of Latin America, President Franklin D. Roosevelt repealed the Platt Amendment with the signing of the Treaty of Relations in 1934, leaving only the continued control over the Guantánamo Bay naval base in the hands of the United States.

TERM PAPER SUGGESTIONS

1. What relationship does the Platt Amendment of 1901 have with the Monroe Doctrine of 1823? In what ways does President Theodore Roosevelt use the Monroe Doctrine to create policies with neighboring Cuba through his Roosevelt Corollary? Take a position on the political and military actions of the U.S. government in the Caribbean at the start of the 20th century.

2. Article III of the Platt Amendment provides that the United States reserves "the right to intervene for the preservation of Cuban independence, the maintenance of a government adequate for the protection of life, property, and individual liberty, and for discharging the obligations with respect to Cuba." Explain how and why the United States militarily intervened in Cuban affairs in 1906, 1912, 1917, and 1920. Determine whether there was a pattern to this intervention and discuss how each intervention shaped Cuba throughout the first half of the 20th century.

3. The Platt Amendment not only provided the United States government with vast control over Cuban society, it also allowed U.S. sugar-producing corporations to dictate Cuba's economy. Argue whether the Platt Amendment helped the island nation politically, economically, and socially, and describe how Cubans did or did not benefit from the rapidly growing sugar industry.

4. In 1934, President Franklin D. Roosevelt signed the Treaty of Relations with the Republic of Cuba. Summarize the new relationship

the United States had with Cuba, and compare Roosevelt's diplomatic approach to the island nation in contrast to the earlier policies of his fifth cousin, Theodore Roosevelt. What does the Treaty of Relations suggest about a shift in U.S. policy and its attitude toward Cubans?

ALTERNATIVE TERM PAPER SUGGESTIONS

1. Acting as Senator Henry M. Teller, author of the Teller Amendment of 1898, write a letter to President Theodore Roosevelt on the eve of passing the Platt Amendment of 1901 conveying your concern over its provisions and the integrity of Cuban independence.

2. Create a series of hyperlinks and include several interactive maps and graphs briefly discussing and illustrating the following events that occurred after the adoption of the Platt Amendment by Cuba in 1903: expansion of the railroad, the growing regions of sugarcane, location of naval bases and military outposts, and sites of U.S. military interventions during the first half of the 20th century.

SELECTED SOURCES

Primary Sources

"Modern History Sourcebook: The Platt Amendment, 1901." http://www.fordham.edu/halsall/mod/1901platt.html. Includes the entire amendment passed by Congress in 1901.

"The Strenuous Life." http://www.theodoreroosevelt.org/research/speech%20strenuous.htm. A reproduction of Theodore Roosevelt's speech to the Hamilton Club in Chicago on April 10, 1899. Roosevelt outlines his vision of the U.S. role in foreign affairs and discusses what should be done with the newly acquired island of Cuba.

"Treaty of Relations between the United States and Cuba, signed May 29, 1934." http://www.latinamericanstudies.org/us-cuba/treaty-5-29-34.htm. Provides original treaty signed by President Franklin D. Roosevelt and Provisional President of Cuba Dr. Manuel Márquez Sterling that eradicates much of what the Platt Amendment installs.

Secondary Sources

Hernández, José M. *Cuba and the United States: Intervention and Militarism, 1868–1933*. Austin: University of Texas Press, 1993. Outlines the political and military relationship the United States had with Cuba until Franklin D. Roosevelt took office.

Lockmiller, David. *Magoon in Cuba: A History of the Second Intervention, 1906–1909*. Westport, CT: Greenwood Press, 1969. Details the occupation governorship of U.S. diplomat and administrator Charles E. Magoon over Cuba to ensure that revolutionaries and U.S. interests were being maintained.

Pérez, Louis, A. *Cuba under the Platt Amendment, 1902–1934*. Pittsburgh, PA: University of Pittsburgh Press, 1991. Part of the Pitt Latin American Series, this is a well documented work on early U.S.-Cuban relations and the emergence of various groups and classes in Cuba stemming from the exercise of the Platt Amendment provisions.

Suchlicki, Jaime. *Cuba: From Columbus to Castro and Beyond*, 5th ed. Dulles, VA: Potomac Books, 2002. While providing a comprehensive history of Cuba, the text includes several chapters on early U.S.-Cuban relations and one specifically devoted to the impact of the Platt Amendment on Cuban society and politics.

Zanetti, Oscar, and Alejandro García. *Sugar and Railroads: A Cuban History, 1837–1959*. Chapel Hill: University of North Carolina Press, 1989. Investigates the close relation between these two industries in Cuba, and explores the economic and cultural impact they had on the everyday lives of Cubans and immigrant workers across the island.

World Wide Web

"History of Cuba: Presidential Gallery." http://www.historyofcuba.com/gallery/PresGal.htm. Includes photographs of Cuban leaders from Carlos Manuel de Cépedes to Fulgencio Batista.

"Platt Amendment (1903)." http://www.usnews.com/usnews/documents/docpages/document_page55.htm. Part of *U.S. News'* "100 Documents That Shaped America," this site provides an overview of the amendment and its impact, and includes PDF images of the actual amendment ratified by the U.S. Congress in 1901.

Multimedia Source

Crucible of Empire: The Spanish-American War. New York: Great Projects Film Company, 2007. DVD. 120 minutes. http://www.pbs.org/crucible/frames/_film.html. Investigates the role race and the media played in igniting this war. It also includes an examination of the aftermath of the war and the impact of the Platt Amendment on Cuba. PBS.org additionally features background information on the film with links to a timeline, popular war songs of the time, teacher/student activities, and a discussion of yellow journalism.

13. Panama Canal Constructed (1904–1914)

Cutting through the isthmus of Panama, the Panama Canal was an intense engineering project supported by the United States and supervised by Chief Engineer John Frank Stevens, which immeasurably improved the shipping trade between the Pacific and Atlantic Oceans. Originally, French engineer Ferdinand de Lesseps, who completed the Suez Canal in 1869, attempted the lockless construction of the canal in Panama but failed; however, the U.S. endeavor was successful because locks were installed to address the change in sea level between the two oceans. The site was selected over a Nicaraguan location mainly due to Panama's newly declared independence from Colombia that had initially owned the land as one of its provinces, and also because of a railroad line that had been constructed through Panama. In 1904, the United States and Panama signed the Hay-Bunau Varilla Treaty giving the United States full control over the Panama Canal in exchange for protection of this newly established republic in Central America. Construction began in 1904 and was supported by a number of nations that trusted the United States would keep the canal neutral. During the construction, medical advances were made to address the outbreak of malaria and yellow fever in the Canal Zone, diseases that had claimed the lives of well over 20,000 laborers when the French attempted to build it. While the canal eventually cut in half the time it took ships to cross from one ocean to the next and made overhead costs manageable for shipping companies, politically Panamanians wanted the Canal Zone returned. The animosity reached its zenith on January 9, 1964, when Panamanians living in the U.S.-controlled Canal Zone and throughout Panama City rioted. The event resulted in the death of 22 Panamanians and 4 U.S. soldiers. Eventually, President Jimmy Carter signed a treaty in 1977 with the Commander of Panama's National Guard, General Omar Torrijos, thus ensuring Panamanian control over the Panama Canal by the end of 1999.

TERM PAPER SUGGESTIONS

1. What role did the United States play in establishing Panama's independence from Colombia at the beginning of the 20th century, and

thus securing control over the construction and ownership of the Canal Zone until 1999?

2. The living and working conditions for outside versus indigenous laborers during the 10-year construction project were imbalanced. Argue how racist policies contributed to unequal pay and treatment between the workers. Provide a comparison between labor conditions during the French phase of the project and the U.S. phase.

3. Despite the U.S. control over the Panama Canal, riots occurred over the canal's sovereignty in January 9, 1964, which culminated in the death of 22 Panamanians and 4 U.S. soldiers. This became known as Martyrs' Day in Panama. Explain the background of this riot and its aftermath that resulted in the signing of the Torrijos-Carter Treaty in 1977.

4. In December 1989, President George H. W. Bush ordered military forces to invade Panama and depose General Manuel Noriega. One of the reasons the White House justified the invasion was to protect the integrity of Panama Canal Zone's neutrality, which was one of the provisions of the Torrijos-Carter Treaty of 1977. Argue whether the United States was justified in claiming that it was protecting this provision of the canal treaty, and discuss how the canal served as a pivotal issue during the invasion.

ALTERNATIVE TERM PAPER SUGGESTIONS

1. Use Google Earth and historical documents and images to demonstrate how the Panama Canal was constructed. Emphasize how this project was an engineering marvel.

2. As the hypothetical leader of one of the resistance groups who participated in the January 9, 1964, riots in the Canal Zone, write a detailed letter to President Lyndon B. Johnson demanding that sovereignty over the Panama Canal be given to Panamanians. Use articles from the time period to support your approach to the letter.

SUGGESTED SOURCES

Primary Sources

Keller, Ulrich. *The Building of the Panama Canal in Historic Photographs.* Mineola, NY: Dover Publications, 1984. Contains extensive coverage of the canal's development with over 160 photographs.

"Panama Canal Authority." http://www.pancanal.com/eng/index.html. Official site for the Panama Canal includes history, photographs, videos, Web cameras, and animated images to demonstrate the operations of the canal.

Secondary Sources

Kinzer, Stephan. *Overthrow: America's Century of Regime Change from Hawaii to Iraq*. New York: Henry Holt and Company, 2006. Provides critical examination of U.S.-foreign involvement during the 20th century. Chapter 11 focuses on Panama including Martyrs' Day and the 1989 invasion.

McCullough, David. *The Path between the Seas: The Creation of the Panama Canal, 1870–1914*. New York: Simon and Schuster, 1977. Examines the French attempt to construct the canal, the U.S. involvement in Panama's independence, and the U.S. supervision of the canal's construction.

Parker, Matthew. *Panama Fever: The Epic Story of the Building of the Panama Canal*. New York: Anchor Books, 2009. Focuses on the lives and roles that laborers played during the construction of the canal.

World Wide Web

"The 1903 Treaty of Qualified Independence." http://countrystudies.us/panama/8.htm. Consists of detailed background information regarding the Hay-Bunau Varilla Treaty of 1903, which guaranteed controlling rights over the construction and supervision of the canal.

"Canalmuseum.com." http://www.canalmuseum.com/. Comprises relevant links, photographs, bibliography, and historical articles on aspects of the Panama Canal.

"Panama Maps: Map of Panama Canal." http://panama-maps.com/display-panama-canal-map.htm. Includes several links to various maps of the canal, some of which are interactive.

Multimedia Sources

A Man, a Plan, a Canal, Panama. Boston, MA: WGBH Production, 2004. DVD. 60 minutes. Includes rare footage of the canal's construction process and in-depth historical narratives.

Panama Canal. Burbank, CA: Warner Home Video, 2000. VHS. 60 minutes. Provides recreated scenes and focuses on the laborers who built the canal.

Seven Wonders of the Industrial World. New York: British Broadcasting Corporation, 2003. DVD. 50 minutes. Includes a profile of the Panama Canal as an engineering marvel and highlights the project's contribution to the shipping trade.

14. Roosevelt Corollary (December 1904)

Concerned over the colonial influence Europe had in the Western Hemisphere, President James Monroe declared in 1823 that Europe should no longer desire to increase their influence nor attempt to re-colonize regions through the Caribbean and Latin America. By 1904 President Theodore Roosevelt wanted to underscore the growing political and economic power of the United States by proposing greater police action throughout the Western Hemisphere. This began with Venezuela's complicated relationship with international creditors. Roosevelt feared that this financial instability would draw concern from the Europeans and ignite an invasion. As such, the Roosevelt Corollary provides that the United States would intervene in Western Hemispheric nations only to ensure that they were fulfilling their financial responsibilities to these creditors and that U.S. interests and rights were not being violated. However, starting in Roosevelt's administration, this "Big Stick" policy translated into a number of overt and covert military invasions throughout the 20th century by subsequent U.S. administrations including Cuba, Panama, Nicaragua, Haiti, the Dominican Republic, and countless others.

TERM PAPER SUGGESTIONS

1. Read both speeches James Monroe and Theodore Roosevelt gave to the U.S. Congress during their presidencies. In what ways does Roosevelt's policy establish a "corollary" to the Monroe Doctrine? Discuss this using the historical context of the United States in 1823 and in 1904 when these annual messages to Congress were delivered.

2. Theodore Roosevelt's Roosevelt Corollary of 1904 and Franklin D. Roosevelt's Good Neighbor Policy of 1933 are contrasting interpretations of the Monroe Doctrine. Describe the background and historical context for these two policies, and articulate how each one was received and interpreted by Latin American countries during the 20th century.

3. Select one of the Latin American or Caribbean nations that experienced a U.S. invasion during the 20th century. Explain the circumstances and draw parallels between the Roosevelt Corollary and the rhetoric

employed by the U.S. administration that authorized the invasion at the time. What does this suggest about U.S. foreign policy?

ALTERNATIVE TERM PAPER SUGGESTIONS

1. Using maps, video clips from digital videos, letters, speeches, and illustrations, create a Web site that highlights a critical examination of Theodore Roosevelt's application of the Roosevelt Corollary in the Western Hemisphere.

2. Examine the various political cartoons depicting President Theodore Roosevelt during his tenure in office. As a result of the Roosevelt Corollary and other policies associated with this one, discuss how the media satirized him. What sort of a presidential figure was he perceived as? Use this Web site, which archives a multitude of political cartoons of Roosevelt: http://www.theodore-roosevelt.com/ trcartoonsprompt.html.

SUGGESTED SOURCES

Primary Sources

Notgrass, Ray. *American Voices: A Collection of Documents, Speeches, Essays, Hymns, Poems, and Short Stories from American History.* Cookeville, TN: Notgrass Company, 2007. Includes central excerpts from Roosevelt's Corollary speech.

Romero, Frances Sanders. *Presidents from Theodore Roosevelt through Coolidge, 1901–1929: Debating the Issues in Pro and Con Primary Documents.* Westport, CT: Greenwood Press, 2002. Includes the Corollary speech of Roosevelt as well as speeches that critique this policy.

"The Roosevelt Corollary to the Monroe Doctrine: President Theodore Roosevelt's Annual Message to Congress, December 6, 1904." http:// www.latinamericanstudies.org/us-relations/roosevelt-corollary.htm. Provides reproduction of Roosevelt's speech.

Tuathail, Gearóid O., Simon Dalby, and Paul Routledge, eds. *The Geopolitics Reader.* London: Routledge, 1998. Chapter 2 provides a reproduction of Roosevelt's 1904 speech to Congress.

Secondary Sources

Collin, Richard H. *Theodore Roosevelt's Caribbean: The Panama Canal, the Monroe Doctrine, and the Latin American Context.* Baton Rouge: Louisiana

State University Press, 1990. Investigates the role the Roosevelt Corollary played in redefining the Monroe Doctrine in Latin American at the beginning of the 20th century.

Coyne, Christopher, and Stephen Davies. "Nineteen Public Bads of Empire, Nation Building and the Like." *Econ Journal Watch* 4, no. 1: 3–35. http://econj watch.org/articles/empire-public-goods-and-bads. Critiques the impact that the Roosevelt Corollary has had throughout Latin America.

Dent, David W. *The Legacy of the Monroe Doctrine: A Reference Guide to U.S. Involvement in Latin America and the Caribbean.* Westport, CT: Greenwood Press, 1999. Geared toward upper-level high school and undergraduate audience, this work is divided into chapters by country and analyzes pivotal events involving U.S. intervention since 1823.

Holmes, James R. *Theodore Roosevelt and World Order: Police Power in International Relations.* Dulles, VA: Potomac Books, 2006. Analyzes the notion of the United States exercising police order abroad and the implications this has had throughout the 20th century.

Vesser, Cyrus. *A World Safe for Capitalism: Dollar Diplomacy and America's Rise to Global Power.* New York: Columbia University Press, 2002. Closely examines how Roosevelt initiated his corollary to the Monroe Doctrine as a result of the conflict rising between public policy and private interests.

World Wide Web

"The Monroe Doctrine and the Roosevelt Corollary." http://www.theodoreroose velt.org/life/rooseveltcorollary.htm. Places the two policies side-by-side with brief overview and quotes from the respective presidents initiating their new U.S. foreign policies in the Western Hemisphere.

"Roosevelt Corollary to the Monroe Doctrine." http://www.u-s-history.com/pages/h1449.html. Discusses the two foreign policies in conjunction with one another and includes relevant links for further research.

"Roosevelt Corollary to the Monroe Doctrine, 1904." http://www.state.gov/r/pa/ho/time/ip/17660.htm. Contains a brief overview of the Corollary and the Latin American nations who were impacted by this policy.

"Theodore Roosevelt, the Roosevelt Corollary (1904)." http://www.pinzler.com/ushistory/corollarysupp.html. Provides a brief summary of the Corollary and excerpts from the 1904 speech to the U.S. Congress.

Multimedia Sources

America's Documents of Freedom: 1896–1916 An Emerging Power. Camarillo, CA: Goldhil Entertainment, 2007. DVD. 30 minutes. The third section investigates the Roosevelt Corollary.

"American Experience: The Presidents: Historian Walter LeFeber on the Roosevelt Corollary." http://www.pbs.org/wgbh/amex/presidents/26_t_roosevelt/filmmore/ra_lafecoro.html. Includes links to program transcript, audio presentation, and bibliographic information for further research.

United States History: Origins to 2000. Wynnewood, PA: Schlessinger Media, 2003. DVD. 30 minutes. Volume 15, "U.S. & the World, 1865–1917," examines a segment on the implications of the Roosevelt Corollary to the Monroe Doctrine.

15. Jones-Shaforth Act (1917)

Once Puerto Rico became a U.S. possession after the Spanish American War in 1898, Congress established limited civilian rule of government on the island through the Organic Act of 1900. However, a growing desire for greater autonomy and political voice from Puerto Rican leaders such as Resident Commissioner Luis Muñoz Rivera eventually led to the creation of the Jones-Shaforth Act and its subsequent signing into law by President Woodrow Wilson on March 2, 1917. The new law, often referred to as the Jones Act of Puerto Rico, provided the citizenry of the island with some of the rights and privileges imparted to U.S. citizens. Additionally, the Act established a form of government similar to a U.S. state. Puerto Rico would now have a triune body of governance, comprised of an executive branch with a U.S. presidentially appointed governor and a U.S. Senate-approved cabinet, a judiciary branch, and a legislative branch made up of a 39-member House of Representatives and a 19-member Senate. The office of Resident Commissioner remained intact; however, this role still involved a vote-less representation in the U.S. House of Representatives. In terms of legal power, the U.S. Congress would be allowed to veto any law passed by Puerto Rico's legislative branch, the island would not be given any electoral votes in the Electoral College, and control over the island's economy and general services such as defense, mail, or immigration would all be the U.S. federal government's responsibility. However, by 1948 the position of governor became an elected one, and by 1952 Puerto Rico was permitted to draft its own constitution.

TERM PAPER SUGGESTIONS

1. Discuss the impact the Jones-Shaforth Act of Puerto Rico had on conscripting over 20,000 new soldiers for World War I, which the

United States had just entered a month after the act was signed into law. Was this looked on with favor by Puerto Rican citizens or with hostility?

2. Explain the details of Puerto Rico's structure of government under the Foraker Act of 1900. What were some of the significant features Puerto Rican leaders wanted to amend? Did the Jones-Shaforth Act of 1917 appease Puerto Ricans?

3. Prior to the U.S. invasion of Puerto Rico in July 1898, the island secured the Charter of Autonomy from Spain, giving the island greater control over its affairs. However, the Spanish American War changed all of this. Argue whether the United States should have recognized Puerto Rico's Charter of Autonomy. Discuss how the independence movement in Puerto Rico came about as a result of the U.S. invasion, and discuss whether the Jones-Shaforth Act addressed any of these concerns.

4. Compare the systems of civilian government established in Puerto Rico versus Cuba and the Philippines, the other two former Spanish colonies that the United States took possession of after the Spanish American War. Describe the conditions of these former colonies and why the respective system of government was imposed there.

ALTERNATIVE TERM PAPER SUGGESTIONS

1. Prepare a series of persuasive speeches to both Puerto Rico's Chamber of Delegates and the U.S. Congress based on your desire for greater autonomy as a Puerto Rican citizen. Be convincing in your case, and use appropriate sources from Puerto Rican leaders at the start of the 20th century who argued for greater autonomy and civil liberties.

2. Design a Web quest with appropriate links to the features of the Jones-Shaforth Act of 1917. Provide conclusions about their relevance and significance to Puerto Rico's history.

SUGGESTED SOURCES

Primary Source

Vásquez, Francisco H. *Latino/a Thought: Culture, Politics, and Society*, 2nd ed. Lanham, MD: Rowman & Littlefield, 2009. A copy of the Jones-Shaforth Act is available on pages 372–374. Text is available on Google books.

Secondary Sources

Ayala, César J., and Rafael Bernabe. *Puerto Rico in the American Century: A History since 1898*. Chapel Hill: University of North Carolina Press, 2007. First part of text includes a detailed examination of the Jones Act and its lasting impact on political, economic, and cultural identity for the island.

Go, Julian. *American Empire and the Politics of Meaning: Elite Political Cultures in the Philippines and Puerto Rico during U.S. Colonialism*. Durham, NC: Duke University Press, 2008. Compares the forms of post-Spanish American War governments established in these two territories.

Picó, Fernando. *Puerto Rico, 1898: The War after the War*. Princeton, NJ: Markus Wiener, 2004. Written by Puerto Rico's leading historian, this work examines the role of resistance groups during the early years of U.S. occupation.

Trías Monge, José. *Puerto Rico: The Trials of the Oldest Colony in the World*. New Haven, CT: Yale University Press, 1997. Provides a compelling study of the impact of the Jones-Shaforth Act and outlines a plan for decolonization.

World Wide Web

"Jones Law." http://www.topuertorico.org/reference/jones.shtml. Includes a chart that illustrates the new form of government to take place in Puerto Rico.

"Luis Muñoz Rivera." http://www.loc.gov/rr/hispanic/congress/munozrivera. html. Provides the Library of Congress' detailed biography of this important leader in early Puerto Rican politics.

"Puerto Ricans Become U.S. citizens, Are Recruited for War Effort." http://www.history.com/this-day-in-history.do?action=Article&id=330. Brief article discusses the conscription of 20,000 soldiers from Puerto Rico to fight for the United States during World War I.

"View of Congress, the Courts, and the Federal Government." http://www.puertoricousa.com/english/views.htm. Provides contemporary analysis on the meaning of Puerto Rican citizenship established under the Jones-Shaforth Act of Puerto Rico.

Multimedia Source

Chicago's Puerto Rican Story. Chicago, IL: New Film Productions, 2008. DVD. 80 minutes. While this documentary focuses primarily on migration issues to the Chicago area, the opening part covers the Foraker Act of 1900 and the Jones-Shaforth Act of 1917.

16. U.S. Border Patrol Established (May 28, 1924)

The flow of immigrants into the United States during the turn of the 20th century prompted U.S. lawmakers to establish stricter regulations to curtail the number of immigrants entering the country from Europe, Asia, and Latin America. During the 1920s, a series of laws limited the number of southern and eastern Europeans permitted to enter while favoring those emigrating from northern Europe. However, Latin American countries, especially Mexico, were left out of the official quota system, and this contributed to the widespread hiring of illegal immigrants from Mexico to work in U.S. factories and fields. In most cases, U.S. companies preferred hiring illegal Mexican workers since they were a source of cheap labor and could easily be taken advantage of. To ensure the flow of illegal workers, companies would often recruit coyotes, or human smugglers, who would escort undocumented laborers across the border as a means to guarantee a workforce. Coyotes would frequently exploit the workers themselves by charging exorbitant fees for the escort while exposing workers to dangerous conditions. In the early years of the 20th century, the United States created a series of mounted guard regiments to secure the international border between California and Texas. However, the number of border guards were few compared to the flood of immigrants entering from Mexico. Therefore, on May 28, 1924, the U.S. Congress created the Border Patrol as part of the Department of Labor. It was their principal task to prevent illegal crossings and drug trafficking between the United States and Mexico.

TERM PAPER SUGGESTIONS

1. Up until 2003, the U.S. Border Patrol was a part of the Department of Justice's Immigration and Naturalization Service (INS). Explain how the September 11th terrorist attacks transformed the organization of the Border Patrol.

2. The Minuteman Project was established in 2005 by U.S. citizens who unofficially monitor the border between the United States and Mexico. Discuss why this group was formed, what their methodology has been, and what makes it a controversial organization.

3. Often agents of the U.S. Border Patrol and members of the Latino community living along the U.S.-Mexico border clash. Investigate some of the key issues surrounding these two groups and provide an in-depth study of how they have also made progress in working with each other.

4. How was the security system along the U.S.-Mexico border organized prior to 1924? Consider the history of border patrolling from 1848 until the establishment of the U.S. Border Patrol in 1924, and analyze some of the key issues for both the U.S. and Mexican governments.

ALTERNATIVE TERM PAPER SUGGESTIONS

1. Design an interactive map illustrating the checkpoints along the U.S.-Mexico border as well as the 33 interior checkpoints that have been established within the United States. Provide details such as number of legal versus illegal crossings that take place at key checkpoints, amount of guards present, and other relevant statistics. Argue whether changing U.S. Border Patrol policies has effectively fulfilled the agency's mission since 1924.

2. Called before a U.S. Congressional committee on immigration, present a research report arguing whether the U.S. Border Patrol has been effective in curtailing illegal crossings of humans and drugs or whether the agency fosters xenophobia in the United States by criminalizing the immigrant community as a whole. Address relevant concerns and propose key resolutions.

SUGGESTED SOURCES

Primary Sources

Moore, Alvin Edward. *Border Patrol.* Santa Fe, NM: Sunstone Press, 1988. Provides first-hand discussion of a border officer's life and duties between 1926 and 1928.

Pacheco, Alex, and Erich Krauss. *On the Line: Inside the U.S. Border Patrol.* New York: Citadel Press Books, 2004. Provides first-hand account of the training process of agents and includes the agency's history and field narratives.

Secondary Sources

Conover, Ted. *Coyotes: A Journey across Borders with America's Illegal Migrants.* New York: Vintage, 1987. Focuses on the author's one-year immersion into lives of Mexicans crossing into the United States.

Denelo, David J. *The Border: Exploring the U.S.-Mexican Divide.* Mechanicsburg, PA: Stackpole Press, 2008. Investigates the life and political culture of agents and immigrants along the border with a particular emphasis on the United States.

Martinez, Ruben. *Crossing Over: A Mexican Family on the Migrant Trail.* New York: Picador, 2002. Documents the underground culture of illegal immigration by profiling a Mexican family crossing the border and highlighting their encounters with coyotes and border agents.

Perkins, Clifford Alan. *Border Patrol: With the U.S. Immigration Service on the Mexican Boundary, 1910–1954.* El Paso: Texas Western Press, 1978. Explores the early U.S. patrol units at the start of the Mexican Civil War and ends with the first 30 years of the U.S. Border Patrol at the start of "Operation Wetback" in 1954.

World Wide Web

"Friends of the Border Patrol." http://www.fobp.us/. Includes relevant articles regarding the agency's policies, strategies, and programs.

"Jim Gilchrist's Minuteman Project." http://minutemanproject.com. Official Web site includes links to various U.S. chapters and articles covering the group's activity along the U.S. border.

"United States Border Patrol." http://www.cbp.gov/xp/cgov/border_security/border_patrol/. The agency's official Web site includes relevant links to policies, history, and detailed statistics.

"U.S. Border Patrol.com." http://www.usborderpatrol.com/Border_Patrol90.htm. Non-government site features detailed information on the border checkpoints, overview of the agency's history, and discussion of its post September 11, 2001, reorganization.

Multimedia Sources

Border Patrol: America's Gatekeepers. New York: A&E Home Video, 2008. DVD. 50 minutes. Follows a team of agents and includes interviews from government officials including former Attorney General Janet Reno.

The Time Has Come! An Immigrant Community Stands Up to the Border Patrol. El Paso, TX: El Paso Border Rights Coalition, 1996. DVD. 40 minutes. Interviews members of the Latino immigrant community of El Paso, Texas, on border patrol abuses.

17. League of United Latin American Citizens Founded (1929)

The League of United Latin American Citizens (LULAC) is the oldest and largest Latino advocacy organization in the United States. Founded on February 17, 1929, in Corpus Christi, Texas, from the merging of several, smaller Latino groups, LULAC's focus has focused its energies on the role of education and economic and civil rights for Latinos. In May 1929, the group drafted a constitution and a formal statement of its principles, often called the LULAC Code, which all members and local chapters must adopt. Among the duties that the code enumerates for its members are to respect U.S. citizenship, to take pride in one's origins, to educate oneself, to serve one's country, and to further the efficiency and capability of each subsequent generation. In the 1950s and 1960s, LULAC played a significant role in Latino civil rights through its sponsorship of voter registrations and of lawyers in several court cases. Among LULAC's most famous cases were *Hernández v. Texas*, which guaranteed Mexican Americans 14th Amendment rights, and *Méndez v. Westminster*, which prevented the segregation of children in schools based on race. LULAC was also one of the lead plaintiff's against California's Proposition 187, which would have required public agencies such as hospitals and schools to reject and report suspected illegal aliens. Over the years, LULAC has faced criticism for its politically moderate perspective. Civil rights organizations of the 1960s onward argued that LULAC was too assimilationist in nature, favoring the integration of Latinos into Anglo-American culture, while other groups criticized LULAC for favoring federal protections for Latinos at the expense of such integration. LULAC today remains one of the most politically viable organizations in the United States, with over 115,000 members in 28 states and Puerto Rico and more than 700 local councils. Among the services that LULAC offers are congressional scorecards, national education agendas, and significant financial aid grants to students.

TERM PAPER SUGGESTIONS

1. As an organization, LULAC is often compared with the NAACP in its approach to Latino advancement. Compare these two organizations and their platforms. What notable similarities and differences do you observe?

2. Examine the role that LULAC has played in Latino Civil Rights. How do cases such as *Hernández v. Texas* and *Méndez v. Westminster* factor into this role? Has this role altered or shifted across the decades?

3. Explore the changes LULAC has undergone as an organization over the decades. What was the group's central focus in the 1930s and 1940s? How did this focus shift in the 1950s and 1960s, and beyond?

4. Critics of LULAC often argue that its methods are assimilationist, favoring integration into Anglo-American culture over maintenance of traditional Latino culture. Examine LULAC's platform, code, and other official documents and determine whether you believe LULAC's platform and positions should be perceived as such.

5. Discuss the role of education in LULAC's philosophy and charitable gift giving. What function does education play in the organization? How does LULAC promote education in its political and social agenda?

6. Given that LULAC has, for years, had a separate organization for women, examine the role that women play in LULAC. Why was there a women's LULAC? What role do women play in the organization today?

ALTERNATIVE TERM PAPER SUGGESTIONS

1. Create a PowerPoint presentation of LULAC's most famous moments in legal advocacy. Be sure to include its role in Supreme Court cases such as *Méndez v. Westminster* and Proposition 187 as well as its sponsorship and endorsement of various politicians.

2. Over the years, LULAC has noted a decrease in membership. Imagine you have been hired as a consultant to increase the organization's membership and efficacy. Develop a written strategy for improving the organization's membership. Be sure to include demographics, statistics, and other data to support this strategy as well.

SUGGESTED SOURCES

Primary Sources

"2008–2009 LULAC National Legislative Platform." http://www.lulac.org/advocacy/platform.html. Features LULAC's official stance on political topics such as affirmative action, education, social security, and workers' rights.

"LULAC Code, Philosophy & Aims and Purposes." http://www.lulac.net/about/code.html. Provides the original code developed in 1929.

Secondary Sources

Gómez-Quiñones, Juan. *Chicano Politics: Reality and Promise, 1940–1990.* Albuquerque: New Mexico University Press, 1990. Chapters 2 and 3 address LULAC's contributions to political and social change.

Gutiérrez, David G. "LULAC and the Assimilationist Perspective." *The Latino Condition: A Critical Reader,* edited by Eds. Richard Delgado and Jean Stefancic. New York: NYU Press, 1998, pp. 421–426. Gutiérrez offers an in-depth background on the history of LULAC's formation.

Kaplowitz, Craig A. *LULAC, Mexican Americans and National Policy.* College Station: Texas A&M University Press, 2005. Kaplowitz discusses the paradoxical nature of LULAC as it both worked for Latino civil rights and assimilation of Latinos into American culture.

Márquez, Benjamin. *LULAC: The Evolution of a Mexican American Political Organization.* Austin: University of Texas Press, 1993. Márquez offers a history of LULAC, based on primary sources from the University of Texas library system archives.

———. "The Politics of Race and Assimilation: The League of United Latin American Citizens 1929–1940." *Political Research Quarterly.* 42, no. 2 (1989): 355–375. Márquez's article focuses on the initial goals and strategies of LULAC prior to the Civil Rights Movement.

Yarsinske, Amy Waters. *All for One, and One for All: A Celebration of 75 Years of the League of United Latin American Citizens.* Virginia Beach, VA: Donning Company, 2004. Yarsinske's book focuses on LULAC's platform development and its role in the arena of education and civil rights.

World Wide Web

"LULAC—League of United Latin American Citizens." http://www.lulac.org/index.html. The official Web site for LULAC offers Webinars, multimedia links, and articles on topics such as Latino employment, education, housing, research, and public service.

"LULAC Urges Renegotiation of Core Text of Peru and Columbia FTAs." http://www.citizenstrade.org/pdf/lulac_PeruColombialetter_01192007.pdf. Features LULAC's official letter regarding the Central American Fair Trade Agreement.

Muñoz, Ernestina, Alma Fajardo, Mayra J. Garcia, and Alisandra Mancera. "LULAC Fought Hard to Guarantee Rights." http://www.epcc.edu/nwlibrary/borderlands. Offers a history of LULAC's participation in various movements to promote Latino livelihood.

"Texas League of United Latin American Citizens." http://www.tx-lulac.org/. Local chapter's Web site offers links to community events and corporate partnerships as well as official documents of the national organization.

Multimedia Source

"LULAC Documentary." http://www.lulac.org/gallery69.html. 24:31 minutes. Features four-part documentary with interviews with several former LULAC presidents about LULAC's founding and its work to counteract Latino discrimination.

18. Dennis Chávez Elected to Congress (1930)

As the first Latino to serve a full term in the U.S. Senate after two terms in the U.S. House of Representatives, Dennis Chávez enjoyed a long political career as an activist who championed the rights of Latinos and Native Americans. Born and raised in New Mexico, Dionisio Chávez (1888–1962) studied engineering, American history, and politics as a youth at the local library while holding down various jobs to support the family. An advocate of the philosophies of Thomas Jefferson, Chávez recognized early on the importance of placing human rights over individual property rights. Having worked for U.S. Senator A.A. Jones as a Spanish interpreter and aide beginning in 1916, Chávez moved to Washington, D.C., to continue working for Jones and to attend Georgetown University Law School. After acquiring a law degree in 1920, he returned to Albuquerque, New Mexico, to practice law and entered the state political scene two years later. With this introduction into politics, Chávez recognized that his desires to serve as a voice for the disenfranchised members of the Latino community could be better served on the federal level. As such, he was elected to two terms as a Democrat in the U.S. House of Representatives in 1930 and again in 1932. After a close senatorial election with incumbent Republican Bronson Cutting, Chávez contested the results; however, Chávez was appointed to the seat by New Mexico Governor Clyde Tingley after Sen. Cutting was killed in a plane crash in 1935. Chávez, however, won the election the following year and secured his place within the Senate until his death in 1962. Throughout his career, Chávez supported the New Deal policies of President Franklin D. Roosevelt. This was further underscored by his support for entering the North Atlantic Treaty Organization (NATO) and by his role as a Spanish-speaking emissary for the U.S. State Department who carried out Good Neighbor policies throughout Latin America, including the development of the Pan American Highway. He supported civil rights and coauthored an early form of the Civil Rights Bill called the Fair Employment Practices Commission Bill. In the 1950s, he publicly denounced the interrogative methods of Republican Senator Joseph McCarthy and demanded decency and professionalism to be returned to the Senate. As the first Latino senator and one of the top-ranking members until his death in 1962, Chávez has been a significant and influential figure in the growing roster of Latino political leaders in the United States.

TERM PAPER SUGGESTIONS

1. Compare the Fair Employment Practices Commission Bill first co-authored in 1944 by Chávez with the 1964 Civil Rights Bill. Discuss the reception of these bills in Congress and highlight their significance by drawing parallels between them.

2. While serving in Congress, Chávez was a strong advocate for water rights within New Mexico. Analyze the legislation he championed and discuss what lasting impact this had for a state where water sources are scarce and coveted.

3. By examining the life and career of Dennis Chávez, discuss how his involvement in the arena of U.S. politics was influenced by thinkers such as Thomas Jefferson. What other important figures had an impact on his life and career?

4. As an advocate of civil rights, discuss how Chávez introduced and supported laws that honored and protected the rights of Latinos and Native American nations. Include a discussion of important civil and labor rights leaders he worked with, especially Luisa Moreno.

ALTERNATIVE TERM PAPER SUGGESTIONS

1. Design a Web quest that profiles the political work of Dennis Chávez. Include important links to relevant information and present conclusions about their significance regarding what Chávez accomplished during his political career.

2. Imagine you are a civil and labor rights leader invited to speak at a Latino youth conference on future leaders in the United States. Prepare a speech that focuses on the life and work of the late Sen. Dennis Chávez.

SUGGESTED SOURCES

Primary Source

"Chavez Is Named to Cutting's Seat." *New York Times,* May 12, 1935: 2. Article announces Chávez's succession to the U.S. Senate seat after rival is killed in airplane crash.

Secondary Sources

Crouch, Barry A. "Dennis Chavez and Roosevelt's 'Court-Packing' Plan." *New Mexico Historical Review* 42 (October 1967): 261–280. Details the position Chávez took regarding President Franklin D. Roosevelt's plan to add to the U.S. Supreme Court through the "Judiciary Reorganization Bill of 1937."

Garcia, Ignacio M. *Viva Kennedy: Mexican Americans in Search of Camelot.* College Station: Texas A&M University Press, 2000. Provides a section on Dennis Chávez and his role during the Kennedy administration.

Leonard, Kevin Allen. "Dennis Chavez: The Last of the Patrones." In *The Human Tradition in America between the Wars, 1920–1945*, edited by Donald W. Whisenhunt. Wilmington, DE: SR Books, 2002, pp. 105–119. Articulates Chávez's extensive political role and the policies he supported and opposed between Word War I and II.

Perrigo, Lynn Irwin. *Hispanos: Historic Leaders of New Mexico.* Santa Fe, NM: Sunstone Press, 1985. Chapter 27 includes discussion on Dennis Chávez's political contributions.

U.S. Government Printing Office. *Acceptance of the Statue of Dennis Chavez Presented by the State of New Mexico: Proceedings in the Rotunda, United States Capitol, March 31, 1966.* Washington, D.C.: U.S. Government Printing Office, 1966. Provides the official proceedings of the dedication ceremony for the statue of Chavez placed in the Capitol.

World Wide Web

"Biographical Directory of the United States Congress: Dennis Chavez." http://bioguide.congress.gov/scripts/biodisplay.pl?index=C000338. Contains official years of service and titles held.

Boeck, Jim. "Dennis Chavez Was an Early Civil Rights Activist." *Valencia County New Bulletin,* Sept. 9, 2006. http://www.news-bulletin.com/lavida/64579-09-09-06.html. Focuses on Chávez's political activism for Latinos and other disenfranchised groups in the United States.

"Dennis Chavez." http://www.notablebiographies.com/Ch-Co/Chavez-Dennis.html. Includes bibliographic information of the life and career of the congressman.

"The Dennis Chavez Foundation." http://www.dennischavez.org/index.html. Site is dedicated to the legacy of Chávez and incorporates biographical information, photographs, and links to archival sources for further study.

"The First U.S. Stamp Made Outside the United States." http://www.nytimes. com/1991/03/29/us/the-first-us-stamp-made-outside-the-us.html?page wanted=1. Covers the honor given to Chávez in 1991 by creating a stamp with his image.

Multimedia Source

"Dennis Chávez: Notable New Mexican." http://video.google.com/videoplay? docid=-400142989977351879&hl=en/#. Five-minute documentary contains interviews with notable Latinos and others who discuss the life and work of Senator Chávez.

19. Good Neighbor Policy toward Latin America (1933)

At his first inaugural address on March 4, 1933, President Franklin D. Roosevelt changed the direction of U.S. foreign policy in the Western Hemisphere by announcing that the United States would no longer engage in acts of intervention and interference with its neighboring nations. This Good Neighbor Policy was a reversal from the Roosevelt Corollary of the 1910s and 1920s, in which the United States maintained that it had a right to ensure that nations beyond the Western Hemisphere would not interfere with the politics of Central and South American governments and that those nations who needed to be stabilized would be through U.S. military intervention. Roosevelt's policy emphasized cooperation and trade rather than the unbridled use of military force to sustain peace and stability through the hemisphere. In December 1933, U.S. Secretary of State Cordell Hull participated in the Montevideo Conference in Uruguay and signed a treaty with Latin American nations solidifying this political commitment. To demonstrate the seriousness with which the Roosevelt administration would take this new policy, it suspended its military presence in Haiti in 1934 and dissolved the 1903 Platt Amendment, which gave the United States far-reaching control over Cuba. After Roosevelt's death in 1945, the policy began to erode, and the United States no longer respected free trade agreements with Latin American nations. Moreover, the United States slowly returned to the earlier policy of intervention and interference that were integral to the Monroe Doctrine and Roosevelt Corollary; during the Cold War era, the United States saw itself more and more as the sole protector of democratic and capitalist endeavors in the Western Hemisphere.

TERM PAPER SUGGESTIONS

1. The term and concept of a "good neighbor" policy between the United States and Latin America were originally initiated by President Herbert Hoover during a speech he gave while visiting Honduras. Describe the previous political conditions such as the criticism of the Coolidge administration for armed intervention in Haiti and Nicaragua in the 1920s that brought about the establishment of Franklin Roosevelt's new policy. How did President Hoover initially pave the way for the Good Neighbor Policy?

2. During World War II, much of the United States' attention was directed toward the European and Pacific theaters of war. Explain how the United States maintained its Good Neighbor Policy with Latin American nations during a period when many of them were ruled by military generals who were influenced by the fascist governments of Europe.

3. Argue whether the Good Neighbor Policy of nonintervention and noninterference during the second half of the 20th century eventually led to the policy's weakness by making matters worse both economically and politically throughout Latin American or whether exterior circumstances and forces, such as the role of oil production and consumption, led to the policy's irrelevance.

4. Select three different pivotal events that transpired during the Roosevelt administration that were directly influenced by the Good Neighbor Policy and that demonstrate how this policy was put into effect. Be sure to illustrate how each event has an interconnection in defining this policy.

5. Compare the Good Neighbor Policy with the North American Free Trade Agreement signed in 1994. What are the commonalities with and differences between these two political and economic approaches? Argue whether you maintain one policy was more effective than the other in terms of the U.S. foreign relations approach.

ALTERNATIVE TERM PAPER SUGGESTIONS

1. As a representative of the newly formed Organization of the American States in 1948, create a series of podcasts that address the important issues occurring in the Western Hemisphere at the time. Base them on actual speeches originally made, but also address how the Organization is responding to the Good Neighbor Policy.

2. Create a comprehensive timeline that illustrates the most significant interactions and decisions created between the United States and specific Latin American nations as a direct result of the Good Neighbor Policy.

SUGGESTED SOURCES

Primary Source

"Document: Franklin D. Roosevelt: The Good Neighbor Policy." http://www. britannica.com/bps/additionalcontent/8/116962/Document-Franklin-D-Roosevelt-The-Good-Neighbor-Policy. Features part of the August 14, 1936, speech Roosevelt delivered at Chautauqua, New York, explaining the new approach to foreign relations.

Secondary Sources

Pike, Fredrick B. *FDR's Good Neighbor Policy: Sixty Years of Generally Gentle Chaos.* Austin: University of Texas Press, 1995. Explores Roosevelt's policy and its influence lasting to the end of the 20th century. Also focuses on how FDR and Eleanor Roosevelt's public activism resonated throughout Latin America.

Wood, Bryce. *The Dismantling of the Good Neighbor Policy.* Austin: University of Texas Press, 1985. Offers details on how the policy slowly declined after the death of President Franklin Roosevelt in 1945 and how factors such as the interference in Guatemala in 1954 dissolved the policy.

———. *The Making of the Good Neighbor Policy.* New York: Columbia University Press, 1961. Outlines the origins of the policy and incorporates a critical examination of the impacts this change in U.S. foreign policy had throughout the Western Hemisphere.

World Wide Web

"Good Neighbor Policy." http://www.u-s-history.com/pages/h1646.html. Presents a comprehensive overview of the policy, its origins and 21st century legacies. Also includes links to other historical sites associated with this policy.

"Good Neighbor Policy." http://history.sandiego.edu/gen/ww2timeline/08/goodneighbor.html. Contains a detailed list of integral events and conditions during the pivotal years of the policy.

"Good Neighbor Policy, 1933." http://www.state.gov/r/pa/ho/time/id/17341.htm. Offers the U.S. Department of State's brief, but official, summary of Roosevelt's foreign policy.

Multimedia Sources

Isolationism vs. Interventionism. Hawthorne, NY: Sunburst Visual Media, 2007. DVD. 30 minutes. Includes a segment on Franklin Roosevelt's Good Neighbor Policy as a means for curtailing American isolationism.

"President Franklin Roosevelt 1933 Inauguration." http://www.youtube.com/watch?v=MX_v0zxM23Q&feature=channel. Provides C-SPAN's 20-minute footage of Roosevelt's March 4, 1933, speech outlining his policies for his administration, including the Good Neighbor Policy.

20. Diego Rivera's Mural Removed from Rockefeller Center (February 10, 1934)

One of the most celebrated muralists of the 20th century, Diego Rivera (1886–1957) was revered worldwide for his innovative, yet highly controversial, Post-impressionistic images of Aztec culture, socialism, and industrialism. Born in the central highland city of Guanajuato City, Mexico, to a wealthy family, Rivera studied art in Mexico City and throughout Europe. Among all of his work, no other commission generated greater controversy and public reaction than the mural in the RCA building in Rockefeller Center in Manhattan. Working through their board of managers, the Rockefellers petitioned Pablo Piccaso, Henri Matisse, and Diego Rivera in May 1932 to paint original frescos in the lobby of their new and grand building. The proposed theme was "Man at the Crossroads Looking with Hope and High Vision to the Choosing of a New and Better Future." It was an ambitious project, and the managers along with Raymond Hood, who was the RCA building's architect, requested that the artists submit samples of their work before signing a contract. Offended by such a request and believing it to be a violation of artistic license, Picasso and Matisse refused to accept these terms; however, after some protests, Rivera agreed to participate in the project. After preliminary sketches of the proposed mural were submitted and approved, Rivera and several assistants commenced the project in March 1933. Work progressed as scheduled, and there was little dispute over content until a reporter from the *New York World-Telegram* published his April 24th interview with Rivera regarding the content of the muralist's choice of imagery. The article was entitled "Rivera Paints Scenes of Communist Activity—and John D., Jr. Foots Bill." Indeed, a section of the mural depicted Vladimir Lenin, a founder of the Soviet Union, clasping hands with an American and a Russian. Rivera maintained that this was symbolic of an inevitable alliance that would have to be created between the United States and the Soviet Union if fascism, which was sweeping through Europe in the 1930s, was to be eradicated. The growing publicity of this politically charged mural and the disagreements that rose between Rivera and the Rockefellers' managers quickly ended in the suspension of the project on May 9, 1933. The arguments continued for several more months; however, Rivera was paid in full and eventually returned to Mexico without being permitted to complete the project or amend it. Nevertheless, his reputation as a respected artist was negatively impacted by the incident. Soon after Rivera had returned to Mexico, the Rockefellers had the nearly completed mural pulverized on February 10, 1934.

TERM PAPER SUGGESTIONS

1. Before accepting the commission at the Rockefeller Center, Diego Rivera had just completed a set of murals in Detroit at the Detroit Institute of Arts for Edsel Ford, the Ford Motor Company's president. True to his art form, Rivera generated a great deal of controversy for choosing socially and politically charged images for his work; however, despite the large public outcry against these murals for being "pornographic" or "pro-communist," Ford did not have Rivera alter his work. Study the Detroit frescos, the controversy surrounding them, and the descriptions of the Rockefeller Center mural, and discuss why one prominent capitalist of the time would

find no fault in Rivera's work, while another would. What do these different reactions suggest about Ford and Rockefeller? What do they suggest about the social and political climate of mainstream United States in the mid-1930s?

2. Even though Rivera and his assistants were expelled from the RCA building on May 9, 1933, the mural was not destroyed until nearly a year later. What transpired during that time? Which groups and prominent individuals became involved in the Rivera controversy? Examine how the aftermath of Rivera's expulsion contributed to the mural's destruction rather than its relocation or alteration.

3. Later in 1934, Diego Rivera had the opportunity to regenerate the Rockefeller Center mural on the second floor of Mexico City's Palace of Fine Arts. The work was entitled *Man, Controller of the Universe*. Examine the work closely and interpret what changes were made from the original one in New York and why. Also, in this analysis describe how the mural loses some of its original meaning and context in terms of its depictions and location, and what this essentially meant for Rivera.

4. Rivera admired the United States for its freedom of expression and openness; however, through the Rockefeller Center project, he realized that his ideas were not necessarily welcomed. Argue for or against the role of artistic license in the case of Rivera's destroyed mural. Compare this event with more recent occurrences of artwork receiving controversial publicity and deemed offensive in the United States such as in the Robert Mapplethorpe's erotic photographic exhibitions in the late 1980s or the Brooklyn Museum of Art's exhibit "Sensation" in 1999, which included a contemporary portrait of the Virgin Mary.

ALTERNATIVE TERM PAPER SUGGESTIONS

1. Based on primary sources, recreate a series of interviews in which you present the ideas of Diego Rivera and other prominent individuals involved in the Rockefeller Center controversy. In this exposé, determine whether Rivera's arguments concerning his original sketches submitted and the claims made by the Rockefeller Center's managing group, the board of Todd, Robertson, Todd Engineering Corporation, justify the actions taken against the mural project.

2. As an art historian and expert on Diego Rivera, present the life and work of this renowned Mexican artist to your class. Using Power-Point with hyperlinks, create a presentation that reflects the pivotal moments in Rivera's private and public life with a special focus on the incident at Rockefeller Center in the 1930s as a dramatic turning point in the artist's career. Be sure to emphasize Rivera's artistic intentions and influences.

SUGGESTED SOURCES

Primary Sources

"Diego Rivera's *Man at the Crossroads.*" http://www.pbs.org/wgbh/culture shock/flashpoints/visualarts/diegorivera.html. Provides a short description of the Rockefeller mural including a black-and-white image taken of the actual work in progress in 1933.

Rivera, Diego. *My Life, My Art: An Autobiography.* New York: Dover Publications, 1991. Based on 13 years of extensive interviews with Gladys March, this work compiles the life work and experiences of Rivera from his own words. Special attention is given to the Rockefeller Center controversy. Includes photographs and reproduced images of key works of art.

Secondary Sources

Kettenmann, Andrea. *Diego Rivera, 1886–1957: A Revolutionary Spirit in Modern Art.* Cologne, Germany: Taschen, 2001. Covers Rivera's life as a political artist with a focus on how his work became a revolutionary language for his worldviews and visions.

Lozano, Luis Martin, and Juan Coronel Rivera. *Diego Rivera, The Complete Murals.* Cologne, Germany: Taschen, 2008. A comprehensive collection of Rivera's murals includes essays from scholars interpreting each one of the pieces. Also provides a broad selection of private and public documents and drawings, period photographs, and the artist's canvas paintings.

Marín, Guadalupe Rivera. *Diego Rivera the Red.* Trans. Dick Gerdes. Houston, TX: Arte Público Press, 2004. Written by the artist's daughter, this work traces the early life of Diego Rivera from his involvement with socialist revolutions to encounters with avant-garde artists throughout Europe.

Marnham, Patrick. *Dreaming with His Eyes Open: A Life of Diego Rivera.* New York: Alfred A. Knopf, 1998. An extensive biography of Rivera's life and work includes color images of his work. Chapter 11 is devoted to the controversies in Detroit and New York.

Scott, Robert L. "Diego Rivera at Rockefeller Center: Fresco Painting and Rhetoric." *Western Journal of Speech Communication* 41 (Spring 1977): 70–82. http://personal.lse.ac.uk/Morett/Papers/Scott-RiveraEssayon.pdf. Article examines the broader impacts on art through a critical examination of the Rockefeller controversy in the 1930s.

Wolfe, Bertram D. *The Fabulous Life of Diego Rivera*. New York: Stein and Day, 1963. Written by a close friend of Rivera and a key player in the Rockefeller Center battle, Wolfe has created a rich biography of the artist that includes over 160 black-and-white reproductions of his canvas work and frescos.

World Wide Web

"Artist Diego Rivera." http://www.pbs.org/newshour/bb/entertainment/july-dec99/rivera_7-15.html. Features transcript of *News Hour with Jim Lehrer* reporter Jeffrey Kaye's interview with curator of the Los Angeles County Museum of Art's 1999 exhibit "Art and Revolution," which showcased Rivera as a revolutionary artist. Includes link to audio version and images of the exhibit.

"Diego Rivera: A Man and His Murals." http://www.yale.edu/ynhti/curriculum/units/1999/2/99.02.06.x.html. From the Yale-New Haven Teaching Institute, this site features an extensive overview of Rivera's life and work and draws connections with Franklin D. Roosevelt's New Deal Cultural program in the 1930s. Includes a brief bibliography and lesson plans.

"Diego Rivera Prints." http://www.diego_rivera.org/bibliography.html. Includes extensive biography with links to museums and exhibitions that sponsor Rivera's work as well as links to his murals and controversial events during his career.

"Man at the Crossroads." http://www.manatthecrossroads.com/lucienne.pdf. Provides 2007 interview transcript of Lucienne Allen, granddaughter of Lucienne Block, one of Rivera's assistants and the one who took copious photographs of the Rockefeller Center mural before Rivera was expelled from the building.

"The Virtual Diego Museum." http://www.diegoriver.com/index.php. Extensive site provides streaming videos of actual footage from Rivera's life, images of his work, biographical information, and relevant links for further study of his life.

Multimedia Sources

Diego Rivera. Princeton, NJ: Films for the Humanities, 2002. DVD. 12 minutes. *News Hour with Jim Lehrer* correspondent Jeffrey Kaye hosts this brief segment on the artist's revolutionary work.

Diego Rivera: I Paint What I See. Corrales, NM: New Deal Films, 2003. DVD. 58 minutes. Examines Rivera's pivotal moments in his career including the Rockefeller Center project and 19 minutes of silent footage of the artist at work in Detroit.

A Portrait of Diego: The Revolutionary Gaze. Mexico City: Alfhaville Cinema, 2007. 80 minutes. Explores the artist's life and philosophy behind his often-controversial work.

21. Ponce Massacre (March 21, 1937)

To protest the arrest of Puerto Rican Nationalist Party leader Pedro Albizu Campos, the Party decided to organize a march through the streets of Ponce, Puerto Rico. As the proposed event was widely publicized, police had time to interfere and prevent the march from taking place. Despite having obtained proper permits to assemble, the members of the Nationalist Party were banned from marching by the ranks of police officials and Governor Blanton Winship himself. They had characterized the march as military in nature and therefore inappropriate. To ensure that a march would not take place, police forces were sent early in the morning of March 21 equipped with rifles, machine guns, and tear gas. Feeling pressure from police, government, and church officials, Ponce Mayor Tormos Diego revoked his permission for the Nationalist Party to conduct their march. Nevertheless, party members, who comprised the Cadets of the Republic, the Nurses Corps, and a small marching band, assembled unarmed just outside of their national headquarters building. Also in the streets were family members of party members who came to see the parade. As soon as the band began playing "La Borinqueña," the national song of Puerto Rico, the police moved in quickly to surround and prevent the march from continuing. After police officer Armando Martínez fired into the air, a series of shots were volleyed, and in the end around 19 people were killed with over 100 wounded.. Many of the victims were bystanders and passersby. Governor Winship had blamed the Nationalist Party for the violence and ordered the arrest of a large number of party members. However, the American Civil Liberties Union became involved and helped to establish what later became known as the Hays Commission to investigate the incident closely. Using first-hand testimonies and photographic evidence taken at the scene, the commission found that the police were responsible for attacking not only the unarmed marchers but also the innocent crowd of bystanders. The Ponce Massacre has always been a pivotal event that represented the ongoing struggle for Puerto Rican independence from the United States.

TERM PAPER SUGGESTIONS

1. Discuss how the Ponce Massacre served to further the causes and agenda of the Puerto Rican Nationalist Party throughout the 20th century. What did the event ultimately symbolize for the Puerto Rican struggle for independence from the United States?

2. One of the reasons the Nationalist Party march took place in Ponce was to protest the unlawful arrest of party leaders, including Pedro Albizu Campos. What was Campos' role in the Nationalist Party at the time of the massacre? Why were his ideas so dangerous as to warrant his arrest and the march that followed?

3. What role did the media play in the Ponce Massacre both in terms of publicizing it and in the outcome of the trial?

ALTERNATIVE TERM PAPER SUGGESTIONS

1. As a reporter witnessing the Ponce Massacre on March 21, 1937, create a podcast that details the event. Include quotes from fictional bystanders, participants, and police and government agents whom you interviewed to convey a sense of realism and accuracy to the report.

2. Take a close look at Puerto Rican poet Martín Espada's poem "Rebellion Is the Circle of a Lover's Hands," about the Ponce Massacre in 1937. Research the poem and Espada's work, and discuss how the event is retold through this art form. What does it suggest about the legacy of this event?

SUGGESTED SOURCES

Primary Sources

"7 Die in Puerto Rican Riot: 50 Injured as Police Fire on Fighting Nationalists." *New York Times,* March 22, 1937: 1. The article reports on the massacre directly.

Hull, Harwood. "Clash Rekindles Puerto Rican Feud." *New York Times,* March 28, 1937: 11. Covers the disparity between Puerto Rican Nationalists and the United States through the event of the Massacre.

"Ponce Massacre 1937." http://www.latinamericanstudies.org/ponce-1937.htm. Includes three photos of police firing on Puerto Rican Nationalists during the march.

Secondary Sources

Ayala, Cesar J., and Rafael Bernabe. *Puerto Rico in the American Century: A History since 1898.* Chapel Hill: University of North Carolina Press, 2007. Chapter 6 discusses the turbulent times of the 1930s and includes a discussion of the 1937 massacre.

Corretijer, Juan Antonio. *Albizu Campos and the Ponce Massacre.* New York: World View Publishers, 1965, pp. 377–406. Documents the background and circumstances that culminated in the 1937 Massacre and the symbolic role Puerto Rican Nationalist Party leader Pedro Albizu Campos played.

———— "Albizu Campos and the Ponce Massacre." In *Latino/a Thought: Culture, Politics, and Society,* edited by Francisco H. Vázque. Lanham, MD: Rowman & Littlefield, 2009. Reproduces the essential highlights of Corretijer's work published in 1965.

Delgado, Linda C. "Jesús Colon and the Making of a New York City Community, 1917 to 1974." In *The Puerto Rican Diaspora: Historical Perspectives,* edited by Carmen Teresa Whalen and Victor Vazuez-Hernandez. Philadelphia: Temple University Press, 2005, pp. 68–87. Includes a discussion of how the Ponce Massacre impacted the continued development of the Puerto Rican enclave in New York City.

World Wide Web

"Dr. Pedro Albizu Campos." http://www.nl.edu/academics/cas/ace/resources/campos.cfm. Contains autobiographical information on the national leader, including photographs and images as well as a biographical timeline.

"Ponce Massacre." http://www.yasminhernandez.com/ponce.html. Puerto Rican artist Yasmin Hernandez's artwork depicts images of the Ponce Massacre with a discussion of the cultural significance the event has for Puerto Ricans.

"The Ponce Massacre." http://www.associatedcontent.com/article/119025/the_ponce_massacre.html?cat=37. Contains a brief overview of the event.

"The Ponce Massacre (1937)." http://www.enciclopediapr.org/ing/article.cfm? ref=06102005&page=1. Provides a detailed account of the massacre and the legal aftermath undertaken by the Hays Commission.

"The Ponce Massacre, Com. of Inquiry, 1937." http://www.llmc.com/ TitleLLMC.asp?ColID=3&Cat=136&TID=7037&TName=Ponce% 20Massacre,%20Com.%20of%20Inquiry,%201937. Details the official U.S. investigation into the massacre.

"Remembering Puerto Rico's Ponce Massacre." http://www.pslweb.org/site/ News2?JServSessionIdr004=xi1nt36q72.app7b&page=NewsArticle& id=6559&news_iv_ctrl=1261. Focuses on the role of the Puerto Rican Nationalist Party in the occurrence and aftermath of the massacre.

Multimedia Source

"Remembering Puerto Rico's Ponce Massacre." http://www.democracynow. org/2007/3/22/remembering_puerto_ricos_ponce_massacre. *Democracy Now!* radio show provides video, audio, and written transcript of an interview with Puerto Rican experts discussing Puerto Rico's status on the 70th anniversary of the Ponce Massacre.

22. Emma Tenayuca and the Southern Pecan Shelling Company Strike (1938)

Since the 1880s, San Antonio, Texas, had been the center of the pecan industry and a constant source for labor among Mexican American and Mexican national workers. Because of these groups' marginalized status in the city, they had little control over their working conditions and relationship with management. However, in January 1938, Emma Tenayuca, a Latina labor activist and outspoken member of the Communist Party, led a massive strike of Latino workers against the Southern Pecan Shelling Company in San Antonio. Still reeling from the stock market crash in 1929 and, in an effort to cut costs, the company mandated a wage reduction to 1 cent per pound of shelled pecans, which greatly angered workers. Tenayuca and other union organizers encouraged several thousand workers at 130 plants to walk out. The strike received national attention not only because of Tenayuca's passionate speeches and communist ties, but also for the brutality of the police who gassed, arrested, and incarcerated hundreds of workers including Tenayuca herself. The strike lasted for five weeks and ended with a slight increase in wages for workers. Soon after, however, many workers were laid off due to the company's conversion from physical hand labor to machines to shell and package the pecans. Nevertheless, the pecan strike and Tenayuca were instrumental in bringing national attention to the labor conditions of Mexican Americans and Mexican nationals alike and encouraged many Latinos to actively participate in U.S. labor unions.

TERM PAPER SUGGESTIONS

1. Compare this strike with other labor strikes throughout the United States that involved large numbers of Latino workers such as the 1937 Republic Steel Mill Strike in Chicago. What do the different strikes suggest about how the Latino communities were organizing themselves during the 1930s?

2. Discuss how labor strikes such as the one at the Southern Pecan Shelling Company brought the needs and concerns of the Mexican-American community to the public's attention and confronted the Jim Crow laws of the Southwest.

3. Explain how Latinas were integral to labor strike movements in the 1930s. Draw parallels between the political philosophies of Emma Tenayuca and Josefina Fierro de Bright and Luisa Moreno who were leaders in the Congress of Spanish Speaking Peoples.

4. Tenayuca was a passionate speaker and an outspoken member of the Communist Party in the United States. Discuss how and why Tenayuca's ties to communism fueled strong opposition to the strike by significant groups such as the Archdiocese of San Antonio, the Mexican Chamber of Commerce, and the police.

ALTERNATIVE TERM PAPER SUGGESTIONS

1. Design a Webography of the life and times of Emma Tenayuca with special focus on the pecan strike and her role in it.

2. Create a detailed timeline of U.S. labor strikes in the first half of the 20th century that predominantly comprised Latino laborers. Draw parallels between the strikes to emphasize their relevance to Latino civil rights.

SUGGESTED SOURCES

Primary Sources

"La Pasionaria de Texas." *Time,* February 28, 1938: 17. http://www.time.com/time/magazine/article/0,9171,931073,00.html. Features original article profiling Tenayuca and her participation in the pecan strike.

Tenayuca, Emma, and Homer Brooks. "The Mexican Question in the Southwest." *The Communist* 18 (1939): 257–268. Argues that Mexican Americans and Mexican nationals are not a separate nation but are in fact a conquered people whose culture, labor, and role in U.S. society have been made invisible.

Secondary Sources

Schmidt Camacho, Alicia. *Migrant Imaginaries: Latino Cultural Politics in the U.S.-Mexico Borderlands.* New York: NYU Press, 2008. Provides an overview of the Latino community's role in U.S. labor movement beginning in the 1920s and includes a segment on pecan strike.

Shapiro, Harold A. "The Pecan Shellers of San Antonio, Texas." *The Southwestern Social Science Quarterly* 32 (1952): 229–230. Details the strike itself and the impact of its aftermath.

Vargas, Zaragosa. *Labor Rights Are Civil Rights: Mexican American Workers in Twentieth-Century America.* Princeton, NJ: Princeton University Press, 2007. Focuses on Mexican American communities in Texas, Colorado, and California and presents a comprehensive background on labor strikes in the United States, particularly the pecan strike. Digital version is available through Google Books.com.

———. "Tejana Radical: Emma Tenayuca and the San Antonio Labor Movement during the Great Depression." *Pacific Historical Review* 66, no. 4 (1997): 553–580. Provides close examination of the four significant phases in Tenayuca's activist career from 1933 to 1939.

World Wide Web

"Emma Tenayuca." http://www.sat.lib.tx.us/Latino/emma.htm. Provides an extensive bibliography on the life of Tenayuca compiled by the San Antonio Public Library.

"History of ACLU in Texas." http://www.aclutx.org/projects/article.php?aid=387&cid=33. Features brief description of how the strike led to the formation of the ACLU in Texas and includes discussion of Tenayuca's involvement and photo of her during the event.

"'Por la raza y para la raza': A Look at Tejana Activists, 1900–1998." http://utminers.utep.edu/yleyva/Tejana%20Activists.htm. Provides transcript of Yolanda Chávez Leyva's speech, September 1998, at the University of Texas, San Antonio, and includes a discussion of Tenayuca as well as several other early Latina labor activists in Texas.

"Unintended Consequences: The San Antonio Pecan Shellers Strike of 1938." http://www.uiw.edu/sanantonio/gower.html. Patricia Gower's detailed article in *The Journal of the Life and Culture of San Antonio* gives a detailed synopsis of this event.

Multimedia Sources

"Development of Labor Unions in San Antonio, 1930s." http://texancultures.com/library/tenayucaInterview.htm. Contais Institute of Texan Cultures' collection of photographs of Tenayuca and the pecan strike. An audio interview with Tenayuca and a written transcript are also available.

The Emma Tenayuca Story: Texas Civil Rights Leader. San Antonio: Institute of Texan Cultures, 2006. DVD. 9 minutes. Features brief overview of Tenayuca's role during the pecan strike.

23. Almighty Latin King Nation Formed (1940s)

First formed by Gino Gustavo Colon in Chicago, Illinois, during the 1940s, the Almighty Latin King Nation has become one of the most powerful and populated Latino urban gangs in the United States with nearly 50,000 members in and around the Chicago area alone. Initially created to protect Puerto Ricans and Mexicans first arriving in the United States, the Latin Kings soon developed into a well-organized entity that has established chapters in over 40 states and several European and Latin American nations. Besides being notorious for violence and drug trafficking, various chapters of the Latin Kings will often engage in community service in an effort to uplift their respective neighborhoods and foster a sense of Latino pride and self-expression. The organization is different from other urban gangs in that it has generated a Latin King Manifesto or Constitution, which is a philosophical tract that charts the three principal phases of consciousness a Latin King member is said to pass through. The first is the Primitive Stage whereby a member is expected to engage in gang-banging and the culture of violence. The next phase is the Conservative/Mummy Stage when a member begins to recognize the institutionalization of racism and starts to move away from urban gang culture. The final phase of "Kingism" within the organization is called the New King Stage, which uses tenets of Christianity, Confucianism, and Marxism and entails members seeking greater unity between warring factions and the championing of the poor and oppressed. By 1994, the New York chapter became the Almighty Latin King and Queen Nation (ALKQN) and set about becoming more public and politically active in the Latino community.

TERM PAPER SUGGESTIONS

1. Present the details of the intensive three year investigation (2003–2006) into the Latin Kings called "Operation Broken Crown," which involved government agencies, such as the U.S. Bureau of Alcohol, Tobacco, Firearms and Explosives. What were the successes and failures of this investigation? Compare this with in-depth investigations conducted in the United States of other organized urban gangs.

2. While the Latin Kings have been associated with violence and drugs, argue how the organization has participated in cultural programs in various cities around the world and how particular chapters have attempted to give back to their communities.

3. Compare the organization, philosophies, and culture of the Almighty Latin King and Queen Nation with other Latino gangs such as the Norteños, the Young Lords, or the 18th Street gang.

4. Articulate how life and expectations are different for female gang members, particularly those who are a part of the ALKQN, compared with male counterparts.

ALTERNATIVE TERM PAPER SUGGESTIONS

1. Create a timeline that details the hierarchical organization and evolution of various key Latin King chapters around the world, including the inclusion of Latin Queens into what became the Almighty Latin King and Queen Nation.

2. One of the most publicized crimes in the Latin King organization was the 1983 murder of Carlos Robles, a North Side Chicago Latin

King, by the order of Gustavo Colon. Imagine you are called before a judicial committee interested in the inner political turmoil of gang structure. Use images, testimonies, and charts to profile the balance of power that exists between different chapters of the Latin Kings.

SUGGESTED SOURCES

Primary Sources

"The Almighty Latin King and Queen Nation." http://people-nation.com/almighty-latin-king-and-queen-nation/. Contains background information on the organization and includes the Almighty Latin Kings and Queens Nation Manifesto and Constitution.

Mission, King. *The Official Globalization of the ALKQN.* King Mission, 2008. This important self-published work provides an in-depth discussion of the group's history, reorganization, and activity beyond the United States.

Sanchez, Reymundo. *My Bloody Life: The Making of a Latin King.* Chicago: Chicago Review Press, 2000. Recounts a former gang member's life in the Latin Kings.

Sanchez, Reymundo, and Sonia Rodriguez. *Lady Q. The Rise and Fall of a Latin Queen.* Chicago: Chicago Review Press, 2008. A provocative memoir offers the perspective of a female gang member.

Secondary Sources

Brotherton, David, and Luis Barrios. *The Almighty Latin King and Queen Nation: Street Politics and the Transformation of a New York Gang.* New York: Columbia University Press, 2004. Chronicles the gang's transformation from an underground society to a public, community-based organization.

Kontos, Louis, David Brotherton, and Luis Barrios, eds. *Gangs and Society.* New York: Columbia University Press, 2003. Comprehensive anthology includes several key articles on the Almighty Latin King and Queen Nation.

Mendoza-Denton, Norma. *Homegirls: Language and Cultural Practice among Latina Youth Gangs.* Malden, MA: Blackwell, 2008. Provides an overview of gangs that many Latinas are involved in, including the ALKQN.

World Wide Web

"Almighty Latin King and Queen Nation." http://www.alkqn.org/index.php. Official Web site incorporates links to career and educational resources and philosophies from different organization leaders.

"The Almighty Latin King Nation." http://www.knowgangs.com/gang_resources/profiles/kings/. Provides brief background on the organization and includes a video with images and footage of gang members and events.

"Gang Profile: The Latin Kings." http://www.ngcrc.com/ngcrc/page15.htm. Features the National Gang Crime Research Center's comprehensive study of the Latin King Nation's origins, methodologies, gang leaders, and statistics.

"An Investigation into the Latin Kings: No Tolerance for Gangs in Public Schools." http://docs.google.com/gview?a=v&q=cache:4LFcpC-A7kUJ:www.nycsci.org/reports/10-97%2520Latin%2520Kings%2520Rpt.PDF+almighty+latin+king+constitution&hl=en&gl=us&sig=AFQjCNFAo6Wcs9o5-s17NXylOIODjlPOfw. Contains a New York City police report on the indictment of a Safety Officer's connection with the Latin King organization.

Multimedia Source

Black and Gold: The Story of the Almighty Latin King and Queen Nation. New York: Big Noise Films, 2008. DVD. 76 minutes. Profiles the group's 1994 transformation into an activist organization.

24. Bracero Program Created (1942)

Formally called the Mexican Farm Labor Program, the Bracero Program was initiated between the United States and Mexico to respond to the vast labor shortage occurring in the United States and the widespread unemployment throughout Mexico during World War II. According to the initial program, Mexican workers would be given temporary visas to work for U.S. agricultural companies as field hands or for U.S. railroads laying track across the continent. The program was amended a few times during its 22-year duration. Between 1942 and 1948, the U.S. Department of Agriculture organized all contracting and recruitment of laborers. Then from 1948 to 1951 amendments to the program turned this duty over to individual U.S. companies, which were required to pay a laborer's round-trip ticket between harvests, guarantee consistent wages, and ensure standard working and housing conditions. In many cases, this feature of the program created greater problems since the laborers were often taken advantage of by the companies. In 1951 during the Korean War (1950–1953), President Harry S Truman signed Public Law 78 after the Mexican government asked for greater guarantees and protection of Mexican laborers. This returned the contracting and recruitment duties to the U.S. government. While the Bracero Program aided in supplying a demand for workers during World War II and the Korean War and brought to the public's eye the vast rural poverty in Mexico, it also became a method for institutionalizing cheap labor and exploitation of immigrant Mexican workers throughout the United States. By the 1960s, the Bracero Program continued to become unpopular for "braceros" and agriculture companies alike. This was because of more mechanized farms, competition with a growing population of undocumented workers, the protestations of labor unions over exploiting Braceros, and the expense of paying laborers a $1 per hour minimum wage. The Bracero Program was finally ended in 1964.

TERM PAPER SUGGESTIONS

1. There were over 50,000 field workers compared with over 75,000 railroad workers that made up the Bracero Program by the end of World War II in 1945. Describe the daily lifestyles of these two types of Braceros in terms of wages, living and working conditions, community structure, and migration patterns. What were important distinctions between these two types of workers in the program?

2. Argue whether the Bracero Program benefited the immigrant workers more or the companies and government agencies that employed them. Highlight some of the central conflicts and controversies surrounding this program, including the disputes that arose in El Paso, Texas, in October 1948 and directly involved U.S. growers, the Immigration and Naturalization Service, and the government of Mexico.

3. Compare the Bracero Program of the mid-20th century with the guest worker program proposed during the George W. Bush administration. What were significant parallels and distinctions between these policies? Why did the Bracero Program succeed in being implemented while President Bush's policy was widely criticized and never realized?

4. Explain the relationship between the Bracero Program and Operation Wetback in 1954. How did these two U.S. government programs respond to the issue of immigration from Mexico into the United States?

ALTERNATIVE TERM PAPER SUGGESTIONS

1. Design a timeline of the Bracero Program at its various stages. Include hyperlinks that provide further explanations of the program's evolution, general statistics, and maps of where concentrations of workers occurred, and photographs from this time period.

2. As a labor organization leader of either the National Farm Laborers Union or the Agricultural Workers Organizing Committee, create a PowerPoint presentation with statements, graphs, and images that you will present to U.S. leaders to demonstrate how the Bracero Program has only exploited the immigrant farm worker and should be ended.

SUGGESTED SOURCES

Primary Sources

"Bracero History Archive." http://braceroarchive.org/. Features first-hand accounts of participants in the program and includes links to photographs, important documents, and teaching lessons.

Jacobo, José Rodolfo. *Los Braceros: Memories of Bracero Workers 1942–1964.* San Diego, CA: Southern Border Press, 2004. Extensive compilation of letters, testimonies, and photographs highlight the experience of many Mexican laborers who participated in the program.

Secondary Sources

Craig, Richard B. *The Bracero Program: Interest Groups and Foreign Policy.* Austin: University of Texas Press, 1971. Features a comprehensive study of various phases in the Bracero Program and the difficulties arising from the amendments made to the original policy during the mid-20th century.

Driscoll, Barbara A. *The Tracks North: The Railroad Bracero Program of World War II.* Austin, TX: Center for Mexican American Studies Books, 1999. Details the other feature of the Bracero Program that contracted laborers to expand railroad lines across the United States.

Garcia y Griego, Manuel. "The Importation of Mexican Contract Laborers in the United States 1942–1964." In *Between Two Worlds: Mexican Immigrants in the United States*, edited by David G. Gutiérrez. Wilmington, DE: Scholarly Resources, 1996, pp. 45–85. Discusses how both United States and Mexico articulate their respective bargaining positions and suggests that, after the 1940s, Mexico had little bargaining advantage.

Navarro, Armando. *Mexican Political Experience in Occupied Aztlán.* Walnut Creek, CA: Altamira Press, 2005. Focuses on the Braceros' perspective and describes the situations and circumstances affecting them.

World Wide Web

Mexican Labor Importation: Los Braceros 1942–1964." http://www1.american. edu/TED/bracero.htm. Presented as a case study, this site offers insight into the program in terms of geographical, economic, and cultural impact and provides relevant charts and statistics.

"Opportunity or Exploitation: The Bracero Program." http://americanhistory. si.edu/ONTHEMOVE/themes/story_51_5.html. Provides historical information and thoughtful discussion grounded in the fieldworker's experience. Also includes photographs of farmhands through various stages of the program with relevant links for further research.

"Snapshots in a Farm Labor Tradition." http://are.berkeley.edu/APMP/pubs/ lmd/html/winterspring_93/snapshots.html. Provides general overview of the Bracero Program and its practices and includes link to photographs of Braceros going through the documentation process with relevant photo captions and bibliography for further research.

"U.S. Temporary Worker Programs: Lessons Learned." http://www.migration information.org/USFocus/display.cfm?ID=205. Compares former President Bush's guest worker program with the Bracero Program in the context of migration.

Multimedia Sources

Bracero Stories. El Paso, TX: Cherry Lane Productions, 2008. DVD. 56 minutes. Focuses on five former farm laborers who took part in the Bracero Program.

The Braceros. Portland, OR: Oregon Public Broadcasting, 2007. DVD. 29 minutes. Presents overview of the program itself and the immediate impact on the U.S. economy and lives of Mexican workers.

"President Bush Proposes New Temporary Worker Program." http://georgewbush-whitehouse.archives.gov/news/releases/2004/01/20040107-3.html. Features Bush's first introduction outlining his guest worker policy during his administration. Includes written transcript, audio and video versions.

25. Zoot Suit Riots (May–June 1943)

The Zoot Suit Riots were sparked by one of the largest and most sensationalized trials in California's history: the Sleepy Lagoon Case. On August 2,

1942, the body of José Diaz was found at Sleepy Lagoon reservoir in southeast Los Angeles, a popular swimming hole among Latinos who were forbidden to use public pools. The discovery set off a series of arrests by Los Angeles police who rounded up over 600 mostly Latino youths in connection with the Diaz murder. The trial, which was covered by major newspapers across the nation, violated a number of the defendants' civil rights including lack of due process. In the end, an all-white jury convicted 12 of the defendants in association with the murder. An East Los Angeles grassroots organization called the Sleepy Lagoon Defense Committee was immediately created to appeal the verdicts, and in October 1944, the case was reversed. Following the 1942 convictions, however, tension between Anglos and Latino youth grew, and on May 31, 1943, a full-blown riot occurred between U.S. servicemen on shore leave in Los Angeles and young Latinos, calling themselves "pachucos" wearing zoot suits. Several days of confrontation between servicemen and zoot suiters continued, which eventually led to Latino neighborhoods being invaded and men and women being attacked in street cars, movie theaters, and bars. Newspapers and the Los Angeles City Council praised the servicemen for "cleaning up" this subculture, while the police did very little to stop the attacks that were now flaring up in many U.S. cities including Chicago, Detroit, and Philadelphia. Eventually, the commanders of the U.S. Navy and Marines ordered servicemen back to ships and bases on June 7, 1943, when the attacks began to involve more and more Latinos and other minorities not connected with the zoot suit youth culture.

TERM PAPER SUGGESTIONS

1. Discuss the broad impact the Sleepy Lagoon Trial and the Zoot Suit Riots had on developing a stronger sense of Chicano identity in the United States.

2. The zoot suit itself became a controversial symbol that represented different things to many people. Explain the various cultural meanings behind wearing the suit and why it was one of the things the rioting servicemen destroyed when accosting the hundreds of Latinos who were attacked.

3. Just prior to the arrest of over 600 Mexican American youths in connection with the Sleepy Lagoon trial, over 120,000 Japanese Americans had been rounded up and sent to internment camps. Many scholars have closely connected these two events as institutionalized illustrations

for controlling domestic minority communities during World War II. Argue whether there are larger cultural and political connections between these events and respond to what scholars have asserted regarding the association made.

4. Examine several of the public statements made by city, press, police, and military officials regarding the Zoot Suit Riots. Determine how Mexican American youths were perceived in the public imagination and argue how such perceptions further divided Anglos from Latinos.

ALTERNATIVE TERM PAPER SUGGESTIONS

1. Develop a PowerPoint presentation whereby you draw associations between the "pachuco" cultural figure of the World War II era and the "cholo" image that developed later in the 20th century. Explain what larger parallels can be made between these Mexican American subcultures in terms of youth expression, challenge to traditional Latino mores, and contemporary gang culture. Also include the role of females involved: the pachucas and cholitas.

2. Create a comprehensive iMovie with images, film clips, photographs, and charts that compare the Zoot Suit Riots in 1943 with the Los Angeles Riots in 1992. Provide commentary on how the two are being associated and what larger issues concerning U.S. race relations are being raised.

SUGGESTED SOURCES

Primary Sources

McWilliams, Carey. *Fool's Paradise: A Carey McWilliams Reader.* Berkeley, CA: Heyday Books, 2001. Provides a comprehensive and unique historical examination of California. McWilliam's chapter, "Blood on the Pavements," relays his experiences as one of the lawyers during the Sleepy Lagoon trials and his participation in the Sleepy Lagoon Defense Committee.

"Zoot Suit Riots." http://web.viu.ca/davies/H324War/Zootsuit.riots.media. 1943.htm. Contains many reprinted articles from West and East Coast U.S. newspapers describing the riots as they took place.

Secondary Sources

Alvarez, Luis. *The Power of the Zoot: Youth Culture and Resistance during World War II.* Berkeley: University of California Press, 2008. Articulates the importance of style and body politics in creating race relations in the United States and compares the Zoot Suit Riots with later 20th-century race riots.

Mazón, Mauricio. *The Zoot Suit Riots: The Psychology of Symbolic Annihilation.* Austin: University of Texas Press, 1988. http://books.google.com/ books?id=NdEQEOA-2AMC&dq=zoot+suit+riots&printsec=front cover&source=bl&ots=rJMcc_-wcf&sig=TUBWXZzIwilEWdeARIQ bqb1jdt8&hl=en&ei=NJSlSp7tCYqksgO4ufmMDw&sa=X&oi= book_result&ct=result&resnum=8#v=onepage&q=&f=false. Investigates the psychodynamics and meaning behind the trial and riots, moving beyond court testimonies and press headlines to define the cultural consequences of the events.

Pagán, Eduardo Obregón. *Murder at the Sleepy Lagoon: Zoot Suits, Race and Riots in Wartime L.A.* Chapel Hill: University of North Carolina Press, 2003. Analyzes in detail the Sleepy Lagoon Trial and the series of cross-country riots that followed.

Ramírez, Catherine Sue. *The Woman in the Zoot Suit: Gender, Nationalism, and the Culture Politics of Memory.* Durham, NC: Duke University, 2009. Explores the complex role of the female zoot suiter, the pachuca, during the Zoot Suit Riots.

Valdez, Luis. *Zoot Suit and Other Plays.* Houston, TX: Art Público Press, 1992. Contains Valdez's celebrated play that fictionalizes the trial and riots, while emphasizing an emerging Chicano identity.

World Wide Web

"Old Memories Los Angeles." http://www.oldmemorieslosangeles.us/zootsuit truestory.htm. Features a collection of historical pictures from Los Angeles' zoot suit subculture and riots.

"The Pachuca Panic: Sexual and Cultural Backgrounds in World War II Los Angeles." http://www.historycooperative.org/cgi-bin/justtop.cgi?act= justtop&url=http://www.historycooperative.org/journals/whq/38.2/ escobedo.html. Focuses on the role of the female zoot suiter, the pachuca, and articulates the changing role of the Mexican American woman in the United States.

"Sleepy Lagoon Trial: 1942–1943—Zoot Suit Riots." http://law.jrank.org/ pages/2971/Sleepy-Lagoon-Trials-1942-43.html. Provides general overview of the trial and riots and incorporates names of those participating in the trial process with their specific convictions.

"World War Two and the Zoot Suit Riots." http://w3.usf.edu/~lc/MOOs/ zootsuit/index.html. Profiles the trial and riots and provides study questions for further analysis.

"The Zoot Suit and Style Warfare." http://invention.smithsonian.org/center pieces/whole_cloth/u7sf/u7materials/cosgrove.html. Includes details of the background and cultural significance of the zoot suit itself and how the suit became a symbolic target during the riots.

Multimedia Sources

Zoot Suit. Universal City, CA: Universal Studios, 2003. This is Luis Valdez' film version of his play, which he wrote and directed. It stars Edward James Olmos as "El Pachuco," the lead character in the original play.

Zoot Suit Riots. Alexandria, VA: PBS Video, 2007. 60 minutes. http://www.pbs.org/wgbh/amex/zoot/index.html. Provides background for the riots and Sleepy Lagoon trial and a discussion of the cultural clashes Mexican Americans were experiencing in the first half of the 20th century. Includes link to PBS interactive site that includes further discussion of film's content, images, and teacher's guide.

26. Great Puerto Rican Migration (1945–1955)

When the U.S. Congress passed the Jones-Shafroth Act in 1917, residents of Puerto Rico were given U.S. citizenship that permitted them to travel to the mainland without a passport. This encouraged a number of Puerto Ricans to migrate between the United States and the island, while others chose to settle permanently in U.S. cities such as New York or Chicago. However, it was not until the post-World War II period that greater numbers of Puerto Ricans migrated to the mainland and formed their own enclaves. With the establishment of airplane travel, it became easier for many Puerto Ricans to come to the United States and begin new lives. Most Puerto Ricans settled in the New York area, and by 1946 nearly 40,000 Puerto Ricans had migrated there. These numbers continued to rapidly increase, especially during the industrialization program called Operation Bootstrap implemented by the United States. By 1953, there were an estimated 75,000 Puerto Ricans living in regions such as the South Bronx, Spanish Harlem, and Brooklyn. Because of the Great Migration of Puerto Ricans during the mid-20th century, New York, along with a number of other U.S. cities, had been dramatically transformed in terms of urban politics, culture, and artistic expression.

TERM PAPER SUGGESTIONS

1. When Puerto Ricans migrated to U.S. cities during the mid-20th century, many of them were unable to find adequate work because of the language barrier, ethnic discrimination, and few technical skills. Identify some of the community-based programs or organizations such as the Puerto Rican Nationalist Party (ASPIRA) that emerged to aid Puerto Rican families succeed both financially, socially, and politically on the mainland and discuss some of the key obstacles many of these organizations faced.

2. Discuss the role and impact Operation Bootstrap had on migration from Puerto Rico to the United States. Argue what its successes were as well as its shortcomings.

3. Define who "Nuyoricans" are and explain what relationship the Nuyorican Movement has had with the concept of migration between New York City and Puerto Rico.

4. Explain the difference in migration patterns between Puerto Ricans and Cubans to the United States during the 20th century. Why did Puerto Ricans principally settle in and around New York City whereas Cubans generally immigrated to Miami?

ALTERNATIVE TERM PAPER SUGGESTIONS

1. Create an interactive map that indicates the regions throughout the United States to which Puerto Ricans were migrating. Show not only general statistics but also illustrate areas from where notable Puerto Ricans have come.

2. As a socio-political activist living in New York City during the height of the Great Migration, write a series of speeches for your organization that advocate the experiences and circumstances surrounding working-class Puerto Rican migrants. Use writings, speeches, and publications from community-based programs and organizations at the time to substantiate your position.

SUGGESTED SOURCES

Primary Source

"Tolan Committee on Internal Migration." http://newdeal.feri.org/tolan/tol02.htm. The 1940 testimony of Florentino Irizarry, who migrated from Puerto Rico to New York just before the Great Migration.

Transcript from the U.S. House Committee to Investigate Migration of Destitute Citizens.

Secondary Sources

Flores, Juan. *Divided Borders: Essays on Puerto Rican Identity.* Houston, TX: Arte Público Press, 1993. Anthology includes a section on working-class perspectives of the Great Migration.

Perez, Gina. *The Near Northwest Side Story: Migration, Displacement, and Puerto Rican Families.* Berkeley: University of California Press, 2004. This ethnography describes the lives of Puerto Ricans migrating between the island and Chicago. Focuses on the struggle to maintain transnational connections with family and friends.

Sánchez Korrol, Virginia. *From Colonia to Community: The History of Puerto Ricans in New York City.* Berkeley: University of California Press, 1994. Explores what led to the mass migration of Puerto Ricans and how enclaves evolved in New York.

Soto-Crespo, Ramón E. *Mainland Passage: The Cultural Anomaly of Puerto Rico.* Minneapolis: University of Minnesota Press, 2009. Charts the political and literary articulation of Puerto Rican identity and representation.

World Wide Web

"Immigration: Puerto Rican/Cuban." http://international.loc.gov:8081/learn/features/immig/cuban3.html. Library of Congress' overview of the migration patterns of Puerto Ricans and Cubans. Features artistic and cultural contributions as a result of the Great Migration. Includes period photographs.

"Latino Education Network Service." http://www.palante.org/History.htm. Includes brief information on early migration and the Great Migration.

"The Puerto Rican Exodus: Media Representations of the Great Migration, 1945–1955." http://www.allacademic.com//meta/p_mla_apa_research_citation/1/0/5/5/2/pages105521/p105521-1.php. Features lengthy examination of how newspapers chronicled the cultural and social impact Puerto Rican migration had on the island and the mainland United States.

"Puerto Ricans: Immigrants and Migrants." http://74.125.155.132/search?q=cache:_1LjVFj_F30J:www.americansall.com/PDFs/02-americans-all/9.9.pdf+puerto+rico+migration+to+us&cd=7&hl=en&ct=clnk&gl=us. Provides historical perspective that details how the communities were formed throughout the United States and incorporates photographs, maps, and statistical charts.

Multimedia Source

Sugar Pathways: A Documentary Film on the Migration of Boricus to the Virgin Islands. U.S. Virgin Islands: Cane Bay Films, 2008. DVD. 80 minutes. Profiles over 50 families who unwillingly migrated from Vieques, Puerto Rico, to the U.S. Virgin Islands during the 20th century.

27. *Méndez v. Westminster* (1946)

Preceding *Brown v. Board of Education* by seven years, *Méndez et al. v. Westminster School District of Orange County* (abbreviated as *Méndez v. Westminster*) was a California court case that ended the segregation of Mexican American school children. Legal scholars often consider *Méndez v. Westminster* to be a precursor to *Brown v. Board of Education*, and the two cases do have many similarities. The Méndez case originated when, in 1943, Gonzalo and Felicitas Méndez tried to enroll their daughter Sylvia and their nephews into the same elementary school that Sylvia's cousin, Alice Méndez Vidaurri, attended. The Méndezes were told that Sylvia and her cousins had to attend a segregated school because of their Hispanic surnames and darker complexions. Other families had experienced similar discrimination, and, on March 2, 1945, Gonzalo Méndez, along with four other fathers (Thomas Estrada, William Guzman, Lorenzo Ramírez, and Frank Palomino) filed a lawsuit against the four Orange County school districts (Westminster, Garden Grove, Santa Ana, and El Modena) whose segregation practices impacted their children. Civil rights lawyer David Marcus represented the plaintiffs, and Thurgood Marshall, who would later become the first African American Supreme Court Justice, wrote an amicus curiae brief for the case. Marcus argued that Orange County's segregation practices violated the Fifth and Fourteenth Amendments to the U.S. Constitution and that such segregation caused academic, sociological, and psychological distress for Latino children. Senior District Judge Paul J. McCormick concurred, finding in favor of the plaintiffs on February 18, 1946. Although the school districts appealed the decision, the Ninth Federal District Court of Appeals upheld McCormick's ruling on April 14, 1947. *Méndez v. Westminster* became a major turning point in ending U.S. segregation. In 2007, the U.S. Postal Service created a stamp to commemorate the 60th anniversary of the case.

TERM PAPER SUGGESTIONS

1. Research and evaluate *Méndez v. Westminster's* influence on *Brown v. Board of Education.* How did the Méndez case serve as a precursor to the Brown ruling? What key issues and people do these two cases share in common? Why, in comparison, is *Méndez v. Westminster* so relatively unknown?

2. Examine the key role played by the League of United Latin American Citizens (LULAC) in *Méndez v. Westminster.* Discuss the contributions that LULAC made to this legal case. What unique evidence and testimonies did the league and lawyer David Marcus acquire for evidence that segregated schools were harmful to Mexican American children?

3. Evaluate the decisions of Judge Paul J. McCormick and the court of appeals. How did McCormick's ruling reinterpret the Fourteenth Amendment? What reasons did McCormick offer to reject the "separate but equal" precedent set by the Supreme Court case of *Plessy v. Ferguson*? Why did the court of appeals reject McCormick's stances on the Fourteenth Amendment but still uphold McCormick's verdict?

4. Investigate *Méndez v. Westminster's* effect on the education system of California. Did California integrate schools after this? What role did the Méndez case play in generating California's 1947 Anderson Bill, which eliminated all racial segregation in public schools? What role did de-facto segregation continue to play in public schools after the Méndez verdict?

5. Scrutinize the use of racial stereotypes and prejudice in the arguments made by the defendants for the four Orange County school districts. What reasons did they give for wanting to maintain segregated schools? How would their statements about Latino children, hygiene, morals, and educational skills be perceived today?

ALTERNATIVE TERM PAPER SUGGESTIONS

1. Controversial and landmark court cases often have several amicus curiae briefs attached; these are "friends of the court" letters written by individuals and organizations offering specialized information on a case. Research the amicus curiae briefs associated with *Méndez v.*

Westminster, including the one co-authored by Thurgood Marshall. Write your own amicus curiae brief for *Méndez v. Westminster.* Be certain to focus on a particular aspect of the case and provide evidence from sources to support your stance.

2. Watch *The Lemon Grove Incident* (1985), a documentary about another, earlier school desegregation case that directly impacted the *Méndez v. Westminster* ruling. Create a PowerPoint presentation comparing the similarities between the two cases. Be sure to note that while both plaintiffs were successful in ending discrimination, the verdicts resulted in two different interpretations of Latinos as a marginalized group.

SUGGESTED SOURCES

Primary Sources

Méndez v. Westminster: 9th Circuit Opinion. http://w3.uchastings.edu/wingate/ Méndez%20v.htm and http://www.learncalifornia.org/doc.asp?id=1508. Offers the Ninth Circuit's original ruling.

Méndez v. Westminster: Trial Court Opinion. http://www.learncalifornia.org/doc. asp?id=1508. Provides the Supreme Court ruling.

Secondary Sources

Aguirre, Frederick P. "Méndez v. Westminster School District: How It Affected Brown v. Board of Education." *Journal of Hispanic Higher Education* 4, no. 4 (2005): 321–332. Discusses the link between these two court cases and how *Méndez v. Westminster* gave the Supreme Court a precedent in *Brown.*

Arriola, Christopher. *Knocking on the Schoolhouse Door: Méndez v. Westminster, Equal Protection, Public Education, and Mexican Americans in the 1940's.* Berkeley, CA: Boalt Hall School of Law, 1995. This article examines the legal implications of the case.

De Genova, Nicholas. *Racial Transformations: Latinos and Asians Remaking the United States.* Durham, NC: Duke University Press, 2006. De Genova's fourth chapter focuses on a reexamination of the interracial coalitions created by this legal case.

Valencia, Richard. *Chicano Students and the Courts: The Mexican American Legal Struggle for Educational Equality.* New York: NYU Press, 2008. Valencia's chapter on "School Segregation" discusses the legal case, with a particular emphasis on the appeal.

World Wide Web

"Méndez v. Westminster: A Look at Our Latino Heritage." http://www. Méndezvwestminster.com/ Web site dedicated to this court case has links to Stanford University's *Méndez v. Westminster* archive and other associated resources.

"Méndez v. Westminster Case." http://Méndezwestminstercase.blogspot.com/ Offers detailed summaries of wide variety of court cases that preceded the Méndez ruling and links to scholarly articles.

Ruiz, Vicki. "We Always Tell Our Children They Are Americans: Méndez v. Westminster." *The Brown Quarterly* 6, no. 3 (Fall 2004). http:// brownvboard.org/brwnqurt/06-3/. Ruiz's article recounts the history of segregation in California prior to Méndez and the work of David Marcus, attorney for the plaintiffs.

Stanford Méndez Collection. http://www-sul.stanford.edu/depts/spc/xml/ m0938.xml. Details Stanford University's archive of interviews, abstracts, and other historical case materials.

Multimedia Sources

The Lemon Grove Incident. The Cinema Guild, 1985. DVD. 57:44 minutes. Focuses on *Roberto Alvarez v. The Board of Trustees of Lemon Grove School District,* another California antisegregation ruling that directly preceded *Méndez et al. v. Westminster.*

Méndez v. Westminster: Desegregating California's Schools. Teachers' Domain, 2002. Quicktime Video. 8:36 minutes. http://www.teachersdomain. org/asset/osi04_vid_Méndez/. Short film covers the origins of the case and its impact on California schools and law.

Méndez v. Westminster: For All the Children. KOCE-TV, 2006. DVD. 29 minutes. Emmy Award-winning short film explores the case and its lasting legacy.

Uprising Radio. "The Sixtieth Anniversary of Méndez v. Westminster." http:// uprisingradio.org/home/?p=1896. Features audio recording of interviews with Sylvia Méndez and Gonzalo Méndez about the 60th anniversary of *Méndez v. Westminster.*

28. Puerto Rican Independence Party Founded (October 20, 1946)

To champion the independence of Puerto Rico from the United States and ensure its political, social, and economic sovereignty as a nation,

Gilberto Concepción de Gracia (1909–1968) founded the Partido Independentista Puertorriqueño (Puerto Rican Independence Party) in 1946, in part because he maintained that the Popular Democratic Party had digressed from its support of sovereignty and had settled on Puerto Rico's commonwealth status as being a satisfactory compromise. Throughout his career as party president, Concepción spoke out for civil and political rights for Puerto Ricans before a number of august bodies such as the United Nations and the Organization of American States. It is the largest pro-independence party in Puerto Rico and the only one that officially appears on the Puerto Rican electoral ballot along with other mainstream or pro-U.S. parties. By the 1970s, Rubén Berríos Martínez assumed the presidency of the Independence Party and continued to grow the party membership fueled by a pro-labor and pro-economically disenfranchised platform. Berríos led a measure in the party that would officially declare the party an advocate of social democracy and not one that was representing a Marxist-Leninist agenda. He participated in the 1971 Navy-Culebra protests, which sought for the removal of the U.S. Navy from Puerto Rico's archipelago of Culebra, and also the 1999 protests against the U.S. Navy in Vieques. One of the important features of the Independence Party's platform is that Puerto Rico's commonwealth status does not allow its citizens to vote in the U.S. presidential election or send a voting member to the U.S. Congress. This, among other political and economic issues, has long been a major point of contention for the party as it continues to struggle for complete independence from the United States.

TERM PAPER SUGGESTIONS

1. Present the Puerto Rican Independence Party platform and highlight how pivotal events in Puerto Rico's history since World War II have solidified or modified the causes and agenda of the party.

2. In 2003, the FBI admitted to infiltrating and sabotaging the political efforts of the Puerto Rican Independence Party. This had been an ongoing effort especially during the 1960s under then Director J. Edgar Hoover. Discuss the role the FBI played in undermining the efforts of the Independence Party and examine what the U.S. Congress did in response to this discovery.

3. In addition to the Independence Party, the two other major political parties in Puerto Rico are the Popular Democratic Party and the

New Progressive Party. Analyze these parties' respective histories and explain what their fundamental differences are. How does each of them represent an ideological aspect of Puerto Rico's political climate?

4. What role did members of the Puerto Rican Independence Party play in the Culebra Island protests in 1971 and the dispute on Vieques Island in 1999 regarding the U.S. Navy?

ALTERNATIVE TERM PAPER SUGGESTIONS

1. Develop an interactive timeline with hyperlinks to articles and images that charts the transformation of Puerto Rico's political status since its acquisition by the United States at the close of the Spanish American War in 1898. Use the platforms and ideologies of various pro-independence parties in Puerto Rico to inform the tone of this timeline.

2. Create a detailed Internet pamphlet or a wiki that outlines the history, beliefs, and current platform of the Puerto Rican Independence Party. Be sure to include illustrations, tables, and graphs to enhance its presentation.

SUGGESTED SOURCES

Primary Sources

Berríos Martínez, Rubén. "Puerto Rico's Decolonization." *Foreign Affairs* 76, no.6 (Nov.-Dec. 1997): 100–114. Outlines Berríos' plan for removing the U.S. colonial system in Puerto Rico.

"Statement Submitted by Rubén Berríos Martínez before the Subcommittee on Insular Affairs." http://www.youtube.com/watch?v=sZzidjV0NxI&feature= related. Independence Party President addresses the U.S. Congressional committee regarding H.R. 900, the Puerto Rican Democracy Act of 2007.

Secondary Sources

Gosse, Van. *Rethinking the New Left: An Interpretive History.* New York: Palgrave Macmillan, 2005. Chapter 10 explores how the Independence Party transformed during the turbulence of the 1960s.

Lopez, Alfredo. *Dona Licha's Island: Modern Colonialism in Puerto Rico.* Cambridge, MA: South End Press, 1999. Investigates the realities of Puerto Rican independence considering the colonial system imposed by the United States and speculates how the Independence Party's platform would succeed.

Rivera Ramos, Efrén. *American Colonialism in Puerto Rico: The Judicial and Social Legacy.* Princeton, NJ: Markus Wiener, 2007. Chapters 5 and 8 examine how the criminalizing of the independence movement in Puerto Rico creates a colonial sense of legal and political stability on the island.

Santana, Maria. *Puerto Rican Newspaper Coverage of the Puerto Rican Independence Party: A Content Analysis of Three Elections.* New York: Routledge, 2000. Focuses on the media coverage of three Puerto Rican gubernatorial elections and the role of the Independence Party.

Torres, Andres, ed. *The Puerto Rican Movement: Voices from the Diaspora.* Philadelphia: Temple University Press, 1998. Assembles a critical anthology of political perspectives that examine the parties and movements throughout Puerto Rico including the Puerto Rican Independence Party.

World Wide Web

"Decades of FBI Surveillance of Puerto Rican Groups." http://www.third worldtraveler.com/Caribbean/FBI_PuertoRicanGroups.html. *New York Times* reporter Mireya Navarro details how the FBI targeted and sabotaged pro-independence groups in Puerto Rico, particularly the Puerto Rican Independence Party.

"Puerto Rico Independence Party." http://www.puertoricousa.com/english/pip. htm. Presents brief overview of the party's beliefs and platform.

"Puerto Rico Political Flags." http://www.crwflags.com/FOTW/flags/pr%7D. html#ind. Analyzes the origin and meaning of various pro-independence movement flags including the green and white-crossed Independence Party's flag.

"Rubén Berríos Martínez." http://www.peacehost.net/WhiteStar/Voices/. Includes a profile of the life and work of this Independence Party president.

Multimedia Source

"Puerto Rico Independence Party's English Site." http://www.independencia. net/ingles/welcome.html. Main Web site for Independence Party provides links to current articles affecting the party's platform and videos, including one featuring Independence Party leader Rubén Berríos Martínez's 1985 speech at Harvard University.

29. Héctor P. García Establishes the American GI Forum (1948)

Héctor P. García (1914–1996) is revered as an early proponent for the protection and empowerment of the Latino community and internationally recognized as a leader in civil rights. García immigrated to Texas from Mexico with his parents as a young child to begin a new life. He earned an M.D. in 1940 from the University of Texas at Galveston and volunteered to serve in World War II two years later. In Europe, he achieved the rank of major while serving in the medical corps and earned the Bronze Star for his military accomplishments. After the war, he opened up a medical practice in Corpus Christi, TX, and soon became involved with the League of United Latin American Citizens (LULAC), an early advocacy group for Latinos. After he was elected their president in 1947, García continued to address the needs of fellow Latinos. He aided Mexican American war veterans in filing claims with the U.S. Department of Veterans Affairs and organized investigative committees to look into living conditions and legal abuses concerning migrant laborers from Mexico. In 1948, he formed the American GI Forum (AGIF) that principally advocated the rights of Latinos in the United States, thus establishing one of the first prominent civil rights organizations in the United States. Because of its patriotic status and associations, the FBI largely avoided probes into the organization during the Cold War when most Latino organizations were under close scrutiny of this agency. García was further instrumental in the 1960 election with organizing "Viva Kennedy" clubs around the nation and in bringing 85 percent of the Latino vote to the Democratic Party. He also served in representing the United States in a number of international and domestic capacities that earned him great attention and respect, namely his appointment as alternate Ambassador to the United Nations in 1967 and to the U.S. Commission on Civil Rights in 1968. García has also been a recipient of countless awards and honors including the Presidential Medal of Freedom in 1984 from President Ronald Reagan and the Order of St. Gregory the Great in 1990 from Pope John Paul II.

TERM PAPER SUGGESTIONS

1. Examine Héctor García's association with Lyndon B. Johnson when Johnson was a Texas state senator. In what ways did these two leaders share a common vision of civil rights in the United States? How did they digress from a single mission?

2. In 1953, the AGIF and LULAC sponsored attorneys who argued *Hernandez v. Texas* before the U.S. Supreme Court and won the case. Explain what the case entailed, why the AGIF/LULAC defense won, and what civil rights implications this had in the United States as a result of the court ruling. What influence did this have on the

Supreme Court's landmark ruling *Brown v. the Board of Education* the following year?

3. Discuss who Félix Longoria was and how he was able to launch the AGIF onto the national stage in the civil rights movement in 1948. How did this incident bring greater notoriety to not only Héctor García but also then Texas Senator Lyndon B. Johnson as champions of civil rights?

4. While Héctor García has earned national attention as a civil rights advocate for the Latino community, examine his efforts toward Latin America and how he served as a conduit for peace between the United States and its Latin American neighbors.

ALTERNATIVE TERM PAPER SUGGESTIONS

1. Scan photographs, illustrations, letters, maps, and other relevant primary and secondary sources and create a two-minute iMovie on the life and achievements of Héctor P. García.

2. Pulitzer Prize recipient Edna Ferber interviewed Héctor García in 1950 to profile the Latino experience in Texas. Two years later, she wrote her novel *Giant* based in part on this interview. Compare the novel with the 1950 interview and the life work of García and provide a creative response that illustrates the significance between history, Latino culture, and U.S. literature.

SUGGESTED SOURCES

Primary Sources

"Hector P. Garcia: A Texas Legend." http://www.utmb.edu/drgarcia/. Provides links to background information on Garcia's life and career, including reproductions of letters he wrote and photographs.

United States. Mission to the United Nations. *Statement by Ambassador Hector P. García, United States Representative in Committee 1, on the Treaty for the Prohibition of Nuclear Weapons in Latin America.* New York: U.S. Delegation to the General Assembly, 1967. Features García's address to the United Nations on October 26, 1967, regarding his concern over the proliferation of nuclear arms throughout the Western Hemisphere.

Secondary Sources

García, Ignacio M. *Hector P. García: In Relentless Pursuit of Justice.* Houston, TX: Arte Público Press, 2002. Documents García's life journey to prominence in the civil rights movement.

Kells, Michelle Hall. *Héctor P. García: Everyday Rhetoric and Mexican American Civil Rights.* Carbondale: Southern Illinois University Press, 2006. Articulates how García established a socio-political discourse for civil rights and justice through the establishment of the American GI Forum.

Powers, Thomas J., and José L. Galvan. *Champions of Change: Biographies of Famous Hispanic Americans.* Austin, TX: Steck-Vaughn, 1989. The seventh entry in this collection focuses on Héctor P. García.

Ramos, Henry A.J. *The American GI Forum: In Pursuit of the Dream, 1948–1983.* Houston, TX: Arte Público Press, 1998. Discusses how the GI Forum was formed in 1948 and continued to grow into over 500 chapters nationwide.

World Wide Web

"American G. I. Forum." http://www.agifusa.org/. The organization's main Web page contains important links, background information, and current events.

"American GI Forum." http://www.pbs.org/kpbs/theborder/history/timeline/19.html. Presents background on AGIF and Garcia's involvement. Incorporates significant links for further profiling and research.

"*Corpus Christi Caller Times*: Hector P. Garcia." http://www.caller2.com/drhector/. Assembles a large number of useful links to various articles on Garcia.

"Hispanic America USA Dr Hector P. Garcia." http://www.neta.com/~1stbooks/forum.htm. Includes important links to relevant resources on the career and contributions of Garcia.

"Justice for My People." http://www.pbs.org/justiceformypeople/. Features a detailed description of the documentary depicting the career of Garcia.

Multimedia Sources

"Justice for My People: Dr. Hector P. Garcia Biography." http://www.justiceformypeople.org/drhector.html. Provides extensive biography and links to audio and visual footage concerning the life and work of Garcia.

Justice for My People: The Dr. Hector P. Garcia Story. Corpus Christi: South Texas Public Broadcasting System, 2002. DVD. 90 minutes. Documents the life and career of a prominent Latino medical doctor, war veteran, and civil rights activist.

30. Operation Bootstrap (1948–1960s)

After World War II, Puerto Rico's economic system began to shift from an agrarian economy and one monopolized by the sugarcane industry to one predicated on an industrialized economy. The U.S. government initiated Operation Bootstrap to facilitate this massive overhaul of the island's economic structure and serve as a model for Latin American countries making a similar shift. It was also supported by Luis Muñoz Marín, who was the first governor of Puerto Rico, and Teodoro Moscoso, the architect of the program. According to the plan, small farms and sugar plantations would be phased out and replaced by strings of factories that would manufacture products such as textiles, tobacco, and various food products. In order for the program to succeed, the Puerto Rican government attracted investors by ensuring a cheap factory labor force, a trustworthy political system, rights to an open U.S. market, and countless subsidies. By the 1960s, the program began to fail and required a change in industry from one that was labor intensive to one that was more highly capital intensive, such as pharmaceutical and petrochemical industries. There was also a great deal of pressure coming from labor unions regarding minimum wage and opposition from civil rights groups and the Roman Catholic Church regarding sterilization policies among the new working-class population.

TERM PAPER SUGGESTIONS

1. In what ways were the new Puerto Rican factories created during the beginning years of Operation Bootstrap similar in purpose and set-up to many of the *malquilodoras* or cross-border plants that presently exist along the U.S.-Mexico border?

2. Argue how effective Operation Bootstrap was for Puerto Rico's economy. Who benefited most in the short-term and long-term? What impact did this have on the newly created industrial working class of the island? Were these new industrial factories models for the rest of Latin America or were they glorified sweatshops?

3. Governor Muñoz Marín has been criticized for his participation in Operation Bootstrap as sacrificing Puerto Rico's dream of independence for closer links to U.S. corporations. Argue whether you agree or disagree with this characterization of the island's popular governor.

4. What relation did Operation Bootstrap have with the political and rhetorical climate of the Cold War, especially during the Kennedy administration?

ALTERNATIVE TERM PAPER SUGGESTIONS

1. Create an iMovie in the spirit of a mid-20th century newsreel that either supports the efforts of Operation Bootstrap or critiques it. Use footage, photographs, maps, and text to assemble this project.

2. Imagine you run a U.S. corporation and want to create a new factory in Puerto Rico to generate a product. Detail a plan of action that would take your company through the process of making this happen. Research what is involved in a company starting up a new industry on the island. Write up a legal contract with explanations of what your company would be willing to do and what compromises would be made.

SUGGESTED SOURCES

Primary Source

"Puerto Rico Aids Fifty Industries." *New York Times,* Jan. 3, 1950: 87. *ProQuest Historical Newspapers.* Article introduces the newest industries that were emerging in Puerto Rico in the earliest years of Operation Bootstrap.

Secondary Sources

Ayala, César J., and Rafael Bernabé. *Puerto Rico in the American Century: A History since 1898.* Chapel Hill: University of North Carolina press, 2007. Includes a chapter detailing the impact of Operation Bootstrap.

Maldonado, Alex W. *Teodoro Moscoso and Puerto Rico's Operation Bootstrap.* Gainesville: University Press of Florida, 1997. Profiles the architect of the industrial economic program and credits Moscoso for the successes.

Safa, Helen Icken. *The Myth of the Male Breadwinner: Women and Industrialization in the Caribbean.* Boulder, CO: Westview Press, 1995. Offers detailed examination of the role Puerto Rican women played during the years of Operation Bootstrap.

World Wide Web

"The First Privatization Policy in Democracy: Selling State-Owned Enterprises in 1948–1950 Puerto Rico." http://www.ub.edu/irea/working_papers/2009/200915.pdf. Features a report analyzing the transformation of the state-owned enterprise sector into a private one and choices made to privatize these state-owned industries as a result of Operation Bootstrap.

"Operation Bootstrap." http://lcw.lehman.edu/lehman/depts/latinampuer torican/latinoweb/PuertoRico/Bootstrap.htm. Provides in-depth analysis of event leading up to the U.S. policy as well as an analysis of the policy itself in relation to the monopoly of the sugarcane industry.

"Operation Bootstrap (1947)." http://www.enciclopediapr.org/ing/article.cfm? ref=06102003&page=1. Features detailed report on the economic growth and industrial patterns of the program and the impact of the Cold War. Includes several photographs of the new industries that were established on the island.

"Operation Bootstrap: The Industrialization of Puerto Rico." http://ngnewsarti cles.blogspot.com/2006/06/operation-bootstrap-industrialization.html. Analyzes the intention behind the program and what led to its eventual decline.

Multimedia Source

Manos a la Obra: The Story of Operation Bootstrap. New York: Cinema Guild, 1983. VHS. Examines the program implemented in Puerto Rico that was supposed to serve as a model throughout Latin America for generating broader industrial growth.

31. Luis Muñoz Marín Elected Governor of Puerto Rico (January 2, 1949)

As a poet, a journalist, and then a politician, Luis Muñoz Marín (1898–1980) became regarded as the "father of modern Puerto Rico" by many for his reforms and for becoming the first democratically elected governor of the island in 1949. His father, Luis Muñoz Rivera, a long-time supporter of Puerto Rican autonomy, had been politically important since he held a number of influential positions including Resident Commissioner of Puerto Rico. Raised in Puerto Rico and educated in Washington, D.C., Muñoz Marín had first-hand exposure to socioeconomic systems existing in both the United States and Puerto Rico. He recognized that the only way for his homeland to thrive would be through independence from the United States. In 1932, Muñoz Marín joined the Liberal Party, which supported political and economic autonomy from the United States. He served as a senator in Puerto Rico until disputes with the party leader caused his expulsion in

1937. In 1938, he helped form the Popular Democratic Party, which won a majority in the Puerto Rican Senate, thus making Muñoz Marín president of the Senate from 1941 to 1949. Much to the resentment of other pro-independence leaders, Muñoz Marín's political ideologies changed, for he realized that a commonwealth status for Puerto Rico would be more favorable than complete independence. In the 1940s, the U.S. Congress allowed Puerto Rico the right to elect its own governor, and on January 2, 1949, Muñoz Marín was sworn in after winning the first gubernatorial election. He was instrumental in drafting a constitution for Puerto Rico, which eventually granted the island a commonwealth status. To modernize Puerto Rico, he implemented Operation Bootstrap, which facilitated a massive overhaul of the island's economic structure and served as a model for Latin American countries making a similar shift. Serving three consecutive terms as governor (1949–1965), this popular leader made a lasting mark on Puerto Rico's history. This was further underscored when Muñoz Marín received the Presidential Medal of Freedom in 1963.

TERM PAPER SUGGESTIONS

1. As governor, Muñoz Marín had been criticized for his participation in Operation Bootstrap as sacrificing Puerto Rico's dream of independence for closer links to U.S. corporations. Argue whether you agree or disagree with this characterization of the island's popular leader.

2. Explain how and why Muñoz Marín began to change his political ideology regarding Puerto Rico from pro-independence to a commonwealth status with the United States. Also describe some of the political fall-out that resulted, namely with the reactions from the Nationalist Party.

3. Muñoz Marín was instrumental in drafting Puerto Rico's constitution and ushering in the island's commonwealth status. Examine the constitution and the ratification process and explain the form of government and the political standing of Puerto Rico that had been created in the mid-20th century. Decide whether you maintain this political system is still a fair and appropriate one now in the 21st century.

4. While Operation Bootstrap focused on reforming the economic structure of Puerto Rico, Operation Serenity was launched to focus

on art and education. Compare these two systems of reform and discuss the impact the latter had in transforming Puerto Rico during Muñoz Marín's tenure as governor.

ALTERNATIVE TERM PAPER SUGGESTIONS

1. Imagine you are a high-ranking member of the pro-independence Puerto Rican Nationalist Party, the one responsible for various attacks such as the Blair House and U.S. Capitol shootings during the 1950s. Prepare a series of podcasts analyzing the life's work of Muñoz Marín. Determine whether the former governor has brought more harm to Puerto Rico than good.

2. Design an interactive timeline of the life and career of Luis Muñoz Marín. Use images to enhance the presentation and text to annotate the key events. Conclude with a summary of the historical significance of Muñoz Marín's contributions to the modernization of Puerto Rico.

SUGGESTED SOURCES

Primary Sources

"Department of Education Press Commonwealth of Puerto Rico 1956." http://www.flmm.org/discursos/1956-04-07.pdf. Features speech given by Muñoz Marín on the state of Puerto Rico during the Annual Convention of the Associated Harvard Clubs at Coral Gables, Florida, on April 7, 1956.

"Speech Delivered by Governor Luis Muñoz Marín at the University of Kansas City, April 23, 1955." http://www.flmm.com/pags_nuevas_folder/discursos_folder/dis_ingles_b.html. Muñoz Marín discusses what Puerto Rico's new commonwealth status means to the Puerto Rican people, as well as the island's relationship with the United States and Latin America.

Secondary Sources

Aitken, Thomas. *Poet in the Fortress: The Story of Luis Muñoz Marín*. New York: New American Library, 1964. Includes an extensive discussion of Muñoz Marín's life and the influences that shaped his political career.

Maldanado, A.W. *Luis Muñoz Marín: Puerto Rico's Democratic Revolution*. San Juan, PR: Editorial Universidad de Puerto Rico, 2006. Documents Muñoz Marín's life and rise to power in Puerto Rico.

Mann, Peggy. *Muñoz Marín: The Man Who Remade Puerto Rico.* New York: Coward, McCann, and Geohegan, 1976. Documents the strategies used by Muñoz Marín during the implementation of Operation Bootstrap.

Rivera, Jose A. *The Political Thought of Luis Muñoz Marín.* Bloomington, IN: Xlibris Corporation, 2002. Articulates the ideological challenges Muñoz Marín faced as president of the Puerto Rican Senate and then as governor while transforming Puerto Rico in the mid-20th century.

Tugwell, Rexford G. *The Art of Politics, as Practiced by Three Great Americans: Franklin Delano Roosevelt, Luis Muñoz Marín, and Fiorello H. La Guardia.* Garden City, NY: Doubleday, 1958. Written by the last U.S.-appointed governor of Puerto Rico, this work profiles the progressive ideologies of three statesmen and underscores the socio-political transformations their actions had in the Western Hemisphere.

World Wide Web

"Governor Luis Muñoz Marin." http://www.nps.k12.nj.us/marin/governor.htm. Contains brief biography of Muñoz Marín with several photographs.

"Luis Muñoz Marín Biography." http://www.biography.com/articles/Luis-Mu%C3%B1oz-Mar%C3%ADn-40337. Provides a brief overview of the life and career of Muñoz Marín.

"Puerto Rico: The Bard of Bootstrap." http://www.time.com/time/magazine/article/0,9171,810360,00.html. The June 23, 1958, article outlines Operation Bootstrap spearheaded by Muñoz Marín to industrialize Puerto Rico and discusses what is happening since the program was initiated.

Multimedia Source

"Interview with Gov. Luis Munoz Marin." http://www.veoh.com/collection/peterp41/watch/v232555zBDZjGex#. Features an interview with Muñoz Marín regarding the 1954 attacks at the U.S. Capitol by Nationalists, Puerto Rico's vote to approve commonwealth status, and the pardoning of Nationalist Party leader Pedro Albizu Campos.

32. Battle of Chávez Ravine/Dodger Stadium (1949–1962)

Just outside of the downtown district of Los Angeles was the Chávez Ravine, a small valley region inhabited by several generations of Mexican Americans.

This rural neighborhood, which was just over 300 acres, became a site of conflict between residents and city leaders, and resulted in an ongoing media saga of displacement and disenfranchisement of a Latino community. In 1949, Los Angeles was making plans for expansion to address the post-World War II housing crisis and accommodate a rapidly growing population. Through a grant from the Federal Housing Act of 1949, Los Angeles Mayor Fletcher Brown proposed 10,000 new homes, most of which were to be constructed in Chávez Ravine. Most Angelenos living outside Chávez Ravine regarded this area as a poor squatter camp, and by July 1950, around 1,200 families received notices to sell their homes to make room for the proposed community of Elysian Park Heights. While many residents relocated after being poorly compensated for their houses, others refused to abandon their homes despite the declaration of eminent domain by the city. Although the city continued to pursue its development plans for new public housing in Chávez Ravine, it soon came under fire by opponents from the business community and city leaders who began to see the project as too communist-like. Norris Poulson became the new mayor in 1953 and vowed to stop the public housing project; however, the city was unable to reverse the contract it generated with the federal government. At the same time, Los Angeles was looking to attract a major league sports team to the area. A deal was struck between city officials and the Brooklyn Dodgers, and after more controversy and legal battles, Dodger Stadium was officially opened on April 10, 1962.

TERM PAPER SUGGESTIONS

1. Create a detailed and well-researched profile featuring several key players in the Chávez Ravine controversy including members of the city as well as groups of displaced Angelenos such as *Los Desterrados* or "the Uprooted."

2. Frank Wilkinson, the assistant director of the Los Angeles City Housing Authority, was targeted in 1952 by the House Un-American Activities Committee, fired, and incarcerated for harboring "communist" objectives in the Elysian Park Heights project. Write an essay that highlights this case and argue whether these accusations were unconstitutional and whether his opponents had ulterior motives for removing Wilkinson from his position.

3. Compare the geographical displacement that transpired in the Battle of Chávez Ravine with other urban projects in U.S. cities during

the 1950s and 1960s that were destroying minority neighborhoods. How did other communities address the cities' actions? What were some of the outcomes?

4. How did the media contribute to the controversy? Consider high-profile members of the Los Angeles community, such as Ronald Reagan; federal entities like the House Un-American Activities Committee; or the various residents from the Ravine who were caught on camera being pulled from their homes by police. Did the media sway public opinion one way or another?

5. Write an essay comparing the impact Don Normark's photography of Chávez Ravine in 1949 had on the general public with what photojournalist Jacob Riis set out to achieve in 1890 with his collection of photographs and profiles of New York City's poorer classes in *How the Other Half Lives: Studies among the Tenements of New York.*

ALTERNATIVE TERM PAPER SUGGESTIONS

1. Create an iMovie that features news footage, documentary clips, photographs, and interviews that examine the controversy surrounding the uprooting of the Mexican American community in Chávez Ravine. Through your presentation, demonstrate how the action taken by city officials was a miscarriage of justice against the community and their individual dignity.

2. Use Google Earth and historical documents and photographs to show where the Mexican American community resided at the time of the Chávez Ravine battle. Be sure to compare the plans for the Elysian Park Heights project with the eventual construction of Dodger Stadium.

SUGGESTED SOURCES

Primary Sources

Normark, Don. *Chávez Ravine: 1949: A Los Angeles Story.* Vancouver, BC: Chronicle Books, 1999. This is a book of photographs of the community prior to its destruction and also provides profiles of residents.

"Orphans of the Ravine." http://articles.latimes.com/2008/mar/29/sports/sp-ravine29. Features Kevin Baxter's interview with former residents of Chávez Ravine and their perceptions of the event nearly 50 years later.

Secondary Sources

Aven, Ken. *Chavez Ravine Echoes.* Pittsburgh, PA: Rosedog Books, 2006. Using diary excerpts from those involved in the event, this fictionalized work retraces the process of the controversy.

Avila, Eric. *Popular Culture in the Age of White Flight: Fear and Fantasy in Suburban Los Angeles.* Berkeley: University of California Press, 2004. Chapter 5 provides an in-depth analysis of the ravine battle and construction of Dodger Stadium.

World Wide Web

"Chávez Ravine: A Los Angeles Story." http://www.pbs.org/independentlens/ chavezravine/index.html. PBS site provides background information on the film and a preview and incorporates a number of Don Normark's photographs of Chávez Ravine prior to the city's takeover.

"Recalling the Roots of Chavez Ravine." http://www.philly.com/inquirer/ breaking/sports_breaking/20091016_Recalling_the_roots_of_Chavez_ Ravine.html. Frank Fitzpatrick's article profiles how former residents of Chávez Ravine have used sections of Dodger Stadium when referring to the former locations of their homes.

Multimedia Sources

Chávez Ravine: A Los Angeles Story. Oley, PA: Bullfrog Films, 2004. DVD. 24 minutes. Narrated by Cheech Marin, this documentary uses Don Normark's photographs and other footage to provide background on the altercation.

Cooder, Ry. *Chávez Ravine.* Perf. Ry Cooder. Nonesuch, 2005. CD. 76:43 minutes. This CD is a musical homage to the events surrounding the families impacted by the Chávez Ravine event.

Culture Clash. *Chávez Ravine.* Perf. Richard Montoya, Ric Salinas, and Herbert Siguenza. Los Angeles Theatre Works, 2005. CD. 76:43 minutes. This is an audio recording of the famous Chicano theater group's recreation of testimonies from former residents of the ravine.

33. Blair House Terrorist Attack (November 1, 1950)

Throughout the first half of the 20th century, Puerto Rico was an epicenter for political protests, nationalist movements, and social violence. Events such as the Río Piedras Massacre in 1936, the Ponce Massacre and first incarceration of nationalist leader Pedro Albizu Campos in 1937, and the Jayuya Uprising and Utuado Uprising in 1950 created a difficult relationship between the Puerto Rican government, the U.S. government, and Puerto Rican nationalists who viewed their island as a weakened colony under the yoke of imperialism. In an effort to respond to the violence against Puerto Rican nationalists, political activists Oscar Collazo and Griselio Torresola attempted to assassinate President Harry S Truman to gain global attention for Puerto Rico's cause. While the White House was undergoing structural renovations, President Truman relocated to Blair House, which was situated just across Pennsylvania Avenue from the White House. Torresola, whose family members had been involved in the failed Jayuya Uprising just a few days earlier, decided along with Collazo to shoot their way into the presidential residence and kill Truman on November 1, 1950. During the shootout, several guards and officers were wounded, and one, Private Leslie Coffelt, eventually died. President Truman had been upstairs taking a nap and was awoken by the gunfire downstairs; however, he was unharmed by the attackers. Torresola was killed instantly, while Collazo was arrested and sentenced to death. Truman, however, changed the sentence to life imprisonment. The assassination attempt lasted less than a few minutes, but it ensured that Puerto Rico's cause for independence was not in vain. It added greater fuel to the tensions between Puerto Rican nationalists and the governments of the island and the United States. In 1979, President Jimmy Carter pardoned Collazo, who was then allowed to return to Puerto Rico.

TERM PAPER SUGGESTIONS

1. Even though the Truman assassination attempt failed, argue whether the actions of Torresola and Collazo strengthened the cause of the Puerto Rican nationalist movement or hurt it.

2. Discuss what innovative security measures were established for protecting high-profile leaders and addressing counterterrorist methodologies after the Blair House attack occurred in 1950.

3. Explain why Oscar Collazo, the surviving assassin, was shown clemency first by President Truman on Collazo's sentencing, and again by President Carter years later through a presidential pardon. How do these actions characterize executive points of view regarding the Puerto Rican nationalist cause?

4. Compare the Blair House attack with other Nationalist Party revolts taking place at the same time, such as the armed uprisings in Jayuya, Utuado, San Juan, and other Puerto Rican cities on October 30, 1950. Discuss how this chain of events impressed on the United States that the Puerto Rican Nationalist Party operated under a united front.

ALTERNATIVE TERM PAPER SUGGESTIONS

1. Cressie E. Coffelt, the widow of the slain Blair House guard Leslie Coffelt, traveled to Puerto Rico after the assassination attempt where she formally articulated that she did not blame Puerto Ricans for the actions of Torresola and Collazo. Acting as a Puerto Rican nationalist, write a response to Coffelt's letter that is sensitive to her loss, but underscores the greater injustices suffered on the island.

2. Create an interactive map of the location and positions for guards, officers, assassins, and President Truman during the terrorist attack at Blair House. Include photographs and links that provide relevant background and context for what transpired on November 1, 1950.

SUGGESTED SOURCES

Primary Sources

"The President Spared." *New York Times,* November 2, 1950: 30. Provides a brief article addressing the attack when it occurred.

Truman, Harry S. *Off the Record: The Private Papers of Harry S. Truman.* Ed. Robert H. Ferrell. Columbia: University of Missouri Press, 1997. Provides short reference to the Blair House assassination attempt from the President's point of view.

Secondary Sources

Hunter, Stephen, and John Bainbridge. *American Gunfight: The Plot to Kill Harry Truman—And the Shoot-Out That Stopped It.* New York: Simon & Schuster, 2005. Includes a play-by-play description of what happened between the assassins and the Blair House security on the day of the attack.

Smith, Elbert B. "Shoot-Out on Pennsylvania Avenue." *American History* 32, no. 1 (August 1997): 16–24. Explains how the assassins attempted to kill Truman, the altercation with guards, and Truman's reactions to the event.

World Wide Web

"President Harry S. Truman: Survived Assassination Attempt at Blair House." http://www.historynet.com/president-harry-s-truman-survived-assassi nation-attempt-at-the-blair-house.htm. Includes an in-depth discussion of the event and its aftermath.

"Private Leslie Coffelt." http://www.statemaster.com/encyclopedia/Private-Leslie-Coffelt. Focuses on the Blair House guard who was killed during the assassination attempt.

"Remember 1950 Uprising of October 30: Puerto Rico." http://www.third worldtraveler.com/Caribbean/Puerto_Rico-Uprising_1950.html. Contains a lengthy overview of the event and discusses its meaning in the context of the pro-independence movement in Puerto Rico.

Multimedia Sources

American Gunfight: The Plot to Kill Harry Truman. Washington, DC: C-SPAN, 2006. DVD. 66 minutes. Presents Stephen Hunter, who co-authored the book *American Gunfight,* and discusses the attempted assassination and the methodologies used in detail.

Failed Assassinations. New York: A & E Television Network, 1999. DVD. 50 minutes. Using interviews, live footage, and re-enactments, this documentary profiles a number of presidential assassination attempts including Truman's in 1950.

"The Truman Assassination Attempt." https://www.whitehousehistory.org/whha_ tours/citizens_soapbox/protest_03-truman.html. Provides background on the attack as well as photographs and includes a narrated audio clip with excerpts from writer Stephen Hunter and his analysis of the event.

34. U.S. Capitol Shooting by Puerto Rican Nationalists (March 1, 1954)

Four months after U.S. President Harry Truman signed Public Law 600 in July 1950 allowing Puerto Rico to create its own constitution, Puerto Rican nationalists made an attempt on his life. When Puerto Rico voted for their commonwealth status on July 1952, over a year and a half later, four Puerto Rican nationalists attacked members of the U.S. Congress in a shooting rampage. On March 1, 1954, Lolita Lebrón, Rafael Cancel Miranda, Andres Figueroa, and Irving Flores Rodríguez expressed their dismay over U.S. control over Puerto Rican affairs by opening fire from the Ladies' Gallery (now the Visitors' Gallery) above the U.S. House of Representatives main chamber. Reports state that the four nationalists, using their automatic pistols, fired nearly 30 shots. As they fired, Lebrón, the 35-year-old leader, unfurled a Puerto Rican flag and yelled in Spanish, "Long live free Puerto Rico." Caught in the crossfire were U.S. Representatives Alvin Bentley of Michigan, Ben Jensen of Iowa, Clifford Davis of Tennessee, George Fallon of Maryland, and Kenneth Roberts of Alabama, but all five congressmen survived the shooting. Three of the shooters were captured immediately. The other was arrested shortly after. Soon after the incident, the backs of chairs in the House and Senate chambers were made bullet proof, and consideration of separating the gallery from the House chamber with bulletproof glass was made, though never followed through. The shooters were each sentenced to 75 years in prison; however, Lebrón was acquitted of assault with intent to kill because she claimed that she fired in the air rather than at the floor where the congressional representatives were in session. On September 10, 1979, U.S. President Jimmy Carter pardoned the four shooters.

TERM PAPER SUGGESTIONS

1. Study the agenda of the Puerto Rican Nationalist Party during the 1930s and 1950s, and explain what motivated the four party members to open fire in the U.S. House of Representatives in March 1954.

2. Discuss what Lolita Lebrón's role was in the Puerto Rican Nationalist Party. What did the 1954 shooting do for her reputation in Puerto Rico? How did this event further the cause of the party?

3. In addition to pardoning the four Puerto Rican nationalists in September 1979, President Carter also pardoned Oscar Callazo, one of the assassins involved in the attempt on Truman's life in November 1950. What were Carter's justifications for these pardons? What does this suggest about U.S. policy or Executive Branch attitude toward the Puerto Rican nationalist movement? Do you agree with the pardoning?

4. Since the September 11th terrorist attacks in New York and Washington, DC, the U.S. perception toward terrorist actions has undergone a vast transformation. Argue whether public and judicial opinion would be different if the March 1, 1954, U.S. Capitol shooting were to occur today. Explain how and why you maintain this position.

ALTERNATIVE TERM PAPER SUGGESTIONS

1. Decide to represent either the defense or the prosecution for the trial of the four U.S. Capitol shooters. Write a legal brief and cite existing laws to defend your claims.

2. Assume you are Puerto Rican nationalist Lolita Lebrón, called before an independent committee on international law. Create a PowerPoint presentation that addresses your concerns as a party member and conclude with resolutions that explain your actions at the U.S. Capitol and the role of the United States in Puerto Rican affairs.

SUGGESTED SOURCES

Primary Sources

Kihss, Peter. "Puerto Rico Head Call It 'Lunacy.'" *New York Times,* March 2, 1954: 19. Interviews Puerto Rican Governor Luis Muñoz Marín regarding the incident and conveys the idea that the vast majority of Puerto Ricans do not support the Nationalists or their actions.

Knowless, Clayton. "Five Congressmen Shot in the House by 3 Puerto Rican Nationalists; Bullets Spray from Gallery." *New York Times,* March 2, 1954: 1, 16. Outlines the play-by-play circumstances of the event and includes detailed interviews from eyewitnesses.

"This Past Weekend in Puerto Rican History: March 1, 1954 Puerto Rican Nationalist Attack on Congress—54 Years Later." http://vivirlatino.com/2008/03/03/this-past-weekend-in-rican-history-march-1-1954-puerto-rican-nationalist-attack-on-congress-54-years-later.php. Presents a photograph of the Nationalists arrested moments after the shooting.

Trussell, C.P. "Four Are Indicted in House Shooting; Plot Plans Barred." *New York Times,* March 4, 1954: 1, 10. Discusses the charges against the four attackers and the motive behind the Puerto Rican nationalists.

Secondary Sources

Abrams, Jim. "Congress Meets in a Bull's-Eye: 50 Years Ago, Terrorists Sprayed House with Gun Fire." *San Antonio Express-News,* Feb. 29, 2004: 16A. Details the shooting and actions taken by those involved. Sets it in the context of various acts of violence in the Capitol since the mid-19th century.

Quintanilla, Ray. "From Rebel to Peacemaker: A Puerto Rican Nationalist Who Shot Up the U.S. House in 1954 Now Touts Peaceful Road to Change." *Chicago Tribune,* January 9, 2006: A-1. Covers 86-year-old

Lolita Lebrón's life since the shooting and how she publically has not condoned the use of violence to achieve political goals.

Roig-Franzia, Manuel. "A Terrorist in the House." *The Washington Post,* Feb. 22, 2004: W-12. Explores the cult-like status of Lolita Lebrón for Puerto Rican nationalists and details the shooting event at the U.S. Capitol.

Vilar, Irene. *The Ladies Gallery: A Memoir of Family Secrets.* New York: Other Press, 2009. Written by the granddaughter of Lolita Lebrón, the work examines Lebrón's life in the context of the shooting and the familial legacy of violence.

World Wide Web

"Puerto Rican Nationalists Wound Five Representatives." http://www.history. com/this-day-in-history.do?action=tdihArticleCategory&id=4802. Provides a short description of the motive behind the attack, the shooters, and the wounded.

Roig-Franzia, Manuel. "Post Magazine: When Terror Wore Lipstick." *The Washington Post,* Feb. 23, 2004. http://www.washingtonpost.com/wp-dyn/articles/A58564-2004Feb20.html. Includes Roig-Franzia's response to questions regarding Puerto Rican nationalism and Lebrón's role in this movement.

"Security Measures Could Not Stop Capitol Hill Shooting." http://www. cnn.com/ALLPOLITICS/1998/07/24/security.shooting/. Discusses the 1998 shooting that left two U.S. Capitol police officers dead and two wounded in light of other security breaches in the Capitol from the past, including the March 1954 incident.

Multimedia Source

"Strange Congress: 1954, Puerto Rican Nationalists Gang Shoot Up the House of Representatives." http://dcrepublican.com/2009/02/10/trange-congress-1954-puerto-rican-nationalists-gang-shoot-up-the-house-of-rep-resentative/. Provides a brief description of the event and includes a link to a two-minute newsreel of the March 1, 1954, shooting.

35. *Hernández v. Texas* (1954)

Hernández v. Texas' origins as a Supreme Court case began in Jackson County, Texas, on September 20, 1951. An agricultural worker named

Peter Hernández, 26, was found guilty of murdering coworker Joe Espinosa and was sentenced to life in prison. However, every person on the grand jury that convicted Hernández was white, a fact that Hernández's lawyers, Gus García and John Herrera, argued was a violation of the U.S. Constitution's Fourteenth Amendment and its guarantee of "equal protection under the law." García and Herrera contended that while over 15 percent of Jackson County was of Latino descent, not a single Mexican American had been asked to serve in the county's jury system for over 25 years. García and Herrera appealed Hernández's case to the Texas Court of Appeals, which rejected their arguments, claiming that the Fourteenth Amendment recognized only two races: black and white. Accordingly, the court held that Mexican Americans were not covered by this Constitutional Amendment. García and Herrera appealed the case to the U.S. Supreme Court and on May 3, 1954, Chief Justice Earl Warren delivered the unanimous opinion that the Fourteenth Amendment applied to all citizens who suffer discrimination for their race or class, including Latinos. Thus, the exclusion of Mexican Americans from jury service was a clear violation of the Fourteenth Amendment. *Hernández v. Texas* stands today as the first Supreme Court case that ruled that Mexican Americans were assured the same Fourteenth Amendment rights as other Americans and the first time lawyers of Latino descent organized and argued a case before the Supreme Court.

TERM PAPER SUGGESTIONS

1. Explain how the Supreme Court's decision in *Hernández v. Texas* changed the application and perception of the Fourteenth Amendment to the U.S. Constitution.

2. Research the discrimination faced by Mexican Americans as noted in the *Hernández v. Texas* ruling. How did Latino civil rights groups use the Hernández decision to challenge discrimination in the 1960s?

3. Although there are many differences between the two cases, *Hernández v. Texas* is often referred to as the "Latino *Brown v. Board of Education*." Discuss the similarities and differences between these two court cases.

4. Hernadez's lawyers, García and Herrera, worked for the League of United Latin American Citizens (LULAC). Examine the role that

LULAC played in *Hernández v. Texas* and its role in other Latino civil rights issues of the time.

5. *Hernández v. Texas* is one of the first Supreme Court cases to acknowledge what is called "de facto" discrimination (what happens in practice) instead of merely "de jure" discrimination (what the law states). Explain how the Warren court used what is called "the rule of exclusion" to acknowledge de facto segregation practices in *Hernández.*

6. Examine the impact of *Hernández v. Texas* on the United States jury selection process. Has Latino participation on juries changed as a result of this case?

ALTERNATIVE TERM PAPER SUGGESTIONS

1. *Hernández v. Texas* is one of the few Supreme Court cases where the transcripts of the lawyers' arguments have been lost. Take a position, pro or con, as a lawyer arguing the case before the Supreme Court. Write a legal brief or orally record your arguments on this case.

2. Design a PowerPoint presentation on *Hernández v. Texas.* Be sure to include details of the case, as well as the legal implications that resulted from the Supreme Court decision.

SUGGESTED SOURCES

Primary Sources

Hernández v. Texas, 347 U.S. 475 (1954). http://caselaw.lp.findlaw.com/cgi-bin/getcase.pl?court=US&vol=347&invol=475. Chief Justice Warren's opinion can be found here along with hyperlinks to some of the other cases referenced in the opinion.

Munguia, Ruben. *A Cotton Picker Finds Justice: The Saga of the Hernández Case.* Publisher unknown, 1954. http://www.law.uh.edu/Hernández50/saga.pdf. This pamphlet created by Mexican American political leaders in Texas offers original photos and testimonies on the case.

Secondary Sources

López, Ian F. Haney. "Race and Erasure: The Salience of Race to Latinos/as." *The Latino Condition: A Critical Reader.* Eds. Richard Delgado and

Jean Stefancic. New York: NYU Press, 1998. 180–195. López's essay discusses the Supreme Court decision and its implications for the understanding of race.

Olivas, Michael A., ed. *"Colored Men" and "Hombres Aquí": Hernández v. Texas and the Emergence of Mexican-American Lawyering.* Houston: Arte Público Press, 2006. Features 10 essays on the case as well as appendices with the Supreme Court transcripts.

Soltero, Carlos R. *Latinos and American Law: Landmark Supreme Court Cases.* Austin: University of Texas Press, 2006. Soltero's chapter on *Hernández v. Texas* discusses how the case changed perceptions of the Fourteenth Amendment and Mexican American civil rights.

Valencia, Reynaldo Anaya, et al. *Mexican Americans and the Law.* Tucson: University of Arizona Press, 2004. Section on "Criminal Justice Issues" focuses on the *Hernández* case and equal protection.

World Wide Web

Johnson, Kevin R. *"Hernández v. Texas*: Legacies of Justice and Injustice." http://papers.ssrn.com/sol3/papers.cfm?abstract_id=625403. Johnson's 2004 paper for the University of California-Davis Law and Legal Studies department provides a thorough overview of the case.

López, Ian F. Haney "Hernández v. Brown." http://www.nytimes.com/2004/05/22/opinion/Hernández-v-brown.html. In this 2004 article for the *New York Times*, López discusses the differences between *Hernández v. Texas* and *Brown v. Board of Education.*

Multimedia Sources

American Experience: A Class Apart. PBS. 2009. Television program focuses on *Hernández v. Texas*. A Web version of the episode can be watched online at http://www.pbs.org/wgbh/americanexperience/class/.

"Michael Olivas to Discuss *Hernández v. Texas* Case." http://ylsqtss.law.yale.edu:8080/qtmedia/lectures07/YLSDeanOlivas100107_s.mov. Features quicktime video of University of Houston Law Professor Michael Olivas' 2007 lecture on the unique aspects of *Hernández v. Texas* as a legal case.

Rodriguez, Marc. "The Jury Right in Comparative Context: Reconsidering *Hernández v. Texas.*" http://www.havenscenter.org/audio/by/title/the_jury_right_in_comparative_context_reconsidering_Hernández_v_texas. 93.27 min. Rodriguez's Havens Center audio lecture discusses how Hernández's case impacted jury selection.

36. Operation Wetback (1954)

To combat the increase in undocumented Mexican laborers being hired by U.S. businesses, President Dwight D. Eisenhower authorized the U.S. Immigration and Naturalization Service (INS) to arrest and deport thousands of undocumented workers from Mexico, who were referred to as "wetbacks," for crossing the Rio Grande River into the United States. In the past, the INS permitted Mexican citizens open access through the borders as a way to retaliate against Mexico for making greater demands from the United States regarding the Mexicans participating in the Bracero Program. The undocumented workers who were permitted to enter the United States were quickly arrested and sent to Texas where growers who refused to comply with labor agreements under the Bracero Program hired them. Eventually, the INS put a stop to this by arresting undocumented workers and sending them as far into the interior of Mexico as they could by airplane, truck, bus, or ship. On the first day of the operation, July 15, 1954, nearly 4,800 undocumented workers were arrested. There was great opposition from the agricultural community who accused the INS of denying them a cheap labor force. However, by the fall of 1954, the INS ran out of funding for the costly operation and discontinued the program.

TERM PAPER SUGGESTIONS

1. Discuss in detail how Operation Wetback conflicted with the Bracero Program, which was going on at the same time. What were the central conflicts and complications for agricultural growers in hiring contracted Braceros versus undocumented workers from Mexico?

2. What role did Texas play in the hiring of undocumented workers from Mexico and the institution of Operation Wetback in mid-July 1954? Why was it excluded from participating in the Bracero Program?

3. How was Operation Wetback similar to the Mexican Repatriation process during the Great Depression in the United States? Emphasize the social and political climate at the time and articulate how these events were characterized by the time period in which they respectively occurred.

4. Two outspoken proponents of Operation Wetback were the American G.I. Forum and the Texas State Federation of Labor. Articulate how they not only encouraged a repatriation policy for undocumented Mexican laborers but also fostered what many regarded as a culture of xenophobia in the United States toward the Mexican.

ALTERNATIVE TERM PAPER SUGGESTIONS

1. Called before a U.S. Presidential Committee on investigating illegal workers entering from Mexico, prepare a PowerPoint report either advocating a program similar to Operation Wetback or offering a different solution that will address the legality and ethics of controlling the flow of immigrants over the U.S.-Mexico border.

2. Assume the role of an undocumented Mexican laborer during the mid-1950s in the United States and prepare a series of podcasts addressing your circumstances in Mexico and your reasons for crossing into the United States illegally.

SUGGESTED SOURCES

Primary Source

Mintz, Steven. *Mexican American Voices: A Documentary Reader,* 2nd ed. Malden, MA: Blackwell Publishing, 2009. Chapter 8 includes testimonies from Mexican migrant workers impacted by Operation Wetback.

Secondary Sources

Cavazos, Sylvia. *The Disposable Mexican: Operation Wetback, 1954: The Deportation of Undocumented Workers in California and Texas.* Ann Arbor: University of Michigan Press, 1988. Provides a critical examination of Eisenhower's program and the immediate repercussions on the Latino communities in California and Texas.

Egendorf, Laura K. *Immigration.* Farmington Hills, MI: Greenhaven Press, 2006. Comprehensive anthology includes an article on the background and intention behind this program.

Garcia, Juan Ramon. *Operation Wetback: The Mass Deportation of Mexican Undocumented Workers in 1954.* Westport, CT: Greenwood Press, 1980. Well-researched text focuses on the issues surrounding Mexican labor in the United States during the mid-20th century.

Hadley, Eleanor M. "A Critical Analysis of the Wetback Problem." *Law and Contemporary Problems* 21 (Spring 1956): 334–357. This detailed article explores the legal repercussions for illegal immigration and the policy of Operation Wetback.

Hoffman, Abraham. *Unwanted Mexican Americans in the Great Depression: Repatriation Pressures, 1929–1939.* Tucson: University of Arizona Press, 1974. Provides background information and central arguments surrounding the voluntary and involuntary exodus of nearly half a million Mexican citizens to Mexico.

World Wide Web

"How Eisenhower Solved Illegal Border Crossing from Mexico." http://www. csmonitor.com/2006/0706/p09s01-coop.html. John Dillin's article includes background information on the policy that was implemented and makes parallels to immigration policies in the late 20th and early 21st century.

"Operation Wetback." http://www.pbs.org/kpbs/theborder/history/timeline/ 20.html. Contains a very brief synopsis of this program.

" 'Operation Wetback': Illegal Immigration's Golden-Crisp Myth." http:// www.commondreams.org/archive/2007/04/05/318. Pierre Tristam provides a critical examination of President Eisenhower's policy.

"Pearce Calls on 'Operation Wetback' for Illegals." http://www.eastvalleytribune. com/story/75335. Highlights U.S. Representative Russell Pearce's September 2006 proposal to recreate a 21st-century Operation Wetback to address immigration.

Multimedia Sources

" 'Wet Backs': Hundreds of Alien Workers Rounded Up." http://www.youtube.com/watch?v=vl3b7Q_ExMU. Silent newsreel from Universal International News of Mexican show workers outside of Stockton, California, being arrested and prepared for deportation.

37. Rise of Ritchie Valens (1958)

Often called both the "Father of Chicano Rock and Roll" and the "First Latino Rock Star," Ritchie Valens (May 13, 1941–February 3, 1959) is considered by musical scholars to be one of the 20th century's most important Latino musicians. Valens' status is even more remarkable when one considers that his national career lasted a mere eight months before his death at age 17. Born Richard Steven Valenzuela, Valens began his musical career in Pacoima, California, a small, predominantly Mexican

American, agricultural area in greater Los Angeles. Playing local venues, Valens was discovered by Bob Keane, who recorded Valens under his Del-Fi label and served as his manager/producer. Within those eight months, Valens appeared several times on national television and had three hit singles, including "Come On, Let's Go," and "Oh, Donna," the latter of which reached number two on the Billboard charts. Valens' overnight success led to his invitation to join a national tour called "The Winter Dance Party," which featured headliner Buddy Holly, along with Waylon Jennings and Jiles Perry Richardson Jr. ("The Big Bopper"). On this tour, Valens, Richardson, and Holly were killed when the plane crashed only a mile from takeoff in the Clear Lake, Iowa, airport on February 2, 1959. The date of their deaths is often referred to as "The Day the Music Died." Today, Valens is best remembered for "La Bamba," a Spanish-language song inspired by a traditional Mexican wedding ballad called the "Huapango." "La Bamba," ironically, was the lowest-ranked of Valens' songs during his lifetime but offers the clearest vision of his unique fusion of Latino influences and American Rock and Roll. Moreover, of *Rolling Stone's* "500 Greatest Songs of All Time," "La Bamba" is the only Spanish-language song. Valens was inducted into the Rock and Roll Hall of Fame in 2001 and a semi-autobiographical film, *La Bamba,* was made of his life in 1987.

TERM PAPER SUGGESTIONS

1. Discuss how Valens' work influenced several musical genres (such as Rockabilly, Latino Alternative, R&B, and Punk) as well as individual bands and musicians (such as Los Lobos, Los Lonely Boys, Chris Montez, and The Ramones).

2. Research the history of "La Bamba," and the "Huapango," the traditional Mexican wedding song on which "La Bamba" is based. Describe Valens' transformation of this musical style into a Rock and Roll hit.

3. Several scholars have noted the role that Southern California, particularly East Los Angeles and the San Fernando Valley, has played in generating mainstream Latino music. Investigate this region and its influence on Latino thought, music, and culture.

4. Many critics have noted substantial differences between Luis Valdez's film version of Valens' life, *La Bamba*, and Valens' actual biography and the film's stereotypes of Latinos. Discuss *La Bamba's* portrayal

of Valens, as well as its interpretation of Latino life and culture in the 1950s.

5. Given that Valens did not speak Spanish and yet he is most remembered for his Spanish-language song, Valens' life and music are often discussed in terms of "assimilation" and "acculturation." Research these terms and discuss which elements of Valens' life and music exemplify elements of European American assimilation and which elements, in contrast, demonstrate an acculturation of Chicano and European American cultures.

6. Explain how Valens' career and instant success paved the way for other Latino musicians in the 20th and 21st centuries.

ALTERNATIVE TERM PAPER SUGGESTIONS

1. Design a Webography for Ritchie Valens, focusing on his musical influences and his legacy to Rock and Roll. Be sure to include Valens' contributions to various musical genres as well as his influence on particular musical groups.

2. Artists as diverse as The Ventures, Los Lobos, Conjunto Medelin de Lino Chavez, and the Mormon Tabernacle Choir have all recorded versions of Valens' "La Bamba." Create an iMovie documentary featuring some of these versions and discussing the song's origins. Be sure to add commentary on the song's status in Latino music and culture.

SELECTED SOURCES

Primary Sources

The Complete Ritchie Valens. Whirlwind Media, 1999. DVD. 161 minutes. This package includes a documentary of Valens' life called *Viva Ritchie: The Ritchie Valens Story* and a CD of Valens' studio recordings.

Valens, Ritchie. *In Concert at Pacoima Jr. High.* Audio CD. Wounded Bird Records, 2006. Includes live renditions of Valens' greatest hits, including "La Bamba" and "Oh Donna."

Valens, Ritchie. *The Lost Tapes.* Audio CD. Del-Fi, 1995. Includes studio tapes and demos of Valens' work.

Valens, Ritchie. *The Ritchie Valens Story.* Audio CD. Rhino, 2005. In addition to his studio recordings, this CD includes an introduction by Valens' producer and manager, Bob Keane, and a radio commercial Valens made for the Winter Dance Party Tour.

Secondary Sources

Ben-Yehuda, Ayala. "Livin' La Vida Bamba." *Billboard* 120, no. 38 (Sep. 20, 2008): 23–23. Discusses Valens' most influential song and its Latino musical influences.

Lehmer, Larry. *The Day The Music Died: The Last Tour of Buddy Holly, The Big Bopper, and Ritchie Valens.* New York: Music Sales Group, 2004. Lehmer, an Iowa journalist, details Valens' last tour. Book includes photos of Valens and interviews with his family and associates.

Mendheim, Beverly. *Ritchie Valens: The First Latino Rocker.* Austin: University of Texas Press, 1987. Mendheim, a music professor, explores the history of Valens' songs and their Latino and African American influences.

World Wide Web

Garfias, Robert. *Latino Music: A View of Its Diversity and Strength.* http://www.pps.k12.or.us/depts-c/mc-me/be-hi-mu.pdf. Forty essays written for the Portland Public Schools Hispanic Baseline Series feature a discussion of Valens' "La Bamba" and its Veracruz origins.

La Bamba Bobs' Official Ritchie Valens Web site. http://www.ritchievalens.org/home.html. Valens' brother, Bob Morales, created this Web site that features articles about Valens' music and career, as well as photos and links to other Web sites featuring Valens.

Ritchie Valens Official Web site. http://www.ritchievalens.com/index.html. Features photos, biographic information and a virtual jukebox that plays many of Valens' hit songs.

Multimedia Sources

Chicano Rock!: The Sounds of East Los Angeles (2008) Dir. Jon Wilkman. Public Broadcasting Corporation. 60 minutes. This documentary of East Los Angeles singers and songwriters features Ritchie Valens and his rise to fame.

La Bamba. Sony Pictures, 1987. 108 minutes. Features director and writer Luis Valdez's biopic of Valdez's life and music.

"Oh Donna Live." http://www.youtube.com/watch?v=1mKHkz6A3Fk. Pictures of Ritchie Valens accompany a live 1958 recording of Valens playing his biggest hit.

"Richie Valens: Ooh My Head." http://www.youtube.com/watch?v=xaTO MsrVg5s&feature=related. 1:05 minutes. Is one of the few video recordings of Valens performing live for Dick Clark's television show.

"Ritchie Valens Performs La Bamba Live." http://vids.myspace.com/index.cfm?fuse action=vids.individual&videoid=24905271#video_details. 4:26 minutes. This audio clip of Ritchie Valens features his most influential song.

38. Fidel Castro Visits New York (April 1959)

After successfully taking control over Cuba in January 1959 and sending the dictator Fulgencio Batista into exile, Fidel Castro visited the United States in April at the invitation of the American Society of Newspaper Editors. Despite the U.S. government's concern and suspicion over Castro's anti-American speeches and sympathies toward communist ideology and leftist leaders like Che Guevara, the U.S. press and public were quite taken by this mythic figure who recited tales of revolution and appeared before cameras in military fatigues, with a beard and a large Cuban cigar. Ambiguous about the relevance of Castro's visit, President Dwight D. Eisenhower did not meet with the Cuban leader and instead spent his time on a golf course. On his 11-day tour of the United States, Castro met with a variety of progressive and moderate leaders and organizations, and he gave a number of speeches outlining Cuba's new role in the Western Hemisphere. While at a meeting with the New York-based Council on Foreign Affairs, he walked out abruptly in anger after insisting that Cuba did not need the United States to economically support his nation, and during the question-and-answer period at Harvard University, he was hissed at one point by the crowd. However, overall both the U.S. press and public received Castro warmly and with visible interest and enthusiasm. Wherever he went, whether in Washington, D.C.; New York; Princeton; Boston; Montreal; or Houston, Castro was greeted by crowds that often numbered in the thousands. The good-will tour presented Castro in a different light; however, it did very little to strengthen diplomatic ties between the United States and Cuba. After his meeting with the Cuban leader, Vice President Richard M. Nixon wondered whether Castro was either deeply imbedded with communist associations or simply naïve about communism. Soon after the April tour, the United States began putting together what eventually would be known as the Bay of Pigs invasion of Cuba.

TERM PAPER SUGGESTIONS

1. When Fidel Castro visited the United States as the new leader of Cuba, he did not adhere to traditional diplomatic protocol during the planning of the trip or on the trip itself. Explain how the Castro delegation broke with protocol and assert whether this contributed to the negative impressions formed by high-level U.S. government officials.

2. In 1960, Fidel Castro again visited New York to deliver a speech before the United Nations. Discuss how this trip was different from the one in April 1959. What did Castro do differently during his stay? Compare these two visits with his 1979, 1995, and 2000 visits as well.

3. Argue why the U.S. press and public were so fond of Castro during his visit. Consider his speeches delivered at various organizations and television interviews. What captured the public's interest in this figure? Analyze the way the U.S. press followed the Cuban leader and how it reported on his activity.

4. Outline the concerns that the United States government had with Fidel Castro seizing control of Cuba in 1959. Link this to the level of reception he received when he visited the United States in April 1959.

ALTERNATIVE TERM PAPER SUGGESTIONS

1. Generate a timeline of Castro's 11-day visit to the United States in April 1959, and using audio and video clips indicate specific encounters and situations that may have served as important marks in the emerging leader's career.

2. As Fidel Castro's press secretary on his April 1959 trip to the United States, create a report that outlines the purpose of the Cuban leader's visit, what he hopes to accomplish by visiting various cities in North America, and what the Western Hemisphere can expect from this emerging leader.

SUGGESTED SOURCES

Primary Sources

"Fidel Castro." http://www.flickr.com/photos/pritheworld/sets/721576039406 30494/detail/. Provides several photographs of Castro's 1959 visit to the United States.

"Fidel Castro's Visit." *New York Times,* April 15, 1959: 32. Includes a summary of Castro's tour and U.S. perceptions of it.

"Hissed at Harvard." *New York Times,* April 26, 1959: 3. Brief article reports on Castro's visit and reception at Harvard University during his 11-day tour.

Secondary Sources

Coltman, Leychester. *The Real Fidel Castro.* New Haven, CT: Yale University Press, 2003. Examines the transformative role Castro underwent as the Cuban leader and provides discussion of his 1960 speech before the U.N. General Assembly in Chapter 10.

DePalma, Anthony. *The Man Who Invented Fidel: Castro, Cuba, and Herbert L. Matthews of the New York Times.* New York: Public Affairs Books, 2006. Explores the famous and controversial U.S. news correspondent's relationship with Fidel Castro. Chapter 9 includes a discussion of Castro's visit to the United States.

McPherson, Alan. "The Limits of Populist Diplomacy: Fidel Castro's April 1959 Trip to North America." *Diplomacy and Stagecraft* 18, no. 1 (January 2007): 237–268. In-depth article examines the nontraditional protocol the Cuban delegation exercised during the Castro visit in 1959 and the impact this had on U.S.-Cuban relations.

Mealy, Rosmari. *Fidel & Malcolm X: Memories of a Meeting.* New York: Ocean Press, 1993. Documents the historic meeting between Castro and Malcolm X during the 1960 visit to New York.

Quirk, Robert E. *Fidel Castro.* New York: W.W. Norton, 1995. Comprehensive biography of Castro includes a discussion of the meeting that took place with Vice President Nixon in April 1959 in Chapter 8.

World Wide Web

"Castro Back Then: After the Revolution, the Leader Visited Houston in 1959 Amid Hopes That He Would Build a Democracy." http://www.chron.com/disp/story.mpl/metropolitan/4140419.html. Interviews various civic leaders in Houston, Texas, who met with Castro during his visit and reports on their 21st-century reflections.

"Castro Visits the United States." http://www.history.com/this-day-in-history.do?action=Article&id=2638. Presents a brief overview of the visit.

"Fidel Castro Visits New York." http://www.hartford-hwp.com/archives/43b/205.html. Teresa Gutierrez's article from the *Workers World* profiles Castro's September 2000 visit to Riverside Church in New York City.

Multimedia Source

Fidel Castro. Alexandria, VA: PBS Home Video, 2005. DVD. 110 minutes. Provides overview of Castro's life and career and includes footage from his April 1959 visit to the United States as well as other U.S. visits.

39. Cuban Immigration to the United States (1959–1994)

Cubans have been immigrating to the United States since the 19th century, but it was not until Fidel Castro's political takeover of Cuba at the start of 1959 that the larger, more prominent waves of immigrants began to appear in the United States. Desiring broader democratic freedoms and economic opportunities for themselves and their families, most Cuban émigrés came to the United States to escape Fidel Castro's socialist policies and mandates. However, at first many thought their political exile would be a temporary situation. The first of these exoduses occurred between 1959 and 1962. Widely regarded as the "Golden Exile," these Cubans were members of the upper classes. Nearly 200,000 of them were physicians, lawyers, prominent businessmen, as well as political and military supporters of the ousted dictator Fulgencio Batista. Most of them left behind extended family as well as personal possessions and property, believing that Castro would soon be overthrown. Because the United States did not support the Castro regime, these initial immigrants were allowed to enter this nation unbarred by restrictions and conditions traditionally imposed on other immigrant groups. The next massive exodus, known as the Cuban Airlift, took place between 1965 and 1973. During this period, the Cuban government decided to permit its citizens whose families had previously immigrated to the United States to join them. To maintain an orderly exodus, Cuban and American officials jointly organized one-way airlifts, also known as "freedom flights," that would transport Cubans twice daily to Miami. While this process gave the Cuban government greater control and regulation over the applicants wanting to leave, Cuba still saw as many as 260,500 of its citizens flee its shores. This was the largest exodus period in Cuban history. By 1980, desperate economic conditions generated a resurgence of Cuban immigration into the United States. On April 1 of that year, nearly 10,000 Cubans stormed the Peruvian embassy, seeking asylum. Castro's government responded by allowing over 125,200 people to leave the country in over 2,000 various sea vessels from the port of Mariel. This exodus, primarily from the lower socioeconomic class, became known as the Mariel Boatlift. Because of the disorderliness of this exodus and the fact that convicted felons were now entering Florida, the U.S. government was prompted to place thousands of asylum-seeking Cubans in internment camps. Nearly 1,000 of the felons who came to the United States during this time were ultimately returned to Cuba. The final chapter in mass exoduses from Cuba to the United States occurred in 1994. As in 1980, there were dramatic and often tragic attempts to leave Cuba, so by August 1994 the Castro government announced that it would not prevent people from emigrating. In just a month's time, nearly 37,000 refugees floated out toward the Florida shores only to be intercepted by the U.S. Coast Guard and sent to Guantánamo Bay, the U.S. Naval Base in southeastern Cuba. The Rafter Crisis ended when Cuba agreed to prevent rafters from setting out if the United States would admit around 20,000 Cubans to its shores through established visa processes. Cuban American communities, especially in Miami, have grown strong and resilient and often take an active political role in American relations toward Cuba.

TERM PAPER SUGGESTIONS

1. Today, a growing segment of the Cuban American population is less sympathetic to the conservative nationalism of the traditional community of exiles. Who is this segment, and how are they changing the image of Cuban Americans?

2. In what ways have Cubans enjoyed special immigration policies and privileges in the United States, like the "wet feet, dry land" policy, compared with other Caribbean and Latin Americans?

3. Many Cuban Americans make a clear distinction between the "exiled" Cubans and the "immigrant" Cubans living in the United States. Discuss the difference between these groups and how it contributes to the larger demographic identity of the community. Is the distinction more generational or ideological, or both?

4. Discuss the role Cuban American political groups and organizations, such as the Cuban American National Foundation, have played in American politics, both on a state and federal level, since the dawn of the Golden Exile.

5. Before 1959, Cubans had long been immigrating to American shores. Outline some of the major events and circumstances that led Cubans to seek asylum in the United States before this period. How do their stories compare with the ones who immigrated after the fall of Batista?

ALTERNATIVE TERM PAPER SUGGESTIONS

1. Create a PowerPoint presentation that profiles the everyday lifestyle of a modern-day Cuban American living in "Little Havana," south Florida, and one residing in Havana, Cuba. Consider their respective access to food, medical attention, information, employment, and education, and underscore the similarities and differences that exist between them. In what ways is one better off than the other?

2. Closely examine the way the U.S. media handled the Elián González news affair in 1999. Create an iMovie that showcases how television, newspaper, and magazine images, articles, and interviews were influential in demonstrating a national perception of Cuban Americanism. In this piece, emphasize what issues or significant arguments in this case were hypersensationalized and/or distorted by the media and other groups.

SUGGESTED SOURCES

Primary Source

Fernández, Alina. *Castro's Daughter: An Exile's Memoir of Cuba.* Trans. Dolores Koch. New York: St. Martin's Griffin, 1998. Written by Castro's illegitimate child, Fernández, now exiled in Spain, recounts what her life was like growing up in revolutionary Cuba by providing intimate portraits of her father and the men with whom he surrounded himself, such as brother Raul or compadre Ché Guevara.

Secondary Sources

García, María Cristina. *Havana USA: Cuban Exiles and Cuban Americans in South Florida, 1959–1994.* Berkeley: University of California Press, 1996. This comprehensive study of the Cuban exile community in the United States not only redefines how the community can and should be articulated, but also discusses the consequences of what living with an exile identity has done to Cuban Americans in terms of culture, language, art, and ideology.

Gonzalez-Pando, Miguel. *The Cuban Americans.* Westport, CT: Greenwood Press, 1998. With a brief historical background on pre-Castro Cuban history, this work provides a stage-by-stage account of how the various layers of the Cuban exile community was established between 1959 and the 1990s.

Grenier, Guillerma J., and Lisandro Pérez. *The Legacy of Exiles: Cubans in the United States.* Boston: Allyn and Bacon, 2003. Part of the "New Immigrant

Series," this source charts the historical details and causes of Cuban migration to the United States from the 19th to the 21st centuries.

Herrera, Andrea O'Reilly, ed. *Remembering Cuba: Legacy of a Diaspora*. Austin: University of Texas Press, 2001. Through an eclectic assembly of letters, artwork, recipes, photographs, and creative stories, Herrera has collected over 100 narratives from both known and unknown Cuban American writers on what exile from Cuba means to the individual and the community as a whole.

Portes, Alejandro, and Alex Stepick. *City on the Edge: The Transformation of Miami*. Berkeley: University of California Press, 1993. This is an urban studies approach to examining how Cuban Americans alone have transformed the politics, economics, and culture of the city of Miami despite the strong presence of the Jewish, African American, Nicaraguan, and Anglo communities.

Torres, María de los Angeles. *In the Land of Mirrors: Cuban Exile Politics in the United States*. Ann Arbor, MI: University of Michigan Press, 1999. Complemented by photographic illustrations, Torres' study explores the political and ideological impacts Cuban migration has had on the ever-growing exile communities in the United States.

Tweed, Thomas A. *Our Lady of the Exile: Diaspora Religion at a Cuban Catholic Shrine in Miami*. Oxford: Oxford University Press, 1997. Profiling the popular shrine of Our Lady of Charity in Miami, Tweed takes a historical and ethnographic approach toward exploring how Cuban Americans view their role as exiles and how they manage to sustain a diasporic culture through religious traditions.

World Wide Web

"Cuban American National Foundation." http://www.canf.org. An American-based Web site comprises multiple members of the exile community who promote human rights and causes for democratic freedom, particularly with respect to Cuba. Although it is an anti-Castro site, it does include a multitude of useful resources, such as news videos, news articles, legal documents, events and is accessible in both English and Spanish.

"The Cuban Experience." http://library.thinkquest.org/18355/index.shtml. Including forums for discussion and debate, this interactive site comprises news articles, historical information, resources for students and teachers of Cuban history and culture, and people profiles that support the further understanding of Cuba and Cuban exiles through an anti-Castro lens.

"Cuban Immigration to the United States." http://www.usimmigrationsupport .org/cubaimmigration.html. Covering general history of Cuban migration, this article examines the motivation behind the waves of immigration from Cuba to the United States since 1959 and includes useful links to further articles on this topic.

"Cuban Information Archives." http://cuban-exile.com/menu1/quikidx.html. This comprehensive site provides details of past and existing Cuban American political organizations as well as speech excerpts, articles, and interviews concerning pivotal events and definitions of the Cuban Exile Community in the United States.

Multimedia Sources

Balseros. New York: New Video Group, 2005. DVD. 120 minutes. This documentary, nominated for an Oscar in 2004, profiles seven different Cuban rafters (*balseros*) and their families who made the journey to Florida during the Rafter Crisis of 1994. In Spanish with English subtitles.

"Elian." http://www.cbsnews.com/stories/2005/09/28/60minutes/main888950. shtml. Covers the Elián González news affair in 1999 and includes a video interview by *60 Minutes*' correspondent Bob Simon, footage of Gonzalez and Castro, and an article that details the event.

40. Dominican Immigration to the United States (1961–2000)

Dominicans have been immigrating to the United States since the late 19th century, and while New York City has always been home to a large Dominican American community since the 1930s, it was not until 1961 that more significant waves of immigration from the Dominican Republic to the United States began. During the dictatorship of Rafael Trujillo, which began in the mid-1930s, it was very difficult to emigrate from the Dominican Republic because of tight control over immigration rights. However, after Trujillo's assassination in 1961, these bans were relaxed, and many nations including the United States became home to Dominicans seeking economic and political refuge. As such, New York, Massachusetts, New Jersey, and south Florida became U.S. destination points for Dominicans seeking new opportunities and a better life outside of the island republic. The largest waves of immigration occurred during the 1980s and 1990s. High unemployment with fewer opportunities encouraged many Dominicans to find work in the United States. Between 1981 and 1990, over 250,000 Dominicans entered the United States legally according to immigration records. The 1990 U.S.

Census reported that there were over 506,000 Dominicans living in the United States, the vast majority being Dominican born. This further suggests that the Dominican community in the United States has principally been an immigrant community (two out of every three Dominicans are foreign born). While many Dominicans come to the United States or Puerto Rico looking for work and new opportunities, most maintain a strong connection with their island nation. In fact, remittances are one of the largest foreign currency industries enjoyed by the Dominican Republic, second only to tourism. By the late 1990s, the trend of immigration began to slow down, and around half of Dominican American households were single-parent systems, the brunt of this duty being placed on the Dominican female. However, between 1990 and 2000, the population of Dominicans in the United States grew 89 percent with estimated numbers reaching over 1.1 million. As the Dominican immigrant population continues to grow, the community faces new challenges in terms of assimilation in the United States and association with the island republic.

TERM PAPER SUGGESTIONS

1. In the late 1990s, many Dominicans participated in the Pro-Vote movement, which allowed Dominicans residing in the United States to participate in the politics of the Dominican Republic. Explain the origins of this movement and the legal processes that finally-granted Dominicans voting rights.

2. In a well-researched paper, discuss how Dominicans have faced the challenges in relocating to the United States. How were these experiences different from economic and political conditions that have brought other Latino groups including Puerto Ricans, Cubans, Mexicans, and Central and South Americans to the United States? Emphasize what circumstances were unique to the Dominican community.

3. A large percent of Dominicans are of African origin. Discuss what role skin complexion has played among Dominican Americans, and what difficulties this group of Dominican Americans has experienced in assimilating to U.S. culture.

ALTERNATIVE TERM PAPER SUGGESTIONS

1. As a newly arrived immigrant from the Dominican Republic, write a series of letters back home to relatives that relate what life is like for a

Dominican immigrant. Consider describing important things such as community support and identity, family stability, economic and social opportunities, and the relationship between Dominican immigrants and second-generation Dominican Americans. Also describe how Dominicans fit into the larger pan-Latino ethnic community in the United States.

2. Create a detailed PowerPoint presentation with text and illustrations highlighting the political and cultural contributions of the Dominican American community. In addition to historical information, include elements of culture such as music, art, literature, and other aspects of popular culture such as sports and fashion. Emphasize how these components have created a multifaceted identity for Dominican Americans.

SUGGESTED SOURCES

Primary Source

Peña-Gratereaux, Mary Ely. *Voices of Diaspora: Stories and Testimonies of Dominican Immigrant Women.* Trans. Elizabeth Figueroa. New York: Cayena Publications, 2008. Profiles the lives and experiences of Dominican women who have left their island home for a new life.

Secondary Sources

Cadelario, Ginetta E. B. *Black behind the Ears: Racial Identity from Museums to Beauty Shops.* Durham, NC: Duke University Press, 2007. Articulates the complex role race and ethnicity play in defining the Dominican in terms of blackness, U.S. culture, and Latino designation.

Gilbertson, Greta. "Caregiving across Generations: Aging, State Assistance, and Multigenerational Ties among Immigrants from the Dominican Republic." In *Across Generations: Immigrant Families in America,* edited by Nancy Foner. New York: NYU Press, 2009, pp. 135–159. Analyzes the difficulties faced by Dominican families whose value systems, needs, and priorities change with each subsequent generation.

Pessar, Patricia R. *A Visa for a Dream: Dominicans in the United States.* Boston: Allyn and Bacon, 1995. Covers the broad exodus of Dominicans to the United States and the challenges Dominican families face in relocating.

———, and Pamela M. Graham. "Dominicans: Transnational Identities and Local Politics." In *New Immigrants in New York,* edited by Nancy Foner. New York: Columbia University Press, 2001, pp. 251–274. Details how Dominican Americans maintain a cultural and political identity both in the United States and in the Dominican Republic.

Torres-Saillant, Silvio, and Ramona Hernandez. *The Dominican Americans.* Westport, CT: Greenwood Press, 1998. Contains comprehensive overview of the history of Dominican Americans in the United States.

World Wide Web

"Dominican Americans." http://www.everyculture.com/multi/Bu-Dr/Dominican-Americans.html. Provides a detailed overview of the history, culture, and immigration patterns of Dominican Americans with relevant links.

"The Dominican American National Roundtable." http://www.danr.org. Main Web page for this nonprofit, nonpartisan advocacy group includes numerous links and videos.

"Dominican Migration to USA." http://www.un-instraw.org/index.php?option=com_content&lang=en&id=338&task=view&Itemid=449. Includes relevant background information on migration history and current trends with statistics.

"The Foreign Born from the Dominican Republic in the United States." http://www.migrationinformation.org/Feature/display.cfm?id=259. Charts relevant statistics and information regarding Dominicans in the United States.

Multimedia Sources

Dreams Ensnared: The Dominican Migration to New York. New York: Cinema Guild, 1994. DVD. 22 minutes. Using profiles of female immigrants, the film charts the difficulties Dominicans have faced in their home country and in the United States.

My American Girls: A Dominican Story. New York: Filmakers Library, 2001. DVD. 62 minutes. Focuses on the everyday lives of the Ortiz family and their struggles with assimilating into the culture of New York.

41. Bay of Pigs Invasion (April 1961)

Toward the end of his tenure in office, President Dwight D. Eisenhower initiated "Operation Pluto" in March 1960, which gave the Central Intelligence Agency (CIA) permission to train members of the Cuban exile community for a future deposing of Fidel Castro in Cuba. President John F. Kennedy actually set the operation in motion shortly after taking office in January 1961. He renamed Eisenhower's scheme "Operation Zapata" in March 1961 and turned the plan into an airstrike and amphibious invasion. Kennedy wanted to ensure that U.S. involvement was undetectable, and air and sea craft would be disguised to deflect U.S. identity. In addition, the CIA trained over 1,400 members of the anti-Castro Cuban exile community in and around the Miami area who were committed to overthrowing Castro and reinstating José Miró Cardona as the prime minister. Cardona had served as prime minister for six weeks beginning in January 1959 before he was replaced by Castro. Most of the members of Brigade 2506, the name the Cuban exiles gave to themselves, were trained in air, sea, and land tactics by CIA operatives in south Florida, Panama, and Guatemala in preparation for the attack against Castro's revolutionary forces. When the airstrike against strategic airbases in Cuba failed during the April 14th attack, the United States launched its amphibious assault on April 17, 1961. This phase of the operation sent nearly 1,300 CIA-led members of Brigade 2506 into *Bahía de Cochinos*, or Bay of Pigs. Like the airstrikes, the amphibious assault was delayed, which gave Castro's forces enough time to prepare for a counterattack. Although more than 100 members of Brigade 2506 were killed during the invasion, most of the original 1,400 surrendered by April 19. The invasion was called a failure and served only to bolster Castro's position of power in the eyes of his supporters. Fearing future assaults from the United States, Castro declared his government a Marxist-Leninist one and asked for the support and protection of the Soviet Union.

TERM PAPER SUGGESTIONS

1. Explore the role that the Cuban Democratic Revolutionary Front played in supporting the Bay of Pigs invasion and include how this organization's military wing, the Cuban Revolutionary Council, was pivotal in working alongside the CIA.

2. Fidel Castro's government had ample warning prior to the invasion. Discuss how this information was generated and how it circulated, thus providing Castro with enough time to prepare and respond to the waves of attack.

3. Closely critique the plans of Operation Zapata implemented by the Kennedy administration, and examine the military and diplomatic pitfalls that made the Bay of Pigs invasion a failure. Compare this with Eisenhower's Operation Pluto ordered just a year earlier.

4. U.S. Ambassador to the United Nations Adlai Stevenson and U.S. Secretary of State Dean Rusk had not been told that the CIA sponsored

the Bay of Pigs invasion. As a result, they publicly denied any U.S. involvement, much to their personal embarrassment. How did the U.S.-led invasion play out on the diplomatic stage? How did the Kennedy administration articulate its position, and did this impact U.S. credibility within the world community or among its allies?

ALTERNATIVE TERM PAPER SUGGESTIONS

1. Design a series of regional maps that include military operations of the Castro regime and Brigade 2506 during the Bay of Pigs invasion of April 1961. Highlight troop movements and battles with hyperlinks that provide researched information.

2. Write a letter from the point of view of a pro-Castro military commander to Fidel Castro himself, highlighting the aftermath of the U.S.-led invasion. Suggest what this action means to the Cuban Revolution and the future of Cuba's diplomatic position in the Western Hemisphere. Draw your response from what Cuban leaders and pro-Castro publications were reciting at the time.

SUGGESTED SOURCES

Primary Sources

Lynch, Grayston L. *Decision for Disaster: Betrayal at the Bay of Pigs.* Dulles, VA: Potomac Books, 2000. Includes in-depth examination of the attack and its aftermath from the perspective of a top CIA operative who participated in the event.

"Robert F. Kennedy Statement on Neutrality Laws, April 20, 1961." http://upload.wikimedia.org/wikipedia/commons/a/af/JFK.jpg. This is Attorney General Robert F. Kennedy's official statement addressing the legality of the United States assisting Cuban exiles in replacing the Castro regime.

Topping, Seymour B. "Moscow Blames U.S. for Attack." *New York Times* April 18, 1961: 1+. Covers the Soviet accusations against the Kennedy administration and underscores the Cold War tone between the two superpowers.

Secondary Sources

Jones, Howard. *The Bay of Pigs.* New York: Oxford University Press, 2008. Part of the Pivotal Moments in American History series, this work suggests that the Bay of Pigs invasion shifted U.S. policy in a new direction, one that included employing military tactics with political assassination.

Kornbluh, Peter. *Bay of Pigs Declassified: The Secret CIA Reports on the Invasion of Cuba*. New York: The New Press, 1998. With interviews and declassified documents, Kornbluh closely critiques the failed 1961 attack organized by the CIA.

Quesada, Alejandro. *The Bay of Pigs: Cuba 1961*. New York: Osprey Publishing, 2009. Quesada, the nephew of a Brigade 2506 veteran, incorporates unpublished photographs and illustrations of the war and includes several engaging interviews with veterans of the conflict.

World Wide Web

"Bay of Pigs Invasion." http://www.u-s-history.com/pages/h1765.html. Includes a brief examination of the event with hyperlinks for further research.

"JFK in History: The Bay of Pigs." http://www.jfklibrary.org/Historical+Resources/ JFK+in+History/JFK+and+the+Bay+of+Pigs.htm. Provides an overview of the invasion and includes several photos of the Kennedys attending the December 1962 celebration of the event at the Orange Bowl in Florida.

"Two Views of the Cuban Invasion." http://www.archive.org/details/TwoViews OfTheCubanInvasion. This online text underscores the perspectives of the invasion by providing two informed positions from prominent historians: Max Shachtman supports it, while Hal Draper opposes it.

Multimedia Sources

Bay of Pigs Declassified. New York: New Video Group, 2002. DVD. 50 minutes. Investigates the invasion through an in-depth analysis of declassified reports.

From the Bay of Pigs to the Brink. Princeton, NJ: Films for the Humanities and Sciences, 2004. DVD. 16 minutes. Contains a brief sketch of the U.S. invasion of Cuba and the foundation it establishes for the Cuban Missile Crisis shortly after.

42. United Farm Workers of America Formed (1962)

Founded by Philip Vera Cruz, Dolores Huerta and César Chávez in September 1962, the United Farm Workers of America (UFW) was formed from the merging of two former associations, the Agricultural Workers Organizing Committee (AWOC) and the National Farm Workers Association (NFWA). The NFWA was an organization founded by Chávez and

Huerta to help agricultural workers obtain unemployment insurance. The UFW, however, functioned as a labor union, intent on improving the working conditions, wages, and lives of its members. In 1965, the UFW became immediately recognizable throughout the United States when UFW members voted to join a strike against grape growers in Delano, California, who refused to offer labor contracts to workers. The strike and subsequent boycott lasted five years, and the UFW's methods of organizing workers, holding rallies and marches, and urging consumers to avoid purchasing grapes were ultimately successful, leading to worker contracts. At the forefront of the movement's public face was Chávez, an articulate leader whose background in community organizing proved instrumental to the UFW. Among the UFW's other successful campaigns was a 1970s lettuce strike/boycott in Salinas, California, and Chávez's 1988 36-day hunger strike to protest the poisoning of farmer workers and their children through pesticide use in McFarlane, California. Another central victory of the UFW occurred in the early 1980s, when over 40,000 agricultural workers held UFW contracts with their employers. After Chávez's death in 1993, Arturo Rodriguez, a veteran UFW organizer, succeeded him as union president. Since that time, the UFW has been active in securing contracts and improving working conditions for agricultural workers, and their strategy of nonviolent, well-publicized strikes and boycotts has continued, including a 1990s protest against Coastal Berry, the largest employer of U.S. strawberry laborers, and a 22-month contract negotiation with Gallo Winery in 2005.

TERM PAPER SUGGESTIONS

1. Research the Delano Grape Strike of 1965, its key players, and issues. How did the UFW incorporate the principles of nonviolence favored by Mahatma Gandhi and Martin Luther King Jr.? Why did the strike last for five years? What role did American consumers play in ending the strike? Ultimately, do you think the strike was successful?

2. Examine the role played by Latinas in the UFW, particularly Dolores Huerta, its co-founder. Would you consider the UFW to be a feminist, gender-neutral organization? Why or why not?

3. Discuss the difficulties experienced by the UFW in organizing agricultural workers. How do issues such as migration, documentation, health, education, and class relations impact the organization? What were the UFW's solutions to make organizing and contract negotiations easier?

4. Appraise César Chávez's 1988 "Wrath of Grapes Campaign" and his 36-day hunger strike in protest over the pesticide poisoning of California's farmworkers and their children. What links were found between pesticide poisoning and cancer? What strategies did Chávez and the UFW use to publicize this issue?

5. Examine the UFW-led campaigns between 2000 and 2009. What issues drive the UFW in this decade? What new strategies have been used by the UFW?

6. Investigate the UFW contract and discuss the contributions made by UFW to U.S. agricultural workers. Be sure to examine such issues as wages, safety, exposure to toxins, and other employee rights that the UFW contract offers.

ALTERNATIVE TERM PAPER SUGGESTIONS

1. Design an interactive Web timeline of the UFW, including the lives of its founders César Chávez and Dolores Huerta. Be sure to offer hyperlinks to the UFW's many campaigns, union initiatives, and court cases. Provide a detailed summary of major events such as the 1965 Delano Grape Strike, the 1988 "Wrath of Grapes" Campaign, the 2002 150-Mile March, and the 2005 Agjobs Congressional bill that failed to overcome a senatorial filibuster.

2. Create an iMovie documentary of a particular strike organized by the UFW. In your iMovie, be sure to provide historical footage as well as a focus on the key issues and participants involved. Provide a bibliography of your sources for viewers interested in researching the topic further.

SUGGESTED SOURCES

Primary Sources

Chávez, César. *The Words of César Chávez*. College Station: Texas A&M Press, 2002. Features a collection of Chávez's major speeches and publications.

Ferriss, Susan, and Ricardo Sandoval. *The Fight in the Fields: César Chávez and the Farmworkers Movement*. New York: Mariner Books, 1998. This companion piece to the PBS video offers photographs, interviews, and an in-depth history of the UFW.

García, Mario, ed. *A Dolores Huerta Reader.* Albuquerque: University of New Mexico Press, 2008. Features a biography of Huerta, as well as her interviews, speeches, and writings.

Secondary Sources

Daniel, Cletus E. "Cesar Chavez and the Unionization of California Farm Workers." In *Labor Leaders in America,* edited by Melvyn Dubofsky and Warren R. Van Tine. Chicago: University of Illinois Press, 1987, pp. 350–382. Chapter offers interviews with and biographical information about César Chávez, along with a focus on the UFW's most successful campaigns.

Gonzales, Manuel G. *Mexicanos: A History of Mexicans in the United States.* Bloomington: University of Indiana Press, 2009. Chapter on the Chicano Movement discusses the formation of UFW, featuring a discussion of its history and a close reading of the Delano Strike.

Jenkins, J. Craig, and Charles Perrow. "Insurgency of the Powerless: Farm Worker Movements (1946–1927)." *American Sociological Review* 42, no. 2 (April 1977): 249–268. Article situates UFW among other collective movements, arguing that such organizations empower agricultural workers who would otherwise be disempowered.

Shaw, Randy. *Beyond the Fields: Cesar Chavez, the UFW, and the Struggle for Justice in the 21st Century.* Berkeley: University of California Press, 2008. Examines UFW's history, focusing on the efficacy of its boycotts, strikes, and collective bargaining as a model for 21st-century organizations.

World Wide Web

"Cesar E. Chavez Foundation." http://www.CesareChavezfoundation.org/. Established in 1993 after Chávez's death, the foundation's Web site offers links to news and events, media resources, and learning resource guides associated with UFW.

Mullikin, M. Christie, and Carol Larson Jones. "Dolores Huerta: César Chávez's partner in Founding the United Farm Workers of America." http://www.csupomona.edu/~jis/1997/Mullikin.pdf. Article focuses on the leadership role of Huerta and other women in labor movements.

"United Farm Workers Official Web site." http://www.ufw.org/. Offers links for news and events, research, and activism along with video and audio clips of historical events.

Multimedia Source

The Fight in the Fields: Cesar Chavez and the Farmworkers' Struggle. PBS, 1997. VHS. 116 minutes. Film offers original footage and interviews with participants in the movement.

43. Cuban Missile Crisis (October 1962)

Wary of an imminent U.S. invasion of Cuba, as had previously occurred during the Bay of Pigs in 1961, the Soviet Union began to construct military sites along the perimeter of Cuba and equip them with nuclear missiles for what was called defensive purposes. U.S. naval reconnaissance aircraft discovered the missile sites on October 14, 1962, and despite Soviet denial, most nuclear warheads had the potential to reach U.S. soil. While Cuba declared before the United Nations its right to defend itself from U.S. attacks, the Kennedy administration carefully weighed its options. On October 22, President John F. Kennedy addressed the United States publicly regarding the discovery of the Soviet missile sites in Cuba. Almost immediately, he placed the military on DEFCON 3, and days later DEFCON 2, and initiated a U.S. naval blockade of Cuba to prevent further missile site material from entering the island nation. Over the next several days, tensions continued to mount as both the United States and the Soviet Union could not come to an acceptable resolution. Through public and private diplomatic channels, both the White House and the Kremlin continued to maintain their standoff. However, by October 28, Soviet Premier Nikita Khrushchev had agreed to the dismantling of the missiles in Cuba if Kennedy promised to remove missiles in Southern Italy and in eastern Turkey and not interfere in Cuba's politics. Soon after, relations between Cuba and the Soviet Union soured because Fidel Castro had been left completely out of the crisis negotiating process.

TERM PAPER SUGGESTIONS

1. When discussing the Cuban Missile Crisis, historians and Cold War experts tend to focus on the role the United States and Soviet governments played during the event. Write a report from the perspective of Cuba during the crisis, underscoring the role that Castro and his leaders played and what effect this was having throughout Cuba.

2. Although the United States was very close to engaging in a nuclear conflict with the Soviets, explain how diplomatic channels were used to avert a war. What compromises were made by all nations involved? How did this impact the climate of the Cold War and U.S./Soviet relations?

3. Although Castro was not completely in support of missile installations in Cuba, he believed that this was a viable solution to curtail future U.S. invasions of the island. Likewise, Khrushchev argued that U.S. nuclear warheads were geographically close to his nation and by placing Soviet ones close to the United States, a balance of power could be achieved during the Cold War. Write an essay arguing for the strategic necessity of placing missiles in Cuba for both the protection of the island nation and the Soviet Union.

4. From a military point of view, evaluate the varied options the Kennedy administration considered during the October Crisis and decide which alternative courses of action would have been more viable than others given the sensitive political and cultural implications between the United States and Soviet Union during the Cold War.

ALTERNATIVE TERM PAPER SUGGESTIONS

1. Create an iMovie with historical video clips and commentary evaluating the nuclear crisis in Cuba. Use excerpts from speeches and images from documentaries and streaming videos to convey your presentation.

2. Design an interactive timeline with hyperlinks that provide textual detail of the events that transpired during the Cuban Missile Crisis. Include photographs to establish visual context, too.

SUGGESTED SOURCES

Primary Sources

"The Cuban Missile Crisis, 1962: The Photographs." http://www.gwu.edu/~nsarchiv/nsa/cuba_mis_cri/photos.htm. Contains the actual images taken by U-2 planes during reconnaissance missions over Cuba between August and November 1962.

Kennedy, Robert, and Arthur Schlesinger. *Thirteen Days: A Memoir of the Cuban Missile Crisis.* New York: W.W. Norton, 1999. Discusses the intricate and complex decisions that were made by the Kennedy administration during the intense days of the crisis, emphasizing Robert Kennedy's pivotal role.

"The World on the Brink: John F. Kennedy and the Cuban Missile Crisis." http://www.jfklibrary.org/jfkl/cmc/cmc_correspondence.html. Features a collection of the correspondence between Kennedy and Khrushchev during October 1962.

Secondary Sources

Dobbs, Michael. *One Minute to Midnight: Kennedy, Khrushchev, and Castro on the Brink of Nuclear War.* New York: Knopf, 2008. Reveals that the United States was closer to a nuclear exchange with the Soviet Union than the public imagined.

Fursenko, Aleksandr, and Timothy J. Naftali. *One Hell of a Gamble: Khrushchev, Castro, and Kennedy, 1958–1964: The Secret History of the Cuban Missile Crisis.* New York: W.W. Norton, 1998. Explores the documents of previously sealed archives from the Soviet Politburo and provides a behind-the-scenes investigation from the Kremlin to the White House to Havana.

Munton, Don, and David A. Welch. *The Cuban Missile Crisis: A Concise History.* New York: Oxford University Press, 2006. Crisis is examined from the perspectives of the United States, the Soviet Union, and Cuba to provide insight into and context for the event.

World Wide Web

"Castro Shows at Cuban Missile Crisis Film." http://www.latinamericanstudies.org/kennedy/costner.htm. Details Fidel Castro's 2001 screening of and thoughts on Kevin Costner's film *Thirteen Days* about the crisis.

"Cuba, Castro, and the Cuban Missile Crisis." http://www.globalsecurity.org/wmd/library/report/1995/LMM.htm. A lengthy report by Lt. Col. Maureen Lynch focuses on Cuba's role during the crisis and sheds light on how U.S. policy has evolved with Cuba since the Kennedy administration.

"The Cuban Missile Crisis: Fourteen Days in October." http://library.thinkquest.org/11046/days/index.html. Presents an overview of the event with links to Kennedy's October 22 speech to the nation and reconnaissance images and maps of the Soviet missile sites.

"Thirteen Days and History." http://www.cubanmissilecrisis.org/. Comprehensive site from Harvard University provides historical context for the film *Thirteen Days* and includes an outstanding series of links to bibliographic sources pertaining to the crisis.

Multimedia Sources

"American Rhetoric: Top 100 Speeches." http://www.americanrhetoric.com/speeches/jfkcubanmissilecrisis.html. Includes President Kennedy's October 22, 1962 address to the nation regarding the discovery of Soviet missile sites on Cuba and a transcript of the same speech.

"Audio Clips from the Kennedy White House." http://www.gwu.edu/~nsarchiv/nsa/cuba_mis_cri/audio.htm. Provides audio clips from the Kennedys

and key Cabinet members during the crisis, accompanied by brief introductions and background information regarding these clips.

"The Cuban Missile Crisis, October 18–29, 1962." http://www.globalsecurity.org/
wmd/library/report/1995/LMM.htm. Comprises a detailed timeline of
the conflict with audio clips interspersed for additional historical context.

44. El Teatro Campesino Founded (1965)

Established by Luis Valdez, El Teatro Campesino, or the Farmworkers'
Theater, emerged out of the United Farm Workers Association during the
mid-1960s to generate pride in Chicano art and culture. Originally, the
theater company was located in the Delano region of California's central
valley. However, by 1971, the company relocated to San Juan Bautista further north, and it continues to host live performances while sponsoring
workshops and venues that promote Chicano culture. The first troupe
members, who were often local farmworkers, would perform *actos* (one-act
plays) on the backs of trucks for their fellow farmworkers in the open
fields. Many of the plays the company performed have been influenced by
medieval dramatic forms of improvisation, such as the 16th century tech-
nique of commedia dell'arte or ritual dramas from Aztec and Mayan civili-
zations. Although the plays themselves were political in nature, humor was
an integral aspect of El Teatro Campesino's work since it helped lighten
many of the difficult experiences farmworkers encountered in their everyday lives. Through parody, the farm owners were depicted as oppressors
who would ultimately lose out to the causes of the workers. Thus, a strong
sense of solidarity was established among workers themselves who participated in or observed the plays, for they were able to recognize the common threads of language, culture, and values they shared as a community.
Throughout his extensive career, Valdez has directed films, written, and
acted in his own plays, and taught at universities, all the while working
through Teatro Campesino to articulate the various identities within the
Mexican American community.

TERM PAPER SUGGESTIONS

1. Many of El Teatro Campesino's plays have been connected with ritual
   dramas from Europe as well as "commedia dell'arte," a 16th-century
   Spanish and Italian method of dramatic improvisation. Discuss the

parallels that exist between Teatro Campesino's "actos" and the influence of medieval drama.

2. Examine *Zoot Suit*, one of Valdez's most celebrated plays, and compare it to the 1981 film version that Valdez wrote and directed. Analyze how these two versions, which are based on the Sleepy Lagoon Trial and Zoot Suit Riots of the early 1940s, present different artistic aspects of these events.

3. Discuss how El Teatro Campesino participated in the political strikes and cultural changes prevalent during the 1960s and 1970s. How did the company move beyond the fields and enter a larger social discourse in the United States? Explain how this involvement helped define the Chicano community.

4. Explore the role El Teatro Campesino plays today in the 21st century. How has its original vision adapted to the transformations in the Latino community and the broader U.S. society? Compare how its role has changed since its inception in the 1960s.

ALTERNATIVE TERM PAPER SUGGESTIONS

1. Create a comprehensive Web site for El Teatro Campesino that incorporates photographs, biographical information, audio and visual clips, your own text, and background that provide an in-depth understanding of how and why this theater company was created.

2. Generate a detailed timeline for El Teatro Campesino that indicates specific events that have served as important marks of transformation and development in the company.

SUGGESTED SOURCES

Primary Sources

"El Teatro Campesino." http://www.elteatrocampesino.com/home.html. The theater company's official Web site.

"Interview with Luis Valdez." http://www.dailymotion.com/video/xhjv7_interview-with-luis-valdez. Video interview of the playwright discusses the background of his theater company.

Valdez, Luis. *Zoot Suit and Other Plays.* Houston, TX: Art Público Press, 1992. Includes four different plays produced by the theater company. Also provides an introduction to the company's history.

Secondary Sources

Broyles-González, Yolanda. *El Teatro Campesino: Theater in the Chicano Movement.* Austin: University of Texas Press, 1994. Explores issues of race, class, culture, and gender in the company's works and provides interviews, original play production notes, and diary selections.

Fava, Antonio. *The Comic Mask in the Commedia dell'Arte: Actor Training, Improvisation, and the Poetics of Survival.* Evanston, IL: Northwestern University Press, 2007. Written by one of the most respected experts on commedia dell'Arte, this work provides extensive discussion and background on this medieval dramatic style.

Huerta, Jorge. *Chicano Drama: Performance, Society, and Myth.* New York: Cambridge University Press, 2000. Contains discussions on the company and critiques its approach to the plays it generates.

Jacobs, Elizabeth. "The Theatrical Politics of Chicana/Chicano Identity: from Valdez to Moraga." *New Theatre Quarterly* 23, no. 1 (2007): 25–34. Articulates the associations between ethnic identity and popular culture and provides background on Valdez's theater company.

Morton, Carlos. "Corridos!! Ballads of the Borderlands." *Theatre Journal* 59, no. 2 (2007): 307–309. Reviews Valdez's play that was performed at El Teatro Campesino Playhouse in 2006.

Sponsler, Claire. *Ritual Imports: Performing Medieval Drama in America.* Ithaca, NY: Cornell University Press, 2004. Includes background information and detail on how ritual dramas and performative historiographies have influenced theater and theater companies in the United States.

World Wide Web

"El Teatro Campesino: An Interview with Luis Valdez." http://www.communityarts. net/readingroom/archivefiles/2002/09/el_teatro_campe.php. Features published transcript of Carl Heyward's 1985 interview with the theater's founder.

"Luis Valdez: 1940—: Playwright, Director, Writer, Actor, Teacher—El Teatro Campesino." http://biography.jrank.org/pages/3230/Valdez-Luis-1940-Playwright-Director-Writer-Actor-Teacher-El-Teatro-Campesino.html. General biographical information includes Valdez's career, memberships, awards, and involvement with the theater company.

"San Diego Latino Film Festival Pays Tribute to Luis Valdez." http://www.sdlatinofilm.com/trends19.html. Discusses the playwright's life and work as well as his vision for his theater company.

Multimedia Source

"Theater—El Teatro Campesino Video Collection." http://cemaweb.library. ucsb.edu/ETCList.html. Includes over 100 streaming videos of speeches related to the theater company and live performances of a number of the company's plays.

45. United States Invades Dominican Republic (April 28, 1965)

Juan Bosch, a former professor of political science, was democratically elected as president of the Dominican Republic in December 1962 after the 30-year dictatorship of Rafael Trujillo ended with Trujillo's assassination in May 1961. The Dominican military grew concerned over Bosch's election because of his communist sympathies and his action that led to the legalization of the Communist Party. Therefore, on September 1, 1963, the senior members of the military, led by Col. Elías Wessin y Wessin, staged a coup and replaced Bosch's administration with a triumvirate that was headed by Gen. Donald Reid Cabral who had the support of the United States. However, the triumvirate outlawed the Communist Party and alienated members of the Dominican military. Angered by the violation of the Dominican Constitution, younger military officers and politicians who supported Bosch established the Rio Piedra Pact on September 25, 1963, calling themselves the Constitutionalists. They directly opposed the triumvirate and marshaled the public to support a general revolt to restore Bosch to his presidency. Likewise, other influential factions in the military community opposed Reid's leadership and eventually ousted him in a secondary coup in April 1964. President Lyndon B. Johnson became concerned over the Dominican Republic's growing instability. These fears were further augmented by reports from the U.S. embassy in Santo Domingo calling for military support for U.S. citizens living in the republic. Not wanting to sit back and watch "another Cuba," as he called it, come to fruition during his term, Johnson decided to invade the country. On April 28, 1965, Johnson ordered over 42,000 marines and paratroopers to enter the Dominican Republic. Although publicly, the administration claimed that the invasion occurred to secure the safety of U.S. citizens, it soon became clear to the U.S. media that Johnson sent troops to prevent the republic from becoming a communist state. With the aid of the Organization of American States peacekeeping force, the United States was able to subdue the revolt throughout the republic, and in July 1966 Joaquín Balaguer took office as the newly elected president.

TERM PAPER SUGGESTIONS

1. Convinced that he did not want the Dominican Republic to become a second Cuba, President Johnson ordered an invasion to suppress a communist takeover of the government. Argue how involved the various factions of the Communist Party were with participating in the Dominican Revolt, and determine how much of a threat they actually were during the political chaos of the 1960s in the republic.

2. Present the fundamental distinctions between the "Constitutional-ists," who supported Juan Bosch's reinstatement, and the "Loyalists," who were backed by the U.S. military. What were their ideological tactics that gained them support? Explain their respective military decisions that fueled the revolt.

3. What impact did President Johnson's decision to invade the Dominican Republic have on public opinion of his governing policies, and how did the invasion affect his role in the Vietnam War?

4. Discuss how the Johnson administration decided to reject the "Good Neighbor Policy" established by Franklin D. Roosevelt in favor of Theodore Roosevelt's "Roosevelt Corollary" as the answer to U.S. foreign policy in the Dominican Republic. Include background on both presidential policies and interpret how the "Johnson Doctrine" enacted the Roosevelt Corollary in the decision to invade and con-tinue policing the Western Hemisphere during the Cold War.

ALTERNATIVE TERM PAPER SUGGESTIONS

1. Prior to the 1965 U.S. invasion of Dominican Republic, the United States had invaded the nation several times throughout the 20th century: 1903, 1914, and 1916. Develop a detailed timeline with hyperlinks that present the situation and aftermath of each of these invasions.

2. Create an interactive map of the Dominican Republic during the Dominican Revolt and the U.S. invasion. Illustrate key areas controlled by various forces and chart the revolt from its start to completion.

SUGGESTED SOURCES

Primary Sources

Buhite, Russell. *Calls to Arms: Presidential Speeches, Messages, and Declarations of War.* Wilmington, DE: Scholarly Resources, 2003. Case number 13 in Chapter 3 includes Lyndon Johnson's explanation for invading the Dominican Republic in 1965.

"Dominican Republic Intervention, 1965: Online Documentation." http://www.history.navy.mil/wars/domrep2.htm. Assembles various official reports from U.S. defense agencies regarding the orders and process of the 1965 invasion.

Secondary Sources

Grow, Michael. *U.S. Presidents and Latin American Intervention: Pursuing Regime Change in the Cold War.* Lawrence: University Press of Kansas, 2008. Consists of detailed descriptions and analyses of Latin American invasions by U.S. presidents. Chapter 4 focuses on the Dominican Republic invasion.

Slater, Jerome. *Intervention and Negotiation: The United States and the Dominican Revolution.* New York: Harper & Row, 1970. Provides a comprehensive overview of the various military and civilian factions involved during the 1965 U.S. invasion.

World Wide Web

"Cascon Case DOM: Dominican Republic 1965–66." http://web.mit.edu/cascon/cases/case_dom.html. Incorporates a map of Dominican Republic and a timetable of the events of what led up to the U.S. invasion and the political aftermath.

"The Dominican Crisis: Intervention by the United States." http://bernard1616.tripod.com/Bernard.html. Includes a detailed, but slanted, account of what brought 42,000 U.S. Marines to Dominican Republic. It also presents the context for the invasion and reports from an eyewitness.

"U.S. Invaded Dominican Republic 44 Years Ago." http://www.dominicantoday.com/dr/local/2009/4/28/31819/The-US-invaded-Dominican-Republic-44-years-ago. Provides a very brief overview of the invasion.

"The U.S. Invasion of the Dominican Republic: 1965." http://fuentes.csh.udg.mx/CUCSH/Sincronia/dominican.html. Contains Salvador E. Gomez's detailed account of the 1965 invasion within the context of earlier U.S. invasions of Dominican Republic in the 20th century.

Multimedia Source

Crandall, Russell. *Gunboat Democracy: U.S. Interventions in the Dominican Republic, Grenada, and Panama.* Princeton, NJ: Recording for the Blind and Dyslexic, 2007. This audio CD presents the invasion of these three nations in a broad context of U.S. foreign policy.

46. National Voting Rights Act (1965)

In 1965, Congress overwhelmingly passed the National Voting Rights Act, a law designed to enforce provisions of the U.S Constitution's Fifteenth Amendment. The Voting Rights Act gave federal oversight of state elections, particularly in areas with high concentrations of minority voters and where minority registration and voting was scarce. Prior to the Voting Rights Act, many states and counties, particularly in the South, employed discriminatory practices that disenfranchised minority voters; unfairly administered literacy tests, grandfather clauses, and poll taxes all served to keep minorities from casting ballots. Although the original 1965 Voting Rights Act is often analyzed for its impact on African Americans, the act also improved conditions for Latino voters as well. In 1975, Congress further expanded the Voting Rights Act to include provisions specifically addressing language-minority groups, with new provisions requiring bilingual ballots and interpreters in districts where language-minority groups made up more than 5 percent of the population or 10,000 people. Although it remains one of the most court-contested pieces of legislation, the Voting Rights Act is also considered landmark legislation, which has increased minority voting and civil rights exponentially.

TERM PAPER SUGGESTIONS

1. Investigate the commonplace discriminatory practices against voters of color prior to the Voting Rights Act. How did discriminatory practices, such as poll taxes, grandfather clauses, and literacy tests, all serve to disenfranchise people of color? How did the Voting Rights Act alter conditions for Latino voters specifically?

2. Examine the connection between the U.S. Constitution's Fifteenth Amendment and the Voting Rights Act. Take a position on whether

the Voting Rights Act is the legislative enforcement of the amendment or whether the act places an undue burden on states.

3. Analyze how the Voting Rights Act of 1965 impacted Latino voters. What changes occurred in the number of voters and the number of those registering to vote? How did the act's language provisions impact Latinos?

4. Assess each section of the act and explain why some of the provisions are permanent and some require reauthorization from Congress. Be sure to discuss Congress' extensions and amendments to the act, including the 2006 and 2007 renewals.

5. The Voting Rights Act has many critics who contest the act for three key reasons: Section 5's preclearance requirements, bilingual balloting requirements, and potential for voting district gerrymandering. Investigate these concerns and take a position on the validity of their criticisms and whether the Voting Rights Act is still needed today.

6. Examine a court case that has arisen as a result of challenges to or enforcement of the Voting Rights Act such as *Terry v. Adams, Bartlett v. Strickland, Allen v. State Board of Election*, or *Northwest Austin Municipal Utility Number One v. Holder*. Be sure to discuss how the case impacted or was impacted by the Voting Rights Act.

ALTERNATIVE TERM PAPER SUGGESTIONS

1. Although some sections of the Voting Rights Act are permanent, others, such as Section 5, require reauthorization. Imagine you are an attorney asked to argue for or against Section 5's renewal. Write a brief explaining your position and discussing the reasons this provision is still necessary or why it is no longer needed.

2. Design a PowerPoint presentation that explains the provisions of the Voting Rights Act and its history. In your presentation, be sure to discuss the many legal challenges to the Voting Rights Act and the court cases that have arisen as a result of its provisions.

SUGGESTED SOURCES

Primary Sources

United States Department of Justice. "Civil Rights Division Voting Section." June 19, 2009. http://www.justice.gov/crt/voting/misc/faq.php. Answers frequently asked questions about the Voting Rights Act and its enforcement.

"Voting Rights Act (1965)." http://www.ourdocuments.gov/doc.php?flash=old &doc=100&page=transcript. Contains the law as written by the 89th Session of Congress.

Secondary Sources

Epstein, David, et al. *The Future of the Voting Rights Act.* New York: Russell Sage Foundation, 2006. Focuses on a wide range of topics related to the Voting Rights Act.

Grofman, Bernard, and Chandler Davidson, eds. *Controversies in Minority Voting: The Voting Rights Act in Perspective.* Washington, DC: Brookings Institution Press, 1992. Offers 17 chapters devoted to different aspects of the Voting Rights Act, along with an appendix containing the law and an index of legal cases central to the act.

Hudson, David M. *Along Racial Lines: Consequences of the 1965 Voting Rights Act.* New York: Peter Lang, 1998. Focuses on the court interpretations of the Voting Rights Act. Hudson provides a sociological investigation of the law's impact on voting in Latino, African American, and Native American communities.

Thernstrom, Abigail. *Voting Rights—and Wrongs: The Elusive Quest for Racial Fair Elections.* Washington, DC: American Enterprise Institute, 2009. Thernstrom's book focuses on the connection between Barrack Obama's election to the presidency and the court battles surrounding the Voting Rights Act.

Zelden, Charles L. *Voting Rights on Trial: A Handbook with Cases, Laws, and Documents.* Santa Barbara, CA: ABC-CLIO, 2002. Discusses the court cases associated with the Voting Rights Act.

World Wide Web

Ross, Michael E. *The Voting Rights Act Turns 40.* MSNBC.com. http://www.msnbc.msn.com/id/8487686/ns/us_news-race_and_ethnicity//. Ross' article examines the legacy of the Voting Rights Act and offers charts comparing minority voting patterns between 1968 and 2000.

"Voting Rights Act." *A Voice: African American Voices in Congress.* http://www.avoiceonline.org/voting/history.html. Provides a brief overview of the Voting Rights Act's history, a timeline of events, and a summary of legislation and debates surrounding the law.

Multimedia Sources

"Andrew Young and the Voting Rights Act of 1965." *Weekend Edition.* National Public Radio. August 6, 2005. 37:06 minutes. http://www.npr.org/templates/player/mediaPlayer.html?action=1&t=1&islist=false&

id=4788074&m=4788215. Features *Weekend Edition*'s interview with Andrew Young, a drafter of the Voting Rights Act.

"The Voting Rights Act: Past, Present, and Future." *Justice Talking*. National Public Radio. 51:00 minutes. http://www.justicetalking.org/ShowPage. aspx?ShowID=518. Program interviews Voting Rights Act scholars and discusses the act's history and challenges.

"Voting Rights Act Signed." Streaming Video. 1:55 minutes. http://www.msnbc. msn.com/id/21134540/vp/8645974#8645974. Features original television news footage of President Johnson signing this legislation into law.

47. United Farm Workers Grape Boycott (1965–1970)

In 1965, the mostly Mexican American National Farm Workers Association and American Workers Organizing Committee, which comprised Filipino farmworkers, merged to establish the United Farm Workers (UFW) in light of the problems farmworker rights leaders were having with grape growing corporations in California. The UFW was instrumental in organizing farmworkers in California and advocating civil rights. Workers, particularly those associated with the former "Bracero Program," were still being subjected to poor wages, a lack of sanitation facilities, and tents instead of appropriate shelters for entire families who labored in the fields of California's central valley. In an effort to strengthen their position against grape companies who were exploiting workers, the UFW initiated boycotts of specific companies. In 1967, a boycott was organized against Giumarra Vineyard Corporation, which was California's largest grape producer. It became known as the Delano Grape Boycott, after the central valley community in California where the farmworkers were organizing, and was in full swing by 1968. Employing the nonviolent tactics of Mahatma Gandhi and Martin Luther King Jr., UFW leaders such as César Chávez, Dolores Huerta, and Philip Vera Cruz gained national attention for their cause through nationwide marches, consumer boycotts, and labor strikes. Chávez's hunger strikes, in particular, brought the plight of the farmworkers to the media's attention and encouraged nearly 14 million U.S. consumers to boycott the purchase of table grapes. By July 29, 1970, the UFW succeeded in negotiating a contract with grape growers that secured broad rights and benefits to farmworkers. The success of the Delano Grape Boycott continues to be a landmark in Latino history and the civil rights of farmworkers.

TERM PAPER SUGGESTIONS

1. During the Grape Boycott, various labor organizations were established and merged. Identify some of the key organizations in the boycott that were a part of this process and discuss whether this strengthened the ultimate cause, harmed it in some ways, or shifted the movement in different directions.

2. The Grape Boycott provided opportunities for Latinas, such as Dolores Huerta, to emerge as prominent labor organizers. Examine the role women played in the Grape Boycott and how they were able to distinguish themselves in a traditionally patriarchal Latino culture.

3. In 1982, California Republican Governor George Dukmeijian was elected and transformed the agency responsible for executing the Agricultural Labor Relations Act of 1975. It shifted to favor growers rather than labor organizations. How were Chávez and the labor organizations affected by this shift in policy and how did they appeal to the public for their causes?

4. Compare the circumstances and strategies of the UFW's Grape Boycott in 1968 with the Southern Pecan Shelling Company's strike in San Antonio, Texas, that Emma Tenayuca and others led in 1938.

ALTERNATIVE TERM PAPER SUGGESTIONS

1. Establish a timeline of the Grape Boycott that includes photographs and captions of strikers and key participants from labor, government, and religious organizations.

2. Assume the role of Dolores Huerta or César Chávez and create a series of podcasts that are directed toward not only the laborers in your organization, but also the U.S. public. Structure your messages based on the actual words of Huerta or Chávez and rally others to your cause.

SELECTED SOURCES

Primary Sources

"Boycott of Grapes Is Fought on Coast." *New York Times,* September 3, 1968: 60. Brief article discusses retaliatory effort against grape growers in the first year of the strike.

"Grape Boycott Urged." *New York Times,* March 28, 1968: 43. Brief article articulates the UFW's message and appeal to boycott grapes.

Huerta, Dolores. "Proclamation of the Delano Grape Workers for International Boycott Day." http://www.tolerance.org/activity/allies-justice-lesson-viva-la-causa. Part of the *Teaching Tolerance* Web site, the original document created by Dolores Huerta is reproduced in both English and Spanish.

Rosensweet, Alvin. "Albert Rojas Says Pickers Subjugated: Grape Boycott Drive Explained." *Pittsburgh Post-Gazette,* December 5, 1968: 1. Describes point of view of Albert Rojas, a Latino immigrant who participated in the boycott and worked with César Chávez.

Secondary Sources

Araiza, Lauren. "'In Common Struggle against a Common Oppression': The United Farm Workers and the Black Panther Party, 1968–1973." *Journal of African American History* 94, no. 2 (Spring 2009): 200–223. Details how the UFW and Black Panthers established a partnership during the Grape Boycott.

Davis, Barbara J. *The National Grape Boycott: A Victory for Farmworkers.* Minneapolis, MN: Compass Point Books, 2008. A part of the Snapshots in History series, this work profiles the Grape Boycott and is aimed at a juvenile audience.

"Exploring the United Farm Workers' History." http://library.thinkquest.org/26504/. Provides brief account of the Grape Boycott along with photos and links to other UFW resources.

Ferris, Susan, and Ricardo Sandoval. *The Fight in the Fields: Cesar Chavez and the Farmworkers' Movement.* New York: Mariner Books, 1998. This is a companion book to the 1996 documentary of the same title by Rick Tejada-Flores and Ray Telles.

Rose, Margaret. "'Woman Power Will Stop Those Grapes': Chicana Organizers and Middle-Class Female Supporters in Farm Workers' Grape Boycott in Philadelphia 1969–1970." *Journal of Women's History* 7, no. 4 (Winter 1996): 6–36. Profiles Mexican American women in the 1969 Philadelphia Grape Boycott and explores the emergence of Chicana activism in the UFW movement.

Shapiro, Harold A. "The Pecan Shellers of San Antonio, Texas." *The South-western Social Science Quarterly* 32 (1952): 229–230. Details the 1938 strike in San Antonio, Texas, by Mexican Americans and the impact of its aftermath.

World Wide Web

"The Fight in the Fields: César Chávez and the Farmworkers' Struggle." http://www.pbs.org/itvs/fightfields/cesarchavez1.html. Presents over-view of events leading up and including the Grape Boycott. Links to timeline of the boycott's events and pictures of the UFW strikers. Also profiles the Rick Tejada-Flores' documentary with this same title.

"United Farm Workers." http://www.ufw.org/. Official Web site of the UFW offers historical and contemporary articles on the organization, photo-graphs, and videos.

"Veterans of Historic Delano Grape Strike Mark 40th Anniversary with Two-Day Reunion in Delano and La Paz." http://www.ufw.org/_page.php?menu=research&inc=history/05.html. Includes excerpts from speeches given by veteran members who organized and participated in the Grape Strike.

Multimedia Sources

"César Chávez Speaks at Harvard University." http://farmworkermovement.org/media/video/players/boycott.swf. A part of the *Farmworker Move-ment Documentation Project*'s collection, this video clip includes Chávez speaking at Harvard University about the UFW's Grape Boycott and its significance.

The Fight in the Fields: Cesar Chavez and the Farmworkers' Movement. New York: Cinema Guild, 1996. DVD. 116 minutes. Archival footage of Chávez, Huerta, Attorney General Robert F. Kennedy, and Governor Jerry Brown during the Grape Boycott.

48. Immigration and Naturalization Act (1965)

In 1965, Congress passed the most comprehensive revision to U.S. im-migration policy in its history. Sponsored by Senator Philip Hart and Representative Emanuel Celler, the Immigration and Naturalization Act (also known as the Hart-Celler Act) was strongly supported by Senator

Edward M. Kennedy, who saw the bill as a lasting legacy to the Civil Rights Movement. The impetus behind the 1965 Immigration and Naturalization Act was to eliminate long-held immigration policies that favored Europeans. In fact, prior to this 1965 legislation, an estimated 70 percent of all immigrants came from Germany, Ireland, or the United Kingdom. The 1965 Immigration and Naturalization Act abolished the previous system's national origin quotas in favor of a hemispheric system. Under this act, the United States would award 300,000 visas for immigrants on a first-come, first-served basis; 170,000 would be granted to immigrants from the Eastern Hemisphere and 120,000 from the Western Hemisphere, with no more than 20,000 visas awarded to immigrants from any specific country. Additionally, the act established a seven-category hierarchical immigrant preference system that favored family reunification. The bill also, for the first time, established legal language that immigrants should not replace U.S. workers. Amendments to this 1965 legislation have largely held the same standards as this transformative law, although the number of visas awarded annually increased in 1990 to 700,000. Since its passage, the Immigration and Naturalization Act has shifted U.S. immigration demographics considerably, resulting in increasing Asian and Latin American eligibility and changing the face of U.S. immigration for decades to come.

TERM PAPER SUGGESTIONS

1. Examine the changes that the 1965 Immigration and Naturalization Act created for immigrants. How did this legislation alter the earlier immigration laws, such as the 1952 act? How did the law change the composition of immigrants to the United States?

2. Analyze how the Immigration and Naturalization Act resulted in new patterns of immigration, particularly for non-European immigrants and those of Asian and Latin American origins. How did the act alter the ethnic composition of immigrants, and, in turn, the ethnic composition of the United States itself?

3. Discuss the role that the Civil Rights Movement played in the 1965 Immigration and Naturalization Act. What common tenets and interests are manifest in this legislation? How did this 1965 act increase equality and representation for immigrants of color, particularly Latinos?

4. The United States has a long history of exclusionary immigration policies, usually directed toward particular ethnic groups. Discuss the exclusionary policies such as the 1882 Chinese Exclusion Act, the Scott and Geary Acts of the 1920s, the Immigration Act of 1924, and Mexican Repatriation policies of the 1930s. How did these policies serve to restrict the immigration of particular nationalities and ethnicities? How then did the 1965 act serve to reverse this long-standing trend?

5. Examine the 1965 Immigration and Naturalization Act's seven-category preferential system for immigrants. What are the seven categories? How do these categories favor family reunification and how do they lead "chain migration," where the immigration of one family member gives preference to the immigration of another family member?

ALTERNATIVE TERM PAPER SUGGESTIONS

1. Design a timeline and PowerPoint presentation detailing U.S. immigration law, past and present. In your presentation, be sure to discuss the 1965 Immigration and Naturalization Act and how it changed immigration to the United States.

2. Create an iMovie explaining the historical significance of the 1965 Immigration and Naturalization Act and detailing its connections to the Civil Rights Movement as well as its political, social, and economic effects.

SUGGESTED SOURCES

Primary Sources

Kennedy, Edward M. "The Immigration Act of 1965." *American Academy of Political and Social Science* 367, no. 1 (1966): 137–149. Features Senator Kennedy's argument in favor of the 1965 Immigration and Nationality Act.

"President Lyndon B. Johnson's Remarks at the Signing of the Immigration Bill." http://www.lbjlib.utexas.edu/Johnson/archives.hom/speeches.hom/651003.asp. Transcript features President Lyndon B. Johnson's October 3, 1965, speech on Liberty Island, New York.

"Public Law 89–236." http://library.uwb.edu/guides/USimmigration/79%20stat%20911.pdf. Features complete text of the October 3, 1965, law passed by Congress.

Secondary Sources

Chin, Gabriel J. "The Civil Rights Revolution Comes to Immigration Law: A New Look at the Immigration and Nationality Act of 1965." *North Carolina Law Review.* 75 (Nov. 1996): 273–345. Discusses the links between the Immigration and Nationality Act and other civil rights legislation, including the 1965 Voting Rights Act.

Graham, Hugh Davis. *Collision Course: The Strange Convergence of Affirmative Action and Immigration Policy in America.* New York: Oxford University Press, 2003. Examines the connections between and the unintended consequences of Affirmative Action and immigration law.

Reimers, David M. *Still the Golden Door: The Third World Comes to America,* 2nd ed. New York: Columbia University Press, 1992. Details the economic and social history of U.S. immigration, with a chapter devoted to the 1965 act.

Shanks, Cheryl. *Immigration and the Politics of American Sovereignty, 1890–1990.* Ann Arbor: University of Michigan Press, 2001. Focuses on the political and public arguments surrounding immigration with a chapter on the 1965 act.

World Wide Web

Congressional Budget Office. "Immigration Policy in the United States." February 2006. http://www.cbo.gov/ftpdocs/70xx/doc7051/02-28-Immigration.pdf. Discusses the legal history of immigration laws as well as the most current U.S. immigration statistics and laws.

Ludden, Jennifer. "Q&A: Senator Kennedy on Immigration, Then and Now." May 9, 2006. http://www.npr.org/templates/story/story.php?storyId= 5393857&ps=rs. Interview with Senator Edward M. Kennedy focuses on the sociopolitical forces behind the 1965 Immigration and Naturalization Act and its legacy.

"Three Decades of Mass Immigration: The Legacy of the 1965 Immigration Act." *Center for Immigration Studies.* September 1995. http://www.cis.org/articles/1995/back395.html. Online article charts the background and the effects of this 1965 legislation.

Multimedia Sources

"The Immigration Act of 1965 and Its Effects." 4:50 minutes. http://www.youtube.com/watch?v=1qohGn7vM0c. Examines how the act impacted Asian American and Latino communities.

Ludden, Jennifer. "1965 Immigration Law Changed Face of America." *National Public Radio.* May 9, 2006. 11:58 minutes. http://www.npr.org/templates/player/mediaPlayer.html?action=1&t=1&islist=false&

id=5391395&m=5394461. With historical audio clips from Presidents Kennedy and Johnson, radio segment provides a comprehensive overview of the act and its lasting impact.

49. Our Lady of Charity Shrine Founded in Miami, Florida (1966)

Founded in 1966 by Cuban refugees fleeing the aftermath of Fidel Castro's revolutionary reforms, the Our Lady of Charity shrine, or "Ermita de la Caridad," in Miami, Florida, honors the Virgin Mary as the Patroness of Cuba. In 1961, thousands of Cuban refugees sought asylum in Miami. At the same time, a replica of the Our Lady of Charity statue from Cuba was smuggled into the United States and brought to Miami. The Archdiocese of Miami, at the time, began to raise money to build a chapel surrounding the Our Lady of Charity Shrine statue along the shoreline of the Biscayne Bay. This location has geographical and cultural significance because it faces toward Cuba and has long been the site of Cuban refugees arriving by sea. The shrine, which was finally consecrated in 1973, was designed so that every aspect of it reflected the Cuban homeland and heritage. Beneath the shrine's altar is a mixture of soil from the six provinces of Cuba and water from the Florida Straits. One famous mural painted by Teok Carrasco is on the eastern wall with portraits of events from Cuban history, including its Spanish colonial period, the role of patriots such as Fr. Félix Varela and José Martí, and the role of the Roman Catholic Church there. Missing from the shrine is any reference to Fidel Castro and his revolution. The shrine has long served as a spiritual and political center for Cuban Americans. With its detailed liturgical calendar, the shrine sponsors a number of pilgrimages and devotional events throughout the year as a way to keep the Cuban American community throughout the United States unified. As such, the shrine functions as one of the most prominent centers of Cuban American identity. In September 2000, the U.S. Conference of Catholic Bishops declared the shrine a national sanctuary; today, it continues to be one of the most visited shrines in the United States and a predominant site for Cuban Americans to pray for their homeland.

TERM PAPER SUGGESTIONS

1. Compare the two traditional Catholic narratives detailing the Marian apparitions in El Cobre, Cuba, around the 17th century and the Virgin

of Guadalupe outside of Mexico City in the early 16th century. Discuss how both apparitions have become significant symbols of devotion, cultural identity, and political expression for Cuban Americans and Mexican Americans, respectively, especially in the 20th century.

2. In his 1998 visit to Cuba, Pope John Paul II crowned the original statue of Our Lady of Charity, identifying her as Queen and Patron Saint of Cuba. What impact did the pope's visit have for Cuban Americans? How did his attention to the Our Lady of Charity address the deep-seated divide that exists between the Castro regime and the Cuban exiles in Florida?

3. Analyze the dual role that Our Lady of Charity plays as the Marian apparition in Cuba and the Santeria goddess Ochun for Cubans and Cuban Americans who are Catholic and practitioners of Santeria. How does the Roman Catholic Church reconcile the syncretism of Catholicism and Santeria with respect to this Marian devotion?

ALTERNATIVE TERM PAPER SUGGESTIONS

1. Design a PowerPoint presentation that focuses on the artwork, murals, and architecture of the Our Lady of Charity shrine in Miami. Interpret what the images and structures represent.

2. Using relevant images and news footage, create an iMovie that examines the role that the Our Lady of Charity shrine in Miami has played as a sanctuary and political voice for anti-Castro Cubans in the United States by featuring significant events such as the Mariel Boatlift in 1980, Pope John Paul II's Cuban visit in 1998, the Elían González situation in 2000, and others.

SUGGESTED SOURCES

Primary Source

"Ermita de la Caridad—National Sanctuary." http://www.ermitadelacaridad.org/. Official site for the shrine provides current information on activities as well as links to the shrine's history and artwork (in English and Spanish).

Secondary Sources

Davidson, Linda Kay, and David Martin Gitlitz. *Pilgrimage: From the Ganges to Graceland: An Encyclopedia.* Santa Barbara, CA: ABC-CLIO, 2002.

Volume one includes a detailed entry on the Miami shrine and its architectural, historical, cultural, and spiritual significance to the Cuban community in Florida and throughout the United States. A brief bibliography follows.

Sharp, Deborah. "Exiles Find Comfort in Shrine Facing Motherland." *USA Today*, Jan. 21, 1998: 13A. Offers background on part of the shrine's unique architecture and role as a community center for exiled Cubans and refugees throughout the waves of immigration.

Tweed, Thomas A. "Diasporic Nationalism and Urban Landscape: Cuban Immigrants at a Catholic Shrine in Miami." In *Gods of the City: Religion and the American Urban Landscape*, edited by Robert A. Orsi. Bloomington: Indiana University Press, 1999, pp. 131–154. Examines how the Roman Catholic Church has used the shrine to maintain a Cuban exile identity in the United States.

————. *Our Lady of the Exile: Diasporic Religion at a Cuban Catholic Shrine in Miami*. New York: Oxford University Press, 2002. Expansion of Tweed's 1999 article in *Gods of the City*. Focuses on the Our Lady of Charity shrine and how exiled Cubans throughout the United States visit the shrine to pray for their homeland. Also discusses the uniqueness of Cuban American Catholicism.

World Wide Web

"Cubans Honor Our Lady of Charity." http://www.miamiarchdiocese.org/ip.asp?op=H1000090911M. Provides photographs of the annual procession of the Our Lady of Charity statue.

"Our Lady of Charity." http://www.kofc.org/un/eb/en/publications/columbia/detail/printer_friendly/458998.html. Presents a detailed account of the devotion Cubans and Cuban Americans have had for Our Lady of Charity or "La Caridad." Charts the history of the original Cuban shrine in El Cobre, Cuba, devoted to her and the various shrines that Cuban American communities have created throughout the United States to this aspect of the Virgin Mary.

"Shrine of Our Lady of Charity." http://www.catholicshrines.net/states/fl3.htm. Includes a short history of the shrine along with several photographs featuring the artwork that decorates the site both inside and out.

Multimedia Source

"Caridad del Cobre—Our Lady of Charity." http://www.examiner.com/x-7785-Miami-Alternative-Religions-Examiner~y2009m5d18-Caridad-del-Cobre–Our-Lady-of-Charity. Documents the history of devotion to

Our Lady of Charity and compares her with the Santeria goddess of rivers and waters, Ochun. Also includes a slide show of the Miami shrine and a short video of the first shrine in Cobre, Cuba, which ends with Pope John Paul II crowning the famous statue during his 1998 visit to Cuba.

50. INTAR Theatre Founded (1967)

In 1967, Max Ferra founded INTAR, one of the United States' oldest Latino theater organizations. Originally called Agrupation de Arte Latino Americano (ADAL), the name INTAR, derived from an acronym for International Arts Relations, became the organization's new working title in 1977, when INTAR achieved equity status as an off-Broadway theater in New York City. From its origins, INTAR has been instrumental in helping Latino actors and playwrights craft, workshop, and stage their works, and, to date, INTAR has showcased the world premieres of over 70 new Latino plays and the works of over 175 individual composers and playwrights. These accomplishments match INTAR's foundational goals of nurturing Latino artists and producing innovative, diverse Latino plays for the general American public. INTAR is also unique for its production of Spanish, English, and bilingual works written by both Latinos and Latin American artists. INTAR has also formed several interdisciplinary and experimental programs, such as its Actor's Collective, Latin American Gallery, Music Theater Program, and in-school touring productions. Among these programs, INTAR is particularly noted for its Playwrights-in-Residence Laboratory, which was directed by award-winning Cuban playwright Maria Irene Fornes from 1979 to 1992. Through this laboratory, some of the best-known Latino playwrights have developed seminal works, including Cherríe Moraga, Migdalia Cruz, Octavo Solis, Denise Chávez, and Nilo Cruz. Nearly all of today's Latino playwrights have participated in at least one of INTAR's workshops. In 2004, playwright Eduardo Machado replaced Max Ferra as artistic director, and the theater relocated to the Cherry Lane Theatre in New York City. Today, INTAR continues to showcase and develop dramatic works focused on Latino history and culture.

TERM PAPER SUGGESTIONS

1. Discuss INTAR's contributions to Latino theater. What role has INTAR played in staging world premieres of Latino works? How

have the organization's various laboratories and programs helped to further a Latino dramatic presence in American theater?

2. Explain the goals of INTAR's first artistic director Max Ferra in forming INTAR. How are those goals reflected in the organization's philosophy, programs, and productions? What experimental and interdisciplinary approaches did Ferra encourage, particularly in the areas of Latino art history and music?

3. Examine Maria Irene Fornes' contributions to INTAR, particularly through the Playwrights-in-Residence Laboratory. Be sure to discuss Fornes' concept of an "Hispanic sensibility" and the visualization and writing techniques she developed for the lab.

4. Investigate INTAR's cross-theater programs and connections with organizations such as Mark Taper Forum's Latino Theater Initiative and the Hispanic Playwrights Series.

5. Analyze INTAR's contributions to the careers of one or more Latino playwrights, such as John Leguizamo, Nilo Cruz, Cherríe Moraga, Jose Rivera, Luis Alfaro, Carmen Rivera, Maria Irene Fornes, and Josefina López.

6. Analyze how INTAR has been particularly instrumental in helping Latina playwrights achieve an equal voice in drama. Give examples from the Latina playwrights who have worked with INTAR and their interviews regarding this organization.

ALTERNATIVE TERM PAPER SUGGESTIONS

1. Design an interactive timeline and Webography focused on INTAR's contributions to Latino theater, culture, and history. Be sure to mention specific plays and artists involved with INTAR, as well as key programs fundamental to INTAR's mission and success.

2. Create an iMovie describing INTAR's history, accomplishments, and various programs and activities, including its Playwrights-in-Residence, Actor's Collective, Latin American Gallery, and Music Theatre Program.

SUGGESTED SOURCES

Primary Sources

"INTAR Theatre." http://www.intartheatre.org/. The main Web site contains links to its programs, history, and Hispanic residency program.

"INTAR Theatre on Facebook." http://www.facebook.com/pages/INTAR-Theatre/8214964500. Contains links to news articles, photos, information, and events centered on INTAR.

Secondary Sources

De la Roche, Elisa. *Teatro Hispano!: Three Major New York Companies*. New York: Taylor & Francis, 1995. Chapter 1 focuses on INTAR, discussing its history, structure, philosophy, goals, and stages of growth.

Delgado, Maria M., and Caridad Svich, eds. *Conducting a Life: Reflections on the Theater of Maria Irene Fornés*. Lyme, N.H.: Smith and Kraus, 1999. Describes Fornes' workshops for INTAR and her influence on Latino playwrights.

Kanellos, Nicolás. *Hispanic Literature of the United States: A Comprehensive Reference*. Westport, CT: Greenwood Press, 2003. Hispanic drama chapter details INTAR's history and contributions to Latino art, culture, and theater.

Lopéz, Tiffany Ana. "Writing beyond Borders: A Survey of U.S. Latina/o Drama." In *Companion to Twentieth-Century American Drama*, edited by David Krasner. Oxford: Wiley-Blackwell, 2007, pp. 370–387. Discusses the impact of INTAR, particularly Fornes' laboratory, on a wide variety of Latino playwrights and their works.

Ramos-Garcia, Luis A., ed. *The State of Latino Theater in the United States: Hybridity, Transculturation, and Identity*. New York: Routledge, 2002. Discusses INTAR's contributions to 1970s through 1990s Latino theater.

World Wide Web

"INTAR & NYU to Present the 2010 New York Maria Irene Fornes Festival." *Broadway World,* Feb. 19, 2010. http://www.broadwayworld.com/article/INTAR_NYU_to_Present_The_2010_New_York_Maria_Irene_Fornes_Festival_20100219. Discusses INTAR's most recent production.

"INTAR Begins New Season Sunday Feb 15th." *David Gersten & Associates.* Feb. 14, 2009. http://gerstenassociates.wordpress.com/2009/02/14/intar-begins-new-season-sunday-feb-15th/. Offers biographies of the organization's administration and discusses INTAR's relocation to the Cherry Lane Theatre.

"Intar Theatre Records, 1966–004." http://proust.library.miami.edu/findingaids/?p=collections/controlcard&id=126. University of Miami's Cuban Heritage Collection houses INTAR's theater records, which contain photographs, audiovisual materials, posters, and scripts.

Svich, Caridad. "INTAR." http://www.jrank.org/cultures/pages/4011/INTAR. html. Examines INTAR's role in promoting Latino theater worldwide and provides a comprehensive history and bibliography for the organization.

Multimedia Source

"Off Broadway." *The American Theatre Wing Seminars.* February 2005. 90 minutes. http://americantheatrewing.org/wit/detail/off_broadway_02_05. Interview features Eduardo Machado, INTAR's artistic director, discussing the contributions of off-Broadway organizations like INTAR to world drama.

51. Brown Berets Founded (1967)

Originally called the Young Chicanos for Community Action, the Brown Berets were founded in 1967 by David Sánchez, a college student in East Los Angeles, whose growing concern about police brutality and unequal education for Chicanos led him to form the organization. Taking their name from the brown hats and military uniforms members wore, the Brown Berets often used military-like methods to combat social injustices. For this reason, the Brown Berets are often compared with the Black Panther Party, an African American militant community group based in Oakland, California, and Brown Beret founders have acknowledged the Black Panthers' influence on their group. The Brown Berets became famous for their participation in the 1968 Los Angeles Chicano Walkouts. They also drew national attention for the role in the National Chicano Moratorium (an anti-Vietnam protest) and for their takeover of Catalina Island in 1972. The Brown Berets' motto is "To Serve, To Observe, and To Protect," and their Ten Point Program focuses on maintaining U.S. constitutional rights for Chicanos, as well as those rights promised in the Treaty of Guadalupe Hidalgo. Organizational infighting and the arrests of key Brown Beret leaders led to the Los Angeles' group's official disbanding in 1972, yet the Brown Berets maintain an active presence today, through autonomous local chapters throughout the United States.

TERM PAPER SUGGESTIONS

1. Examine the Brown Berets' motto and Ten Point Program. How are the 10 points grounded in the U.S. Constitution, particularly the

Bill of Rights, and the Treaty of Guadalupe Hidalgo? What social and political activities did the Brown Berets participate in that reflect their motto and program?

2. Investigate some of the Brown Berets' political actions in the late 1960s and early 1970s, such as La Caravana de la Reconquista, the Chicano Vietnam War Moratorium, the Catalina Island takeover, the Nuevas Vista Conference, and the Los Angeles student walkouts. How did these actions impact their public image?

3. Discuss the social programs established by the Brown Berets, particularly the free medical clinics in East Los Angeles and Chicago. How did these programs serve to fulfill the Brown Berets' motto and its Ten Point Program?

4. Compare the Brown Berets with the Black Panther Party. How did the Black Panthers serve as a foundation for the Brown Berets? How did these two organizations differ in their philosophies, particularly with regard to socialism and communism?

5. Analyze the connections between the Brown Berets and other Chicano organizations and movements of the 1960s and 1970s, particularly the United Farm Workers Union, Center for Autonomous Social Action (CASA), La Raza Unida, and El Movimiento Estudiantil Chicano de Aztlan (MEChA). How did the Los Angeles region serve as a site for these groups? What divisions and alliances exist between these groups today?

6. Discuss the roles for women in the Brown Berets, including their orchestration of the La Causa newsletter. Did their work challenge conventional notions of the Brown Berets as an organization exclusively for men? What problems did women encounter with sexism within the Brown Berets' organization?

ALTERNATIVE TERM PAPER SUGGESTIONS

1. Create a series of podcasts focused on key Brown Berets' social and political actions. Be sure to include video footage from the National Chicano Moratorium and the Los Angeles High School Walkouts, as well as photos and interviews of key leaders.

2. Create an interactive map showing locations of Brown Beret local chapters. In your map, be sure to note the focus, date of origin, and

major activities of each of the selected chapters, as well as links to their homepages.

SUGGESTED SOURCES

Primary Sources

"National Brown Berets." http://nationalbrownberets.com/. Official national Web site features links to videos on the Chicano Movement, as well as official documents and articles related to the organization's history.

Sánchez, David. "Brown Beret National Policies." In *Latino/a Thought: Culture, Politics, and Society,* 2nd ed., edited by Francisco H. Vázquez. Lanham, MD: Rowman & Littlefield, 2008, pp. 215–242. Offers the 16 articles that represent the Brown Berets' national policies.

———. Brown Power! http://www.networkaztlan.com/history/david_sanchez. html. Sánchez provides an autobiographical history of his experience forming the Brown Berets.

Secondary Sources

Chávez, Ernesto. *¡Mi Raza Primero! (My People First!): Nationalism, Identity, and Insurgency in the Chicano Movement in Los Angeles, 1966–1978.* Berkeley: University of California Press, 2002. Chapter on the Brown Berets discusses the group's origins and major accomplishments.

Espinoza, Dionne. "'Revolutionary Sisters': Women's Solidarity and Collective Identification among Chicana Brown Berets in East Los Angeles, 1967–1970." *Aztlán: A Journal of Chicano Studies* 26, no. 1(Spring 2001): 15–58. Discusses women's contributions to the Brown Berets.

Pulido, Laura. *Black, Brown, Yellow, and Left: Radical Activism in Los Angeles.* Berkeley: University of California Press, 2006. Explores the Brown Berets' connections to other activist groups in Los Angeles in the 1960s to 1970s.

Rosen, Gerald. "The Development of the Chicano Movement in Los Angeles from 1967 to 1969." *Aztlán: A Journal of Chicano Studies* 4, no. 1 (Spring 1973): 155–184. Discusses the Brown Berets' instrumental role in the Chicano Movement.

World Wide Web

Carlson. Mike. "Joining a New Battle: *La Causa* for Brown Berets Switches to the Home Front." *Los Angeles Times,* Nov. 4, 1993. http://articles. latimes.com/1993-11-04/news/ga-52943_1_brown-beret. Covers the Brown Berets' 1990s' reformation to combat gang wars in Los Angeles.

Espinosa, Dionne. "Brown Berets: Philosophy and Influences, Development, Young Citizens for Community Action, La Causa, La Conciencia, Regeneración II." http://www.jrank.org/cultures/pages/3667/Brown-Berets.html. Article discusses the Brown Berets' origins and philosophy.

Fight Back! News. "The Brown Berets: Young Chicano Revolutionaries," Feb. 1, 2003. http://www.fightbacknews.org/2003winter/brownberets.htm. Features an interview with Brown Beret leader Carlos Montes.

"Watsonville Brown Berets." http://brownberets.info/. Oldest local chapter features the organization's history, links to other Brown Beret Web sites, and national news coverage.

Multimedia Sources

Chicano!: Taking Back the Schools. KCET/Galan Productions, 1996. 57 minutes. Documentary focuses on the 1968 Los Angeles and 1969 Denver student walkouts, with particular emphasis on the Brown Berets' contributions.

"Videos: Brown Berets." http://nationalbrownberets.com/videos_brown_berets. National Web site collection of Brown Beret activity in the United States features various regional activities as well as a slide show documentary of the organization.

52. Rudolfo "Corky" Gonzales Publishes "Yo Soy Joaquín" (1967)

Perhaps the most famous of all Chicano poems, "Yo Soy Joaquín" ("I Am Joaquín") by Rudolfo "Corky" Gonzales holds a central place at the forefront of the 1960s' Chicano Civil Rights Movement. The 502-line poem, published in both English and Spanish, became a symbol of Chicano pride and history, and many Chicano organizations opened their meetings with a recital of the poem. What makes "Yo Soy Joaquín" so unique is its use of a Mexican song and storytelling tradition called the *corrido*, a ballad-like structure focused on the life of an infamous person and his or her deeds. Although the Joaquín in the poem references the legendary story of Joaquín Murrieta, a Gold Rush Era "bandit" killed for avenging his wife's rape and murder, "Yo Soy Joaquín" also situates Joaquín as a Mexican American "Everyman," as the poem chronicles events from Mexico's initial conquest to 1960s' discrimination. As with a typical *corrido*, "Yo Soy Joaquín" opens with a description of Joaquín's attempts to survive physically and spiritually in

Anglo society before launching into a history of the Chicano people. The poem details historical injustices and discrimination, as well as famous and infamous figures of Mexican American history such as Emil Zapata, the Espinoza Brothers, and Diego Rivera. Throughout the poem, Joaquín declares himself to be each of these figures, thereby unifying all Chicanos into a singular entity. Near the poem's end, Gonzales calls on Chicanos to unite, take pride, and endure. Both the poem's uplifting tone and references to such a vast array of Chicano historical events, many of which were neither previously discussed nor acknowledged in U.S. educational settings, made the poem incredibly popular among Chicano student and civil rights organizations. Like his poem, Gonzales himself played a pivotal role in forming this new Chicano consciousness. After founding a Chicano organization called the Crusade for Justice, Gonzales led the March 1969 conference of the Chicano National Youth Organization where "El Plan de Aztlán" was written. Today, many scholars credit "Yo Soy Joaquín" for raising Chicano consciousness, which, in turn, made Chicano civil rights progress possible.

TERM PAPER SUGGESTIONS

1. Examine the history of the *corrido* as a storytelling device. How does the *corrido*'s structure function to convey both the life story and a moral lesson? What elements of "Yo Soy Joaquín" do so?

2. Throughout the poem, "Joaquín," (the narrator) claims to be several historical figures. Research the people Gonzales references in "Yo Soy Joaquín." Discuss the role that each plays in Chicano history.

3. Gonzales also references many events in the poem, including Hernán Cortés' conquest of Mexico in 1519 and the Treaty of Guadalupe Hidalgo. Discuss Gonzales' incorporation of these events in "Yo Soy Joaquín." What imagery does Gonzales use to depict these events? How does each contribute to a sense of a united Chicano civilization?

4. Many scholars note that the structure of "Yo Soy Joaquín" begins with a litany of negative moments in Chicano history but ends with the positive statement that Joaquín, the Chicano Everyman, will survive and endure. Trace the poem's subtle transition from pessimism to optimism.

5. Examine the role that "Yo Soy Joaquín" played in the Chicano Civil Rights Movement of the 1960s and 1970s. What influence did the poem and its author have on these events?

6. "Yo Soy Joaquín" was such a popular poem that it was made into a 20- minute film in 1969. Write a review of the film (available online), discussing its visual depiction of the poem's events.

ALTERNATIVE TERM PAPER SUGGESTIONS

1. Create an updated version of "Yo Soy Joaquín" that features people and events from the 1960s onward. Include people and events that you believe are essential to understanding Chicano history.

2. Design a PowerPoint presentation on Rodolfo "Corky" Gonzales and his contributions to the Chicano movements of the 1960s.

3. Using Luis Valdez's 1969 film as an example, create a short iMovie for "Yo Soy Joaquín."

SUGGESTED SOURCES

Primary Source

Gonzales, Rodolfo. *I Am Joaquin: Yo Soy Joaquín; An Epic Poem.* New York: Bantam Books, 1972. Now out-of-print, a Web version of the entire poem can be found at http://www.latinamericanstudies.org/latinos/joaquin.htm.

Secondary Sources

Bruce-Novoa, Juan. *Chicano Poetry: A Response to Chaos.* Austin: University of Texas Press, 1982. Bruce-Novoa's first chapter centers on analyzing Gonzales's poem and its historical references.

Limón, José Eduardo. *Mexican Ballads, Chicano Poems: History and Influence in Mexican American Social Poetry.* Berkeley: University of California Press, 1992. Limón's sixth chapter focuses on "I Am Joaquin," providing a comprehensive analysis of the poem and its place in the forefront of several late 20th-century Chicano movements.

Noriega, Chon A., and Ana M. López. *The Ethnic Eye: Latino Media Arts.* Minneapolis: University of Minnesota Press, 1996. First chapter discusses both the poem and Valdez's film as essential to the Chicano movement.

Vazquez, Francisco H. *Latino/a Thought Culture, Politics, and Society.* Lanham, MD: Rowman & Littlefield, 2008. Vazquez's first chapter offers the poem in its entirety followed by a historical analysis of the images and references Gonzales uses.

World Wide Web

"Chicano Leader Rodolfo 'Corky' Gonzales 1929–2005." http://www.democracy now.org/2005/4/15/chicano_leader_rodolfo_corky_gonzales_1929. Democracy Now's obituary for Rodolfo "Corky" Gonzales features audio and video stream downloads of an interview with Robert Rodriguez about Gonzales' role in the Chicano Movement.

"Exhibit: Rodolfo 'Corky' Gonzales." http://history.denverlibrary.org/news/ gonzales.html. Denver Public Library's 2009 exhibit on Gonzales features photos of Gonzales, a timeline of events, and Gonzales' biography.

Hartley, George. "*I Am Joaquín*: Rodolfo 'Corky' Gonzales and the Retroactive Construction of Chicanismo." http://epc.buffalo.edu/authors/hartley/ pubs/corky.html. Ohio University English professor George Hartley provides this short essay on the role that "I Am Joaquín" played in the founding of the Chicano movement.

"Latino Poetry Review: *I Am Joaquín.*" http://latinostudies.nd.edu/lpr/letters. php?issue=1&letter=2 and http://latinostudies.nd.edu/lpr/letters.php? issue=1&letter=3. Features two letters, one by Javier Huerta and another by Eric Selinger, regarding Selinger's negative review of Gonzales's poem. Both Huerta's disagreement and Selinger's retraction offer critical analysis of the poem's key features.

Multimedia Sources

Chicano! History of the Mexican American Civil Rights Movement Part 1: Quest for a Homeland. NLCC Educational Media, 1996. 82 minutes. Part 1 of this VHS series features a discussion of Rudolfo Gonzales's poem and its place in the Chicano movement.

I Am Joaquin. Dir. Luis Valdez. 1969 (20 minutes). Part1: http://www.youtube. com/watch?v=U6M6qOG2O-o. (9:55 minutes. Part 2: http://www. youtube.com/watch?v=3sCae3qYm9Y. 9:30 minutes). Entire film in two parts.

"I Am Joaquin": A poem recital by Pete Ochoa. Aug. 9, 2009. http://www. mefeedia.com/entry/i-am-joaquin-a-poem-recital-by-pete-ochoa/21678401. This recording from Sacramento Digital Stories, in conjunction with the California State Library, focuses on Pete Ochoa, a performer who has publicly presented "I Am Joaquin" for over 35 years. Ochoa explains his relationship with the poem and its place in Latino history.

"Rodolfo Corky Gonzales: Commemoration." 4:26 minutes. http://www.youtube. com/watch?v=Fpm6wHLGIYU&feature=related. Offers an interview with Gonzales about his work in the Chicano movement.

53. Bilingual Education Act of 1968 (1968)

Introduced by Texas Senator Ralph Yarborough, the 1968 Bilingual Education Act was the first piece of congressional legislation to address the education of minority language speakers directly. Known also as Title VII of the Elementary and Secondary Education Act (ESEA), the Bilingual Education Act established federal funding for bilingual classrooms, teacher training, and curriculum education programs for students with limited English-speaking abilities. Originally, schools could choose whether to apply for the Bilingual Education Act's federal funds, but the Supreme Court case of *Lau v. Nichols* decreed that all U.S. public schools with significant numbers of language-minority students who spoke the same language must be provided with the necessary tools to learn. Subsequent legislation related to the Bilingual Education Act, such as the 1974 and 1988 amendments, further redefined the act's provisions, altering definitions of bilingual education, student eligibility, and expressed goals and standards. In 2001, Congress passed the No Child Left Behind Act, altering ESEA's provisions for bilingual classroom funding and limiting student eligibility, often to one transitional year of bilingual instruction. Today, bilingual education remains controversial, with scholars and critics divided on the funding and success of bilingual classrooms. Historically, however, the Bilingual Education Act exemplifies Congress' first attempt to provide equal education opportunities to language-minority students.

TERM PAPER SUGGESTIONS

1. Investigate the background of the Bilingual Education Act (Title VII). What arguments were made before Congress to demonstrate that bilingual education would benefit language-minority groups, particularly Latinos?

2. Discuss how the 1974 and 1988 amendments to Title VII modified U.S. bilingual instruction. What new definitions and criteria did these amendments provide? How did the 1974 and 1988 amendments broaden who was eligible for Title VII instruction?

3. Explain how the Supreme Court case of *Lau v. Nichols* transformed the 1968 Bilingual Education Act. What changes did the "Lau remedies" make to Title VII?

4. Discuss the role that *Castañeda v. Pickard* played in enforcing the Bilingual Education Act. What role did the courts play thereafter in determining LEP school compliance?

5. Examine the controversy behind the Bilingual Education Act. Why is bilingual education still so controversial in the United States? What arguments and evidence are offered to support these different perspectives on bilingual classrooms?

6. In 2002, Congress passed the No Child Left Behind Act, legislation that altered federal funding for bilingual education. Discuss this act's provisions and its impact on bilingual education. Do you agree or disagree with scholars who argue that the No Child Left Behind Act ended bilingual education in U.S. schools?

ALTERNATIVE TERM PAPER SUGGESTIONS

1. Create an iMovie focused on bilingual education's history in the United States. Be sure to cover pertinent moments such as the 1974 and 1988 amendments to the Bilingual Education act and the 2001 No Child Left Behind Act.

2. Develop a PowerPoint presentation examining and explaining the types of bilingual education learning environments in practice today. How do programs such as double immersion, dual language, sheltered English, late-exit, and transitional English classrooms differ from one another? How do such programs classify minority-language speakers differently? Be sure to explain the often-used terms in bilingual education (such as English as a Second Language (ESL), English Language Learner(ELL), English for Speakers of Other Languages(ESOL) and Limited English Proficiency(LEP)) and which programs have been the most successful.

SUGGESTED SOURCES

Primary Sources

"Elementary and Secondary Education Acts of 1967 (P.L. 90-247)." http://nysl.nysed.gov/Archimages/91341.PDF. Contains the original Bilingual Education Act (Title VII).

"Elementary and Secondary Education Acts of 1974 (P.L. 93-380)." http://nysl. nysed.gov/Archimages/91348.PDF. Contains 1974 legislation amendments to the 1968 Bilingual Education Act.

Secondary Sources

Baker, Colin. *Foundations of Bilingual Education and Bilingualism.* 4th ed. Bristol, UK: Multilingual Matter, 2006. Chapter on "The Foundations of Bilingual Education" covers the act; other chapters discuss the development, effectiveness, and assessment of bilingual education practices.

Engel, Laura C. "Elementary Students and Native Language Instruction." In *The Praeger Handbook of Latino Education in the U.S.,* edited by Lourdes Diaz Soto. Westport, CT: Praeger, 2007, pp. 138–141. Provides a comprehensive overview of the Bilingual Education Act and its modifications.

García, Ofelia, and Colin Baker, eds. *Policy and Practice in Bilingual Education: A Reader Extending the Foundations.* Bristol, UK: Multilingual Matters, 1995. Anthology covers a wide range of political, historical, and pedagogical issues associated with the Bilingual Education Act.

Leibowitz, Arnold H. "The Bilingual Education Act: A Legislative Analysis. 1980." http://www.eric.ed.gov/ERICDocs/data/ericdocs2sql/content_storage_01/0000019b/80/33/0f/b7.pdf. Provides origins and historical analysis of the Bilingual Education Act.

World Wide Web

"Bilingual Education Links." http://jan.ucc.nau.edu/~jar/BME.html. Provides links to an array of educational articles about U.S. bilingual education's definitions and practices.

Crawford, James. "Ten Common Fallacies about Bilingual Education." http://www.ericdigests.org/1999-3/ten.htm. Analyzes bilingual education myths with a comprehensive bibliography.

———. "Obituary: The Bilingual Education Act 1968–2002." http://www.rethinkingschools.org/archive/16_04/Bil164.shtml. Discusses the Bilingual Education Act's nonrenewal, with statistics about its funding and success.

"Double Talk?" PBS http://www.pbs.org/newshour/forum/september97/biling2.html. Features the Sept. 29, 1997, debate between James Lyons of the National Association for Bilingual Education and Ron Unz, author of Proposition 187.

"History of Bilingual Education." *Rethinking Schools Online.* http://www.rethinkingschools.org/archive/12_03/langhst.shtml. Gives a brief history of bilingual education dating back to 1839.

National Association for Bilingual Education. http://www.nabe.org/. Offers links to research, advocacy, publications, and conferences.

Office of English Language Acquisition: United States Department of Education. http://www2.ed.gov/about/offices/list/oela/index.html?src=mr Contains the legal provisions for bilingual education under the No Child Left Behind Act.

Osorio-O'Dea, Patricia. "Bilingual Education: An Overview." June 7, 2001. http://www.policyalmanac.org/education/archive/bilingual.pdf. Congressional Research Service Report contains information on the history, funding, and programs designated by Title VII.

Stewner-Manzanares, Gloria. "The Bilingual Education Act: Twenty Years Later." *New Focus* 6 (Fall 1988): 1–9. http://www.eric.ed.gov/ERIC Docs/data/ericdocs2sql/content_storage_01/0000019b/80/23/2e/28.pdf. Explains how court cases, along with the 1974, 1978, 1984, and 1988 reauthorizations, have modified bilingual education and its funding.

Multimedia Sources

"Bye Bye Bilingual." *Hoover Institution.* 26:48 minutes. http://www.youtube. com/watch?v=j0nbvcoFVTA. Stanford University's Hoover Institution debates the success of bilingual education and English immersion programs.

"A Historical Background on Bilingual Education." 6:01 minutes. http://www. youtube.com/watch?v=0tIppleeIjk&feature=related. Destination Casa Blanca, a Latino political organization, discusses bilingual education's history.

"SFUSD Bilingual Education Lau vs Nichols." *SFGTV San Francisco.* 7:21 minutes. http://www.youtube.com/watch?v=cXhQrJ37gFE&feature= related. Focuses on the changes that *Lau v. Nichols* brought to the Bilingual Education Act.

54. Los Angeles School District Chicano Student Walkouts (1968)

On March 3, 1968, an estimated 20,000 East Los Angeles high school students, along with teacher Sal Castro, walked out of their classes to protest the unfair educational practices and conditions for the area's Latino students. The "walkouts" or "blowouts," as the protests came to be called, lasted one-and-a-half weeks, essentially closing four high schools in Los Angeles, the largest U.S. school system. The walkouts began to protest disparate learning conditions for East Los Angeles' Mexican American students. Prior to their protest, students brought forth to the Los Angeles Unified School Board 36 demands for educational reform. Among these were assertions of racist teachers and inferior educational practices, a critique noting the absence of both Latino teachers and Mexican American history courses, and a call to end school policies that appeared to single out Mexican American students for both punishment and non-college track coursework. In addition to the leadership of several high school students, many college organizations, particularly United Mexican American Students (UMAS), helped to organize the walkouts. Three months later, in June 1968, the Los Angeles Grand Jury had 13 of the participants, including Sal Castro, arrested on charges of conspiracy. Those arrested became known as "The East L.A. 13," and although the charges were later dropped, their arrests fueled the movement further. The walkouts had several lasting effects on the Chicano Movement: they called attention to problems facing Latinos, helped Chicanos to mobilize politically, and ultimately led to national educational reform and to the formation of Chicano studies programs in the U.S. college system.

TERM PAPER SUGGESTIONS

1. Examine the demands made by the Educational Issues Coordinating Committee in their survey brought before the Los Angeles Board of Education. What changes did they seek from the board? Which of those changes have been made since 1968?

2. Discuss the publicity and media tactics that the students used during the walkouts, including the students' meeting with Attorney General Robert F. Kennedy. How effective were these strategies in representing their cause?

3. In 2008, on the 40th anniversary of the walkouts, newspapers published several editorials on the walkouts. Some argued that they were incredibly effective; others took the position that the walkouts changed very little. Investigate the efficacy of the walkouts.

4. Sal Castro, along with several students, was arrested for his role in the student walkouts. Research the civil rights, police brutality, and

constitutional issues surrounding the walkouts, taking a position on these subjects.

5. In 2006, Los Angeles students staged another walkout, this time in protest to a legislative bill with stricter immigration laws. Research this second walkout and compare it with the 1968 events. What similarities and differences are there between the two events?

6. The walkouts are well known for the key role played by women organizers. Investigate the role that women such as Paula Cristostomo, Tanya Mount, Mita Cuaron, Rosalinda Gonzalez, and Vickie Castro played in leading the walkouts. How does their work speak to the larger role women played in the Chicano movement?

ALTERNATIVE TERM PAPER SUGGESTIONS

1. Imagine yourself a student in the Los Angeles School System in February 1968. Write a letter to the board of education explaining why you will or will not participate in the upcoming walkouts in March.

2. Many famous people, including Los Angeles' Mayor Antonio Villaraigosa, participated in the 1968 walkouts. Create a Webography of the key participants such as Antonio Villaraigosa, Moctesuma Esperza, Sal Castro, Harry Gamboa Jr., Vicky Castro, Paula Crisostomo, and Carlos Muñoz. In your Webography, examine how the walkouts impacted their lives and their further contributions to Latino thought and culture.

SUGGESTED SOURCES

Primary Sources

Chicano!: Taking Back the Schools. KCET/Galan Productions, 1996. 57 minutes. Documentary focuses on the 1968 Los Angeles and 1969 Denver student walkouts, featuring interviews with several of the participants and original footage of the events.

Muñoz, Carlos Jr. *Youth, Identity, Power: The Chicano Movement.* New York: Verso, 1989. Muñoz, one of walkout student participants, writes on the strike in Chapter 3, connecting the events in Los Angeles with other movements taking place across the country.

Nava, Julian. *Julian Nava: My Mexican-American Journey.* Houston, TX: Arte Público Press, 2002. As the sole Latino member of the L.A. school board, Nava's 15th chapter concentrates on the walkouts and his reaction to them.

Secondary Sources

Bernal, Dolores Delgado. "Grassroots Leadership Reconceptualized: Chicana Oral Histories and the 1968 East Los Angeles School Blowouts." In *Women's Oral History: The Frontiers Reader*, edited by Susan Hodge Armitage, Patricia Hart, and Karen Weathermon. Omaha: University of Nebraska Press, 2002, pp. 227–257. Bernal's chapter provides a gender analysis of the walkouts with interviews with key female participants.

Donato, Rubén. *The Other Struggle for Equal Schools: Mexican Americans during the Civil Rights Era*. New York: SUNY Press, 1997. Donato's book offers a comprehensive overview of the educational systems, before, during, and after the walkouts.

Haney-López, Ian. *Racism on Trial: The Chicano Fight for Justice*. Cambridge, MA: Harvard University Press, 2004. Second chapter discusses the legal events surrounding the walkouts, particularly the arrest and trials of the "L.A. 13."

Mora, Carlos. *Latinos in the West: The Student Movement and Academic Labor in Los Angeles*. Lanham, MD: Rowman & Littlefield, 2007. Compares the Los Angeles student walkouts in 1968 with those in the early 1990s.

Soldatenko, Michael. "The Mexican Student Movements in Los Angeles and Mexico, 1968." *Latino Studies* 1, no. 2 (2003): 284–300. Article analyzes the walkouts as an example of student self-determination.

World Wide Web

Contreras, Raoul Lowery. "The 1968 Walkout Didn't Matter." March 12, 2008. http://articles.latimes.com/2008/mar/12/opinion/oew-contreras12. Contreras wrote this editorial for the *Los Angeles Times* to discuss the progress still needed in the Los Angeles school system today.

Goodman, Amy. "Walkout: The True Story of the Historic 1968 Chicano Student Walkout in East L.A." http://www.democracynow.org/2006/3/29/walkout_the_true_story_of_the. Features an interview with Esparza about the walkouts; features audio links.

"Interview with Moctesuma Esparza." http://www.hbo.com/films/walkout/interviews/esparza.html. Esparza was one of the original student participants and the executive producer of the film *Walkout*. He discusses both in this interview.

Ochoa, Gilda L. "Pump Up the Blowouts." http://www.rethinkingschools.org/archive/22_04/pump224.shtml. Ochoa discusses the blowouts in their historical context, relating them to other 1960s Civil Rights events.

Multimedia Sources

"Blowout Panel 2." http://www.uctv.tv/search-details.aspx?showID=15024. 129 minutes. University of California Santa Barbara's 2008 Walkout Anniversary Conference featured this panel with Vicky Castro, Harry Gamboa Jr., and other students who led the walkouts.

"Blowout Panel 3." http://www.uctv.tv/search-details.aspx?showID=15025& subject=art. 59:36 minutes. Sal Castro's University of California Santa Barbara 2008 keynote address discusses the L.A. walkouts and their legacy.

Walkout! HBO Films, 2006. DVD. 110 minutes. Features director Edward James Olmos' award-winning drama based on the Los Angeles walkouts.

55. National Council of La Raza Established (1968)

With funding from the Ford Foundation, that National Organization for Mexican American Services (NOMAS) conducted a comprehensive study in the early 1960s on the state of the Mexican American community and ways to address issues of poverty and marginalization. By 1968, those who led the study, which included Herman Gallegos, Julian Samora, and Ernesto Galarza, formed the Southwest Council of La Raza in Arizona. As this organization grew, it became national and changed its name to the National Council of La Raza, then relocating to Washington, D.C. As a nonprofit and nonpartisan organization, the NCLR has been a social and political advocate group for the pan-Latino community throughout the United States since the mid-1970s, having broadened its focus from the Mexican American community. The NCLR has been concerned with issues of health, education, immigration, and housing for members of the Latino community. As the largest Latino organization in the United States, it continues to play a pivotal role in the U.S. political system and establish a voice for the needs, concerns, and welfare of the Latino community. Despite attacks from conservative groups who have called the organization racist, separatist, or elitist, the NCLR continues to remain transparent in its connections with other groups throughout the United States and those who financially support it.

TERM PAPER SUGGESTIONS

1. The NCLR supports a number of education programs and policies that would help not only the Latino youth, but also many underprivileged

students in the United States. One such measure the organization has favored is the DREAM (Development, Relief, and Education for Alien Minors) Act. Explain what this piece of legislation is and why NCLR supports it. Then take a position either supporting or opposing this measure.

2. At the heart of the NCLR's agenda is immigration reform in the United States. Analyze what the current debate is over immigration and present what the NCLR's position is regarding this issue. Articulate your own argument supporting or opposing the NCLR's stance on immigration reform in the United States.

3. What pivotal role did the NCLR play in the 2008 U.S. presidential election? Watch and read about Barack Obama and John McCain's respective appearances at the 2008 NCLR Conference, and chart the two platforms presented by these candidates. What central issues were they emphasizing, how did these candidates envision the place of Latinos in their different visions of the United States, and how did the NCLR respond to these candidates?

4. The organization has been widely criticized by conservative groups and politicians for advocating a separatist agenda and for being anti-United States in its policies concerning immigration and social welfare. Articulate several of the key criticisms aimed against the NCLR and research the organization's responses to them. Determine whether you think the critiques have any merit.

ALTERNATIVE TERM PAPER SUGGESTIONS

1. Assume the role of an important representative from the National Council of La Raza and prepare a series of podcasts that address the criticism the organization has received from other groups and public figures for its agenda and activities. Structure your messages based on responses given by both sides; however, you may include some original positions defending the NCLR.

2. Create several online pamphlets complete with graphic illustrations and captions demonstrating the values and ideals of the NCLR and their positions on key issues.

SUGGESTED SOURCES

Primary Sources

"Mobilizing the Latino Vote: Tapping the Power of the Hispanic Electorate." http://www.nclr.org/content/publications/detail/1398. Offers NCLR's report on the strategies and tactics used to increase political awareness and interest in the 2004 election.

"National Council of La Raza." http://www.nclr.org/. The organization's official homepage provides articles, links, events, and history.

"The *Truth* about NCLR: NCLR Answers Critics." http://www.nclr.org/content/viewpoints/detail/42500/. Features the organization's detailed responses to popular critiques and misconceptions about its policies and activities.

Secondary Sources

Abcarian, Robin, and Nicole Gaovette. "McCain's Turn before La Raza in San Diego," *Los Angeles Times,* July 15, 2008: A-11. Reports on presidential candidate John McCain's speech before the NCLR highlight his platform on border security, economics, immigration, and education.

Jenkins, A. Francesca. "MALDEF Models Teamwork by Joining Forces with NCLR." *The Hispanic Outlook in Higher Education* 18, no. 9 (June 2008): 20–21. Covers Mexican American Legal Defense and Educational Fund (MALDEF) and NCLR's collective efforts to reform education and immigration in the United States.

Marquez, Benjamin. "Mexican American Political Organizations and Philanthropy: Bankrolling a Social Movement." *The Social Service Review* 77, no. 3 (Sept. 2003): 329. Documents the role external funding plays for major Latino organizations in the United States, including the NCLR.

Ramirez, Jessica. "When Hate Becomes Hurt," *Newsweek* (March 10, 2008) http://www.newsweek.com/id/117886. Presents NCLR's campaign to address media outlets that give attention and airtime to ultraconservative anti-immigration groups and spokespersons.

World Wide Web

"A Guide to the Political Left: National Council of La Raza." http://www.discoverthenetworks.org/groupProfile.asp?grpid=153. Offers a critique of the organization and disputes many of its policies as being anti-United States.

"Keeping the Dream Alive: Resource Guide for Undocumented Students." http://www.miracoalition.org/uploads/M9/eZ/M9eZP0hFiHo9839qKlEXpw/NCLR-Student-info-pack.pdf. Explains the role the NCLR has in defining and reaching out to children of undocumented parents in the United States. Provides statistics and strategies for helping these high school students.

"We Can Stop the Hate." http://www.wecanstopthehate.org/. Details NCLR's campaign to address the hateful and violent discourse surfacing around the issue of immigration in the United States.

Multimedia Sources

"Angela Arboleda of the National Council of La Raza." http://www.discover thenetworks.org/groupProfile.asp?grpid=153. Video interview with the organization's Associate Director of Criminal Justice Policy focuses on the judicial system's impact on Latino juveniles.

"Barack Obama at Annual NCLR Conference." http://www.youtube.com/watch? v=M6LuA_S5sP4. Presidential candidate Obama discusses his experience with community action groups at the 2008 conference in San Diego.

Impact of Immigration Raids on Children. Washington, DC: National Cable Satellite Corporation, 2008. DVD. 60 minutes. Profiles the research facilitated by the NCLR on the far-reaching effect raids have on Latino immigrant families and advocacy institutions.

56. California State University Establishes the First Chicano Studies Program (1968)

May 9, 2009, marked the 40th anniversary of California State University Los Angeles' (CSULA) formation of the nation's first Chicano Studies Department in 1968. Originally called the Mexican American Studies Department, CSULA's program sought to redress the invisibility of Chicano culture in U.S. university systems. Demand for the program came from the 1960s' student movements in the Southern California area, and recently created African American studies departments served as blueprints for Chicano Studies. Prior to CSULA's program, few universities had developed curriculum to learn about Latino contributions to U.S. arts, history, or culture, and CSULA's Chicano studies department sought to change that. Other Chicano studies programs, departments, and research centers soon followed, particularly in California and the Southwest. Today, universities across the nation now offer bachelor and graduate programs in Chicano studies. CSULA's own department has expanded to include curriculum focused more generally on Latinos as a whole and now offers majors and minors in Chicano studies, Central American studies, and Mesoamerican studies, as well as master's degrees, and teaching credential programs.

TERM PAPER SUGGESTIONS

1. Explain the origins of Chicano Studies programs, beginning with El Plan de Santa Barbara. How did this conference lay the foundation

for CSULA's own department? How were Chicano Studies departments built from the momentum of 1960s and 1970s student activism?

2. Discuss the key people, events, and organizations responsible for creating and promoting the Chicano Studies Department at CSULA. How did Latino student organizations such as United Mexican American Students (UMAS), and Mexican American Youth Organization (MAYO) provide the impetus for these departments? What contributions did professors such as Rodolfo F. Acuña, Ralph Guzmán, and Carlos Muñoz make?

3. Analyze how Chicano and/or Latino studies programs differ from other college majors in their combination of many different fields of study, namely history, sociology, arts, literature, psychology, and language. How do Chicano Studies departments differ in their focus from more generalized cross-ethnic departments, such as American studies and comparative ethnic studies departments? What unique role does community and community activism play in Chicano studies departments?

4. Chicano studies programs differ considerably depending on their models and curriculum. Compare two Chicano studies departments in the United States today. How, for example, does CSULA's department differ from that of CSUN's, a program started only one year later? In your comparison, be sure to discuss the number of enrolled majors and minors, the departments' histories and the course offerings, and each department's educational focus.

5. Discuss how Chicano Studies Departments have changed in the 40 years since the first department began. How has Chicano Studies grown into Latino studies? What do Chicano studies programs now emphasize for their majors? What role does community activism now play in the departments and the curriculum?

6. Describe how Chicano studies departments have increased the visibility of Latino art, history, and literature in the United States. How did Chicano studies bring visibility to these contributions? What programs, activities, and conferences do Chicano studies departments offer to acknowledge further the contributions of Latinos to U.S. society?

ALTERNATIVE TERM PAPER SUGGESTIONS

1. Create an iMovie detailing the rise of Chicano studies, first at CSULA and then in other universities and colleges nationwide. Be sure to

discuss the growth and changes that have occurred in these programs over the last 40 years as well as the reasons they were initially founded.

2. Write a persuasive letter to a campus school board calling for the formation of a Chicano or Latino studies department for a campus that does not have such a department. In your letter, offer statistics and facts of the local students the program would serve and the courses that would be offered in the department. Be sure to emphasize how such a department would serve the college, the campus, and the community.

SUGGESTED SOURCES

Primary Sources

Chicano Coordinating Council on Higher Education. *El Plan de Santa Barbara.* Oakland, CA: La Causa Publications, 1969. http://www.sscnet.ucla.edu/ 00W/chicano101-1/SBplan.pdf. Outlines the necessity of Chicano Studies Programs and provides several models for forming Chicano Studies departments.

Muñoz, Carlos, Jr. *Youth, Identity and Power: The Chicano Movement.* New York: Verso, 1989. Muñoz, former chair of the CSULA's Chicano Studies, chronicles the program's founding in his chapter, "The Struggle for Chicano/a Studies."

Secondary Sources

Cabán, P.A. "Moving from the Margins to Where? Three Decades of Latino/a Studies." *Latino Studies* 1, no.1 (Mar. 2003): 5–35. Cabán's article discusses the current status of Latino studies departments and the types of educational models they use.

García, Eugene E., Francisco A. Lomelí, and Isidor D. Ortiz, eds. *Chicano Studies: A Multidisciplinary Approach.* Amsterdam, NY: Teachers College Press, 1984. The first book to focus on Chicano Studies theory discusses the departments' origins, organization, and curriculum.

Rosales, F. Arturo. *Chicano! The History of the Mexican American Civil Rights Movement.* Houston, TX: Arte Público Press, 1996. Rosales' chapter on "The Legacy of the Chicano Movement" features the formation of Chicano studies programs in the United States.

Soldalenko, Michael. "Radicalism in Higher Education: How Chicano Studies Joined the Curriculum." In *The Hidden Curriculum in Higher*

Education, edited by Eric Margolis. New York: Routledge, 2001, pp. 193–212. Focuses on the historical events that led to the call for Chicano studies as a college discipline.

World Wide Web

"Department of Chicano Studies at California State University, Los Angeles." http://www.calstatela.edu/academic/chs/. Offers links to course offered and community outreach and events.

"National Association for Chicana and Chicano Studies." http://www.naccs. org. Established in 1972, NACCS holds annual conferences on issues in Chicano studies.

Padilla, Raymond V. "Chicano Studies Revisited." *ERIC: Chicano Studies Occasional Papers.* http://www.eric.ed.gov/ERICDocs/data/ericdocs2sql/content_storage_01/0000019b/80/13/a5/d2.pdf. Discusses the formation of and challenges to Chicano Studies Departments.

Rodriguez, Roberto. "Chicano Studies." *Black Issues in Higher Education,* September 2000. http://findarticles.com/p/articles/mi_m0DXK/is_16_17/ai_66380113/. Rodriguez explores the recent incorporation of a broader Latino studies emphasis in Chicano studies departments.

Multimedia Sources

"Chicana and Chicano Studies Department Video—CSUDH." Video. 9:24 minutes. http://www.youtube.com/watch?v=MCtlAfLP_Mk. Features California State University's Dominguez Hill's video on the history and importance of Chicano studies.

"UCLA Chicano Studies Research Center 40th Anniversary." 3:06 minutes. http://www.youtube.com/watch?v=-llwNYwTaHw. Video contains footage of the student strikes, which led to CSULA's Chicano Studies Department.

57. Mexican American Legal Defense and Education Fund Founded (1968)

One of the oldest nonprofit organizations for Latinos, the Mexican American Legal Defense and Education Fund (MALDEF) originated in 1968 with the goal of serving as the Latino community's nonprofit law firm and educational outreach center. Modeled on the tenets and goals of the National Association for the Advancement of Colored People

(NAACP), MALDEF was founded by four Latino civil rights lawyers, including MALDEF's first executive director, Pete Tijerina, who, with a $2.2 million grant from the Ford Foundation, set out to establish an organization focused primarily on advocating for Latino legal rights in the areas of voting, employment, education, immigration, and political access. MALDEF's first legal victory was *White v. Regester,* the 1973 Supreme court case that challenged a Texas redistricting plan for discriminating against Latino voters. MALDEF was also a key participant in *Plyler v. Doe* (1982), a Supreme Court case that granted Fourteenth Amendment legal protections to undocumented children in the U.S. public education system. MALDEF is also known for its annual Latino State of the Union conference, which gathers key political and business leaders to discuss issues relevant to the Latino community and for its Community Education and Leadership Development program (CELD), which centers on offering free community workshops with instruction on securing access to public education and college admission. In 2008, MALDEF celebrated its 40th anniversary and maintains its headquarters in Los Angeles, California; its program office in Houston, Texas; and regional chapters in Atlanta, San Antonio, Chicago, Sacramento, and Washington, D.C.

TERM PAPER SUGGESTIONS

1. Compare the focus and scope of MALDEF, League of United Latin American Citizens (LULAC), and the NAACP. What similarities and differences are there between these organizations in terms of funding, membership, mission statements, history, and court victories?

2. Explain the educational focus of MALDEF, both in terms of its scholarship and community programs and its emphasis on education as a legal right. What role does MALDEF attribute to education in the betterment of Latino lives? What educational court cases has MALDEF participated in since its founding?

3. Discuss MALDEF's annual Latino State of the Union conference. How are these conferences organized? What key Latino leaders have been invited to speak? What roles do the conferences play in focusing MALDEF's organizational goals for the upcoming year?

4. Examine MALDEF's role in a particular court case focused on Latino civil, voting, and education rights, such as *White v. Regester, Plyler v. Doe, G.I. Forum v. Perry, Velez v. Lindow, Rodriguez v. Malloy,* and *Ramirez v. Desert Community College District.* What arguments did MALDEF make

in the case? How did MALDEF's participation prove instrumental in the case's success?

5. Analyze MALDEF's active role in the 2010 census, discussing the reasons for MALDEF's interest in ensuring Latinos are not under-represented in the poll. What methods and outreach programs, including their infomercials and advertising campaigns, has MALDEF funded to ensure Latino participation?

6. Discuss MALDEF's community programs such as its Community Education and Leadership Development (CELD), Civil Rights Education and Art Toward Empowerment (CREATE!), Immigrant Leadership for Responsible Education and Development (LINDER), and the Los Angeles Multicultural Education Collaborative (LAMEC). What is the goal or focus of each program? What events and outreach activities does each program orchestrate? How do these programs contribute to MALDEF's overall mission?

ALTERNATIVE TERM PAPER SUGGESTIONS

1. Create an interactive timeline for MALDEF, examining pivotal moments in the organization's history. Be sure to discuss MALDEF's leadership and membership, its community outreach programs, its participation in key Supreme Court cases affecting Latinos, and its Latino State of the Union conferences.

2. Imagine yourself to be a political consultant for MALDEF charged with obtaining funding from private organizations such as the Ford Foundation. Design a pamphlet and a fundraising campaign for MALDEF that focuses on the organization's past successes and the current issues and programs MALDEF is championing.

SUGGESTED SOURCES

Primary Source

Mexican American Legal Defense and Education Fund. http://maldef.org/. National web site provides links to the organization's history, mission statement, contemporary legislation, and scholarly resources.

Secondary Sources

Kaplowitz, Craig A. *LULAC, Mexican Americans and National Policy.* College Station: Texas A&M University Press, 2005. The fifth chapter compares

MALDEF and LULAC in terms of each organization's focus and court victories.

Maurilio, Vigil. "The Ethnic Organization as an Instrument of Political and Social Change: MALDEF, a Case Study." *Journal of Ethnic Studies* 18, no. 1 (Spring 1990): 15–31. Article focuses on MALDEF's origins, community participation, and goals.

Navarro, Armando. *Mexicano Political Experience in Occupied Aztlán: Struggles and Change.* Lanham, MD: Altamira Press, 2005. Navarro's book discusses MALDEF's role in political events of the 1960s onward, as well as the organization's relationship with other Latino political groups.

Skerry, Peter. "The Ambivalent Minority: Mexican Americans and the Voting Rights Act." In *Civil Rights in the United States,* edited by Hugh Graham. University Park: Penn State University Press, 2004, pp. 73–95. Examines MALDEF's key role in the Voting Rights Act Reauthorizations.

World Wide Web

Badillo, Miguel A. "MALDEF and the Evolution of Latino Civil Rights." http://latinostudies.nd.edu/pubs/pubs/2005.2BadilloFINAL.pdf. This Institute of Latino Studies article discusses MALDEF's origins and its critical role in securing Latino legal rights.

"Latino Group Holds Its Own State of the Union." National Public Radio. Jan. 27, 2010. http://www.npr.org/templates/story/story.php?storyId=123024713. NPR's interview with MALDEF's President Thomas A Saenz examines MALDEF's third annual State of the Latino Union project.

"MALDEF, ACLU/SC and NDLON File Lawsuit." Feb. 2, 2010. http://www.aclu.org/free-speech-immigrants-rights/maldef-aclusc-and-ndlon-file-lawsuit-challenging-city-costa-mesas-anti. Discusses MALDEF's most recent lawsuit against Costa Mesa City's (California) anti-solicitation law.

Zehr, Mary Ann. "A Scholar's Look at MALDEF's Role in Plyler v. Doe. *Education Week,* Jan. 6, 2007. http://blogs.edweek.org/edweek/learning-the-language/2007/06/a_scholars_look_at_maldefs_rol.html. Focuses on MALDEF's contributions in this pivotal Supreme Court case.

Multimedia Sources

"MALDEF Video Gallery." http://maldef.org/multimedia/video_gallery/. Contains links to over a dozen different podcasts focused on MALDEF.

MALDEF's Channel. http://www.youtube.com/user/maldef. MALDEF's YouTube channel provides video links to MALDEF's most current issues and campaigns, including the 2010 census informercials.

"MALDEF's 40th Anniversary." 7:22 minutes. http://maldef.org/about/40th_anniversary/.Video covers the history of MALDEF from its origins to present.

58. Young Lords Organization Created in Chicago (1968)

Initially composed of Puerto Ricans and their descendants living in Chicago, the Young Lords Organization was informally created in September 1968 as a way to address the urban renewal programs, unfair eviction policies, and widespread police brutality that severely impacted the Puerto Rican community there. Inspired by the Illinois Black Panther Party, Jose "Cha-Cha" Jimenez worked closely with Panther leaders such as Fred Hampton and the Brown Berets to generate a public response to civil rights violations and to inspire community-based programs that would aid deteriorating Puerto Rican neighborhoods. By May 1970, the Young Lords set up a new chapter in New York, calling themselves the Young Lords Party. From the Black Panther Party they adopted formal structures of organization that were highly disciplined in an effort to become more effective in urban neighborhoods and carry out their manifesto called the "13 Point Program and Platform." Believing that Puerto Rico should receive independence from the United States, the Young Lords were also active in their local neighborhoods. Despite being targeted by law enforcement agencies determined to undermine the Young Lords' efforts, they organized and participated in countless marches, sit-ins, and community meetings. At the same time, they sponsored social programs throughout the late 1960s and into the 1970s such as free breakfast programs for children, free medical clinics that could test for tuberculosis and lead poisoning, solidarity initiatives for imprisoned Puerto Ricans, Vietnam Veterans' rights, and cultural events that promoted Puerto Rico's history and traditions.

TERM PAPER SUGGESTIONS

1. Because the Young Lords were active and visible in civic politics, they were constantly the target of the Federal Bureau of Investigation (FBI) and city police investigations and opposition. Discuss the tactics and methodology used by these law enforcement agencies to

block the Young Lords' efforts. What were the effects of this opposition on the organization's ability to maintain their structure and
influence while promoting their 13 Point Program and Platform?

2. Explore some of the key ideologies and values of the Young Lords. Consider some of the specific events and circumstances both in Chicago and
New York to which the chapters were trying to respond during the
1960s and 1970s.

3. The Young Lords were strongly inspired by the organizational tactics
and visibility of the Illinois Black Panther Party movement. Discuss
how the Young Lords generated their own identity as progressive
Latinos based on the Black Panther forum and association with this
community action group.

4. In August 1969, the New York chapter of the Young Lords launched
what they called the "Garbage Offensive." Describe what this campaign
was and argue whether the organization was successful in bringing attention to their causes.

ALTERNATIVE TERM PAPER SUGGESTIONS

1. Using the Young Lords 13 Point Program and Platform, develop a
PowerPoint presentation that incorporates illustrations, quotations from
interviews, and further explanation of what this manifesto meant at the
time it was generated. Compare it with other manifestos or agendas of
similar political groups and organizations like the Black Panther Party or
the Brown Berets that had developed during the 1960s and 1970s.

2. Assume the role of one or more of the Young Lords leaders and prepare
a series of podcasts aimed at addressing the Puerto Rican community.
Structure these messages based on the writings and interviews of these
leaders.

SUGGESTED SOURCES

Primary Sources

Abramson, Michael. *Palante: Young Lords Party.* New York: McGraw-Hill,
1971. Features a collection of photographs and interviews with party
members. This was the first text published about the Young Lords.

Melendez, Miguel. *We Took the Streets: Fighting for Latino Rights with the Young
Lords.* New York: St. Martin's Press, 2003. Written by one of the founding

members of the Young Lords, this work details tactics and ideologies used to promote the organization's agenda.

"Young Lords Party 13 Point Program and Platform." http://www2.iath.virginia. edu/sixties/HTML_docs/Resources/Primary/Manifestos/Young_Lords_ platform.html. Features a copy of the original program for the Young Lords.

"A Young Lord Remembers." http://www.virtualboricua.org/Docs/perez_00. htm. Offers reflections on how the Young Lords Party politicized the Latino community from Richie Pérez, one of the founding members.

Secondary Sources

Pulido, Laura. *Black, Brown, Yellow, and Left: Radical Activism in Los Angeles.* Berkeley: University of California Press, 2006. Chapters 6 and 7 provide a brief analysis on the Young Lords 13 Point Program and Platform as well as positions on gender equality.

Torres, Andrés, and José Velázquez. *The Puerto Rican Movement: Voices from the Diaspora.* Philadelphia, PA: Temple University Press, 1998. Examines pivotal Puerto Rican social and political groups that emerged in New York during the 1960s and 1970s, including the Young Lords Party, the Pro-Independence Movement, and the Puerto Rican Student Union.

Young, Cynthia A. *Soul Power: Culture, Radicalism, and the Making of a U.S. Third World Left.* Durham, NC: Duke University Press, 2006. Chapter 3 includes a detailed section on the Young Lords' contribution as a political action group and advocate for the Latino community.

World Wide Web

"New York Young Lords History." http://palante.org/AboutYoungLords.htm. Features a timeline of the organizations involvement between 1969 and1970.

"Palante, Young Lords." http://younglords.info/. Provides a bibliographic collection of links to primary and secondary sources regarding the Young Lords Party.

"The Past and Present of the Young Lords: A Puerto Rican Social Movement." http://latincul.newark.rutgers.edu/younglords.html. Contains a brief overview on the evolution of the Young Lords Party.

"The Young Lords and Early Chicago Puerto Rican Gangs." http://www.gang research.net/ChicagoGangs/latinkings/lkhistory.html. Part of the Chicago Gang History Project, this site provides detailed history of the Young Lords Party and gang culture among Puerto Rican communities in the United States.

Multimedia Sources

"Latino Education Network Service." http://palante.org/Documentary.htm. Incorporates information on the documentary and book entitled *¡Palante, Siempre Palante; The Young Lords* with a video clip of the documentary. Includes a discussion of the Young Lords organization and additional resources to articles.

"National Young Lords." http://nationalyounglords.com/. Includes poetry, interviews, a timeline, and a series of significant videos charting various cultural, political, and historical elements concerning the Young Lords.

¡Palante, Siempre Palante; The Young Lords. New York: Third World Newsreel, 1996. VHS. 50 minutes. Provides background on this New York group's activities and social legacy through interviews, photographs, archival footage, and music.

59. El Plan Espiritual de Aztlán Drafted (1969)

In March 1969, Rudolfo "Corky" Gonzales' organization, the Crusade for Justice, hosted the National Chicano Liberation Youth Conference in Denver, Colorado. This weeklong conference brought together a collective of young Chicanos to discuss Mexican American civil rights and goals. What emerged from the conference was a document entitled "El Plan Espiritual de Aztlán" (also called "El Plan de Aztlán"). "El Plan Espiritual de Aztlán" takes its name from a poem written and read by Alurista (Alberto Baltazar Urista Heredia) at the conference. The first section of the plan, its preamble or manifesto, features Alurista's poem, which calls for a Chicano brotherhood, "La Raza," to reclaim Aztlán as its homeland. The second section focuses on seven "organizational goals," for enhancing Mexican American "unity," "economy," "education," "institutions," "self-defense," "cultural values" and "political liberation." The final section discusses six actions that the movement can take to realize these goals, including the complete dissemination of "El Plan de Aztlán" and the formation of a Chicano political party. Unlike other documents to emerge from the Chicano Movement, "El Plan Espiritual de Aztlán" is less concrete in its language and its goals. Instead, the plan is focused on providing a sense of ethnic pride and Chicano consciousness. At the heart of this focus is the transformation of Aztlán. Originally, Aztlán referred to the pre-Columbian homeland of Nahuatl-speaking Mexica people, possibly situated on an undetermined area of what is now Texas, Arkansas, and Mexico. "El Plan de Aztlán," and other works inspired by it, resituated Azltán to incorporate the areas the United States obtained from Mexico after the Mexican American War, from Oklahoma and Kansas to California and Oregon. In so doing, the plan transformed Chicanos from immigrants to the area's original inhabitants, creating a sense of ownership and the notion of a collective utopic Chicano homeland in the process.

TERM PAPER SUGGESTIONS

1. Discuss the role of "El Plan Espiritual de Aztlán" in the Chicano Movement. What is the function of the plan? How did the plan influence other historical events?

2. Explain how the concept of Aztlán functions in "El Plan Espiritual de Aztlán." How is the term used to unify Chicanos? How does its usage differ from the Aztlán's original definition?

3. Discuss the use of "nationalism" in "El Plan Espiritual de Aztlán." How does the document define this term? Who is included and excluded by it? How are European Americans portrayed as a result of this definition?

4. Examine the seven organizational goals and the six actions outlined in the plan. Which of these later became priorities for the Chicano movement? Discuss what historical events correlate with these priorities.

5. Several scholars have critiqued "El Plan Espiritual de Aztlán" for its use of masculine and familial terms. Analyze the document's use of "brotherhood," "La Raza," "cultural values," home," and "family." Do you agree or disagree that the plan can be seen as alienating to women, gays, lesbians, and/or individuals with biracial or multiracial backgrounds?

6. Critics have also noted that the plan's poetic language makes it difficult to interpret. Others note how the vagueness of the outlined goals could cause disagreement as to the best course of action. Discuss some of the terms and phrases that could be perceived as vague or difficult to interpret. What wording would you suggest to clarify them?

ALTERNATIVE TERM PAPER SUGGESTIONS

1. Create a PowerPoint presentation on Aztlán as a term, a concept, and a Chicano homeland. Discuss the controversy surrounding these various definitions of the word.
2. "El Plan de Aztlán" and its use of "La Raza" and "nationalism" as unifying terms is highly controversial. Write a letter defending the document.

SUGGESTED SOURCES

Primary Source

"El Plan Espiritual de Aztlán." In Francisco Arturo Rosales, ed., *Testimonio: A Documentary History of the Mexican American Struggle for Civil Rights.* Houston, TX: Arte Público Press, 2000, pp. 361–364. http://student orgs.utexas.edu/mecha/archive/plan.html. The manifesto created by the conference participants contains organizational goals and plans for action.

Secondary Sources

Anaya, Rudolfo A., and Francisco A Lomelí. *Aztlán: Essays of the Chicano Homeland.* Albuquerque: University of New Mexico Press, 1991. All 15 chapters of this book focus on Aztlán and its conceptual emergence from "El Plan Espiritual de Aztlán."

Chávez, John R. *The Lost Land: The Chicano Image of the Southwest.* Albuquerque: University of New Mexico Press, 1984. The chapter, "Aztlán Rediscovered," connects "El Plan Espiritual de Aztlán with a larger portrait of Aztlán as a mythical homeland.

Contreras, Sheila Marie. *Blood Lines: Myth, Indigenism, and Chicana/o Literature.* Austin: University of Texas Press, 2008. The chapter, "The Mesoamerican in the Mexican-American Imagination," discusses the historical and philosophical background of Aztlán.

Jacobs, Elizabeth. *Mexican American Literature: The Politics of Identity.* New York: Routledge, 2006. Jacob's first chapter discusses both the history of the Chicano movement and the gender discrimination in "El Plan Espiritual de Aztlán's" word choice.

Rosales, Francisco Arturo. *Chicano!: The History of the Mexican American Civil Rights Movement.* Rosales' chapter entitled "The Fight for Educational Reform" discusses the Denver conference's origins and events.

Vigil, Ernesto B. *The Crusade for Justice: Chicano Militancy and the Government's War on Dissent.* Madison: University of Wisconsin Press, 1999.

The chapter, "School Protests and Youth Liberation," discusses the vague and poetic wording in "El Plan Espiritual de Aztlán," arguing that these features make the document hard to implement.

World Wide Web

Allen-Taylor, J Douglas. "Wizard of Aztlán." *Metroactive Books.* http://www. metroactive.com/papers/metro/08.05.99/cover/Aztlán-9931.html. This 1999 interview with Alurista examines the poet's reflections on the plan.

"El Movimiento Chicano: The Art of Revolution." http://xroads.virginia.edu/ ~UG01/voss/paper.html. This online essay focuses on the "El Plan de Aztlán" and its role in inspiring Chicano art.

"In Search of Aztlán." http://www.insearchofAztlán.com/preamble.html. Includes photos and commentary on the Denver conference as well as biographies and interviews with some of the conference's most famous attendees.

"Rodolfo 'Corky' Gonzales." http://www.mechacsuf.com/corkynew.html. This page features photos and discussion of the 1969 Denver Conference.

Multimedia Source

Chicano! History of the Mexican American Civil Rights Movement. Part 1: Quest for a Homeland. NLCC Educational Media, 1996. 82 minutes. Part 1 of this series features the Denver Conference.

60. El Plan de Santa Barbara Ratified (1969)

One month after the creation of "El Plan Espiritual de Aztlán," the Chicano Coordinating Council on Higher Education (CCHE) assembled a conference of Chicana/o student and faculty delegates from over 25 California state and community colleges and universities. In April 1969, conference attendees met on the University of California Santa Barbara campus with the goal of outlining the creation of Chicano studies programs in the California college system. *El Plan de Santa Barbara* is the 155-page document produced by the conference. Frustrated with the barriers for Hispanic Americans in higher education, as well as federal Equal Opportunity Programs that focused rather exclusively on African American students, the CCHE sought to establish programs and departments centered on Mexican

American history and culture. In great detail, *El Plan de Santa Barbara* calls for and outlines the formation of such departments and programs, with chapters dedicated to such topics as organizing students, instituting Chicano studies programs, developing recruitment and admissions standards, devising curriculum, maintaining political action, and fostering community involvement throughout the process. What is significant about both the conference and the document is the emphasis on higher education both as an arena for cultural expression and as a lasting solution for Mexican American poverty and cultural isolation. *El Plan de Santa Barbara* is also notable for its role in the founding of El Movimiento Estudiantil Chicano/a de Aztlán (MEChA), a national Chicano student organization whose original by-laws can be found in the book. In May 2009, University of California Santa Barbara hosted a second conference to commemorate the 40th anniversary of this important moment in Chicano history.

TERM PAPER SUGGESTIONS

1. In *El Plan de Santa Barbara*'s manifesto is "Chicanos recognize the central importance of institutions of higher learning to modern progress, in this case, to the development of our community." The written plan also explains the type of education Chicano students should receive. Describe *El Plan de Santa Barbara*'s vision for Chicano studies. What type of curriculum is emphasized in the three program models (Chapters 12 through 14) the plan provides?

2. Discuss the role that *El Plan de Santa Barbara* outlines for student activism. What role in higher education does *El Plan de Santa Barbara* envision for the Chicano community? What role is the community expected to plan in the university system?

3. Prior to the 1960s, "Chicano" was a derogatory term used to describe a lower-classed individual. *El Plan de Santa Barbara* is one of the first documents to redefine and describe the terms "Chicano" and "Chicanismo" as positive. Examine how "Chicano" and "Chicanismo" are being used in the document's manifesto. Why was the term Chicano chosen over Hispanic or Mexican American?

4. At the conference, several separate Mexican American university clubs and organizations were merged into a unified, national Chicano student organization called MEChA. *El Plan de Santa Barbara*'s chapter on "Campus Organizing" explains this process. Discuss some of the benefits

or drawbacks of having a national organization instead of many separate ones.

5. Research the three Chicano studies program and degree models found in *El Plan de Santa Barbara*. Which programs are still in existence? How have these programs changed over the years?

6. In 1996 and 1997, MEChA updated its national constitution. Examine the changes between the new constitution and the one established by *El Plan de Santa Barbara*.

ALTERNATIVE TERM PAPER SUGGESTIONS

1. Create a PowerPoint presentation outlining the history of MEChA. Be sure to include key moments in MEChA political activism and changes that have occurred in the organization since its formation in 1969.

2. Create a short video detailing the importance of *El Plan de Santa Barbara* in the formation of Chicano studies programs and degrees. Be sure to include the historical conditions, such as the Los Angeles Unified School District student walkouts, which influenced faculty and students to plan this conference.

3. In recent years, several individuals and organizations have accused MEChA of promoting Chicano separatism or reverse discrimination. Research this debate online and write a letter to MEChA describing your findings.

SUGGESTED SOURCES

Primary Source

Chicano Coordinating Council on Higher Education. *El Plan de Santa Barbara*. Oakland, CA: La Causa Publications, 1969. This book is now out-of-print, but the complete text can be found online: http://www.sscnet.ucla.edu/00W/chicano101-1/SBplan.pdf.

Secondary Sources

Aguirre, Adalberto, Jr., and O. Ruben Martinez. *Chicanos in Higher Education: Issues and Dilemmas for the 21st Century*. Hoboken, NJ: Jossey-Bass, 1993. Examines some of the challenges facing Chicanas/os in the U.S. university systems, with a historical section on *El Plan de Santa Barbara's* contributions to improving Latino participation in higher education.

Camacho, Alicia R. Schmidt. *Migrant Imaginaries: Latino Cultural Politics in the U.S.—Mexico Borderlands*. New York: NYU Press, 2008. Camacho's chapter, "Bordered Civil Rights," discusses gender inequality present in *El Plan de Santa Barbara*.

Garcia, Ignancio. "Juncture in the Road: Chicano Studies Since '*El Plan de Santa Barbara*.'" In *Chicanas/os at the Crossroads: Social, Economic, and Political Change*, edited by David Maciel and Isidoro D. Ortiz. Tucson: University of Arizona Press, 1996, pp. 181–203. García's article discusses the formation of *El Plan de Santa Barbara* and its complicated educational legacy, particularly for Chicano professors and students in the 1980s.

Mora, Carlos. *Latinos in the West: The Student Movement and Academic Labor in Los Angeles*. Lanham, MD: Rowman & Littlefield, 2007. Mora's second chapter outlines how *El Plan de Santa Barbara* has impacted the struggle to create and maintain Chicana/o studies programs in the California university system.

Muñoz, Carlos, Jr. *Youth, Identity and Power: The Chicano Movement*. New York: Verso, 1989. Muñoz's chapter on "The Struggle for Chicano/a Studies" chronicles the founding of the Chicano Coordinating Committee on Higher Education and the events of the Santa Barbara conference.

Rangel, Javier. "The Educational Legacy of *El Plan de Santa Barbara*: An Interview with Reynaldo Macías." *Journal of Latinos and Education* 6, no. 2 (2007): 191–199. Reynaldo Macías chairs UCLA's Chicana/o studies department. In this interview, Rangel and Macías discuss the original intentions of *El Plan de Santa Barbara* and how Chicana/o studies have moved beyond this seminal document.

World Wide Web

"Common Myths about MEChA." http://www.ohlone.edu/org/lrrc/mecha myths.html. This website debunks popular misunderstandings about MEChA.

"El Congreso's website." http://www.myspace.com/elcongreso. El Congreso, the oldest Latino student association in existence, is the Santa Barbara region's MEChA website. This site offers links to photos, videos, and ongoing MEChA events in the region.

"The Making of MEChA: The Climax of the Chicano Student Movement." http://studentorgs.utexas.edu/mecha/archive/research.html. Discusses *El Plan de Santa Barbara*'s place in the Chicano student movement.

"M.E.Ch.A. de Cornell." http://www.rso.cornell.edu/mecha/Cornell's website offers several links to the history, philosophy, and national constitution of MEChA and includes the manifesto from *El Plan de Santa Barbara*.

"M.E.Ch.A. National web pages." http://www.utpa.edu/orgs/mecha/nat.html. Features the new national constitution, several position papers, and other important documents in the governance of MEChA.

"National M.E.Ch.A." http://wwwnationalmecha.org. The Official National MEChA website offers a national overview of MEChA events and national actions, with links to news articles and archives.

Rodriguez, Roberto. "Chicano Studies: Forging Identity—Development of Chicano Studies as a Discipline." *Black Issues in Higher Education.* Aug. 27, 2009. http://findarticles.com/p/articles/mi_m0DXK/is_n3_v13/ai_18327453/. Rodriguez's article describes the changes that have taken place in Chicano studies since the publication of *El Plan de Santa Barbara.*

Multimedia Sources

"MEChA students, local activists protest Blue Diamond Growers." http://media.www.statehornet.com/media/storage/paper1146/news/2008/03/22/Multimedia/Mecha.Students.Local.Activists.Protest.Blue.Diamond.Growers-3278846.shtml. News clip focuses on one of MEChA's most recent community involvement protests.

"On the 40th Anniversary of El Plan de Santa Barbara: Senior Chicano Studies Faculty Reflections" (Panel 2). 101:30 minutes. http://www.uctv.ucsb.edu/2009/voices/4543Bplan.html. This video of University of California Santa Barbara's 40th Anniversary conference features the November 21, 2008, roundtable discussion of Chicano studies faculty, many of whom attended the original conference.

"Pedro Acevez: MEChA de UW." http://depts.washington.edu/civilr/acevez.htm. Features several streaming video interviews with the former president of MEChA about the organization, the Chicano movement, and the formation of Chicano studies programs in the Pacific Northwest.

61. Santana Performs at Woodstock (1969)

Santana, a San Francisco band named after the Mexico-born lead guitarist Carlos Santana, formed in 1966, three years prior to Woodstock. Although Santana had a small Bay Area following, the band was nationally unknown. This changed after their performance at the Woodstock Music and Art Festival on Saturday, August 16, 1969. As a favor to Santana's producer, Bill Graham, concert organizers added the band to the lineup, making Santana the only group at Woodstock that had not released an album. Playing songs that fused together Latin roots and modern rock, the band took the stage at 2:00 P.M. and played for an audience of nearly 40,000 attendees for 45 minutes. Their extended version of "Soul Sacrifice" is still discussed as one of the concert's finest moments. Their memorable performance and surprise popularity led to a record deal with Columbia music, and their debut album "Santana" appeared that same month. In 1970, Latin-inspired songs such as "Evil Ways" and "Black Magic Woman," reached the Billboard Top 10, returning Latino music and rhythms once again to the mainstream. Since 1972, when the original members of Santana disbanded, the band name has been most closely associated with lead guitarist Carlos Santana who obtained the legal rights to the band name and moved a newly formed group into a new musical direction. Throughout the 1980s and 1990s, Santana focused on creating world music that fused Latin sound with jazz, blues, soul, and salsa musical styles. Carlos Santana and his band also performed at Woodstock '94, an anniversary festival, winning him *Hispanic* magazine's longevity award. In 2000, Carlos Santana returned to top the charts with his album *Supernatural*, which garnered him three Latin Grammy Awards and nine Grammy Awards, including "Album of the Year." In 2003, *Rolling Stone* magazine named him number 15 on their list of "The Greatest Guitarists of All Time." Carlos Santana is still one of the best-known and most influential Latino musicians whose work fuses together many musical traditions.

TERM PAPER SUGGESTIONS

1. Woodstock gave Santana its first national audience. Discuss the importance of the festival in Santana's career and in the history of Latino music.

2. Examine the footage of Santana's Woodstock performance. Discuss the camerawork's focus on the band members and its incorporation of audience members into the footage. How does this camerawork differ from traditional concert footage?

3. Listen to Santana's *The Woodstock Experience*, an album featuring the original lineup and songs played at Woodstock. Analyze the elements of Latin musical rhythms and sound in these songs. How does this create the "Latin Rock and Roll" sound for which Santana is known?

4. Describe the musical departures of Carlos Santana after Woodstock. How does his work in the 1980s fuse jazz and blues with Latin sound?

5. Carlos Santana is known as a collaborative artist who works with other musicians to create new styles and sounds. Examine some of Santana's collaborative musical projects with artists such as Michelle Branch, Run DMC, Babtunde Olatunji, Rueben Blades, and the Neville Brothers.

ALTERNATIVE TERM PAPER SUGGESTIONS

1. In 2008, an interactive museum called the Museum at Bethel Woods opened to commemorate the 1969 Woodstock Music Festival with interactive displays of the concert's legacy. Create a short iMovie and a multi-poster display that features Santana for this museum. Be sure to focus on the band's Latino musical influences and this event's musical legacy.
2. Music scholars often discuss Carlos Santana's incorporation of Latin rhythms and sounds into a variety of standard musical genres, namely jazz and rock. Create a PowerPoint presentation and timeline discussing Santana's work in these genres. Be sure to discuss how each album influenced the musical history of the genre.

SELECTED SOURCES

Primary Sources

Santana: The Woodstock Experience (Remastered). 2-CD set. Legacy/Sony, 2004. Along with live performances, this CD set features the original Woodstock song line-up and alternative takes.

Woodstock: 3 Days of Peace, Love and Music, The Director's Cut. DVD. 184 minutes. Dir. Michael Wadleigh. Warner Home Video, 1970. This Academy Award winning documentary features Santana's live performance at the concert.

Secondary Sources

Graham, Bill, and Robert Greenfield. *Bill Graham Presents: My Life inside Rock and Out*. Cambridge, MA: Da Capo Press, 2004. Chapter entitled "Bringing It All Back Home" features Graham's recollections about Santana's Woodstock performance and includes interview material with Carlos Santana.

McCarthy, Jim, and Ron Sansoe. *Voices of Latin Rock: People and Events That Created This Sound*. Milwaukee: Hal Leonard Corporation, 2004. Several chapters feature examinations of Santana's music and include photos of the band's Woodstock performance.

Morales, Ed. *The Latin Beat: The Rhythms and Roots of Latin Music from Bossa Nova to Salsa and Beyond.* Cambridge, MA: Da Capo Press, 2003. The chapter, "The Hidden History of Latinos and Latin Influence in Rock and Hip Hop," discusses Santana's long-lasting cross-genre musical influence.

Santana, Carlos. "Remembering Woodstock." *Rolling Stone*, August 12, 2009. http://www.rollingstone.com/news/story/29585500/remembering_wood stock_carlos_santana. Carlos Santana discusses his recollections of the festival and his band's performance.

Shapiro, Marc. *Carlos Santana: Back on Top*. New York: Macmillan, 2008. The chapter, "By the Time They Got to Woodstock," recounts the events of the concert alongside personal interviews with the original band members.

World Wide Web

"Carlos Santana Biography." http://www.biography.com/articles/Carlos-Santana-9542276. Biography of both the band and the lead guitarist features links to videos featuring his Woodstock performance.

"Santana: Latin Influence At Woodstock." http://www.woodstockstory.com/santana.html. Along with a clip of Santana playing "Soul Sacrifice," this short article details Santana's contributions to the festival.

"Santana at the Rock and Roll Hall of Fame." http://www.rockhall.com/inductee/santana. Discusses the band's work and has a timeline of its key moments.

"Santana at Woodstock." http://www.youtube.com/watch?v=ojQMTkAYnqY& feature=related. 5:31 minutes. Video clip features Carlos Santana discussing Santana's Woodstock performance.

"Santana's Official Web site." http://www.santana.com/. Features news, tours, photos, and videos of the band, past and present.

Multimedia Sources

"Carlos Santana: At Woodstock." 2:15 minutes. http://video.msn.com/dw.aspx/?mkt=en-us&from=truveo&vid=15ec3695-0d21-4a1e-99ef-c26a7e152b d0&wa=wsignin1.0. Video clip from Bio.com features interviews with the band about the Woodstock Festival.

"Santana Woodstock Restoration Video." 3:13 minutes. http://www.facebook.com/video/video.php?v=231228700376. Details the film and sound restoration of Santana's Woodstock Performance.

62. La Raza Unida Party Founded (January 17, 1970)

The formation of La Raza Unida Party (RUP), the united race/people party, was one of the most significant political endeavors during the Chicano Movement of the 1960s and 1970s. The party encouraged and mobilized thousands of Latinos throughout the barrios to put forward candidates and articulate relevant platforms that would allow for a wider recognition and participation of Latinos in U.S. politics, both locally and nationwide. The party's specific grassroots activism also encouraged greater participation of emerging Latino community leaders. Created during a walkout by Crystal City, Texas, high school students in 1970, RUP was led by José Angel Gutiérrez, who had formed the Mexican American Youth Organization (MAYO) just three years earlier. As a third-party organization, RUP sought to offer an alternative platform and agenda to counter U.S. Southwestern Democratic Party candidates who showed little interest in the needs of the Latino community. Throughout the 1970s, RUP won a number of local elections throughout South Texas and staged three bids for gubernatorial elections throughout the 1970s. More and more RUP chapters began to spread throughout Texas, New Mexico, Colorado, Arizona, Illinois, Wisconsin, and Washington, D.C.; however, each one responded to the individual needs of its community, thus ensuring a loose confederation between the chapters. A pivotal moment in the party's organization occurred during the September 1972 convention in El Paso, Texas, when Gutiérrez won the party's presidency over activist and founder of Crusade for Justice Rodolfo "Corky" Gonzalez, thus resulting in a pronounced ideological split within the party. By the mid-1970s, RUP began to break down and lose membership to other emerging Chicano organizations and political movements. Nevertheless, the party had been successful in forcing the Democratic and Republican parties to restructure their respective platforms and agendas and become more inclusive of Latinos' needs and their participation in the U.S. political arena.

TERM PAPER SUGGESTIONS

1. Discuss the role that La Raza Unida Party played in the 1972, 1974, and 1978 gubernatorial elections in Texas. How did they go about selecting a

candidate and what happened once one was found? How did this candidate conflict with the party platform?

2. Explain the central ideological differences between the two La Raza Unida Party leaders: José Angel Gutiérrez and Rodolfo "Corky" Gonzalez. How does their political split underscore the various interests and agendas within the broader Chicano Movement during the 1960s and 1970s?

3. What transpired during the 1972 La Raza Unida convention in El Paso, Texas? Who were the principal leaders and what was on the agenda? How did the outcome of this convention transform the party and determine courses of action for the Chicano Movement?

4. By the mid-1970s, La Raza Unida Party began to break down and lose momentum. Chart the events and circumstances that led to the Party's eventual decline, but emphasize what it was able to accomplish while active during the early part of this decade.

ALTERNATIVE TERM PAPER SUGGESTIONS

1. Imagine you are campaigning for a local candidate on La Raza Unida Party's ticket. Create a series of campaign posters that promote your candidate and party's platform and develop a podcast that underscores the candidate's agenda.

2. Construct a timeline that charts the momentous events involving La Raza Unida Party's rise to and decline from power. Include photographs, hyperlinks, and background information that provide a comprehensive overview of this important Chicano party.

SUGGESTED SOURCES

Primary Sources

Gutiérrez, José Angel. *The Making of a Chicano Movement: Lessons from Cristal.* Madison: University of Wisconsin Press, 1999. Features a provocative memoir of the beginning stages of La Raza Unida Party from its founder.

"La Raza Unida Organizing Committee—Albuquerque, NM." http://larazaunida. tripod.com/enter.htm. The New Mexico chapter of La Raza Unida's main Web page includes principles and policies.

Secondary Sources

Chávez, Ernesto. *¡Mi Raza Primero!: Nationalism, Identity, and Insurgency in the Chicano Movement in Los Angeles, 1966–1978.* Berkeley: University of California Press, 2002. Chapter 4 provides an in-depth examination of the party's involvement in the Chicano Movement.

García, Ignacio M. *United We Win: The Rise and Fall of La Raza Unida Party.* Tucson: University of Arizona Press, 1989. Charts the formation and eventual disintegration of the party throughout the 1970s.

Muñoz Jr, Carlos. *Youth, Identity, Power: The Chicano Movement.* London: Verso, 2007. Contains extensive sections on the creation and involvement of the party.

Navarro, Armando. *The Cristal Experiment: A Chicano Struggle for Community Control.* Madison: University of Wisconsin Press, 1998. Analyzes one of the early stages of political viability for the Chicano Movement in a small Texas town where La Raza Unida Party emerged.

———. *La Raza Unida Party: A Chicano Challenge to the U.S. Two-Party Dictatorship.* Philadelphia: Temple University Press, 2000. Presents one of the most comprehensive studies into the party's establishment and its organizing methods during the 1970s.

Oropeza, Lorena. *¡Raza Si! ¡Guerra No!: Chicano Protest and Patriotism during the Viet Nam War Era.* Berkeley: University of California Press, 2005. Highlights the struggle the Chicano community had with U.S. participation in the Vietnam War and the role of La Raza Unida Party.

World Wide Web

"Raza Unida Party." http://www.tshaonline.org/handbook/online/articles/RR/war1.html. The Handbook of Texas Online includes a detailed presentation of the party's history and evolution.

"Raza Unida Party Collection, 1969–1979." http://www.lib.utexas.edu/taro/utlac/00102/lac-00102.html. Profiles the University of Texas' archival collection of primary sources from the party and includes a brief historical overview.

"La Raza Unida Party: Mexican American Youth Organization, Chicano Power: The Emergence of Mexican America." http://www.jrank.org/cultures/pages/4057/La-Raza-Unida-Party.html. Offers a lengthy historical background on the party and a useful and extensive bibliography for further research.

Multimedia Sources

Chicano!: The History of the Mexican American Civil Rights Movement. Episode 4 "Fighting for Political Power." Austin, TX: Galán Productions, 1996. DVD. 56 min. Includes a discussion of La Raza Unida Party's formation as a third-party force for political viability in the Chicano Movement.

La Raza Unida. New York: Cinema Guild, 2005. DVD. 32 min. Documents
the first national convention in 1972 and includes important speeches
from party leaders.

63. Chicano Park Founded in San Diego (April 1970)

The history of Chicano Park's origins is intricately embedded in Barrio
Logan, a San Diego neighborhood that has been the home of one of
the largest Mexican American communities since 1940. In the 1950s,
this area was rezoned for industrial use, transforming the neighborhood
into factories and auto junkyards. Subsequently, in 1963, Interstate 5, a
multi-lane freeway, was constructed through the middle of Barrio Logan,
razing an estimated 5,000 businesses and homes and dividing the neighborhood into two districts: Barrio Logan and Logan Heights. Although
the area's residents protested this and the subsequent Coronado Bridge
that was built across Barrio Logan in 1969, they did not prevail. Residents
in 1969 then petitioned the San Diego City Council to convert 7.9 acres
of land beneath the bridge into a park. However, when Mario Solis, a local
resident and member of the Brown Berets, talked with construction workers under the bridge on April 22, 1970, he discovered that the city planned
to build a parking lot for the California Highway Patrol instead. The next
day, the Chicano Park Steering Committee was formed. Organizing fellow
Brown Berets and thousands of participants, the committee and local residents began a 12-day occupation of the area, physically stopping the parking lot's construction. The protest worked and residents won the right to
build Chicano Park on the site. Today, Chicano Park is home to over
73 sculptures and murals featuring images of Mexican American history
and culture. Every April, the steering committee hosts Chicano Park Day
to commemorate the park's founding and to honor participants who create
and save this space.

TERM PAPER SUGGESTIONS

1. Analyze the impact of Chicano Park in Latino history. How was the
   reclamation of this space a victory of the Chicano Movement? How
   has the park functioned as a representative space for Mexican American
   history and art?

2. Compare the founding of Chicano Park with Berkeley's People's Park. How are their histories similar? What role did Latino political activism play in both parks' origins?

3. Discuss the role that the Brown Berets played in the formation of Chicano Park. How was this group instrumental in securing the land for the Barrio Logan community?

4. Chicano Park is home to over 73 sculptures and murals depicting Chicano history. Select a few of these murals and research their connection to historical and mythical figures in Mexican American history. Examine the role that these murals perform in preserving this history.

5. Investigate the history of Logan Heights, describing its origins as a Latino urban space and its transformation after World War II by the San Diego freeway system. How did the founding of Chicano Park reinvigorate the Barrio Logan community once again?

ALTERNATIVE TERM PAPER SUGGESTIONS

1. Create an interactive map of Logan Heights, Barrio Logan, and Chicano Park from origins to present. Be sure to showcase the transformation of this region by key events, such as the introduction of Interstate 5 and the Coronado Bridge. Analyze how these changes altered the area for its residents, socially, politically, and economically.

2. Read and listen to Juan Felipe Herrera's poem, "Logan Heights and the World" and Los Alacranes Mojados' song "Chicano Park Samba." Compare their descriptions of the significant historical events associated with Chicano Park's creation. Be sure to include how each addresses the role of the freeway system above Chicano Park and what the park represents in both works. Play or read both the poem and song for the class to accompany your analysis.

SUGGESTED SOURCES

Primary Sources

"The History of Chicano Park." http://www.chicanoparksandiego.com/. Web site features park photos, history, and virtual tour as well as a discussion of the park's mural restoration project.

"La Tierra Mia—Chicano Park." http://chicano-park.org/ Official Web site for Chicano Park features area maps, history, interactive links, and contact information for the Chicano Park Steering Committee.

Secondary Sources

Avila, Eric. "Turning Structure into Culture; Reclaiming the Freeway in San Diego's Chicano Park." In *The Cultural Turn in U.S. History: Past, Present, and Future,* edited by James W. Cook, Lawrence B. Glickman, and Michael O'Malley. Chicago: University of Chicago Press, 2009, pp. 267–283. Avila's chapter discusses the impact of the park on Chicano identity.

Griswold del Castillo, Richard. *Chicano San Diego: Cultural Space and the Struggle for Justice.* Tucson: University of Arizona Press, 2007. Several chapters feature Barrio Logan and Chicano Park, its history, origins, and role in the Chicano Movement.

Jordan, Jennifer. "Collective Memory and Locality in Global Cities." In *Global Cities: Cinema, Architecture, and Urbanism in a Digital Age*, edited by Linda Krause and Patrice Petro. Piscataway, NJ: Rutgers University Press, 2003. Jordan's article discusses how the park's formation manifested a global Chicano community.

Latorre, Guisela. *Walls of Empowerment: Chicana/o Indigenist Murals of California.* Austin: University of Texas Press, 2003. Latorre's fourth chapter features a discussion of Chicano Park's murals from an art history perspective.

World Wide Web

"Barrio Logan." http://history.sandiego.edu/GEN/projects/178/barriologan00. html. Provides a detailed timeline, maps, and photographs of the area.

Beltran, Raymond. "Restoration Is ahead for Historic Collection of Murals." *La Prensa San Diego*, March 23, 2007. http://www.laprensa-sandiego. org/archieve/2007/march23-07/murals.htm. Discusses the restoration project ahead for the murals in Chicano Park.

"Chicano Park." http://www.carloterlizzi.com/Photojournalism/chicano_park/. Provides jpg photographs of dozens of Chicano Park's murals.

Delgado, Kevin. "Turning Point: The Conception and Realization of Chicano Park" *The Journal of San Diego History.* https://www.sandiegohistory.org/ journal/98winter/chicano.htm. This article from an online journal discusses the history of Chicano Park and the formation of the Chicano Park Monumental Public Mural Program.

Multimedia Sources

Chicano Park. The Cinema Guild, 1989. VHS. 60 minutes. Documentary features the history of Barrio Logan and the formation of the park.

"Chicano Park Documentary." http://www.youtube.com/watch?v=q1Upzodz7cs. 10:07 minutes. Features history and recent footage of the park's murals.

Rebirth of Barrio Logan. Full Focus. KPBS. 2005. 26:39 minutes. http://video. google.com/videoplay?docid=301296838191908483&ei=PkbESormN 4uwqAPFlMiOBg&q=barrio+logan&hl=en#. Local San Diego television show's opening 8 minutes discusses Barrio Logan with historical footage of the demonstrations and an interview with founder and muralist Salvatore Torres.

"Remembering Our Past: The History of Barrio Logan." http://www.mefeedia. com/entry/remembering-our-past-the-history-of-barrio-logan/22957808. Discusses the complete history of the Logan Barrio with resident interviews.

"Scenes of Groundbreaking in Chicano Park." http://www.kpbs.org/videos/ 2009/may/19/4427/#video. Silent film footage captures the original protests and ceremonies.

64. National Chicano Moratorium March (August 29, 1970)

By the start of the 1970s, many Americans had grown disenchanted with the ongoing war in Vietnam. Television had for the first time brought the experience of war's horror and death into the living rooms of families across the nation. Within the growing storm of "*el movimiento*" (the movement), the Chicano activist movement in the United States, came a particular displeasure for the Vietnam War. Mexican Americans throughout the Southwest were angered by the large, disproportionate sacrifice their own communities were making. Unable to participate fully in the predominantly white middle-class antiwar campaigns, Chicano political organizations such as the Brown Berets, El Movimiento Chicano Estudiantial de Aztlán (MEChA), and the Southwest Council of La Raza aided UCLA student leader Rosalío Muñoz in generating the National Chicano Moratorium March on August 29, 1970, in East Los Angeles. Built on a growing wave of Chicano-centered antiwar demonstrations, the Moratorium March in 1970 drew an estimated crowd of 30,000 demonstrators. Despite the peaceful nature of the march, which included food stands, musical groups, and an eclectic roster of public speakers, the Los Angeles Police Department grew concerned that the crowd, most of whom were under the age of 25, could not be controlled and began to break it up once it assembled in Laguna Park. In the wake of beatings, tear-gassing, and hundreds of arrests, three individuals were killed by the police violence, including the popular Chicano news reporter Rubén Salazar, who was well known for his reports on police brutality against the Mexican American community. The tragic outcome of the National Chicano Moratorium March in August 29, 1970, fueled "el movimiento" throughout the 1970s and 1980s and brought about greater political, economic, and educational awareness of and reforms for Chicanos throughout the United States.

TERM PAPER SUGGESTIONS

1. Why did Rubén Salazar, a man not directly connected to the politics of the Chicano movement, become one of its principal martyrs?

2. Discuss the role of former UCLA student body president Rosalío Muñoz in organizing the Moratorium. How was he able to appeal to both established Mexican American activists like César Chávez and more progressive Chicano groups such as the Brown Berets?

3. The Moratorium March on August 29, 1970, was the largest of its kind. Explain how earlier Chicano-centered antiwar demonstrations influenced it.

4. From the perspective of the Los Angeles Police Department, explain what led up to the eventual dispersal of the Moratorium demonstrators. How did the judicial inquest of the "LA Thirteen" shortly after the tragedies of the march impact the general public's perception of the event?

5. In an argumentative essay, discuss how and why many Chicanos felt alienated by the anti-Vietnam War demonstrations that had been taking place throughout the 1960s.

ALTERNATIVE TERM PAPER SUGGESTIONS

1. You are a reporter for a Los Angeles-based newspaper covering the Chicano Moratorium March on August 29, 1970. Describe your experiences and observations, and write an article, either as a news report or an editorial, that details the event.

2. Imagine that you are one of the demonstration organizers for the Moratorium March in 1970. How will you maintain crowd control over the zealous participants so as to avoid setting off the Los Angeles Police Department? Propose a solution that will ensure peace is maintained during the march. Use the following link on the 1999 World Trade

Organization protests in Seattle, WA, as a contemporary model for understanding a multi-organization march and a violent aftermath: http://www.globalissues.org/article/46/wto-protests-in-seattle-1999.

SUGGESTED SOURCES
Primary Sources

Marín, Marguerite V. *Social Protest in an Urban Barrio: A Study of the Chicano Movement, 1966–1974.* Lanham, MD: University Press of America, 1991. Generating an inclusive array of interviews, case studies, and investigations, Marín explores the detailed accounts of urban Chicanos and their socio-political struggle for empowerment and identity during this time of turbulence in American society.

Mariscal, George. *Aztlán and Viet Nam: Chicano and Chicana Experiences of the War.* Berkeley: University of California Press, 1999. Contains comprehensive collection of speeches, articles, poems, and short stories on an array of attitudes and perspectives concerning the impact the Vietnam War had on the Chicano community.

Muñoz, Carlos. *Youth, Identity, Power: The Chicano Movement: Revised and Expanded Edition.* New York: Verso, 2007. Written by a leader in the Chicano Movement (*movimiento*), this text examines the social and political evolution of Chicano protest in the United States from the perspective of multiple generations.

Secondary Sources

Chávez, Ernesto. *"¡Mi Raza Primero!" ("My People First!"): Nationalism, Identity, and Insurgency in the Chicano Movement in Los Angeles, 1966–1978.* Berkeley: University of California Press, 2002. Focuses on four primary Chicano organizations that consolidated the Los Angeles-based Movement (*movimiento*) including the Brown Berets, the Chicano Moratorium Committee, La Raza Unida Party, and the Centro de Acción Social Autónomo and provides an analysis of their ideas and methodologies.

García, Ignacio M. *United We Win: The Rise and Fall of La Raza Unida Party.* Tucson: University of Arizona Press, 1989. García's study provides detailed background into the personalities, events, and ideologies of the "party of the united people" as it developed and dissolved during the pivotal moment in Chicano history.

Hammerback, John C., Richard J. Jensen, and José Angel Gutiérrez. *A War of Words: Chicano Protest in the 1960s and 1970s.* Westport, CT: Greenwood Press, 1985. The authors explore Chicano activism by comparing the rhetorical strategies of speeches and writings from prominent leaders including César Chávez, Rodolfo "Corky" Gonzalez, José Angel Gutiérrez, and Reies López Tijerina.

Oropeza, Lorena. *¡Raza Sí! ¡Guerra No!: Chicano Protest and Patriotism during the Viet Nam War Era.* Berkeley: University of California Press, 2005. Examines how the military and the Viet Nam war made an adverse impact on the Chicano community and addresses issues of service, nationalism, and citizenship.

Treniño, Jesús Salador. *Eyewitness: A Filmmaker's Memoir of the Chicano Movement.* Houston, TX: Arte Público Press, 2001. Noted filmmaker and writer recounts the most pivotal events of Chicano activism between the 1960s and 1970s including the Moratorium March.

World Wide Web

Chicano Draft Resistance: Speech Refusing Induction: September 16, 1969." http://www.yclusa.org/article/articleview/1609/1/296/. This is Rosalío Muñoz's speech against the Selective Service that launched him into the forefront of Chicano politics.

"The Chicano Moratorium, August 29, 1970, Still Remembered after All These Years." http://www.laprensa-sandiego.org/archieve/august26-05/chicano.htm. Committee on Chicano Rights leader Herman Baca recollects his experiences at the march and discusses the transformations that have occurred in the Chicano community at the 35-year anniversary of the event.

"Heroes of La Raza Series: Rubén Salazar." http://www.aztlan.net/default3.htm. Provides a brief biography of the life and career of this slain journalist.

"The National Chicano Moratorium Committee." http://committeeonraza-rights.org/ncmc/mainindex.html. Originally founded by student activist Rosalío Muñoz and others who organized the 1970 march, this is now the official Web site for the present committee.

Multimedia Sources

Chicano!: The History of the Mexican American Civil Rights Movement. Episode 1 "Quest for a Homeland." Austin, TX: Galán Productions, 1996. DVD. 56 minutes. This installment includes footage from the Moratorium March and a discussion of the riot and death of journalist Rubén Salazar.

Requiem 29. Los Angeles, CA: National Latino Communications Center Educational Media, 1997. VHS. 31 minutes. Covers the march and scenes from the inquest hearing on Salazar's death. Footage and interviews are included.

65. Nuyorican Poets Café Founded (1973)

The Nuyorican Poets Café is a nonprofit organization dedicated to producing, representing, and delivering Nuyorican (New York Puerto Rican) poetry in Manhattan's Lower East Side ("Loisaida"). Because a large number of Puerto Rican poets and writers felt the need to create a representative body that made the Nuyorican Movement more visible, the Café was founded in 1973 in the New York apartment of college professor Miguel Algarín, and with the aid of fellow playwrights and poets such as Miguel Piñero and Bittman "Bimbo" Rivera. The Nuyorican Poets Café became the official forum for the Nuyorican Movement and has emerged as a principal voice of Puerto Rican art, performance, writing, and music in New York City. It is also host to countless poetry slam competitions and has sponsored numerous poets from a variety of ethnic backgrounds who compete in slam competitions throughout the United States. Of the several centers that have fostered and hosted Puerto Rican poetry in the United States, such as El Caney or the New Rican Village, the Nuyorican Poets Café has determined the direction of much of the writing and artistic expression rising out of the Puerto Rican community. What fuels this movement is the Café community's close association with the street and the everyday world of Puerto Ricans residing in "Loisaida." Today, the Nuyorican Poets Café continues to showcase emerging poets, playwrights, comedians, filmmakers, and artists while connecting those with different racial, class, and ethnic histories to produce a larger experience of urbanism and an understanding of the marginalized American artist.

TERM PAPER SUGGESTIONS

1. Discuss the history and practice of the poetry slam and how the Nuyorican Poets Café has been an important organization for promoting and fostering this movement.

2. Analyze three different poems that emerged from the Nuyorican Poets Café since its founding in 1973. Argue how the poems reveal aspects of Nuyorican culture and the development of identities in New York City. Also, consider how these poems have contributed in their own way to transforming the identity of the Café.

3. Originally established to encourage the endeavors of artists and poets active in the Nuyorican Movement, the Nuyorican Poets Café has crossed ethnic boundaries and has become more inclusive of various artists and performers. Explain how this happened.

ALTERNATIVE TERM PAPER SUGGESTIONS

1. In a PowerPoint presentation, recreate an historical account of the Nuyorican Poets Café from its inception in 1973 to the present day. Demonstrate how it has changed from a forum for the Nuyorican Movement into a cross-ethnic, multimedia stage for art and culture. Use relevant images as well as audio and visual clips to enhance your work.

2. Incorporating recordings from past Nuyorican Poets Cafe poetry slam participants or from other slam competitions throughout the United States, develop a creative iMovie in which you have assembled various poets showcasing this movement.

SUGGESTED SOURCES

Primary Sources

Algarín, Miguel, and Bob Holman. *Aloud: Voices from the Nuyorican Poets Café*. New York: Henry Holt, 1994. Contains a rich collection of poetry promoted by the Nuyorican Poets Café.

Bonais-Agard, Roger, et al. *Burning Down the House: Selected Poems from the Nuyorican Poets Cafe National Slam Champions*. New York: Soft Skull Press, 2000. Anthologizes the poetry from the five-member slam team who competed in 1998.

Kane, Daniel. *All Poets Welcome: The Lower East Side Poetry Scene in the 1960s*. Berkeley: University of California Press, 2003. Includes a 35-track CD of audio clips of poetry readings. Kane's text provides an in-depth examination of the poetry emerging from New York's Lower East Side in the 1960s. It is a collection of historical and culture background, interviews, and unpublished letters. There is a final chapter devoted to Bob Holman and the Nuyorican Poets Café.

Secondary Sources

Abu-Lu, Janet L. *From Urban Village to East Village: The Battle for New York's Lower East Side*. Cambridge, MA: Blackwell Publishers, 1995. This collection investigates the social and cultural conflicts that arise out of sharing cross-ethnic space in the neighborhoods of the Lower East Side. It also includes a chapter on the Puerto Ricans and references to the Nuyorican Poets Café.

Foley, John Miles. *How to Read an Oral Poem*. Urbana: University of Illinois Press, 2002. This is a comprehensive study of Foley's experience with Spoken Word poetry from around the world and includes a chapter on the work emerging from the Nuyorican Poets Café.

Maffi, Mario. *Gateway to the Promised Land: Ethnic Cultures on New York's Lower East Side*. Amsterdam: Editions Rodopi, 1994. Is a comprehensive work that charts the evolution of New York's Lower East Side from the Irish and Germans, to the Chinese and Jews, to the arrival of the Puerto Ricans. More than an historical account, this work explores the integral cultural aspects of this changing community including its theater, music, art, literary productions, and cuisine.

World Wide Web

"Nuyorican Poets Café." http://www.nuyorican.org. Official Web site for the Café includes book lists as well as performance schedules for readings, slams, films, plays, and music venues.

"Verbs on Asphalt: the History of Nuyorican Poetry Slam." http://www.verb sonasphalt.com/index.php?option=com_content&task=view&id=1& Itemid=2. Provides historical information on the development of the poetry slam movement, including a discussion of techniques used, video clips of slam performances, and a glossary of terms.

Multimedia Sources

Nuyorican Poets Café. Dir. Ray Santisteban. 1994. DVD. 14 minutes. Best Documentary winner of the 1995 New Latino Film Maker's Festival, this work provides an historical overview of the Café and its functions. Link to film's description: http://www.subcine.com/nuyorican.html.

Slam. Santa Monica, CA: Lions Gate, 1998. DVD. 103 minutes. Features performances of Saul Williams, the 1996 Nuyorican Grand Slam Champion.

SlamNation: The Sport of Spoken Word. New York: Cinema Guild, 1998. 2-Disc DVD. 91 minutes. Follows Bob Holman, the Nuyorican Poets Café Slam founder, and the Café's team of poets as they perform at the 1996 National Poetry Slam competition in Portland, Oregon.

66. The Mexican Museum Founded in San Francisco (1975)

Founded by artist Peter Rodriguez on November 20, 1975, the Mexican Museum, or El Museo Mexicano, began as just two storefront rooms in San Francisco's Mission District on the anniversary of the Mexican Revolution. Rodriguez worked with Galería de la Raza, a Latino artist collective in San Francisco. Concerned and frustrated that Latino art received little recognition from major museums, Rodriguez began El Museo Mexicano with the goal of showcasing the works of Mexican and Mexican American artists. Today, the museum also features the works of Latino and Latin American artists. The museum's permanent collection is divided into five major time periods described by the museum as Preconquest, Colonial, Popular, Modern and Contemporary Mexican and Latino, and Chicano works. To expand their exhibit space and educational programs, the museum moved to a larger complex in San Francisco's Fort Mason area. The increased space allowed the museum to expand its permanent collection and, in 1987, the museum received its first major gift: 500 pieces of Mexican folk art from Nelson A. Rockefeller's private collection. Today, the museum is estimated to hold 12,000 objects in its permanent collection. In 2001, plans began to transition the museum to its third home, a multi-level complex in San Francisco's Yerba Buena Arts District. As of 2010, however, funding for the new building's completion is still in progress, so the museum remains in the Fort Mason area. Since its origin, the Mexican Museum has been instrumental in bringing public awareness to the vast and complex world of Latino and Latin American art, with exhibits featuring some of the world's greatest artists throughout history.

TERM PAPER SUGGESTIONS

1. The museum's history is often described as having three phases: an early period, a developmental period, and an expansion period. Examine the history of the museum and its different objectives in each stage of development. Be sure to discuss how the museum's various collections and exhibits have contributed to these phases as well.

2. The Mexican Museum has played a considerable role in furthering the careers of Latino and Latin American artists, such as Frida Kahlo and Gronk. Describe how the Mexican Museum's emphasis on being a "first voice" in Latino art has helped to launch the careers of such artists.

3. The Mexican Museum's collection now contains Chicana/o and Latina/o art as well as works originating in Mexico. Discuss how this expansion has changed the museum and its focus. How does the museum's pan-American approach differ from that of other Mexican museums in the United States and abroad?

4. The Mexican Museum's collection is noted for its comprehensive historical scope and for accumulating nontraditional works. Analyze how the museum's organization and permanent collection challenge traditional notions of art. Do you agree with scholars who argue that the museum has played a key role in debunking Eurocentrism in the art world?

ALTERNATIVE TERM PAPER SUGGESTIONS

1. Imagine you have been hired to write a persuasive letter to contributors asking for donations for the Mexican Museum's new building. In your letter, explain the museum's history as well as its vital role in Latino history and art.

2. Design an interactive timeline of the museum's history. In your timeline, discuss key figures, such as museum founder Peter Rodriguez and Nelson A. Rockefeller, a chief contributor to the museum's art collection. Likewise, be sure to include key exhibitions hosted by the museum and important artworks added to the permanent collection since 1975.

SUGGESTED SOURCES

Primary Sources

The Mexican Museum. http://www.mexicanmuseum.org/.Bilingual Web site features links to the museum's past exhibits and permanent collection.

Mexican Museum. *The Mexican Museum: Catalog of Selections from Its Collection, with Introductions to Mexican and Mexican American Art*. San Francisco: The Mexican Museum, 1981. Contains a comprehensive review of the museum's permanent collection.

Oetinger, Marion. *Folk Treasures of Mexico: The Nelson A. Rockefeller Collection*. New York: Harry N. Abrams, 1990. Focuses on seminal pieces gifted to the museum, with color photos and a detailed history of key works.

Wagner, Nora. "Oral History Interview with Peter Rodriguez." Archives of American Art, Smithsonian Institution. Oct. 23–24, 2004. http://www.aaa.si.edu/collections/oralhistories/transcripts/rodrig04.htm. Interview with Peter Rodriguez discusses his reasons for founding the Mexican Museum.

Secondary Sources

Aguirre, Rosainés. "San Francisco's Mexican Museum." *Lector* 5, no. 2 (1988): 9–10. Focuses on museum's history and founder Peter Rodriguez.

Dávalos, Karen Mary. *Exhibiting Mestizaje: Mexican (American) Museums in the Diaspora.* Albuquerque: University of New Mexico Press, 2001. Chapter 4 discusses the Mexican Museum's influences and importance.

Kaplan, Flora. "Mexican Museums in the Creation of a National Image in World Tourism." In *Crafts in the World Market*, edited by June C. Nash. New York: SUNY Press, 1993, pp. 103–126. Discusses the problem in balancing cultural awareness with cultural exploitation in museums.

Zamora, Herlinda. "Identity and Community: A Look at Four Latino Museums." *Museums and Their Communities.* Ed. Sheila Watson. London: Routledge, 2007, pp. 324–330. Compares the economic struggles and institutional focus of the Mexican Museum with other Latino museums in New York, Chicago, and Austin.

World Wide Web

Dávalos, Karen Mary. "Mexican Museum, San Francisco: The Permanent Collection, Phases of Historical Development, the Museum's Legacy." http://www.jrank.org/cultures/pages/4187/Mexican-Museum-San-Francisco.html. Discusses the phases of the museum's development and argues that the Mexican Museum differs from traditional public museums in its focus and intentions.

Goodwin-Guerrero, Erin. "From the Mexican Museum to the Palo Alto Art Center." ArtsShift San José, Oct. 6, 2009. http://artshiftsanjose.com/?p=1766. Contains information about the Mexican Museum's traveling exhibit as well as photos of important art pieces.

Hamlin, Jessie. "Mexican Museum Still Searching for a Home." *San Francisco Chronicle Online*, Jan. 27, 2008. http://www.sfgate.com/cgi-bin/article.cgi?file=/c/a/2008/01/27/MNEFUJQ4E.DTL. Discusses the museum's history and stalled efforts to build the new art complex.

Multimedia Sources

"Mexican Museum Structure." 0:27 minutes. http://www.youtube.com/watch?v=Y3F3IaCy6wQ. Features a revolving 3-D image of the museum's future building in downtown San Francisco.

"Mission Eyes: The Mexican Museum." 2:07 minutes. http://www.youtube.com/
watch?v=1iBOpXuPRT4. Reviews the museum's nativity exhibit and
brief interviews with museum advisory board member Eli Aramburo and
San Francisco Art Council member Luis Cancel.

67. Congressional Hispanic Caucus Established (1976)

In 1976, five Latino Congressmen—Herman Badillo (New York), E. Kika
de la Garza (Texas), Henry B. Gonzalez (Texas), Edward Roybal (California),
and Baltasar Corrado del Río (Puerto Rico)—started the Congressional
Hispanic Caucus, a Legislative Service Organization in Congress, to further
the interests and concerns of Latinos through legislative means. Originally,
the Congressional Hispanic Caucus included only members of the House of
Representatives, but the organization today is bicameral, with both senators
and representatives in its membership. The Congressional Hispanic Caucus
also allows for the associate membership of non-Latinos, thereby making
the organization one of the largest minority-group caucuses in Congress.
Although the caucus' interests are far-reaching, organization is centered on
11 task forces, each focused on particular Latino concerns: health, education,
labor, immigration, veteran's affairs, international relations, livable communities, business and economic development, telecommunications and technology, arts and entertainment, and census and civil rights. In 1978, the caucus
created a nonprofit educational foundation called the Congressional Hispanic
Caucus Institute (CHCI) to provide leadership and educational opportunities for Latinos. Although the caucus has been bipartisan since its origins,
several Republican members left in the 1990s and formed their own caucus,
the Congressional Hispanic Conference, in 2003. Today, the Congressional
Hispanic Caucus plays a key role in legislation centered on immigration and
health care reform.

TERM PAPER SUGGESTIONS

1. Explain Congressional Hispanic Caucus' role in U.S. law and politics since 1976. How has this group influenced key Congressional
   decisions, particularly on immigration and welfare legislation?
2. Examine the Congressional Hispanic Caucus' organization and its
   task forces. Which task forces have been the least and the most successful in instituting legislative change for Latinos?

3. Since its origins, the Congressional Hispanic Caucus has been closely linked with the Democratic Party whose leadership often appoints caucus members to key committees and congressional positions. Analyze the relationship between the caucus and the Democratic Party. On what issues have the two groups concurred? On what issues have they differed?

4. In 2003, several Latino Republicans formed the Congressional Hispanic Conference, a parallel to the Congressional Hispanic Caucus. Compare the platforms and central issues of these two organizations. What differences exist between their legislative concerns and their congressional votes? Does the division between these two organizations weaken or strengthen Latino representation in Congress?

5. Investigate the Congressional Hispanic Caucus Institute's role in Latino education and economic policy. Beyond their scholarship programs, how has the institute worked to further the number of Latino-owned businesses and the number of Latinos in higher education?

6. Examine the Congressional Hispanic Caucus' interactions with other caucuses in Congress, such as the Black Caucus or the Asian Pacific American Caucus. How and how often do they work together in coalition? On what issues have these groups worked together? On what issues have they disagreed?

ALTERNATIVE TERM PAPER SUGGESTIONS

1. Create an iMovie documentary about the Congressional Hispanic Caucus' history and its role in U.S. law and policymaking. In addition to a focus on the organization's origins and leadership, be sure to include discussion of the group's 11 task forces and the role played by the Congressional Hispanic Caucus Institute.

2. Many Latino Congresspersons do not join the Congressional Hispanic Caucus, and some scholars note that a significant factor involves the percentage of Latinos in the respective congressperson's district. Create an interactive map of Latinos in Congress, noting who has joined the Caucus and who has not. In your map, create a report of the individual Congress members' key votes on central issues, his or her district's racial demographics, and the top three concerns of the individual congressperson's district.

SUGGESTED SOURCES

Primary Sources

"Congressional Hispanic Caucus." http://velazquez.house.gov/chc/. Provides information about the organization and its current legislative issues, with links to each member's congressional homepages.

"Congressional Hispanic Caucus Reports on Hispanic Health in the United States." *Harvard Journal of Hispanic Policy* 12 (1999): 71–86. Features the Caucus' report on U.S. Latino health issues.

Secondary Sources

Duran, Ingrid. "The Nexus between Race and Policy: Interview with Ingrid Duran, Executive Director of the Congressional Hispanic Caucus Institute." *The Georgetown Public Policy Review* 124 (Spring 1999). Duran discusses the issues of gender and race involved in coalescing Latinos.

Hammond, Susan Webb. *Congressional Caucuses in National Policy Making.* Baltimore: Johns Hopkins University Press, 2001. Hammond's book discusses the key roles caucuses play in American politics with several chapters discussing the Congressional Hispanic Caucus and its history.

Johnson, James B., and Philip E. Secret. "Focus and Style Representational Roles of Congressional Black and Hispanic Caucus Members." *Journal of Black Studies* 26 no. 3 (Jan. 1996): 245–273. Article discusses the legislative role and perceptions of the Caucus.

Menifield, Charles E. "A Loose Coalition or a United Front: Voting Behavior within the Congressional Hispanic Caucus." *Latino Studies Journal* 9, no. 2 (1998): 26–45. Menifield's article discusses the voting tendencies of the Caucus, with a particular focus on economic and international issues.

World Wide Web

"Congressional Hispanic Caucus." http://www.facebook.com/congressional. hispanic.caucus CHC's Facebook page has several links to podcasts, news articles, and associated Web pages.

"Congressional Hispanic Caucus Institute." http://www.chci.org/. Contains information on upcoming events, internships, and scholarships as well as reports on Latino issues from the organization's task forces.

"Congressional Hispanic Caucus Topics Page." *USA Today.com.* http://content. usatoday.com/topics/topic/Congressional+Hispanic+Caucus. Compiles all articles about the Caucus published by *USA Today.*

Multimedia Sources

"CHCI 32nd Gala." http://www.hitn.com/chci/08_gala_part_1.php. Offers links to several streaming videos from the Congressional Hispanic Caucus Institute's 32nd Gala, including President Barrack Obama's speech at the event.

"Congressional Hispanic Caucus Institute Public Policy Conference." Oct. 2, 2006. http://www.kaisernetwork.org/health_cast/hcast_index.cfm?display=detail& hc=1922. Offers links to videos and transcripts of four conference panels of the 2006 conference.

"Congressional Tri-Caucus Press Conference on Health Care Reform." June 9, 2009. 44 minutes. http://www.c-span.org/Watch/Media/2009/06/09/ HP/A/19595/Congressional+TriCaucus+Press+Conference+on+ Health+Care+Reform.aspx. Features C-Span video coverage of the press conference of the Hispanic, Black, and Asian Pacific American Caucuses on health care reform.

68. Cherríe Moraga and Gloria Anzaldúa Publish *This Bridge Called My Back* (1981)

In 1981, Cherríe Moraga and Gloria Anzaldúa published *This Bridge Called My Back: Writings by Radical Women of Color*, an anthology that would remain at the forefront of Latina studies for decades to come. *This Bridge* was the brainchild of Gloria Anzaldúa who began the project in 1979. Tired of women of color occupying an outsider position in both Chicano and feminist movements, Anzaldúa conceived of the book project that would soon become one of the most cited texts in contemporary feminist and Latino studies. *This Bridge* is further credited as helping to shift feminist consciousness from a European American emphasis to one that gathered together women of color from various ethnic backgrounds, much the way *This Bridge* gathered these same voices for the anthology. For its second edition, Moraga and Anzaldúa moved the book to Kitchen Table Press, a small women-of-color publishing house, which Moraga co-founded. The move made *This Bridge*'s second edition a work entirely created and produced by women of color. In 1986, *This Bridge* won the Before Columbus Foundation American Book Award, and an all-Spanish edition was released in 1989. In 2002, Anzaldúa, with co-editor Analouise Keating, created a sequel publication titled *This Bridge We Call Home: Radical Visions for Transformation*, which sought to revisit issues still pertinent to women of color in the 21st century. *This Bridge Called My Back* celebrated its 20th anniversary with a third edition, published by Third Woman Press, in 2002. Despite problems in finding a fourth publisher (all three previous publishers have ceased operation), the book remains a seminal work of Latina thought and culture and is still widely read today.

TERM PAPER SUGGESTIONS

1. Discuss the historic role *This Bridge Called My Back* played in Third Wave Feminism. How did *This Bridge* exemplify feminism's shift in focus from European American concerns to recognizing the different experiences women of color encounter? Why, according to Moraga and Anzaldúa, did *This Bridge* and its authors reject European American feminism's call for women to unite as collective victims of patriarchy? What transformations did *This Bridge* demand to make feminism more inclusive?

2. Analyze *This Bridge* as a model of Latina consciousness. How did the anthology challenge Chicano and Latino political movements that tended to minimize Latina contributions? How does the book challenge machismo and other forms of male domination and privilege in Latino organizations?

3. Examine the works of Latina authors in *This Bridge Called My Back*. How do they challenge historical perceptions both of Latinas and Latino culture, such as the myth of La Malinche (Alarcón), the importance of skin color (Anzaldúa), or silence about one's sexuality (Moraga and Anzaldúa)? How do they grapple with both sexism and racism concurrently in these works?

4. Examine the history of *This Bridge Called My Back* as a seminal academic text. How has the book been studied in Latino and women's studies programs? What role has *This Bridge* played in inspiring Latina writers, artists, and scholars? How does the anthology's cross-genre approach (mixing poetry, essays, and personal writing) reflect Latino studies' own multi-disciplinary approach to academics?

5. Analyze the similarities and differences between *This Bridge Called My Back* and its sequel, *This Bridge We Call Home*. How does the sequel reflect the changing experiences of U.S. Latinos between 1981 and 2002? What elements remain the same in both works?

ALTERNATIVE TERM PAPER SUGGESTIONS

1. Create an iMovie documenting *This Bridge Called My Back*'s history and its influence on feminist, Chicano, and Latino movements. Be sure to include interviews and secondary sources that attest to the anthology's prominent place in feminist and Latino studies, as well as historic conditions under which the book was published.

2. Design a Webography for *This Bridge Called My Back*, focused specifically on the book's contributions to Latino thought, culture, and history. Be sure to include information about the book's editors as well as key contributors such as Norma Alarcón and Jo Carrillo, providing links to their other works in Latino studies.

3. Create a PowerPoint presentation analyzing the poems in *This Bridge Called My Back* that reflect Latina history and consciousness. Consider performing a few of these poems, in person or through podcasts, prior to your PowerPoint analysis.

SUGGESTED SOURCES

Primary Source

Cherríe Moraga and Gloria Anzaldúa, eds. *This Bridge Called My Back: Writings by Radical Women of Color*, 3rd ed. Third Woman Press, 2002. This 20th anniversary edition adds visual artworks by 17 different women of color.

Secondary Sources

Alarcon, Norma. "The Theoretical Subject(s) of *This Bridge Called My Back* and Anglo-American Feminism." In *The Postmodern Turn: New Perspectives on Social Theory*, edited by Steven Seidman. Cambridge, UK: Cambridge University Press, 1994, pp.140–152. Discusses this collection's engagement with European American feminists.

Alexander, M. Jacqui. *Pedagogies of Crossing: Mediations on Feminism, Sexual Politics, Memory and the Sacred*. Durham: Duke University Press, 2004. Chapter 6 focuses on *This Bridge Called My Back*'s central role in Latina feminism.

Anzaldua, Gloria, and Analouise Keating, eds. *This Bridge We Call Home*. New York, Routledge, 2002. Sequel to *This Bridge Called My Back* contains several articles focused on its critical role in Latino history and culture.

Calderon, Hector. "'A New Connection, A New Set of Recognitions': From *This Bridge Called My Back* to *This Bridge We Call Home*." *Discourse* 25, no. 1 (Winter/ Spring 2003): 294–303. Discusses *This Bridge Called My Back*'s history.

Short, Kayann. "Coming to the Table: The Differential Politics of *This Bridge Called My Back*." In *Eroticism and Containment: Notes from the Flood Plain,* edited by Carol Siegel and Ann Kibbey. New York: NYU Press, 1994, pp. 3–44. Provides an overview of *This Bridge*, historical conditions of its publication, and its impact on the feminist movement.

World Wide Web

Agarwal, Nisha. "This Bridge Called My Back: A Retro Look at Women of Color and Power." http://www.huffingtonpost.com/nisha-agarwal/this-bridge-called-my-bac_b_418196.html. Offers a 2010 review of the book's lasting legacy and importance.

"Interview with Gloria Anzaldua by Karen Ikas." http://www.auntlute.com/www.auntlute.com/auntlute.com/GloriaAnzalduaInterview.htm. Anzaldúa discusses her motivation for creating *This Bridge Called My Back.*

Lopez, Lonnie. "Cherrie Moraga at the Intersections of Race, Ethnicity, Gender, and Sexual Orientation." http://www.associatedcontent.com/article/107641/cherrie_moraga_and_the_intersection.html?cat=10. Discusses the impact of *This Bridge Called My Back* on women of color.

Love, Heather. "The Second Time Around." http://www.wellesley.edu/womensreview/archive/2003/01/highlt.html. Compares *This Bridge Called My Back* with its sequel, *This Bridge Called My Home.*

Multimedia Sources

"The Bridge Poem." http://www.youtube.com/watch?v=lMWJoL0Uz74. Contains a performance of Donna Kate Rushin's poem, which opens *This Bridge Called My Back.*

Don't Erase My History. CreateSpace Studios, 2009. DVD. 30 minutes. Features an interview with Cherríe Moraga.

"Mixed Minute: Gloria Anzaldúa." 1:01 minutes. http://www.youtube.com/watch?v=MUPwYtOXx6I. Discusses Gloria Anzaldúa's work and the concept of mestiza consciousness.

This Bridge Called My Back (Selections). Audio Cassette. Los Angeles: Pacifica Tape Library, 1983. 63 minutes. Features 29 excerpts from the book.

69. Cuban American National Foundation Established (1981)

In an effort to organize Cuban Americans and the Cuban exile community in their efforts to establish a free and democratic Cuba, Jorge Mas

Canosa and Raul Masvidal, visible leaders of the exile community, formed the Cuban American National Foundation (CANF) as a political lobbying group that would articulate Cuban American interests in Washington, D.C. Since the group's creation in 1981, it has always supported the trade embargo against Cuba as a means to topple the Castro government and replace it with a democratically elected one. As has been the case with most of those in the Cuban exile community, CANF has traditionally been conservative and has supported the Republican Party to champion its causes. Mas Canosa was also instrumental in encouraging President Ronald Reagan to sign the Radio Broadcasting to Cuba Act in 1983, which established Radio Martí in 1985 and later Television Martí in 1990. CANF also created *La Voz de la Fundación* in the early 1990s, which has served as the organization's official radio station. During the early 1990s, several of CANF's leaders including Mas Canosa and Francisco Jose Hernandez, who had been a veteran of the 1961 Bay of Pigs invasion, wanted to move the organization beyond a political lobbying role and affect real change. As such, they amassed weapons and military equipment with the intention of assassinating Castro and setting up a democratic government in Cuba. However, their plans fell through. With the 1997 death of its dynamic president, Jorge Mas Canosa, the organization began to splinter and disagree ideologically. CANF also began to distance itself from the Republican Party. This, along with other disagreements in policy, created a pronounced division among members in 2001 and led to the formation of the Cuban Liberty Council. In April 2009, CANF made a further radical shift in policy and decided to de-emphasize their campaign against the Castro government and instead encourage an easing of the trade embargo against Cuba. CANF has since supported efforts to send financial aid, supplies, and material to pro-democratic groups in Cuba and to emerging entrepreneurs and businesses on the island.

TERM PAPER SUGGESTIONS

1. CANF has been involved in a number of controversial programs and endeavors, some of which included aiding in terrorist attacks against the Cuban government. Identify some of these controversial efforts and explain how the U.S. and Cuban governments as well as others within the Cuban American community have responded to these activities.

2. Discuss the influential role Jorge Mas Canosa had in steering the agenda of CANF. After his death in 1997, the organization split. What were some of the fundamental differences between CANF and the Cuban Liberty Council that solidified this divisiveness in the Cuban American community?

3. What has been CANF's relationship with the U.S. presidential administrations since the Reagan administration of the 1980s? How would you characterize the political associations that were established between the organization and each individual administration?

4. In April 2009, CANF President Francisco "Pepe" Jose Hernandez released a 14-page proposal outlining the organization's new approach in attitude, tone, and policy toward Cuba and U.S.-Cuban relations. How is this shift different from the group's position in the past, and what has been President Barack Obama's position on this change? More importantly, how has this new proposal been received throughout the Cuban American community?

ALTERNATIVE TERM PAPER SUGGESTIONS

1. Create a timeline with images, footage, and links to relevant articles and Web sites charting the CANF's evolution as the most powerful and influential lobbying group for U.S.-Cuban relations and national policy.

2. As a political consultant hired by CANF, develop a website that promotes the organization's post-2009 identity. The site should be directed toward the Cuban American community, the U.S. government, and the people of Cuba.

SUGGESTED SOURCES

Primary Sources

"Cuban American National Foundation." http://www.canf.org/. Official website for the organization includes articles on current issues involving CANF's agenda, video archives, and relevant links.

Cuban American National Foundation. *The Alternatives of Freedom: A Statement of Principles and Objectives for a Free and Democratic Cuba.* Miami, FL: Cuban American National Foundation, 1992. Outlines the group's official platform for rebuilding Cuba politically and economically after the removal of the Castro government.

————. *Castro and the Narcotics Connection: The Cuban Government's Use of Narcotics Trafficking to Finance and Promote Terrorism.* Washington, D.C.: Cuban American National Foundation, 1983. A special report issued by the organization implicates Fidel Castro's government in involvement with the drug trade.

Secondary Sources

Erlich, Reese. *Dateline Havana: The Real Story of U.S. Policy and the Future of Cuba.* Sausalito, CA: PoliPoint Press, 2009. Chapter 4 outlines CANF's formation and its role as a political lobbying group for the exile community within the United States.

García, Cristina María. *Havana USA: Cuban Exiles and Cuban Americans in South Florida, 1959–1994.* Berkeley: University of California Press, 1996. Chapter 2 examines CANF's establishment and its position as the political voice for the exile community in South Florida.

Haney, Patrick, and Walt Vanderbush. *The Cuban Embargo: Domestic Politics of American Foreign Policy.* Pittsburgh, PA: University of Pittsburgh Press, 2005. Includes extensive discussion throughout Chapter 5 of CANF's influence on U.S.-Cuban relations since the group's formation in 1981.

World Wide Web

"Cuban American National Foundation Calls for New U.S. Cuba Policy." http://havanajournal.com/cuban_americans/entry/cuban-american-national-foundation-calls-for-new-us-cuba-policy/. The April 2009 article describes how CANF has shifted its policy toward U.S.-Cuban relations, de-emphasizing its campaign against the Castro government and directing its efforts to help Cuban citizens more directly.

"Directorio Responds to Cuban American National Foundation Smear Campaign." http://www.latinamericanstudies.org/us-cuba/Directorio_Responds_to_CANF.pdf. This is the Cuban Democratic Directorate's rebuttal to public discrediting by CANF.

"The Jorge Mas Canosa Freedom Foundation." http://www.jorgemascanosa.org/. Provides biographical information on the CANF co-founder and information on its scholarship program, which is the largest awarded to Cuban Americans.

Multimedia Source

Campaign for Cuba. Pensacola: University of West Florida Documentary Institute, 1992. VHS. 58 minutes. Profiles how CANF and the greater Cuban American exile community swayed foreign relations during the 1980s and the start of the 1990s between the United States and Cuba.

70. *Plyler v. Doe* (1982)

In 1982, the Supreme Court ruled on a class action lawsuit called *Plyler v. Doe*. The case centered on a 1975 Texas law that withheld funds to local school districts for the education and enrollment of children who could not prove legal residency in the United States. Lawyers for the state argued that educating noncitizens was cost prohibitive and that the Fourteenth Amendment applied only to U.S. citizens. The Supreme Court disagreed. In a 5 to 4 decision, the justices held that Texas state law violated the Fourteenth Amendment's guarantee of equal protection, placing an undue burden on Latino schoolchildren and their parents. In the majority opinion, author Justice William J. Brennan argued that the Fourteenth Amendment applies to all persons, regardless of their residential status or citizenship. In so doing, Brennan extended the Fourteenth Amendment to include citizens and noncitizens alike. Although the case did concur with early rulings that held that the Constitution does not guarantee education as a fundamental right, *Plyler v. Doe* set a precedent whereby states had to educate all children regardless of their legal status. In May 2007, the Warren Institute at University of California Berkeley's Law School held a 25th Anniversary Conference to commemorate *Plyler v. Doe* and its lasting impact on Latino education.

TERM PAPER SUGGESTIONS

1. The Supreme Court decided *Plyler v. Doe* by a narrow 5 to 4 majority. Examine the majority opinion and dissenting opinions in this case. How did those justices dissenting and those concurring perceive the Fourteenth Amendment's equal protection clause differently? How did *Plyler v. Doe* extend the definition of the Fourteenth Amendment's guarantee of equal protection?

2. Analyze the impact of *Plyler v. Doe* on undocumented Latino schoolchildren. How did the decision affect their access to education in public schools? What problems do undocumented children still encounter in the U.S. school systems, both in the K-12 system and in college?

3. Explain how *Plyler v. Doe* established precedents for future decisions regarding undocumented residents' rights to education, medicine,

and local government services. How did *Plyler v. Doe* later serve as a precedent to overturn California's Proposition 187?

4. Investigate the Mexican American Legal Defense and Education Fund (MALDEF) and its role in *Plyler v. Doe*. How did this organization lay the groundwork for the court case and its legal defense?

5. Analyze why, 25 years after the *Plyler v. Doe* decision, the ruling remains so contested and controversial. What legislative attempts, such as Proposition 187 and the Gallegly Amendment, have appeared to challenge *Plyler v. Doe*? Why have these challenges remained unsuccessful?

ALTERNATIVE TERM PAPER SUGGESTIONS

1. Create a PowerPoint presentation regarding *Plyler v. Doe*, its impact on U.S. education and its interpretation of the Fourteenth Amendment. In your presentation, include audio clips, photos, and news clips from the court case.

2. Design an online pamphlet of Supreme Court cases related to education and Latinos. Include illustrations and website links to famous court cases such as *Plyler v. Doe*, *Méndez v. Westminster*, and others relevant to Latinos.

SUGGESTED SOURCES

Primary Source

Plyler v. Doe, 457 U.S. 202 (1982). http://caselaw.lp.findlaw.com/scripts/getcase.pl?court=US&vol=457&invol=202. Contains transcripts of the U.S. Supreme Court case.

Secondary Sources

Biegel, Stuart. "The Wisdom of Plyler v. Doe." *Chicano-Latino Law Review* (Fall 1995): 47–63. Discusses how *Plyler v. Doe* can serve as a model for 21st century education law.

Soltero, Carlos R. *Latinos and American Law: Landmark Supreme Court Cases.* Austin: University of Texas Press, 2006. Chapter on *Plyler v. Doe* offers a comprehensive background on the case.

Suárez-Orozco, Marcelo, Peter D. Roos, and Carola Suárez-Orozco. "Cultural, Education, and Legal Perspectives on Immigration: Implications for School Reform." In *Law and School Reform: Six Strategies for Promoting Education Equality*, edited by Jay P. Heubert and Martha Minow. New Haven, CT: Yale University Press, pp. 160–204. Discusses the implications of *Plyler v. Doe* and compares the case with California's Proposition 187.

Valencia, Richard R. *Chicano Students and the Courts: The Mexican American Struggle for Educational Equality.* New York: New York University Press, 2008. Discusses *Plyler v. Doe* in conjunction with other Latino education legal struggles.

Wexler, Emily Love, Megan Bucholtz, and Brandy Chance. "Ending the Dream of Plyler v. Doe." In *Current Issues in Education Policy and the Law,* edited by Kevin Grant Welner and Wendy C. Chi. Charlotte, NC: IAP, 2008, pp. 173-187. Discusses the legacy of *Plyler v. Doe* on U.S. education for immigrant children.

Whitson, James Anthony. *Constitution and Curriculum: Hermeneutical Semiotics of Cases and Controversies in Education, Law, and Social Science.* Oxford: Taylor & Francis, 1991. Whitson discusses the limited authority of the *Plyler v. Doe* decision and compares it with two other education-related Supreme Court cases.

World Wide Web

"The 25th Anniversary of Plyler v. Doe." *University of California Berkeley Law School.* http://www.law.berkeley.edu/2913.htm. Features a description of the 25th Anniversary Conference at University of California Berkeley, with links to seven of the conference's papers.

López, María Pabón. "Reflections on Educating Latino and Latina Children." http://biblioteca.rrp.upr.edu/LatCritCD/publications/otherresources/prsa/pabonlopezlcix.pdf. This article, originally written for *Seton Hall Law Review,* discusses how undocumented children are still educationally vulnerable despite *Plyler v. Doe.*

Olivas, Michael A. "Plyler v. Doe, Toll v. Moreno, and Postsecondary Admissions: Undocumented Adults, and 'Enduring Disability.'" *Journal of Law and Education* 15, no. 1 (Winter 1986): 19–55. Examines *Plyler v. Doe*'s impact on post-secondary education.

Rohe, John. "Plyler and Proposition 187." *The Social Contract* 5, no. 3 (Spring 1995). http://www.thesocialcontract.com/artman2/publish/tsc0503/article_448.shtml. Reviews the legal precedents set in *Plyler v. Doe.*

Multimedia Sources

"Plyler v. Doe: Oral Arguments." Audio Clip. 99:39 minutes. http://www.oyez.org/cases/1980-1989/1981/1981_80_1538/. Contains the opening arguments in this Supreme Court case.

"Plyler v. Doe: 25 Years Later." *Dallas Morning News.* http://www.dallasnews.com/s/dws/photography/2007/plyler/. Contains eight videos interviewing key participants, including Justice Brennan and Superintendent Jim Plyler, 25 years after the Supreme Court's decision.

71. Boland Amendments (1982–1984)

From 1982 to 1984, Congress added three restrictions to the U.S government's funding of Nicaraguan "Contras," the name given to a series of armed military groups looking to overthrow Nicaragua's pro-Marxist, Sandinista government. Collectively, these three amendments are called the Boland Amendments, and each was attached to the Defense Appropriations Acts of 1982, 1983, and 1984, respectively. The Boland Amendments prohibited the funding of military operations in Nicaragua from Congress' defense budget, and required that any aid provided by the U.S. government through other means be made public. The bill was originally introduced to limit then-President Ronald Reagan's support of and funding for the Nicaraguan Contras, but scholars later argued that the ambiguous language of the amendments created a legal battleground. In 1986, a media investigation revealed that the Reagan administration had been selling weapons, through Israel, to Iran in exchange for their help in releasing U.S. hostages held by the Lebanese group Hezbollah. With the money received from the weapons sales, the National Security Council, led by Colonel Oliver North, covertly transferred the funds to Nicaraguan Contras. The scandal was soon called the Iran-Contra Affair, and, on November 25, 1986, Reagan announced that a special review board, the Tower Commission, would be investigating the matter. Much of North's testimony, as well as that of other players in the events, was televised, and the Tower Commission's 200-page report criticized the actions of those from the Reagan administration involved in the arms-for-hostages, money-for-Contras events, particularly those of the National Security Council. No criminal charges, however, were ever brought against anyone involved in the Iran-Contra Affair. Central to these debates was the Boland Amendments and whether the language of these amendments made the administration's actions illegal.

TERM PAPER SUGGESTIONS

1. Examine the Boland Amendments and the role it played in the Iran-Contra Affair. What limitations did the Boland Amendments

place on military operations in Nicaragua? Did the money channeled to the Contras through the National Security Council violate these amendments?

2. Scholars have argued whether the Boland Amendments were constitutional. Research the two sides of this debate and take a stance on the constitutionality of the amendments.

3. Discuss the events leading up to the Boland Amendments. What Central Intelligence Agency (CIA) actions caused Congress to want to limit the U.S. involvement with and funding of the Contras? Why did the Boland Amendments pass Congress while other, more stringent amendments, such as New York Senator Patrick Moynihan's, did not?

4. Reagan, who signed the Boland Amendments into law, argued that the events of the Iran-Contra Affair did not violate the provisions because the language of the Boland Amendments was open to interpretation. Examine the language of these amendments and determine whether you find the language ambiguous and open to interpretation.

ALTERNATIVE TERM PAPER SUGGESTIONS

1. Create an interactive timeline and map detailing the events and places involved in the Iran-Contra Affair. Be sure to include a discussion of the rise of the Sandinistas and the Contras in Nicaragua, the creation of the Boland Amendments, and the people and players involved in the Iran-Contra scandal.

2. Assume the role of an attorney defending or prosecuting a member of Reagan's administration accused of violating the Boland Amendments. Write a legal brief detailing his or her actions in relation to the amendments' language, and give specific reasons why he or she is innocent or guilty of the charges.

SUGGESTED SOURCES

Primary Sources

"H.R. 2968." http://thomas.loc.gov/cgi-bin/bdquery/z?d098:HR.2968. Contains description of 1983 Boland Amendments that prohibited covert assistance to Nicaraguan Contras.

Reagan, Ronald. "Speech about Iran Contra," May 4, 1987. http://www.pbs. org/wgbh/amex/presidents/40_reagan/psources/ps_irancontra.html. Transcript of Reagan's May 4, 1987, speech explains his role in the scandal.

Secondary Sources

Church, George J., Hays Gorey, and Barrett Seaman. "But What Laws Were Broken?" *Time*. 1 June 1987. http://www.time.com/time/magazine/ article/0,9171,964501-2,00.html. Discusses the multiple interpretations of the Boland Amendments.

Fisher, Louis. "How Tightly Can Congress Draw the Purse Strings?" *The American Journal of International Law*. 83, no. 4 (Oct. 1989): 758–766. Discusses strict language of the Boland Amendments and its funding limitations for Nicaraguan Contras.

Hamilton, Lee H., and Daniel K Inouye. *Report of the Congressional Committees Investigating the Iran/Contra Affair*. Darby, PA: Diane Publishing, 1995. Chapter 6 discusses the history and the legal implications of the Boland Amendments.

Moreno, Dario. *U.S. Policy in Central America: The Endless Debate*. Gainesville: University of Florida Press, 1990. Discusses Congress' intentions in passing the Boland Amendments.

Risenfeld, Stefan A. "The Powers of Congress and the President in International Relations: Revisited." *California Law Review* 75, no. 1 (Jan. 1987): 405–414. Discusses the constitutional and current legal powers of Congress and the president with regard to war.

Sharpe, Kenneth E. "The Post-Vietnam Formula under Siege: The Imperial Presidency and Central America." *Political Science Quarterly* 102, no. 4 (Winter 1987–1988): 549–569. Discusses the powers of Congress and the president, post-Vietnam, through the lens of the Boland Amendments and the Iran-Contra scandal.

World Wide Web

"Foreign Affairs: Ronald Reagan, 40th President." *American Experience*. http:// www.pbs.org/wgbh/amex/presidents/40_reagan/reagan_foreign.html. Article discusses Reagan's political philosophy regarding foreign affairs and his reaction to the Boland Amendments.

Wolf, Julie. "The Iran-Contra Affair." *PBS*. http://www.pbs.org/wgbh/amex/ reagan/peopleevents/pande08.html. Discusses the Boland Amendments' relationship to the Iran-Contra scandal.

Multimedia Sources

American Experience: Ronald Reagan. PBS Home Video, 2003. DVD. 263 minutes. Documentary of Reagan's life and presidency devotes 20 minutes to discussion of Reagan's rejection of the Boland Amendments and the Iran-Contra scandal that followed.

Coverup: Behind the Iran-Contra Affair. MPI Home Video, 2001. VHS. 72 minutes. Documentary offers footage of the 1988 hearings regarding the Iran-Contra scandal and the related Boland Amendments violations.

Iran-Contra Investigation. National Archives and Records Administration. DVD. 63 minutes. Features the July 14, 1987, meeting of the Senate Select Committee on the Iran-Contra hearings.

72. *El Norte* Debuts (1983)

In 1983, director Gregory Nava released *El Norte*, a film he co-wrote and produced with his wife, Anna Thomas. *El Norte* was the first to depict the struggles of thousands of Guatemalans, who, in the 1980s, were escaping political persecution and military conflicts by migrating to the United States. Melodramatic in nature, *El Norte* centers on Enrique and his sister Rosa, who flee Guatemala after their father, a political dissident, is assassinated and their mother is taken by the police. Through Enrique and Rosa's journey from Guatemala to the United States, Nava depicts their arduous U.S.-Mexico border crossing as well as the cultural, legal, and economic difficulties the protagonists encounter once they reach "El Norte" (the north), the United States. Praised for its honest portrayal of both immigration and the Quiche Mayan culture, *El Norte* was the first independent film to be nominated and to receive an Oscar for Best Original Screenplay. The film also won the grand prize at the Montreal World Film Festival in 1983. Today, *El Norte* serves as an important portrayal of the historical mass exodus of Amerindians from Guatemala in the 1980s and was thus selected in 1995 by the Library of Congress to be included for preservation in U.S. National Film Registry. In 2009, Criterion released a high-definition, 25th anniversary edition of the film, calling it a "landmark independent film."

TERM PAPER SUGGESTIONS

Discuss the impact of *El Norte* on public perceptions of Guatemalan refugees. How did the film's release impact viewers and U.S. policy, including the amnesty portion of the Immigration Reform and Control Act of 1986 and the settlement in the court case *American Baptist Churches v. Thornburgh* (often referred to as "The ABC Decision").

1. Director/writer Gregory Nava has argued that the U.S.-Mexico border is the world's only frontier where a first-world and a third-world country converge. Examine *El Norte*'s representation of the U.S.-Mexican border and border patrol. How does Nava depict both sides of this international boundary? Research the border and determine whether this representation is accurate.

2. Analyze *El Norte*'s portrayal of various Latin American cultural exchanges, particularly those between Guatemalans and Mexicans. How does the film reveal cross-stereotyping between these two Latin American cultures? Likewise, how does the film reveal the common European American conflation of the two cultures?

3. Critics have praised *El Norte* for its accurate portrayal of contemporary Amerindian culture, especially that of the Quiche Mayans. Investigate contemporary Mayan cultural traditions, discussing elements exhibited in the film as well as elements the film neglects.

4. In a 2009 interview at the Smithsonian Institution, Gregory Nava argued that *El Norte*'s message about immigration and immigrants is equally essential today. Appraise *El Norte*'s representation of immigration to the United States and determine whether you think the film's depiction of U.S. immigration and border crossing is still accurate today.

5. Gregory Nava has had a long career in Latino filmmaking, including the films *Selena, Mi Familia, Frida,* and *Bordertown.* Examine Nava's depictions of Latinos and Latino culture across these films. How does he portray the domestic and familial experiences of Latinos? What role does melodrama as a genre play in his work?

ALTERNATIVE TERM PAPER SUGGESTIONS

1. Create an iMovie of the U.S.-Mexico border, comparing *El Norte*'s depiction of its protagonists' border crossing with today. How has the border, its patrol and its crossings changed? What has remained the same since the film was made?

2. Using reviews, video clips, and interviews, create a website about *El Norte* and its historical and cultural impact on Latino history.

SUGGESTED SOURCES

Primary Sources

El Norte. Criterion Collection, 2009. DVD. Nava's 1983 film has been re-re-leased under Criterion's label with several special features, including Nava's first student film and a featurette on the U.S.-Mexico border.

Insdorf, Annette. "*El Norte*: On Screen and in Reality, a Story of Struggle." *New York Times*, Late Edition (East Coast). Jan. 8, 1984. A17+. Insdorf's review features interviews with Gregory Nava and Anna Thomas, director and producer of the film.

Secondary Sources

Ebert, Roger. "Odyssey to *El Norte*." *Mother Jones Magazine* (Feb/Mar. 1984): 28–31. Ebert's article focuses on the making of the film and Gregory Nava's direction.

List, Chris. "*El Norte*: Ideology and Immigration." *Jump Cut*. 34 (Mar. 1989): 27–31. http://www.ejumpcut.org/archive/onlinessays/JC34folder/ElNorte. html. List's article argues that Nava's film exemplifies the Latin American melodrama tradition.

Marciniak, Katarzyna. *Alienhood: Citizenship, Exile, and the Logic of Difference*. Minneapolis: University of Minnesota Press, 2006. Marciniak's first chapter is devoted to a reading of *El Norte* and its characters' transnational identities.

Naficy, Hamid. *An Accented Cinema: Exilic and Diasporic Filmmaking*. Princeton, NJ: Princeton University Press, 2001. Focusing on a postcolonial reading of the film, Naficy offers two close readings of *El Norte*.

World Wide Web

"El Norte." http://www.criterion.com/films/972. Criterion's official Website for the film features the film's trailer along with links to interviews and press notes about the release.

Johnson, Reed. "Gregory Nava's film 'El Norte' Marks 25th Anniversary." *Los Angeles Times Online,* Jan 28, 2009. http://www.calendarlive.com/movies/la-et-el-norte28-2009jan28,0,6636204.story. Johnson's article recounts the lasting impact of the film and its influence on independent cinema.

Santander, Hugo N. "Immigration and Colonization Reflexiones Sobre *El Norte* de Gregorio Nava." 2002. http://www.ucm.es/info/especulo/numero22/north.html. Arguing that *El Norte* is an epic, Santander traces the film's use of biblical motifs and Central American myths in Nava's story of immigration.

Tobar, Héctor. "Promised Land: *El Norte.*" http://www.criterion.com/current/
posts/1005 Tobar's article discusses the film's links with *The Grapes of
Wrath* and *El Salvador,* arguing that *El Norte* continues to hold an important place in immigration history.

Multimedia Sources

"Gregory Nava at Smithsonian." http://www.youtube.com/watch?v=F4_ BQYj8lp4.
1:57 minutes. Nava discusses the lasting impact of *El Norte* today.
"In the Service of the Shadows: The Making of *El Norte.*" *El Norte.* Criterion,
2009. DVD. 58:20 minutes. Special Feature documentary discusses
the making of the film with Gregory Nava, Anna Thomas, and the
film's cast and crew.

73. Culture Clash Created (1984)

Founded on May 5, 1984, on the Mexican American holiday of Cinco
de Mayo, Culture Clash is perhaps the most famous Latino theater
group in the United States. The brainchild of founders Richard Montoya, Ric Salinas, and Herbert Siguenza, Culture Clash was an offshoot
of a larger San Francisco theater collective called Comedy Fiesta. Tired
of the limited parts available for Latinos on the stage, Montoya, Salinas,
and Siguenza started writing their own performance pieces for the theater, beginning with the 1988 play, *The Mission*, about the difficulty Latino actors have in finding good parts. The success of this play led to
other tours and performances, all of which humorously blend together
Latino history and culture with a commentary on mainstream American
popular culture. Their next play, *Bowl of Beings*, for example, features a
sketch of Che Guevara, La Raza, the San Francisco 49ers, and Dominos
Pizza, immediately after a scene uniting the narratives of Christopher
Columbus, La Malinche, and *The Godfather*. Their 1992 play, *S.O.S.:
Comedy for These Uncertain Times*, focuses on the racial tensions associated with the Rodney King beating, the Los Angeles riots that ensued,
and the AIDS epidemic. Many of their most famous plays are available
in print, including *Culture Clash in AmeriCCa, Nuyorican Stories, Radio
Mambo,* and *Water and Power*. In 1998, Culture Clash adapted Aristophanes' ancient Greek comedy, *The Birds*, with modern political and

popular culture characters such as the Marx Brothers, John Lennon, Dick Cheney, and Los Angeles Mayor Antonio Villaraigosa. Along with another adaptation of Aristophanes' *Peace*, Culture Clash's more recent work continues their tradition of blending popular culture with political, social, and cultural commentary. *Anthems: Culture Clash in the District* (2002) discusses the events of September 11, 2001. *Chavez Ravine*, (2003) focuses on the 1959 Latino community displaced when Dodger Stadium was built, and *Bordertown* (2006) centers on the San Diego/ Tijuana border. As one of the few theater performance groups to focus on Latino culture and social issues, Culture Clash is a vital and timely example of Latino influence on American popular culture.

TERM PAPER SUGGESTIONS

1. Examine the use of Latino history and culture in the one of Culture Clash's key plays. Discuss Culture Clash's union of American popular culture with Latino politics and history. What role does each contribute to the other?

2. Discuss the variety of Latino or Mexican American identities created in one of Culture Clash's plays. What types of characters do they create? What role is given to racial, gender, religious, sexual, and class-based identities in these plays? Do you agree or disagree with critics of Culture Clash who argue that their characterizations often rely on stereotypes?

3. Research one of the Latino historical figures such as Father Junipero Serra, Che Guevara, Fidel Castro, or Antonio Villaraigosa used by Culture Clash in one of their plays. What similarities and differences are there in the historical account and in Culture Clash's representations on these figures?

4. Explore one of the contemporary U.S. historical events such as the September 11th terrorist attack, the displacement of Latinos from Chavez Ravine, and the Rodney King riots. Discuss the Latino perspective Culture Clash provides on this historical issue and how they do so.

5. Many scholars consider Culture Clash to be a premier example of West Coast theater. Given that most U.S. theater derives from playwrights living on the East Coast, particularly New York City, how

does Culture Clash's work offer a West Coast theatrical experience? What West Coast social and living conditions does Culture Clash reference in their works? How does this impact the work?

6. Examine the roles available to Latinos in U.S. television, theater, and film prior to Culture Clash's work and compare these with contemporary portrayals. What has changed in the United States in the years that Culture Clash has been in production? What contributions, if any, do you believe this group has made to these changing opportunities?

ALTERNATIVE TERM PAPER SUGGESTIONS

1. Read or watch a Culture Clash play of your choice then create a series of podcasts explaining and detailing your research into the many intertextual references to Latino history and culture. Be sure to provide a bibliography detailing your sources.

2. Watch *The Bronze Screen: 100 Years of the Latino Image in Hollywood* and read Culture Clash's first play, *The Mission*. Create a PowerPoint presentation detailing the stereotypes of Latinos in Hollywood films, noting how Culture Clash's play addresses these stereotypes as well. In your PowerPoint presentation, be sure to discuss how *The Mission* both uses and rejects these stereotypes of Latinos in the media.

SUGGESTED SOURCES

Primary Sources

Aldama, Frederick Luis. *Spilling the Beans in Chicanolandia: Conversations with Writers and Artists.* Austin: University of Texas Press, 2006. Features an interview with founding Culture Clash member Richard Montoya.

Montoya, Richard. *Water and Power.* New York: Samuel French, 2006. This L.A. Drama Circle outstanding new play winner features Latino residents in a neo-noir Los Angeles setting.

Montoya, Richard, Ricardo Salinas, and Herbert Siguenza. *Culture Clash in AmeriCCa.* New York: Theater Communications Group, 2003. Features four of Culture Clash's most recent plays, including *Dreaming of Lincoln* and *Bordertown*.

Montoya, Richard, Ricardo Salinas, and Herbert Siguenza. *Life, Death and Revolutionary Comedy.* New York: Theater Communications Group, 1997.

Collection features three of Culture Clash plays including *The Mission* and *Radio Mambo* and Philip Kan Gotanda's interview with the group.

Montoya, Richard, Ricardo Salinas, and Herbert Siguenza. "Zorro in Hell." *TheatreForum* 30 (2007): 77–104. The complete play can be found in this journal.

Secondary Sources

Huerta, Jorge. "Chicano Theater in a Society in Crisis." In *Text & Presentation, 2007*, edited by Stratos E. Constantinidis. Jefferson, NC: McFarland, 2008, pp. 5–23. Huerta discusses six phases of Chicano theater and Culture Clash's role within those phases.

López, Corina Benavides. "Reflections on Teaching, Learning, and Performing Chicana/o History." *Radical History Review* 102 (2008): 131–135. Article focuses on using Culture Clash's material pedagogically.

Monaghan, Constance. "Mambo Combo." *American Theater* 15, no. 3 (1998): 10–14. Discusses Culture Clash's historical and cultural influences.

World Wide Web

Banks, Gabrielle. "Cultural Chameleons: The Irreverent Sketch Comedy of Culture Clash." *The Free Library,* September 22, 2003. http://www.the freelibrary.com/Cultural chameleons: the irreverent sketch comedy of Culture Clash..-a0108693825. Features interviews with the group about Culture Clash's origins and political works.

"Culture Clash." http://cultureclash.com/. Main website for the group features film clips, history, and upcoming events.

Johnson, Reed. "Culture Clash: Staying Irreverent Yet Relevant after 25 Years." *L.A. Times,* Oct. 25, 2009. http://www.latimes.com/entertainment/ news/la-ca-culture-clash25-2009oct25,0,952157.story. Article highlights the troupe's work and its 25 years of performances.

Multimedia Sources

The Bronze Screen: 100 Years of the Latino Image in Hollywood. Queslar, 2003. DVD. 90 minutes. Film focuses both on the stereotypes of Latinos in Hollywood and on the remarkable contributions of Latinos to Hollywood filmmaking.

Culture Clash. *A Bowl of Beings.* NLCC Educational Media, 1992. VHS. 58 minutes. Features vignettes from their televised PBS performance.

Culture Clash. *Radio Mambo: Culture Clash Invades Miami.* La Theater Works, 2002. Audio CD. Features Culture Clash's performance of the play.

74. *American Baptist Churches et al. v. Thornburgh et al.* and the ABC Decision (1985, 1991)

From 1980 to 1991, an estimated 500,000 to 1 million Guatemalans and Salvadorians fled the civil wars, violence, political instability, and insurrections taking place in their respective countries to seek refuge in the United States. However, over 90 percent of those who applied for refugee status were denied, mostly on the grounds that the 1980 Refugee Act, the current law of the time, was intended to provide amnesty for those fleeing Communist rule, not those leaving Latin American countries. Those rejected for amnesty status had the choice of being deported back to Central America or staying illegally in the United States; many chose the latter. In 1980, several religious organizations began sheltering many of the Central American refugees who stayed. Calling themselves "the Sanctuary Movement," leaders such as Rev. John Fife and Rev. Jim Corbett of Tucson, Arizona, argued that churches could provide safe havens for those fleeing civil war under their First Amendment rights to religious freedom. The Immigration and Naturalization Services (INS) and the U.S. Attorney General disagreed. In 1985, the INS arrested 12 religious leaders harboring illegal aliens. These leaders were convicted but given suspended sentences. In response to their court cases, the Center for Constitutional Rights, on behalf of eight national and dozens of Christian and Jewish religious organizations, filed a 1985 class action lawsuit against U.S. Attorney General Edwin Meese (later, by the time of the trial, Richard Thornburgh replaced Meese) and the INS. The plaintiffs contended that the INS engaged in discriminatory practices against El Salvadorians and Guatemalans seeking refugee status and churches had the First Amendment right to offer sanctuary to refugees. They also argued that the 1980 Refugee Act did not meet the minimum standards set by international law. The plaintiffs lost the case but reached a settlement, called "the ABC Decision" or "the ABC Settlement," in 1991. This settlement called for a temporary protected status for Guatemalans and Salvadorians who entered the country before October 1, 1990, and for the re-examination of over 250,000 refugee cases, reopening and overturning more decisions than any judicial settlement in U.S. history.

TERM PAPER SUGGESTIONS

1. Investigate the living conditions of El Salvadorians and Guatemalans in the 1980s. What was the political and social climate in these two countries? What percentage of the population left the country during this time? What were the causes of this mass migration?

2. Analyze how the ABC Decision altered the terms of the 1980 Refugee Act. Discuss eligibility requirements for refugee status before and after this settlement.

3. Discuss criteria for refugee status enacted under the ABC Settlement. What rules were created with regard to dependents, employment, and stay of deportation? Why was such an emphasis placed on the de novo interview process?

4. Examine the sanctuary movement in the United States and the role it played in the ABC Decision. What ethical arguments did they make with regard to housing refugees? What role did the Sanctuary Movement play in swaying public opinion and convincing the U.S. government to accept the ABC Settlement?

5. The various churches that became plaintiffs in this case argued that they had the constitutional right to house refugees under the First Amendment; the defendants disagreed. In 2007, the issue returned to the news when the New Sanctuary Movement made similar claims about their First Amendment rights. Analyze the First Amendment and take a position on whether the U.S. Constitution gives churches the right to house refugees.

6. Scholars argue that the settlement in *American Baptist Churches v. Thornburgh* came too late to help the vast majority of those who applied for amnesty. Examine why the case took six years to reach a settlement, why the case was settled out of court, and how this delay impacted refugees between 1985 and 1991.

ALTERNATIVE TERM PAPER SUGGESTIONS

1. Using maps, video clips, and diary excerpts, create a website that highlights the human rights violations and living conditions of El Salvadorians and/or Guatemalans in the 1980s. Give reasons why citizens feared for their safety and why they sought refugee status in the United States during this time.

2. Assume the role of an organizational leader who has offered sanctuary to a family from El Salvador or Guatemala in 1985. Write a letter to the U.S. attorney general offering legal reasons why this family should be granted refugee status in the United States.

SUGGESTED SOURCES

Primary Sources

"American Baptist Churches v. Thornburgh (ABC) Settlement Agreement." http://www.peerallylaw.com/en/index2.php?option=com_content& do_pdf=1&id=324. Contains the settlement conditions of the ABC Decision.

"American Baptist Churches v. Thornburgh Settlement Agreement." http://www. uscis.gov/portal/site/uscis/menuitem.5af9bb95919f35e66f614176543f6d1a/ ?vgnextoid=86d796981298d010VgnVCM10000048f3d6a1RCRD&vg nextchannel=828807b03d92b010VgnVCM10000045f3d6a1RCRD. Contains the provisions of the settlement agreement.

U.S. Citizen and Immigration Services. "Making ABC Registration Determinations," June 8, 2006. http://www.nationalimmigrationproject.org/ LegalUpdates/abc_registration_060806.pdf. Provides the updated criteria by which refugees can apply for sanctuary under the ABC Settlement.

Secondary Sources

Blum, Carolyn Patty. "The Settlement of American Baptist Churches v. Thornburgh: Landmark Victory for Central American Asylum-Seekers." *International Journal of Refugee Law*. 3, no. 2 (1991): 347–356. Discusses the reasons why the United States government settled out of court.

Coutin, Susan Bibler. "From Refugees to Immigrants: The Legalization Strategies of Salvadoran Immigrants and Activists." *International Migration Review* 32, no. 4 (Winter 1998): 901–925. Discusses the implementation of the ABC Decision and its impact on Salvadorian immigration.

Kahn, Robert S. *Other People's Blood: U.S. Immigration Prisons in the Reagan Decade*. Boulder, CO: Westview Press, 1996. Kahn's book discusses the human cost of the lengthy judicial process in this case.

Musalo, Karen, Jennifer Moore, and Richard A. Boswell. *Refugee Law and Policy: A Comparative and International Approach*. 2nd ed. Durham, NC:

Carolina Academic Press, 2002. Features chapter on *American Baptist Churches v. Thornburgh* and the settlement.

World Wide Web

Gzesh, Susan. "Central Americans and Asylum Policy in the Reagan Era." *Migration Information Source.* April 2006. http://www.migration information.org/Feature/display.cfm?ID=384. Discusses the overall picture of migration in the 1980s and 1990s, linking the ABC Decision with Reagan's immunity program and other legislation.

Ogletree Jr., Charles J. "America's Schizophrenic Immigration Policy: Race, Class and Reason." http://www.bc.edu/bc_org/avp/law/lwsch/journals/bclawr/41_4/01_TXT.htm. Discusses the history of immigration law in the United States and the ABC Decision's place within it.

Simcox, David, and Rosemary Jenks. "Refugee and Asylum Policy: National Passion versus National Interest." *NPG Forum Series.* Feb. 1992. http://www.npg.org/forum_series/ref&asylum_policy.htm. This article in Negative Population Growth's forum offers a counterargument against the ABC decision.

Multimedia Sources

"El Salvador Migration." http://www.youtube.com/watch?v=630D6v5iZRY. 10:29 minutes. Posted by University of Scranton, this short video discusses the reasons why El Salvador migration has been so prevalent.

"Immigrant Sanctuary Movement." *Religion and Ethnics Newseekly/PBS.* June 15, 2007. Online Video. http://www.pbs.org/wnet/religionandethics/week1042/feature.html#. Examines the "New Sanctuary Movement" that has emerged now that the ABC Settlement has ended.

"Lou Dobbs and the Sanctuary Movement." http://www.youtube.com/watch?v=DGhp8r6BuXQ. 6:23 minutes. Discusses the ongoing debate about the "new Sanctuary Movement" of 2007.

75. Radio Martí's First Broadcast to Cuba (May 20, 1985)

A prominent leader of the Cuban American exile community in Florida, Jorge Mas Canosa, lobbied for the creation and support of a broadcasting station that could transmit news stories and information to the island of Cuba. Believing that Fidel Castro and his communist government suppressed the Cuban people by controlling outside news and information, the Cuban American leader won the support of President Ronald Reagan and members of the U.S. Congress to create such a forum. In September 1983, Congress passed a bill that created Radio Martí, named for the late 19th-century Cuban hero Jose Martí who died during the Cuban War of Independence with Spain and a long-time critic of U.S. involvement in the political affairs of Latin America. A month later, in October 1983, President Reagan signed the Radio Broadcasting to Cuba Act into law. The law provided for funding of station programming, which would be operated and administered by the United States Information Agency, a governmental body that also operates Voice of America. On May 20, 1985, the first broadcast was sent to Cuba from the United States. On March 27, 1990, Radio Martí sent its first televised broadcast. The station, which broadcasts in Spanish, has been accused of tainting its news stories and coverage to denigrate the Cuban government and encourage its overthrow. As such, the Cuban government tries its best to jam or disrupt frequencies that come into Cuba from the outside, especially those broadcasted by Radio y Television Martí.

TERM PAPER SUGGESTIONS

1. Jorge Mas Canosa, who was a co-founder of the Cuban American National Foundation and administrative leader for Radio y Television Martí, has been a controversial figure with respect to his management of the station. Discuss the role he played in establishing the broadcast forum, and explain why a number of individuals and agencies have accused him of maintaining a strong, biased programming agenda at the station.

2. Analyze the government funding of Radio y Television Martí, and highlight the controversy surrounding this.

3. A principal reason for President Reagan's signing the Radio Broadcasting to Cuba Act in 1983 was to provide Cubans with news and information that was not influenced or monitored by Fidel Castro's government. Argue to what degree Radio y Television Martí has been successful or effective in bringing about change within Cuba or awareness among its citizens.

4. The International Telecommunication Union, which is an information and broadcasting agency within the United Nations, has accused Radio y

Television Martí and the U.S. government that funds the station of violating international laws and fanning the flames of hostility. Argue whether you agree with this accusation, and determine whether the broadcasts are meant to create civil unrest and to topple the Cuban government. Is Radio y Televisión Martí a self-serving propaganda machine bent on destroying the Castro regime or does it provide fair news stories as a service to a citizenship whose information is controlled?

ALTERNATIVE TERM PAPER SUGGESTION

1. As a news reporter for Radio y Televisión Martí, write a report on a current issue in the Cuban American community in Miami, Florida, to be broadcasted to Cuba. Create a podcast of this story for the station. Remember that your audience is the citizens of Cuba, and you will want to ensure that your story promotes the important role the exile community plays in wanting Cuba to be liberated from Castro.

SUGGESTED SOURCES

Primary Sources

Radio Broadcasting to Cuba Act. http://ecip.loc.gov/cgi-bin/cpquery/?&sid= cp109b23IJ&refer=&r_n=sr035.109&db_id=109&item=& sel=TOC_ 353813&. Includes the act ratified by the U.S. Congress in September 1983 and signed into law by President Reagan the following month.

"Radio y Televisión Martí." http://www.martinoticias.com/. Both a Spanish and English site is available; this is the official Web site that includes text articles, TV, radio broadcasts, and relevant links and archives.

"Statement of the Radio Broadcasting to Cuba Act." http://www.reagan.utexas. edu/archives/speeches/1983/101183d.htm. Offers President Reagan's justification for signing the bill into law in October 1983.

Secondary Sources

Adams, David. "Time to Scrap TV Marti, Critics Say." *St. Petersburg Times,* Feb. 16, 2009: A1. Reports on the costly endeavor to maintain the program operation and discusses lack of interest among Cubans.

Parker, Laura. "TV Marti: Igniting War of Airwaves." *The Washington Post,* Mar. 27, 1990: A3. Analyzes the radio cold war with Cuba and Cuba's jamming and disruption of Radio y Televisión Martí's broadcasts.

Robles, Frances. "Survey May Not Be Clear Indicator of How Many Cubans Listen to Radio Martí." *McClatchy-Tribune News Service,* Feb. 4, 2009. Discusses a U.S. congressional report questioning the extent of Radio Martí's audience ratings.

World Wide Web

"Privatize Radio and TV Marti." http://www.alvinsnyder.com/privatize_radio_and_tv_marti_54918.htm. *Miami Herald* columnist Alvin Snyder presents background information on Radio y Televisión Martí's founding and funding, and discusses why its headquarters were moved from Washington, D.C., to Miami shortly after its creation.

"Radio and TV Marti." http://www.bbg.gov/broadcasters/marti.html/. Includes a profile of the station and current broadcasting highlights.

"Radio TV Martí: Office of Cuba Broadcasting." http://ibb7-2.ibb.gov/pubaff/ocbfact.html. Provides a general overview of the station's history, programming content, and significant links for further research.

"Radio and TV Martí: Washington Guns after Castro at Any Cost." http://www.coha.org/radio-and-tv-marti-washington-guns-after-castro-at-any-cost/. Detailed article from Katie Herr of the Council on Hemispheric Affairs explains the controversy surrounding the extensive government funding of the broadcast and programming material.

Multimedia Sources

"Should State-Run Media Be Broadcast in the United States? A Debate on Radio and TV Martí Airing in South Florida." http://www.democracynow.org/2007/1/10/should_state_run_media_be_broadcast. Audio and video streams of this January 2007 story explain the controversy with broadcasting propaganda within the United States despite a current law prohibiting this.

"Tom Gjelton Reports on the Controversy over Radio Martí." http://www.npr.org/templates/story/story.php?storyId=1030835. Investigates the 1996 allegations that Jorge Mas Canosa, a prominent leader in the U.S. Cuban exile community, abused his position at the station for self-serving interests.

76. Immigration Reform and Control Act (November 1986)

On November 6, 1986, President Ronald Regan signed into law the Immigration Reform and Control Act of 1986 (IRCA), also known as the Simpson-Mazzoli Act. This law, which took Congress nearly five years and multiple revisions to pass, held far-reaching changes to previous immigration policies and practices. Among the most pivotal changes were IRCA's amnesty provisions, which allowed over 2 million illegal immigrants who had resided continuously in the United States since January 1, 1982, to apply for permanent residence status. Many of those eligible had previously sought and been denied refugee status after fleeing the political instability of Guatemala, El Salvador, and Nicaragua in the 1980s. IRCA now cleared the way for them to apply for legal residency without penalty or punishment. IRCA's second significant change was its new employer provisions. Prior to IRCA, employers were not required to authenticate employees' eligibility for work in the United States; however, under IRCA, all employers were required to file an I-9 employment form for all employees, verifying their employees had appropriate documentation to work. Over the years, IRCA has had many critics—some who thought the amnesty provisions encouraged further illegal immigration, some who believed the employer provisions ultimately discriminated against Latinos if employers presumed them to be illegally in the United States. Yet, IRCA also had many supporters who believed that IRCA placed appropriate controls on employers and allowed one-time undocumented residents to start afresh.

TERM PAPER SUGGESTIONS

1. Examine the history of the IRCA. Why did it take five years for Congress to pass this legislation? What groups favored the reform? What were opponents' concerns? What role did President Reagan play in furthering this legislation?

2. Investigate how IRCA altered employer hiring practices. What changes did IRCA require employers make to their hiring strategies? What practices did IRCA make illegal for employers? How did the act unintentionally lead to a rise in subcontractor employment?

3. Examine IRCA's amnesty provisions. What historical events, particularly in Central America, led to these amnesty provisions? What key players were involved in the law's passage? How did the Sanctuary Movement increase public support for this law?

4. Compare IRCA with a previous U.S. immigration law: the Bracero Program. What similarities and differences exist between these two pieces of legislation? How did IRCA alter long-standing U.S. immigration policies for illegal immigrants?

5. Discuss the impact of the 1994 North American Fair Trade Agreement (NAFTA) on U.S. immigration, particularly from Canada and Mexico. How did NAFTA alter immigration standards that were established under IRCA? What provisions of IRCA are still in place today?

6. Take a position on the success or failure of IRCA. Give specific reasons why you agree or disagree with this law, its amnesty provisions, and its new restrictions on employers.

ALTERNATIVE TERM PAPER SUGGESTIONS

1. Create an iMovie discussing IRCA's historical impact and describing how IRCA impacted immigration patterns and hiring practices. Be sure to discuss the factors that led to this law's amnesty and the employer compliance provisions.

2. Imagine you have been hired to train a corporation's human resources department to comply with IRCA. Create a pamphlet and a PowerPoint presentation training human resources to follow IRCA's employer guidelines. Be sure to discuss the I-9 form and what employee documentation will be necessary for hiring new employees.

SUGGESTED SOURCES

Primary Sources

Immigration Reform and Control Act of 1986. http://www.vec.virginia.gov/vec-portal/employer/pdf/IRCA1986.pdf. Contains complete text of the law.

"Statement on Signing the Immigration Reform and Control Act of 1986." http://www.reagan.utexas.edu/archives/speeches/1986/110686b.htm. Features President Reagan's November 6, 1986, speech on signed IRCA.

Secondary Sources

Baker, Susan Gonzalez. *The Cautious Welcome: The Legalization Program of the Immigration Reform and Control Act.* Lanham, MD: University Press of America, 1990. Baker's data-driven book focuses on the law's goals, implementation, and impact.

Espensoza, Ceclia M. "The Illusory Provisions of Sanctions: The Immigration Reform and Control Act of 1986." *Georgetown Law Journal* 8 (1994): 343–389.

Laham, Nicolas. *Ronald Reagan and the Politics of Immigration Reform.* Westport, CT: Greenwood Press, 2000. Laham's fifth chapter is devoted to the IRCA, with a focus on Ronald Reagan's role in this legislation.

Lowell, Lindsay, Jay Teachman, and Zhongren Jing. "Unintended Consequences of Immigration Reform: Discrimination and Hispanic Employment." *Demography* 32, no. 4 (Nov. 1995): 617–628. Article examines how the IRCA correlates with employer discrimination against Latino workers.

Zolberg, Aristide R. " 'Reforming the Back Door': The Immigrant Reform and Control Act of 1986 in Historical Perspective." In *Immigration Reconsidered: History, Sociology, and Politics,* edited by Virginia Yans-McLaughlin. New York: Oxford University Press, 1990, pp. 315–339. Discusses IRCA's impact on three immigrant groups, including Latinos.

World Wide Web

"Immigration Reform and Control Act." http://www.usimmigrationsupport. org/irca.html. Provides a comprehensive overview of the act with a statistical analysis of the law's effects.

Stumpf, Juliet, and Bruce Friedman. "Advancing Civil Rights through Immigration Law: One Step Forward, Two Steps Back?" http://www1.law. nyu.edu/journals/legislation/issues/vol6num1/stumpf.pdf. Argues that an uneasy relationship exists between immigration and civil rights laws.

"Ten-Year Impact of the Immigration Reform and Control Act of 1986." http://www.numbersusa.com/content/files/pdf/1986%20irca%20chart. pdf. Provides a statistical chart of IRCA's impact on the U.S. population with detailed explanations of IRCA's several provisions.

U.S Equal Opportunity Employment Commission. "Pre-Employment Inquiries and Citizenship." http://www.eeoc.gov/laws/practices/inquiries_ citizenship.cfm. Details what employer practices are illegal under IRCA.

Multimedia Sources

"1986 Law Offers Clues for Immigration Debate." *National Public Radio.* 4:50 minutes. http://www.npr.org/templates/player/mediaPlayer.html?action= 1&t=1&islist=false&id=5324476&m=5324477. Interview with University of California Irvine Professor Louis DeSipio reviews IRCA's history and its problematic employer sanctions.

"Immigration Proposition Brings Echoes of 1986." *National Public Radio.* 5:12 minutes. http://www.npr.org/templates/player/mediaPlayer.html? action=1&t=1&islist=false&id=1589757&m=1589758 Interview with Princeton University Professor Douglass Massey discusses IRCA's enforcement and sanctions.

In the Shadow of the Law. University of California Center for Media and Independent Learning, 1991. DVD. 58 minutes. Discusses economic issues, the impact, and difficulties experienced by illegal aliens applying for legal status under IRCA.

The Other Side of the Border. PBS Video, 1987. VHS. 60 minutes. Discusses illegal immigration and IRCA's potential impact.

77. Republic of Nicaragua v. The United States of America (1986)

On June 27, 1986, The International Court of Justice (ICJ), the judicial branch of the United Nations, ruled in a case called *Republic of Nicaragua v. The United States of America* (commonly called *Nicaragua v. U.S.*). Nicaragua brought the case to the ICJ, arguing that the United States had violated both Article 2 (4) of the United Nations (UN) Charter and a treaty between the United States and Nicaragua. Further, Nicaragua claimed that U.S. financial support, training, and gifting of military weapons to the Contras violated Nicaragua's sovereignty; proof for this was provided in the form of a 90-page 1983 Civil Intelligence Agency (CIA) training manual distributed to the Contras, as well as the U.S. Senate investigations into the Iran-Contra scandal. In response, the United States initially argued that its actions were permitted under the UN's "right of collective self-defense" and that the CIA had merely helped to moderate actions already taken by the Contras. Later, counsel for the United States argued that the ICJ did not have sufficient jurisdiction to hear the case, and, by 1986, the United States had withdrawn completely from the proceedings. The court's ruling in *Nicaragua v. U.S.* rejected the argument that the court had no jurisdiction, citing Article 36 of the 1956 U.S. Treaty with Nicaragua that called for the UN to hold "compulsory jurisdiction." Additionally, the ICJ found the United States guilty of violating Nicaragua's sovereignty through an "unlawful use of force." Although the court ruled in Nicaragua's favor and the UN General Assembly voted (94 to 3) on November

3, 1986, to urge U.S. compliance, the United States refused and blocked all attempts at acquiescence through its permanent position on the UN's Security Council. Nicaragua dropped its pursuit of reparations in 1991, but the case raised important questions regarding U.S.-Latin America policies and the UN's role as a world court.

TERM PAPER SUGGESTIONS

1. Explain the court's findings and ruling in *Nicaragua v. U.S.* What evidence provided the basis for this ruling? What elements of Nicaragua's case did the ICJ reject and which did it support? Why did the United States withdraw from the court proceedings? Summarize the case and its importance in U.S.-Latin American relations and history, discussing the precedents set in *Nicaragua v United States.*

2. Examine the International Court of Justice and its jurisdiction over countries. Who votes on this court? How are the justices selected? How is the ICJ's jurisdiction determined? What penalties exist, if any, for violating the court's rulings?

3. Investigate the 1983 CIA manual distributed to Contras, *Psychological Operations in Guerrilla Warfare,* at the center of Nicaragua's case. Do you agree with the ICJ's finding that this manual violated Nicaragua's sovereignty and reflected an unlawful use of force? Discuss how this manual compares with former U.S. policies toward Latin America, such as the Good Neighbor Policy or the Monroe Doctrine.

4. Discuss the 1956 Treaty of Friendship, Commerce, and Navigation between the United States and Nicaragua. How did this treaty provide the basis for much of the court's ruling in this case? Under what circumstances was the treaty formed?

5. Examine the United States' initial claim to collective self-defense and its assistance of El Salvador. How did 1980s military and political upheavals in El Salvador, Guatemala, and Costa Rica coincide with this argument that other countries sought U.S. protection against Nicaragua? Why did the court reject this argument?

ALTERNATIVE TERM PAPER SUGGESTIONS

1. Imagine yourself a lawyer for either the United States or Nicaragua during *Nicaragua v. U.S.* Write a brief regarding the legal situation

and use evidence to defend your case. Be sure to reference both the UN's charters and conventions as well as the United States and Nicaragua's 1956 Treaty.

2. Create a PowerPoint presentation providing a comprehensive overview of the case, the arguments, and the court's rulings. Be certain to discuss the precedents this case established with regard to international law.

SUGGESTED SOURCES

Primary Source

International Court of Justice. "Republic of Nicaragua v. The United States of America." http://www.icj-cij.org/docket/index.php?sum=367&code=nus&p1=3&p2=3&case=70&k=66&p3=5. Contains the verdict, initial proceedings, and oral and written arguments in the case.

Secondary Sources

Hargrove, John Lawrence. "The Nicaragua Judgment and the Future of the Law of Force and Self-Defense." *The American Journal of International Law* 81, no. 1 (Jan. 1987): 135–143. Hargrove's article discusses the impact of the court's decision as setting a precedent for future disagreements between nations.

Leigh, Monroe. "Nicaragua v. United States of America." *American Journal of International Law* 79(1985): 442–446. Article offers a comprehensive overview of the court case and responses of both countries.

Murphy, John. *The United States and the Rule of Law in International Affairs.* New York: Cambridge University Press, 2004. Murphy's seventh chapter covers the impact of this case on the International Court of Justice's future decisions.

Rosenne, Shabtai, and Terry D. Gill. *The World Court: What It Is and How It Works.* 4th ed. Leiden, Netherlands: Brill, 1989. Chapter 6 discusses *Nicaragua v. United States* and other chapters explain how the world court system works.

Van Dervort, Thomas R. *International Law and Organization: An Introduction.* Newbury Park, CA: Sage, 1997. Discusses the history and implementation of international law with a section devoted to the case.

World Wide Web

"Germain's International Court of Justice Research Guide." http://library.law school.cornell.edu/WhatWeDo/ResearchGuides/ICJ.cfm. Provides an overview of the ICJ and a bibliography for researching this topic.

"Nicaragua v. United States." http://www.economicexpert.com/a/Nicaragua: v:United:States.htm. Provides an overview of the case and the court ruling with a graph of the individual judge's votes in the case.

"Psychological Operations in Guerrilla Warfare." http://www.freewebs.com/ moeial/CIA's%20Psychological%20Operations%20in%20Guerrilla% 20Warefare.pdf. Contains the full 90-page CIA training manual that became a central issue in the *Nicaragua v. United States* ruling.

"United States—Trade Measures Affecting Nicaragua." http://www.worldtrade law.net/reports/gattpanels/nicembargo.pdf. Discusses the economic inter-actions between the United States and Nicaragua leading up to the case.

Multimedia Sources

Nicaragua No Pasaran. Frontline Films, 2008. DVD. 73 minutes. Discusses the rise of the Sandanista Party and the Contras, background events that led to the *Nicaragua v. United States* case.

"Noam Chomsky on Central America." Streaming Video. 10:13 minutes. http://www.youtube.com/watch?v=Irs8urW2Jp4. At Northwestern Uni-versity, public intellectual Noam Chomsky discusses the case and its impact on U.S.-Central America relations.

78. Ileana Ros-Lehtinen Becomes the First Latina Elected to Congress (1989)

In 1989, Ileana Ros-Lehtinen made history when she became the first Lat-ina elected to Congress. Her election to the U.S. House of Representatives also made her Florida's first female Republican Representative, Congress' first Cuban American member, and the first Latino to represent Florida in 166 years. Ros-Lehtinen initially won her seat to Florida's 18th District in a bitterly contested special election to replace the late Claude D. Pepper, but she was easily reelected the next year and has successfully defended her seat in biannual elections thereafter, including an unopposed run for office in 1994. Born in Havana, Cuba, Ros-Lehtinen came to the United States in 1952, at age seven, and grew up in Miami, Florida, where she went to college and graduate school. Prior to serving in government, Ros-Lehtinen founded Eastern Academy, a private elementary school, where she also taught. In 1982, Ros-Lehtinen entered politics, first as a member of Florida's House of Representatives then as a Florida State Senator in 1986. She left the Florida State Senate when she won her position in the U.S.

House of Representatives. As a Representative serving a district with a majority Latino population, Ros-Lehtinen has played a prominent role in issues of concern to her community, such as education; childcare; the environment; lesbian, gay, bisexual, and transgender (LGBT) equality; and senior citizen rights. However, it is in international relations where Ros-Lehtinen's work is best known. A ranking member of the House's Committee on Foreign Affairs, Ros-Lehtinen was an active supporter of the Helms Burton Act, the Cuban Democracy Act, and the Central American Fair Trade Agreement. Today, Ros-Lehtinen is the most senior ranking female Republican in the U.S. House of Representatives and has been actively engaged in a campaign for Honduran civil rights.

TERM PAPER SUGGESTIONS

1. Discuss Ros-Lehtinen's representation on Latino issues in Congress. What policies and issues have characterized her congressional career since 1989? What committees has she served on and what bills has she authored? Describe her impact on Latinos, particularly those in her congressional district.

2. Analyze Ros-Lehtinen's support for the Helms Burton Act and the Cuban Democracy Act. How has her membership in the Cuban American Lobby and the Congressional Cuba Democracy Caucus, as well as her service on the House Committee on Foreign Affairs, made her an active voice in U.S. relations with Cuba?

3. Investigate Ros-Lehtinen's role in the Elián González case and her public remarks about Fidel Castro. How did her experiences as a child emigrant from Cuba impact her position on González's case and Castro's rule?

4. Ros-Lehtinen made the news in 2010 when she wrote a personal letter to President Barrack Obama about Honduras. Examine Ros-Lehtinen's letter and her remarks about Honduran civil rights. How is her letter in keeping with her concerns for Latin American issues? Researching Honduras, do you agree or disagree with Ros-Lehtinen's position on Honduras and the United States' responsibility to help?

ALTERNATIVE TERM PAPER SUGGESTIONS

1. Create a Webography for Ros-Lehtinen. Be sure to discuss her childhood emigration from Cuba to the United States, her career in education, and her work in U.S.-international relations.

2. Create a PowerPoint presentation focused on Ros-Lehtinen's congressional track record on Latin American foreign affairs, environmental concerns, and education. Discuss her support for key areas of legislation in these areas and how each has impacted the Latino population in her district.

SUGGESTED SOURCES

Primary Source

"Congresswoman Ileana Ros-Lehtinen." http://ros-lehtinen.house.gov/. Ros-Lehtinen's official homepage features an autobiography, video and picture galleries, and discussion of key legislation.

Secondary Sources

Cruz, Barbara C. "Ileana Ros-Lehtinen." In *Latinas in the United States*, edited by Vicki Ruíz and Sánchez Korrol. Vol. 1. Bloomington: Indiana University Press, 2006, pp. 645–646. Provides an overview of Ros-Lehtinen's career.

Pachon, Harry, and Louis DeSipio. "Latino Elected Officials in the 1990s." *Political Science and Politics*. 25, no. 2 (June 1992): 212–217. Discusses Ros-Lehtinen in conjunction with a rise in Latino elected officials in the United States.

Rosenthal, Cindy Simon, ed. *Women Transforming Congress*. Norman: University of Oklahoma Press, 2002. Ros-Lehtinen is featured in several chapters of this anthology.

Schmal, John P. *The Journey to Latino Political Representation*. Westminster, MD: Heritage Books, 2007. In addition to a section on Ros-Lehtinen, this book discusses Latino voters and the rise of Latino political organizations.

Telgen, Diane, and Kamp, Jim, ed. *Notable Hispanic American Women*. Detroit, MI: Gale Research, 1993, pp. 356–357. Discusses Ros-Lehtinen as a Latino community member, focusing on key issues in her tenure as House Representative.

World Wide Web

"Congress Debates Elian." PBS.com. Jan. 25, 2000. http://www.pbs.org/news hour/bb/international/jan-june00/cuba_1-25.html. Features interview with Ros-Lehtinen on the Elián González case.

"Hispanic Americans in Congress, 1822–1995." http://www.loc.gov/rr/his panic/congress/introduction.html. Discusses Ros-Lehtinen's place among other prominent Latino Congress members in history.

"Hispanics in Congress: Ileana Ros-Lehtinen." http://www.loc.gov/rr/hispanic/congress/roslehtinen.html. Brief biography from the Library of Congress discusses Ros-Lehtinen's district.

"Ileana Ros-Lehtinen: The First Hispanic Woman in Congress." Women of the GOP. http://gopwomen.blogspot.com/2009/10/ileana-ros-lehtinen-first-hispanic.html. Bio discusses Ros-Lehtinen's voting record and key voting issues.

"U.S. Congresswoman Ileana Ros-Lehtinen Gives Letter to Obama on Honduras." http://www.kirkf.com/2009/07/02/us-congresswomen-ileana-ros-lehtinen-gives-letter-to-obama-on-honduras/. Features Ros-Lehtinen's letter to President Obama on human rights violations in Honduras.

Multimedia Sources

"Congresswoman Ileana Ros-Leihtinen." http://www.youtube.com/user/IleanaRosLehtinen. Ros-Lehtinen's YouTube page features over 20 interviews, press events, and speeches.

"Cuba: 40th Anniversary of Revolution." National Public Radio. Dec. 31, 1998. 47:55 minutes. http://www.npr.org/templates/story/story.php?storyId=1009984. NPR's radio broadcast features Ros-Lehtinen discussing Cuba's status 40 years after Castro came to power.

79. Voting Rights Language Assistance Act (1992)

In 1992, Congress passed the Voting Rights Language Assistance Act, an amendment to the Voting Rights Act of 1965 that extended the language provisions act (Section 203) and provided new criteria for determining language-minority status. Prior to 1992, the Voting Rights Act required assistance if the county's population of a single language minority group was 5 percent or greater and the illiteracy rate was greater than the national average. The 1992 act maintained the 5 percent rule, but added that if the population of single language minority citizens was greater than 10,000, the polling places needed to provide language interpreters and bilingual ballots. This increased the number of eligible regions as large cities where the population of single language minority groups was greater than 10,000 citizens but less than 5 percent of the city's population would not be eligible for voting protections. Likewise, the 1992 legislation revised the illiteracy statutes to focus on limited English proficiency as the new measure for language assistance. Although the Voting Rights Language Assistance Act remains controversial, particularly with English-only advocacy groups, Congress voted 98–0 to renew these provisions in the Voting Rights Act Renewal Act of 2006, which extends Sections 5 and 203 of the Voting Rights Language Assistance Act until 2032.

TERM PAPER SUGGESTIONS

1. Explain how the Voting Rights Language Assistance Act altered the language-minority criteria of the Voting Rights Act. What changes in minority voting and demographics occurred between 1965 and 1992 to convince Congress to make these modifications?

2. Analyze the Voting Rights Language Assistance Act's impact on Sections 5 and 203 of the Voting Rights Act section of the law. Why are these two sections so controversial? How does the Voting Rights Language Assistance Act define Limited English Proficiency (LEP)? How did the act impact Latino voters, particularly in urban areas?

3. Examine the arguments made on behalf of language minority voters to the Voting Rights Language Assistance Act of 1992. What reasons, statistics, and evidence did these groups provide to support their position that the language provisions of the 1965 Voting Rights Act needed renewal? What counterarguments did they address?

4. Critics of the Voting Rights Language Assistance Act argue that its provisions are incredibly costly for states; some even argue that the legislation violates the constitutional rights of states to run elections. In contrast, others argue that the legislation is integral to democracy and equal protection to voters. Take a position on the issue, giving reasons to support your stance. Be sure to examine the U.S. Constitution's Fourteenth and Fifteenth Amendments.

ALTERNATIVE TERM PAPER SUGGESTIONS

1. Assume the role of an elections board member for a voting area with a large Latino population, 5 percent or more who have limited English proficiency. Create an online pamphlet that discusses your area's demographics and how your polling places will comply with the Voting Rights Language Assistance Act.

2. Create a series of podcasts about the passage of the Voting Rights Language Assistance Act and its subsequent renewal in 2006. Examine

the key players in this bill's passage into law. What role did Latino interest groups and governmental agencies (such the Mexican American Legal Defense and Education Fund (MALDEF) and the Congressional Hispanic Caucus) play in 1992 and 2006? What key amendments were introduced to limit or expand Section 203?

SUGGESTED SOURCES

Primary Sources

United States Congress. *Voting Rights Language Assistance Act of 1992: Report Together with Dissenting Views (to Accompany H.R. 4312).* Washington, DC: U.S. Government Printing Office, 1992. Contains this legislation's provisions and the arguments made before Congress.

"The Voting Rights Language Assistance Act of 1992." The Library of Congress. http://thomas.loc.gov/cgi-bin/query/C?c102:./temp/~c102n BGcDV. Features printer-friendly version of the act as passed by the Senate and House of Representatives.

Secondary Sources

de la Garza, Rodolfo, and Louis DeSipio. "Reshaping the Tub: The Limits of the VRA for Latino Electoral Politics." In *The Future of the Voting Rights Act,* edited by David L. Epstein et al. New York: Russell Sage Foundation Press, pp. 139–162. Discusses the impact of language assistance on Latino voters.

Jones-Correa, Michael. "Language Provisions under the Voting Rights Act: How Effective Are They?" *Social Science Quarterly* 86, no. 3 (Aug. 2005): 549–564. Jones-Correa argues that the Voting Rights Language Assistance Act has been instrumental in helping to enfranchise Latinos.

Laney, Garrine P. *The Voting Rights Act of 1965: Historical Background and Current Issues.* Hauppauge, NY: Nova Publishers, 2003. Laney's sixth chapter covers the issues and debates surrounding the 1992 language provisions.

Tucker, James Thomas. "The Politics of Persuasion: Passage of the Voting Rights Act Reauthorization Act of 2006." *Journal of Legislation* 33, no. 2 (2007): 205–267. http://electionlawblog.org/archives/tucker.pdf. Tucker examines the 2006 political process and arguments made during the 2006 renewal of 1992's Voting Rights Language Assistance Act.

World Wide Web

Jones-Correa, Michael, and Karthick Ramakrishnan. "Studying the Effects of Language Provisions under the Voting Rights Act," May 26, 2009.

http://www.allacademic.com//meta/p_mla_apa_research_citation/0/
8/8/3/5/pages88351/p88351-1.php. Article presents data demonstrating
the Voting Rights Language Assistance Act's impact on Latino voting.

"Myths & Facts about Section 203 of the Voting Rights Act." http://www.civil
rights.org/voting-rights/vra/section-203.html. Addresses common misconceptions about the Voting Rights Act's language provisions.

Tucker, James Thomas. "Enfranchising Language Minority Citizens: The
Bilingual Voting Provisions of the Voting Rights Act." http://www1.
law.nyu.edu/journals/legislation/issues/vol10num1/tucker.pdf. Discusses
the Voting Rights Language Assistance Act provisions and its impact on
language minority voters.

United States Department of Justice. "About Language Minority Voting Rights."
http://www.justice.gov/crt/voting/sec_203/activ_203.php. Explains the
legal requirements with guidelines for election compliance.

Multimedia Sources

"Congressmen Look to Extend Voting Rights Act." National Public Radio,
May 3, 2006. 11:53 minutes. http://www.npr.org/templates/player/
mediaPlayer.html?action=1&t=1&islist=false&id=5378847&m=
5378848. Contains audio interview with Congressmen Steve Cabot
and John Lewis on the 2006 legislation to extend the 1992 Voting
Rights Language Assistance Act.

"Debo Adegbile Talks about the Voting Rights Act." *Tavis Smiley,* July 1,
2009. Streaming Video. 11:20 minutes. http://video.pbs.org/video/
1171383920/. Interview with Debo Adegbile, who argued in favor of
Section 5 of the Voting Rights Act before the U.S. Supreme Court,
discusses the constitutionality of the language provisions.

80. *Church of the Lukumi Babalu Aye v. City of Hialeah, Florida* (1993)

In the mid-1980s, Ernesto Pichardo announced his plans to open the
Church of the Lukumi Babulu Aye in the city of Hialeah, a largely
Cuban American community in Florida. Pichardo's church intended to
practice Santeria, a Cuban religion that blends West African religious
practices with Roman Catholicism. At the center of debate were Santeria's religious practices, which call for the ritual sacrifices of animals and,
on occasion, human consumption of the meat. Pichardo's intentions of
opening the first church to practice Santeria openly in the United States

raised an outcry from Hialeah residents, especially within the Cuban community. In response, city officials passed specific ordinances prohibiting ritual animal sacrifices, thus making the Church of the Lukumi Babulu Aye's religious practices illegal. Pichardo and his church sued the city, arguing that these ordinances violated their First Amendment guarantee to religious freedom. In their defense, the City of Hialeah argued that it had a compelling interest to protect the public from both uninspected meat consumption and improper animal carcass disposal; they further contended that local governments had the right to create and enforce zoning laws to limit animal slaughter. Initially, the lower courts agreed with the City of Hialeah, citing another Supreme Court case, *Employment Division v. Smith,* that held that religious freedoms are not guaranteed for illegal activities. However, Pichardo and his church appealed the lower court's decision, and, in 1993, the Supreme Court unanimously ruled in favor of the Church of the Lukumi Babalu Aye, arguing that the Hialeah's ordinances violated the First Amendment's Free Exercise clause because the city's laws against ritual sacrifice exclusively targeted Pichardo's church. Despite having won the case, the Church of the Lukumi Babulu Aye continues to occupy a controversial role for Florida's Cuban American communities, with protests and legal battles continuing between Hialeah's residents, municipal leaders, and church members.

TERM PAPER SUGGESTIONS

1. Describe the role of the First Amendment in *Church of the Lukumi Babalu Aye v. City of Hialeah*. What arguments were made regarding the First Amendment in this case? How did this case set new precedents for the Supreme Court with regard to the First Amendment's Free Exercise clause and the court's own concept of a neutrality test for city laws against religious practices?

2. Explain the religion of Santeria, as practiced by the Church of the Lukumi Babalu Aye. What are the religion's origins? What role does animal sacrifice play in this religion? How does Santeria combine various religious practices from Roman Catholicism and traditional African cultures as these groups met in Latin American countries?

3. Cubans who commonly practice Santeria are often of African heritage and Santeria has been controversial in Cuba as well as the United States. Examine the role of race and perceived racism in the

background to this Supreme Court case. How did the case reflect tensions for Florida's Cuban American community about racial heritage and religious practices?

4. Analyze the impact of Church of the Lukumi Babalu Aye on the Cuban American communities in Florida. How did the case divide Cuban Americans? What concerns did Cuban American leaders express about the case and its affect on mainstream public perceptions of Cuban Americans? Why does Pichardo's church continue to clash culturally with the Hialeah's residents even today?

ALTERNATIVE TERM PAPER SUGGESTIONS

1. Research the amicus curiae briefs of this Supreme Court case and write one of your own supporting either the Church of the Lukumi Babalu Aye or Hialeah's arguments.

2. Create a PowerPoint presentation explaining the practice of Santeria and its place in Cuban and Cuban American culture. Be sure to discuss the various reactions of the Cuban American community in Florida to this Supreme Court case.

SUGGESTED SOURCES

Primary Source

"Church of the Lukumi Babalu Aye v. City of Hialeah, 508 U.S. 520 (1993)." http://caselaw.lp.findlaw.com/scripts/getcase.pl?navby=CASE&court= US&vol=508&page=520. Features full text of Justice Anthony Kennedy's majority opinion for the court.

Secondary Sources

Brown, Steve. "Blood and Precedent: *Church of The Lukumi Babalu Aye v. City of Hialeah* (1993)." In *Creating Constitutional Change: Clashes Over Power and Liberty in the Supreme Court*, edited by Gregg Ivers and Kevin T. McGuire. Charlottesville: University of Virginia Press, 2004, pp. 181–193. Provides a history of Santeria and the practices of the Church of the Lukumi Babalu Aye.

Cruz, R. Ted. "Animal Sacrifice and Equal Protection Free Exercise: Church of the Lukumi Babalu Aye Inc. v. City." *Harvard Journal of Law & Public Policy* 17, no. 1 (1994): 262–274. Analyzes the case and its impact on cases centered on religious freedom.

Drinan, Robert F., and Jennifer I. Huffman. "Religious Freedom and the Oregon v. Smith and Hialeah Cases." *Journal of Church & State* 35, no. 1 (1993): 19–26. Discusses this case and the *Employment Division v. Smith* decision.

O'Brien, David M. *Animal Sacrifice and Religious Freedom: Church of the Lukumi Babalu Aye v. City of Hialeah.* Lawrence: University Press of Kansas, 2004. Provides a behind-the-scenes case investigation with chapters on minority-group religious freedoms and culture clashes caused by religious practices.

Palmié, Stephan. "Whose Centre, Whose Margin? Notes Towards an Archaeology of US Supreme Court Case 91-948, 1993 Church of The Lukumi vs. City of Hialeah, South Florida." In *Inside and Outside the Law: Anthropological Studies of Authority and Ambiguity,* edited by Olivia Harris. New York: Routledge, 1996, pp.144–163. Presents a comprehensive background on the case's foregrounding events, discussing racial tensions in Hialeah.

Patrick, John J., and Gerald P. Long. *Constitutional Debates on Freedom of Religion: A Documentary History.* Westport, CT: Greenwood Press, 1999. Offers an overview of the case, Justice Kennedy's majority opinion, and Justice Souter's concurring opinion.

Willing, Richard. "Courts Asked to Consider Culture." *USA Today,* May 25, 2004. Discusses the culture clashes that continue between the Church of the Lukumi Babalu Aye and Hialeah 11 years after the Supreme Court verdict.

World Wide Web

"Church of the the Lukumi Babalu Aye." http://www.church-of-the-the-Lukumi.org/Site%206/Welcome.html. This is the official Web site of the first Santeria church in the United States.

Doheny, Shannon L. "Free Exercise Does Not Protect Animal Sacrifice: The Misconception of *Church of The Lukumi Babalu Aye v. City of Hialeah* and Constitutional Solutions for Stopping Animal Sacrifice." http://www.animallaw.info/articles/arus2journalanimallaw121.htm. Argues that the Lukumi decision is widely misunderstood and does not prevent government from prohibiting animal sacrifice. Provides an overview of Santeria's history.

"Freedom of Religion—Further Readings." http://law.jrank.org/pages/12435/Freedom-Religion.html. Explains the Free Exercise clause of the First Amendment and the Supreme Court's "Neutrality Test."

"Santeria." http://www.religioustolerance.org/santeri.htm. Provides an overview of Santeria, its customs and practices, as well as links to Internet sources and books.

Willing, Richard. "Courts Asked to Consider Culture." *USA Today*, May 25, 2004. http://www.usatoday.com/news/washington/judicial/2004-05-24-courts-culture_x.htm. Discusses the culture clashes that continue between the Church of the Lukumi Babalu Aye and the City of Haleah.

Multimedia Sources

"Church of the the Lukumi Babalu Aye v. Hialeah—Oral Argument." 58:03 minutes. http://www.oyez.org/cases/1990-1999/1992/1992_91_948/ argument. Features audio recording of Attorney Douglas Laycock before the Supreme Court on November 4, 1992.

Havana Centro: Cuba's Musical and Spiritual Underground. Customflix, 2007. DVD. 32 minutes. Documentary discusses the roots of Santeria as practiced in Cuba.

"Obá Ernesto Pichardo [Hialeah, FL. 05]." 1:09 minutes. http://www.you tube.com/watch?v=VH_VHVKGrQ4. 1993. Features CBS news coverage of the court's decision.

"Obá Ernesto Pichardo [Santeria One, FL 01]." 1:48 minutes. http://www. youtube.com/watch?v=L8jM32AQGSg. Local Florida news coverage discusses the protests and debates that led to the case.

"Obá Ernesto Pichardo [Santeria One]." 1:43 minutes. http://www.youtube. com/watch?v=_Af0Ikn_tCY. Features footage of Pichardo's argument before council members in Hialeah.

81. North American Free Trade Agreement (January 1, 1994)

Evolving from the 1988 Canada-United States Free Trade Agreement, the North American Free Trade Agreement eliminated trade tariffs between Canada, the United States, and Mexico as a way to bolster these nations' economies and labor forces. As the largest and most economically powerful trade bloc, NAFTA was initially signed by Mexican President Carlos Salinas, U.S. President George H. W. Bush, and Canadian Prime Minister Brian Mulroney on December 12, 1992. This was done in part to compete with the signing of the Maastricht Treaty that same year, which established the European Union. After the ceremonial signing, NAFTA underwent a lengthy ratification process by the Mexican and U.S. Congresses and the Canadian Parliament where it stirred an enormous amount of controversy among politicians and economic activists throughout North America. Although economists and trade experts have argued that NAFTA has strengthened Mexico's volatile economy, lowered food prices there, and brought greater prosperity to North American businesses, others contend that the trade agreement has had an adverse impact on Mexican farmers, who cannot compete with cheaper U.S. imports, and on U.S. factories that have relocated to Mexico, resulting in widespread job loss for U.S. citizens. Once it passed in the U.S. Congress, President Bill Clinton signed NAFTA into law on December 8, 1993, and it went into effect on January 1, 1994.

TERM PAPER SUGGESTIONS

1. Explain how NAFTA was initiated and what changes were made by the time it went into effect on January 1, 1994. Discuss why these changes were made and what compromises were created between U.S. congressional leaders.

2. Although NAFTA was supposed to help strengthen Mexico's economy and generate jobs for Mexicans, critics suggest that this part of the trade agreement has failed. Examine the continued flow of Mexicans to the United States who look for work despite the NAFTA provision that should have eliminated this. Take into account policies such as Operation Gatekeeper and the Secure Fence Act initiated by the United States that underscored this failure to bolster Mexico's labor force by militarizing the U.S.-Mexico border.

3. Compare NAFTA with other wide-reaching trade agreements in the Western Hemisphere, particularly the Central American Free Trade Agreement. Determine the relationship between these and broader open trade systems such as the World Trade Organization.

4. Study the impact that NAFTA has had on the agricultural economy in Mexico and determine whether the trade agreement has helped or harmed this industry. Focus on some of the key issues, such as the effects on the meat and corn sub-industries, and detail how Mexico is addressing these issues in the 21st century.

ALTERNATIVE TERM PAPER SUGGESTIONS

1. A by-product of NAFTA has been the relocation of U.S. factories to Mexican border cities such as Tijuana or Ciudad Juarez. These factories, called *maquiladoras*, have been a great source of controversy because

of the substandard working conditions and violation of civil rights. As an advocate for human and labor rights, write a series of letters to various business and governmental leaders articulating your concern for the welfare of Mexican workers who are taken advantage of in these *malquiladoras*. Examine Coalition for Justice, an advocacy watchdog organization that reports on *malquiladoras*: http://coalitionforjustice.info/CJM_Website/New_Sites/Home/Home.html.

2. With a small group of students, create a comprehensive wiki that addresses and profiles the difficult conditions Mexican workers have experienced since the ratification of NAFTA. Include relevant images, useful links, and important texts that present the challenges workers and farmers are facing.

SUGGESTED SOURCES

Primary Sources

"NAFTA Resources." http://lanic.utexas.edu/la/mexico/nafta/#documents. Contains links to primary documents and significant sources compiled by the Latin American Network Information Center.

"North American Free Trade Agreement." http://www.nafta-sec-alena.org/en/view.aspx?x=343. Includes the original NAFTA document.

Secondary Sources

Folsom, Ralph H. *NAFTA and Free Trade in the Americas in a Nut Shell*. St. Paul, MN: Thomson/West, 2008. Offers an in-depth examination of the agreement and references the Central American Free Trade Agreement, as well as other significant free trade agreements.

Geniesse, Peter A. *Illegal: NAFTA Refugees Forced to Flee*. Bloomington, IN: iUniverse, 2010. Profiles a number of undocumented Mexican workers and the effect the trade agreement had on their lives and the Mexican economy.

Hing, Bill Ong. *Ethical Borders: NAFTA, Globalization, and Mexican Migration*. Philadelphia: Temple University Press, 2010. Reviews NAFTA in the context of growing illegal emigration from Mexico to the United States.

Nader, Ralph, and Jerry Brown, eds. *The Case against "Free Trade": GATT, NAFTA, and the Globalization of Corporate Power*. San Francisco: Earth Island Press, 1993. Collection of important articles from trade experts details the original negotiations and predicts the negative outcomes it will have.

Ojeda, Martha A., and Rosemary Hennessy. *NAFTA from Below: Maquiladora Workers, Farmers, and Indigenous Communities Speak Out on the Impact of Free Trade in Mexico.* Missouri City, TX: Coalition for Justice in the Maquiladoras, 2006. Compiles the testimonies and accounts of migrant workers in light of what NAFTA has done.

World Wide Web

"Duke Law Library & Technology: NAFTA." http://www.law.duke.edu/lib/researchguides/nafta.html. Assembles a brief description of the agreement with relevant links to primary and secondary sources associated with NAFTA and includes a useful annotated bibliography.

"Fact Sheet: North American Free Trade Agreement (NAFTA)." http://www.fas.usda.gov/info/factsheets/NAFTA.asp. Details both general information and relevant statistics from the U.S. Department of Agriculture.

Malkin, Elizabeth. "After 15 Years, Nafta's Promise Still Unfulfilled in Mexico." *New York Times,* March 23, 2009. http://www.nytimes.com/2009/03/24/business/worldbusiness/24peso.html. Addresses some of the central issues surrounding flow of workers from Mexico to the United States despite NAFTA's provisions to end this.

"North American Free Trade Agreement (NAFTA)." http://www.ustr.gov/trade-agreements/free-trade-agreements/north-american-free-trade-agreement-nafta. Documents a summary and detailed statistics recorded by the Office of the United States Trade Representative.

"North American Free Trade Agreement (NAFTA)." http://www.citizen.org/trade/nafta/. Presents a general overview and incorporates divergent views on the success of the agreement.

Multimedia Sources

Harsh Reality: Mexico's NAFTA Problem. Princeton, NJ: Films for the Humanities and Sciences, 2008. DVD. 15 minutes. Canadian news show examines how and why NAFTA failed to strengthen Mexico's economy.

NAFTA under Assault: Reassessing Its Impact. Santa Monica, CA: Milken Institute, 2008. DVD. 75 minutes. Panel of experts discusses the impact renegotiating the trade agreement would have on Canadian, Mexican, and U.S. economies, particularly in terms of labor and environmental standards.

82. Operation Gatekeeper (October 1, 1994)

To curtail the growing number of undocumented workers crossing the U.S.-Mexico border and the drug trade, President Bill Clinton established

Operation Gatekeeper to secure the borderlands and had Attorney General Janet Reno make the public announcement on September 17, 1994. It was officially initiated on October 1, 1994. Operation Gatekeeper provided for an increase in border agents, military equipment, and tactics, and a 14-mile long wall that stretched from the Pacific Ocean and eastward along the San Diego, California/Tijuana, Mexico sector. By 1997, the Congress doubled the Immigration and Naturalization Service, increased funds to the U.S. Border Patrol and doubled their agents, and added more fencing and high-tech surveillance equipment along the border. Despite the effort to strengthen the border, migrants continued to cross; however, they did so farther east and through the Imperial Desert of southern California. This led to an increase in deaths and did little to decrease the number of border-crossers. In February 1999, the Organization of American States, the American Civil Liberties Union, and other U.S. legal advocate organizations filed a petition against the U.S. government accusing officials of creating conditions and exercising tactics through Operation Gatekeeper that violated human rights. In 2000, the human rights wing of the United Nations and the U.S. division of Amnesty International underscored this petition by arguing Operation Gatekeeper has led to the unnecessary human rights violation of thousands of migrant workers.

TERM PAPER SUGGESTIONS

1. Although the Clinton administration hailed Operation Gatekeeper as a success during the time of its implementation, a broad spectrum of critics have argued that it was not only a failure, but also a violation of human rights. Argue whether the policy had been successful and to what degree opponents of Operation Gatekeeper raised relevant issues.

2. Explain what the political climate was during the 1990s concerning immigration in California and other U.S. border states. How exactly did this influence the creation and implementation of Operation Gatekeeper and its phases?

3. Compare the important similarities and differences between Operation Gatekeeper, which was initiated by President Bill Clinton in 1994, and the Secure Fence Act, which was signed by President George W. Bush in 2006. Discuss the circumstances behind each policy that led to its initiation, detail its features, and explain whether such approaches have been effective in controlling illegal movement between the U.S.-Mexico border.

4. What were some of the ways Operation Gatekeeper "militarized" the U.S.-Mexico border during the 1990s. How did this new technology differ from what the U.S. Border Patrol had used in the past? Determine how effective these methods and programs were in monitoring the border and curtailing illegal crossing.

ALTERNATIVE TERM PAPER SUGGESTIONS

1. Assume that you are a human rights advocate for families and laborers who cross the U.S.-Mexico border illegally to find work. Study the conditions many crossers endured during the years of Operation Gatekeeper and create a series of podcasts highlighting not only their specific circumstances but also underscoring the need to consider issues of human rights.

2. Develop an interactive map with hyperlinks that illustrates the phases of Operation Gatekeeper along the U.S.-Mexico border. Provide relevant information, such as images, statistics, and links to pertinent articles and sites.

SUGGESTED SOURCES

Primary Sources

"AG Reno Announces New Agents and Resources to Strengthen Operation Gatekeeper and Cut Illegal Immigration." http://www.justice.gov/opa/pr/Pre_96/January95/3.txt.html. January 4, 1995, press release details U.S. Attorney General Janet Reno's intention to continue bolstering efforts toward Operation Gatekeeper, which she officially announced on September 17, 1994.

"Background to the Office of the Inspector General Investigation." http://www.justice.gov/oig/special/9807/gkp01.htm. Features the U.S. Department of Justice's overview of Operation Gatekeeper and implementation of its policy.

U.S. Border Patrol. "Border Patrol Strategic Plan: 1994 and Beyond." *National Strategy,* July 1994. Washington, DC: U.S. Border Patrol. Details the Clinton administration's four-phase policy to militarize the U.S.-Mexico border.

Secondary Sources

Andreas, Peter. *Border Games: Policing the U.S.-Mexico Divide.* 2nd ed. Ithaca, NY: Cornell University Press, 2009. Analyzes the patrolling of the

U.S.-Mexico border and relevant policies like Operation Gatekeeper. This second edition provides a post-September 11 context.

Huspek, Michael. "Why Violence Is Growing along the U.S.-Mexico Border." *Los Angeles Times,* Aug. 24, 1997. http://articles.latimes.com/1997/aug/24/opinion/op-25443. Details Operation Gatekeeper's strategies such as "channeling" immigrants eastward from San Diego and into the dangerous desert. Also explores the increase in deaths among border crossers as a result of the 1994 policy.

Nevins, Joseph. *Operation Gatekeeper: The Rise of the "Illegal Alien" and the Remaking of the U.S.-Mexico Boundary.* New York: Routledge, 2001. Articulates the Clinton administration border and immigrant policy with great detail and introduces the notion of dehumanizing undocumented workers.

World Wide Web

"Militarizing the Border." http://mediafilter.org/caq/CAQ56border.html. Jose Palafox's detailed article explains the significance and relevance of policies such as Operation Gatekeeper in protecting and securing the U.S.-Mexico border.

"Operation Gatekeeper." http://www.globalexchange.org/countries/americas/unitedstates/california/dayofthedead/gatekeeper.html. Includes an overview of the border policy with relevant statistics and links, critiques the program, and emphasizes its shortcomings.

"'Operation Gatekeeper' Claims the Lives of 444 Immigrant Workers in Five Years." http://www.wsws.org/articles/1999/oct1999/immi-o09.shtml. Criticizes U.S. politicians who praise the effectiveness of the Clinton administration border policy by underscoring the increase in deaths among Mexican and Central American immigrants.

"Up Against the Wall." http://www.govexec.com/archdoc/1096/1096s1.htm. Katherine McIntire Peters' in-depth coverage details how Operation Gatekeeper has changed the role of several U.S. Border Patrol agents she interviewed.

Multimedia Sources

Death on a Friendly Border. New York: Filmmakers Library, 2001. Profiles how the militarization of the U.S-Mexico border has transformed the daily implementation of policies for the U.S. Border Patrol.

New World Border. Berkeley, CA: Peek Media, 2001. DVD. 28 minutes. Presents civil rights abuses along the U.S.-Mexico border since the implementation of Operation Gatekeeper. Includes interviews with border activists and immigrants.

83. California Proposition 187 Passes (1994)

In November 1994, a California ballot initiative called "Proposition 187: Illegal Aliens, Ineligibility for Public Services, Verification and Reporting" passed with nearly 59 percent approval among voters. California Assemblyman Dick Mountjoy originally authored the proposition, calling it the "Save Our State (S.O.S.) Initiative," and prominent supporters included then-Governor Pete Wilson who was running for reelection that year. The controversial proposition made public social services, such as health and education, unavailable to illegal aliens in California. The initiative also mandated that state and local agencies must report suspected illegal aliens to federal immigration agencies, while making it a felony to create or sell counterfeit residence or citizenship documents. Proponents of Proposition 187 argued that undocumented workers were costing Californians millions of dollars in services, and its passage into law would send a message to the federal government to tackle illegal immigration. The initiative's opponents, however, countered that Proposition 187 violated federal law and would ultimately cost taxpayers billions in federal monies, particularly in Medicaid. They also noted that the proposition held no penalties for employers who hired illegal aliens and that the initiative held racist overtones, particularly against Latinos, that could harm children who were suspected of illegally attending the state's schools. The day after the election, the American Civil Liberties Union (ACLU), along with the Mexican-American Legal Defense/Education Fund (MALDEF) and the League of Latin American Citizens (LULAC), filed lawsuits to prevent the proposition's passage into law. A temporary restraining order was placed against Proposition 187, and the federal courts held that the initiative did indeed violate the U.S. Constitution, as the federal not state government has exclusive authority on immigration issues. California's attorney general appealed the decision, keeping the initiative in the court system until 1999, when it was voided. Although Proposition 187 was never enacted into law, it became a symbol of the late 20th century's continuing debates about immigration, race, and citizenship.

TERM PAPER SUGGESTIONS

1. Scholars have linked Proposition 187 with earlier anti-immigration movements such as Operation Wetback (1954) and the Chinese Exclusion Act (1882). Research an earlier anti-immigration measure in U.S. history and compare its similarities and differences with Proposition 187.

2. In the U.S. Court System, Proposition 187 was found to violate the federal government's right to regulate immigration. Research the role that state and federal governments have played in immigration in the 19th and 20th centuries and take a position on Proposition 187's constitutionality. Do you agree with the court's decision that Proposition 187 is unconstitutional?

3. Scholars of immigration often discuss the role that political nativism (one's beliefs about immigrants and appropriate ethnicity) was central to pro-Proposition 187 campaign tactics. Examine the written opinions, ballot arguments, and advertisements favoring Proposition 187. State whether there are anti-immigrant sentiments and racial stereotyping in these texts.

4. Examine the role that special interest groups played in Proposition 187's publicity, funding, and endorsement. How did these groups impact the Proposition's success?

5. Proposition 187's provisions held many changes for state and local agencies, particularly public schools, with regard to reporting suspected illegal aliens. Examine the impact that Proposition 187's passage into law would have created for public schools and hospitals. What procedures would have changed? What issues would Proposition 187 have created for these services?

6. Those in favor of Proposition 187 claimed the initiative was race-neutral, whereas opponents claimed the initiative was racist, and targeted Mexican Americans particularly. Analyze the positions of various opponents and proponents of Proposition 187 and argue whether the initiative was race-neutral or racial targeting.

ALTERNATIVE TERM PAPER SUGGESTIONS

1. Imagine you are a California politician running for reelection in 1994. You have been asked by reporters to define your position on

Proposition 187. Write a position statement that will be issued to the press.

2. Imagine you work for an advertising agency and have been asked to create two television commercials for or against Proposition 187. Create two persuasive iMovie commercials to be aired on television to appeal to two different voter demographics. Write a pitch for the agency explaining your marketing choices and how these ads will appeal to their target groups.

SELECTED SOURCES

Primary Sources

Proposition 187: Text of Proposed Law. http://www.usc.edu/libraries/archives/ ethnicstudies/historicdocs/prop187.txt. Contains the legislation passed by California voters.

Proposition 187: Ballot Arguments. http://holmes.uchastings.edu/cgi-bin/star finder/23973/calprop.txt. Contains the ballot arguments and the full text of the proposed law.

Secondary Sources

Garcia, Ruben J. "The Racial Politics of Proposition 187." In *The Latina/o Condition: A Critical Reader,* edited by Richard Delgado and Jean Stefancic. New York: NYU Press, 1998, pp. 118–124. Article questions Proposition 187's racial neutrality and links it with other historical anti-Latino movements.

Gendzel, Glen. "It Didn't Start with Proposition 187: One Hundred and Fifty Years of Nativist Legislation in California." *Journal of the West* 48, no. 2 (Spring 2009): 76–85. http://lawprofessors.typepad.com/files/gendzel-in-jow.pdf. Traces anti-Latino legislation in California from 1848 to present.

Jacobson, Robin Dale. *The New Nativism: Proposition 187 and the Debate over Immigration.* Minneapolis: University of Minnesota Press, 2008. Bucknell University political science professor investigates the roles that race, migration, assimilation, and work ethic played in framing arguments on Proposition 187.

Johnson, Kevin. "Immigration Politics, Popular Democracy and California's Proposition 187." In *The Latina/o Condition: A Critical Reader,* edited by Richard Delgado and Jean Stefancic. New York: NYU Press, 1998, pp. 110–117. Johnson's article discusses the political environment in California under which Proposition 187 materialized.

Ono, Kent A., and John M. Sloop. *Shifting Borders: Rhetoric, Immigration, and California's Proposition 187.* Philadelphia: Temple University Press, 2002. Offers a comprehensive analysis of Proposition 187 and evaluates the debates and the positions offered by both sides.

World Wide Web

"Alien Nation?" http://www.pbs.org/newshour/bb/congress/immigrant_benefits1_3-26.html. Transcript from PBS' *Online NewsHour* features interviews with several California Representatives about Proposition 187.

"California: Proposition 187 Unconstitutional." http://migration.ucdavis.edu/MN/more.php?id=1391_0_2_0. UC Davis' *Migration News* discusses the legal ruling on Proposition 187.

"Federal Judge Issues Final Ruling on Prop. 187: Measure Unconstitutional." https://www.aclu-sc.org/releases/view/100086. The ACLU's newsletter about the court case contains direct quotations from Judge Mariana R. Pfaelzer's ruling on the initiative.

"Point/Counterpoint." http://www.wcl.american.edu/hrbrief/v2i2/point.htm. Features statements of key proponents and opponents of Proposition 187.

Multimedia Sources

"California's Proposition 187." 4:32 minutes. http://www.youtube.com/watch?v=D3x5cFl9Umo. Video features NBC's 1994 coverage on Proposition 187 prior to the vote and during the proposition's court trial.

Fear and Learning at Hoover Elementary. PBS, 53 minutes. 1997. Sundance award-winning documentary directed by Laura Angelica Símon, a 4th-grade teacher in Los Angeles, offers firsthand evidence of Proposition 187's impact on her school.

84. Selena Murdered (1995)

When Tejano singer Selena Quintanilla-Pérez was shot and killed by her fan club president, Yolanda Saldivar, on March 31, 1995, millions of music fans mourned her passing. Equally striking, however, was Selena's relatively unknown status in mainstream American popular culture before her death. Born on April 16, 1971, Selena started singing at an early age, and, by nine years of age, she was the lead singer of Selena and Los Dinos, a band her father formed to showcase her musical skills.

The group recorded its first album in 1984, a second in 1985, and three more in 1987 and 1988. With each record, the band's popularity grew, and Selena soon signed a solo artist record deal with EMI Latin. Selena, also known as the "Queen of Tejano," won her first Tejano music award in 1986 for Best Female Vocalist—the same award she would win every year from 1986 to 1996. With her unique blend of Country-Western, Disco, traditional Latin rhythms and American pop music, Selena transformed the Tejano music scene from a Latino regional venue to worldwide popularity. By February 26, 1995, over 65,000 fans arrived at Houston's annual rodeo to see her perform hits such as "Bidi Bidi Boom Boom" and "Como La Flor." To date, Selena's was the largest concert performance Houston has held. Just as she had transformed Tejano music, so, too, was Selena's career on the brink of transition when she was killed. Slated by EMI Latin to be the next Gloria Estefan, another Latina who crossed from regional to mainstream musical success, Selena had recently recorded *Dreaming of You,* an album featuring several English-language songs. Before the album was released, however, Selena discovered Saldívar had embezzled money. On confrontation, Saldívar shot Selena multiple times, resulting in the singer's death at age 23. Posthumously, Selena remained one of the top-selling female artists in the United States, and her album, *Dreaming of You*, reached number one on the billboard charts in 1995.

TERM PAPER SUGGESTIONS

1. Examine the impact of Selena's musical work on Tejano music. What contributions and alterations did Selena make to this musical genre? What were her influences? How did she alter Tejano music's status in the United States, particularly for those unfamiliar with the genre prior to Selena?

2. Compare the careers of Selena Quintanilla-Pérez and Ritchie Valens. How did both artists work to merge Latino musical influences and traditions with American pop and rock music? Beyond their early deaths, what other similarities can be seen in their childhood influences, their crossover approaches, and their initial entrance into mainstream musical stardom?

3. Selena's career has been discussed as an example of the roles that assimilation and acculturation play in Latino identities. Research

these terms and address the elements of Selena's work that showcase assimilation and those that highlight acculturation.

4. Selena, often called "The Tex-Mex Madonna," had, like Madonna, used controversial images of femininity and sexuality in her performances. Concurrently, Selena had also been marketed as a traditional Latina. How did Selena both use and challenge the traditional roles assigned to women in Latino culture?

ALTERNATIVE TERM PAPER SUGGESTIONS

1. Design an interactive map and timeline of Tejano music, its influences, and key artists. With your map, examine the influences from Europe (particularly Poland, Germany, and Spain), Latin America, and the United States, and the particular instruments and musical traditions each contributed to Tejano music. With your timeline, examine the key hits and awards of artists such as Selena, La Mafia, Little Joe, Los Relampagos del Norte, and Marcelo Tafoyo.

2. Create a Webography of Selena's musical work, focusing on her impact on Latino culture. Analyze three or four of Selena's most important songs for their musical influences and historical importance.

SELECTED SOURCES

Primary Sources

Selena. *Amor Prohibido*. EMI Latin, 1994. CD. Selena's final recorded album prior to her death features several of her most popular Spanish-language hit singles.

Selena. *Live, The Last Concert*. Image Entertainment, 2003. DVD. Captures Selena's final live performance to over 65,000 fans at the Houston Livestock Show and Rodeo as well as a biopic documentary of her life.

Selena. *Ven Conmigo*. EMI Latin, 2002. This 1990 collection was the first Tejano album to achieve gold record status.

Secondary Sources

Anijar, Karen. "Selena—Prophet, Profit, Princess: Cannonizing the Commodity." In *God in the Details: American Religion in Popular Culture*, edited by Eric Michael Mazur and Kate McCarthy. New York: Routledge, 2001, pp. 83–100. Anijar's article explores Selena's post-death image in Latino popular culture.

Patoski, Joe Nick. *Selena: Como La Flor*. Boston: Little Brown, 1996. Unauthorized biography of Selena explores her relationship with family, friends, and Yolanda Salvídar.

San Miguel, Guadalupe. *Tejano Proud: Tex-Mex Music in the Twentieth Century*. Texas Station: Texas A&M University Press, 2002. Chapter features an exploration of Selena's early work with her band, Los Dinos, and their impact on Tejano music.

Vargas, Deborah R. "Bidi Bidi Boom Boom: Selena and Tejano Music in the Making of Tejas." In *Latino/a Popular Culture*, edited by Michelle Habel-Pallán and Mary Romero. New York: NYU Press, 2002, pp. 117–126. Vargas argues that Selena's work, drawing on African American women's disco traditions, creates a new space for women artists.

Willis, Jennifer L., and Alberto Gonzalez. "Reconceptualizing Gender through Dialogue: The Case of the Tex-Mex Madonna." *Women and Language* 20, no. 1 (Spring 1997): 9–12. Article discusses Selena's impact as a cultural symbol for Latinas and the role that her sexualized body played in that process.

World Wide Web

"Official Selena Web site." http://www.q-productions.com. Offers MP3 Downloads of Selena's music as well as a video collage of Selena's performances and pictures.

Strachwitz, Chris. "The Roots of Tejano and Conjunto Music." http://lib.utexas.edu/benson/border/arhoolie2/raices.html. Discusses the early history and musical origins of Tejano and Conjunto musical styles.

Multimedia Sources

Corpus: A Home Movie for Selena. PBS Home Video. 1999. 47 minutes. Director Lourdes Portillo's documentary about Selena features footage of the singer's performances, interviews with her family, and a discussion of her impact on Tejano music.

Selena. Warner Bros. 1997. 127 minutes. Director Gregory Nava's biopic of Selena's life features Edward James Olmos and Jennifer Lopez in her first starring role.

85. Illegal Immigration Reform and Immigrant Responsibility Act (1996)

In 1996, Congress passed the Illegal Immigration Reform and Immigrant Responsibility Act of 1996 (IIRAIRA), which reversed many of the former U.S. immigration policies favoring family reunification and amnesty. IIRAIRA's provisions focused on an array of immigration reforms, mostly focused on amplifying enforcement funding and illegal immigration penalties. IIRAIRA increased funding for border control, authorizing millions of dollars for additional INS and border agents and enhanced barriers between the U.S.-Mexico border. IIRAIRA also added the controversial Section 287(g) to the Immigration and Nationality Act, which allowed local and state law enforcement officers to undertake immigration law enforcement for the first time. IIRAIRA's greatest modifications, however, were its stricter penalties for illegal immigrants. Under IIRAIRA, a person illegally in the United States for 180 to 365 days, unless pardoned, would be deported and could not return to the United States for three years, and a person who has illegally resided in the United States for more than a year could not return for 10 years. The IIRAIRA's new language regarding detention and deportation allowed for indefinite incarceration of noncitizens prior to their immigration board hearing and also called for the deportation of permanent residents for minor criminal offenses such as shoplifting. Further, IIRAIRA eliminated the judicial review process for noncitizens, who could no longer appeal the immigration board's ruling. The IIRAIRA applied all these penalties and provisions to illegal aliens and permanent residents equally, whether or not their spouses or children were U.S. citizens. For these reasons, IIRAIRA was considered the most stringent and controversial U.S. immigration reform to date.

TERM PAPER SUGGESTIONS

1. Explain IIRAIRA's provisions for border security. How did IIRAIRA increase funding for border fences, barriers, border patrol, and INS investigations? What successes and drawbacks has this enhanced security created? Has IIRAIRA reduced illegal immigration?

2. Discuss IIRAIRA's impact on both illegal immigrants and lawful residents. What increased penalties does IIRAIRA hold for illegal immigration and noncitizen criminal activity? How has IIRAIRA affected permanent residents and their status? Has IIRAIRA's penalties for illegal immigration proven to be an effective deterrent or has illegal immigration continued unchanged?

3. Investigate IIRAIRA's controversial provisions for indefinite detention of noncitizens prior to the Supreme Court's ruling on *Zadvydas*

v. Davis (2001). Do you agree with the Supreme Court that IIRAIRA's detention provisions violated the U.S. Constitution?

4. Analyze the international response to IIRAIRA. What protests did the U.S. face from Mexico and Canada particularly? Do you agree with Mexican and Canadian officials who argued that IIRIRA violated the North American Fair Trade Agreement (NAFTA) and international law?

5. Examine Section 287(g) enacted by IIRAIRA. Which states implemented Section 287(g) and which did not? What are the concerns of Section 287(g)'s critics? What are the responses of those who defend Section 287(g)?

6. Discuss IIRAIRA's elimination of judicial process. What changes did IIRAIRA make to the appeals process and judicial review for illegal immigrants? How can a noncitizen protest deportation under IIRAIRA?

ALTERNATIVE TERM PAPER SUGGESTIONS

1. Imagine yourself a politician running for public office, and you have been asked your position on IIRAIRA and its efficacy. Explain your position on this controversial law, offering both reasons and evidence for why you believe IIRAIRA to be effective or ineffective against illegal immigration.

2. Create a PowerPoint presentation comparing IIRAIRA with the Immigration and Nationalization Act of 1965 and the Immigration Reform and Control Act of 1986. What differences exist between the goals, focus, and scope of each of these acts? Which of the three do you believe was the most effective?

SUGGESTED SOURCES

Primary Source

"Pub.L. 104–208." http://frwebgate.access.gpo.gov/cgi-bin/getdoc.cgi?dbname=104_cong_public_laws&docid=f:publ208.104. The act appears in Division C of this public law.

Secondary Sources

Fix, Michael, and Wendy Zimmerman. "All under One Roof: Mixed-Status Families in an Era of Reform." *International Migration Review* 35, no.

2 (Summer 2001): 397–419. Discusses IIRAIRA's effects on families with both citizens and noncitizens in the same household.

Fragomen, Austin T. Jr. "The Illegal Immigration Reform and Immigrant Responsibility Act of 1996: An Overview." *International Migration Review* 31, no. 2 (Summer 1997): 438–460. Fragomen argues that IIRAIRA offers the strictest U.S. measures against illegal immigration to date.

Langenfeld, Amy. "Living in Limbo: Mandatory Detention of Immigrants under the Illegal Immigration Reform and Immigrant Responsibility Act." *Arizona State Law Journal* 31 (Fall 1999): 1041–1069. Discusses IIRAIRA's indefinitive detention policies and its impact.

Medina, Isabel M. "Judicial Review—A Nice Thing? Article III, Separation of Powers and the Illegal Immigration Reform and Immigrant Responsibility Act of 1996." *Connecticut Law Review* 29 (1996–1997): 1525–1563. Discusses how IIRAIRA limits the judicial appeal process for illegal immigrants.

Ramji, Jaya. "Legislating Away International Law: The Refugee Provisions of the Illegal Immigration Reform and Immigrant Responsibility Act." *Stanford Journal of International Law* 37, no. 1 (2001): 117–162. Discusses IIRAIRA's violation of international law.

World Wide Web

"IIRIRA 96—A Summary of the New Immigration Bill." http://www.visalaw.com/96nov/3nov96.html. Tennessee Law Firm Siskind Susser Bland provides this comprehensive summary of the law and its provisions.

"Mexico Criticizes IIRAIRA." *Migration News* 4, no.4 (May 1997). http://migration.ucdavis.edu/mn/comments.php?id=1224_0_2_0. University of California Davis' Migration News outlines Mexico's reaction to IIRAIRA.

U.S. Department of Homeland Security. "Fact Sheet: Section 287(g) Immigration and Nationality Act," Aug. 16, 2006. http://www.ice.gov/doclib/pi/news/factsheets/060816dc287gfactsheet.pdf. Reviews IIRAIRA's addition of Section 287(g) to the Immigration and Nationality Act.

Zadydas v. Davis. 2001. http://caselaw.lp.findlaw.com/scripts/getcase.pl?court=US&vol=000&invol=99-7791. First successful Supreme Court case to challenge IIRAIRA eliminated indefinite detention.

Multimedia Sources

"Citizens Speak Out in Response to Refusal of 287(g) Program." 8:29 minutes. http://www.youtube.com/watch?v=0rVmJJD0l8w. February 16, 2009,

Chatham County's Commissioners meeting features citizens speaking out against IIRAIRA and provision 287g, which the county's commissioners refused to adopt.

"Episode 170: Immigration." *This American Life*, Oct. 13, 2000. 46 minutes. http://www.thislife.org/radio-archives/episode/170/Immigration. Radio television show focuses on IIRAIRA and its impact on deported immigrants, local police, and the U.S. prison system.

Sentenced Home. Indiepix Studios, 2003. DVD. 76 minutes. Documentary tells the story of three adult children of U.S. residents, raised in the United States, who are deported under IIRAIRA's provisions.

86. Helms-Burton Act (March 12, 1996)

Officially called the Cuban Liberty and Democratic Solidarity (LIBERTAD) Act of 1996, the Helms-Burton Act strengthened the Cuban Democracy Act of 1992 through increased commercial, financial, and economic restrictions against Cuba by penalizing foreign companies who trade with the island nation; furthermore, the law prevented international corporations from operating in the United States if they traded with Cuba. The act received a great deal of criticism from political bodies such as the United Nations, the European Union, the Organization of American States, and Russia who claimed that the United States violated international laws and the sovereignty of the Cuban Republic with the ratification of the Helms-Burton Act. More significantly, the international community argued that the stricter embargo provisions would do little to effect regime change in Cuba and only harm the everyday Cuban citizens. According to congressional rhetoric, the act would push Cuba toward a more Western-style democracy, while providing that Cuban Americans, whose property had been confiscated during Fidel Castro's 1959 takeover of Cuba, would receive monetary compensation from non-U.S. companies trading with businesses now occupying those properties. After initially being tabled in Congress, the act received greater attention when on February 24, 1996, Cuban fighter jets destroyed two private planes flown by the anti-Castro Cuban American group Brothers to the Rescue. Cuba stated that the planes illegally entered Cuban airspace and were not in compliance with international law. The attack bolstered conservative Cuban American groups and encouraged the bill's passage into law the following month.

TERM PAPER SUGGESTIONS

1. Some have argued that President Bill Clinton had lost Florida's electoral votes during the 1992 election for his ambivalent stance on the U.S. trade embargo against Cuba. However, once Clinton signed the Helms-Burton Act of 1996, he won the electoral votes from Florida in the next election. What stance did Clinton take regarding the trade embargo during his presidency? How would you characterize his relationship with not only the Cuban government, but also Cuban Americans residing in the United States?

2. Discuss how the long-standing U.S. trade embargo has impacted the everyday lives of common Cuban citizens. How effective has this policy been in crippling the Castro government? Explain how conservative Cuban American organizations, like the Cuban American National Foundation, have begun to alter their anti-Castro opposition and have reconsidered the success of the trade embargo.

3. Compare the Helms-Burton Act of 1996 to the Cuban Democracy Act of 1992. Explain what these acts provide and what initiated them in Congress. How did they characterize the U.S. tone and attitude toward Cuba during the 1990s?

4. Seen as widely unpopular and a grave infraction on the sovereignty of Cuba and the Cuban people, the world community has broadly criticized the U.S. creation and ratification of the Helms-Burton Act. Discuss how non-U.S. nations, world leaders, and international organizations have responded to the act and what, if any, impact this has had on the U.S. trade embargo against Cuba.

ALTERNATIVE TERM PAPER SUGGESTIONS

1. Provide a detailed PowerPoint presentation with multimedia links that outlines the provisions and policies of the U.S. trade embargo since Fidel Castro's ascension to power in 1959. Assess whether it has been effective or unsuccessful in achieving its goals; in this presentation, argue whether the embargo should be strengthened, maintained, reduced, or dissolved. Compare this with contemporary opinion polls in the United States.

2. As a political consultant hired by the Cuban American National Foundation, which has traditionally been a conservative group now changing its position on the long-standing embargo, develop a Web

site that promotes the organization's post-2009 identity. How does their new position respond to embargo policies such as the Helms-Burton Act of 1996? The site should be directed toward the Cuban American community, the U.S. government, and the people of Cuba.

SUGGESTED SOURCES

Primary Sources

"Cuban Democracy Act of 1992." http://www.state.gov/www/regions/wha/ cuba/democ_act_1992.html. Contains an original copy of the act.
"Cuban Liberty and Democratic Solidarity (LIBERTAD) Act of 1996." http://frwebgate.access.gpo.gov/cgi-bin/getdoc.cgi?dbname=104_cong_ public_laws&docid=f:publ114.104. Features an original copy of the Helms-Burton Act.

Secondary Sources

Alexander, Kern. *Economic Sanctions: Law and Public Policy.* New York: Palgrave Macmillan, 2009. Chapter 7 discusses the Helms-Burton Act through a legal lens and analyzes issues of liability and regulations.
Haney, Patrick, and Walt Vanderbush. *Cuban Embargo: Domestic Politics of American Foreign Policy.* Pittsburgh: University of Pittsburgh Press, 2005. Chapter 6 explores how the George W. Bush administration tightened the embargo with Cuba through the ratification of the Act.
Lowenfeld, Andreas F. "Congress and Cuba: The Helms-Burton Act." *American Journal of International Law* 90, no. 3 (July 1996): 419–434. Explores the legal ramifications of this act.
Morely, Morris, and Chris McGillion. *Unfinished Business: America and Cuba after the Cold War, 1989–2001.* New York: Cambridge University Press, 2002. Chapter 3 provides an in-depth examination of the Helms-Burton Act in a post-Cold War context.
Morici, Peter. "The United States, World Trade, and the Helms-Burton Act." *Current History* 96, no. 607 (1997): 87. Investigates the relationship with nations trading with Cuba and the U.S. role in the Cuban embargo.

World Wide Web

"The Cuban Democracy Act of 1992." http://www.associatedcontent.com/ article/590101/the_cuban_democracy_act_of_1992.html?cat=37. Presents an overview of this act of Congress.

"The Godfrey-Milliken Bill." http://web.textfiles.com/politics/NWO/nwo_0012. txt. Features the original bill presented in the Canadian Parliament as a symbolic gesture of protest that satirizes the ratification of the Helms-Burton Act.

"The Helms-Burton Act." http://library.thinkquest.org/18355/the_helms-burton_ act.html. Provides a brief explanation of how the act works and includes a link to the original piece of legislation.

"The Helms-Burton Act." http://www.earlham.edu/~pols/ps17971/weissdo/ HelmsB.html. Includes a brief summary of the act and why it was created.

"The Helms-Burton Act: The Helms-Burton Probe Heats Up." http://www. skralaw.com/Articles/cuba.htm. Presents a detailed description of the act and examines whether it violates existing international laws.

"Helms-Burton Case: Fate of the Cuba Embargo." http://www1.american. edu/TED/helms.htm. Provides a useful breakdown of the act and explains how it is implemented and what larger ramifications exist.

Multimedia Source

"The United States Embargo against Cuba." http://www.youtube.com/watch? v=vQCa0U0d7rM. Includes part of a November 1995 interview with former Central Intelligence Agency agent Phil Agee discussing the Cuban embargo while the Helms-Burton bill was being discussed in Congress.

87. Colombian Immigration to the United States (1996–Early 21st Century)

Although 1996 was a peak year in Colombian immigration to the United States, waves of Colombian immigrants started coming to the United States after World War II, and most went to Jackson Heights in Queens, New York, as well as northern New Jersey and south Florida. As a result of political violence and economic recession in Colombia during the 1960s and mid-1970s, over 116,000 immigrated to the United States for improved working conditions and lives. This large wave was mostly made up of working class Colombians who began to displace the professional class Colombians already in the United States. The Immigration Act of 1965, however, began to curtail the flow of immigrants coming from nations throughout the Western Hemisphere. Between 250,000 to 350,000 undocumented Colombians were living in the United States during the mid-1970s according to calculations made by U.S. government agencies and the Colombian Consulate. This created problems particularly for Colombians who were waiting to enter the United States and escape the rising unemployment. The ongoing warfare in Colombia between guerilla and paramilitary groups as well as powerful drug cartels also added greater tension to life in Colombia. Nevertheless, those who were desperate to leave Colombia continued to enter the U.S. illegally. Between 1996 and 2002, many middle- and upper-middle class Colombian professionals entered the United States to escape the violence, and a large number of them settled throughout south Florida. Because of the drug-trafficking reputation associated with Colombia, many Colombian Americans have worked hard to disassociate themselves from the political turmoil in their home country.

TERM PAPER SUGGESTIONS

1. Because of the political strife in Colombia, many Colombian immigrants to the United States have sought asylum. Those who do not qualify for political asylum in the United States then apply for Temporary Protection Status (TPS) if they have no other legal standing to be in the country. Explain the political process of being granted and/or denied asylum and temporary protection status for immigrants coming into the United States. How have Colombian immigrants faired with regard to applying for these designations?

2. Between 1996 and 2002, a large wave of Colombian immigrants settled in south Florida. They were mainly middle- and upper-middle-class professionals. However, unlike their Cuban counterparts whose professional and working classes came to the region between the 1960s and 1980s and were willing to work together, the Colombian immigrants, a very class-conscious group, were less successful in establishing solid social and economic enclaves. Explain what the differences were between these groups and the factors involved in success and failure.

3. During the mid-1990s, the U.S. federal and various state governments responded to the growing anti-immigrant sentiment throughout the United States. Policies such as Congress' Contract with America or California's Proposition 187 underscored this backlash against the rising number of undocumented workers. How did this legislation and others like it impact the Colombian American community? Did it make them more resilient or fragmented in the long run?

ALTERNATIVE TERM PAPER SUGGESTION

1. As an expert on the growing Central and South American immigrant communities in the United States, create a Web site that discusses fundamental differences between these groups in terms of culture and history, and explain how they (Colombians, Salvadorans, Nicaraguans, and Guatemalans) are becoming part of the pan-Latino community in the United States. Provide relevant images, statistics, links, and maps.

SUGGESTED SOURCES

Primary Sources

Berger, Joseph. "The Making of an American." *New York Times*, late edition, June 4, 2006: WC1. Profiles Aurelio Castano's experience coming from Colombia to New York to become a day laborer and the friction he encounters.

Kinzie, Susan. "A Mother's Dream Is Brothers' Reality; Two Teens Leave Death in Colombia to Pursue Education in Maryland." *The Washington Post,* July 30, 2005: B1. Documents a Colombian American couple who offer their nephews asylum in the United States, away from the danger in Colombia, after their mother is executed by a guerilla death squad.

Saccetti, Maria. "Home in a Strange Land; Teen Starts New Life As Immigrant Parents Return to Colombia." *Boston Globe,* Oct. 15, 2007: A1. Features an interview with a U.S.-born Colombian youth who goes to Colombia to be with recently deported father.

Secondary Sources

Balcazar, Fabricio E., Edume Garcia-Iriarte, and Yolanda Suarez-Balcazar. "Participatory Action Research with Colombian Immigrants." *Hispanic Journal of Behavioral Sciences* 3, no. 1 (Feb. 2009): 112. Presents a study that focuses on the health care and social service needs of Colombian immigrants in Chicago and how they have navigated the city's system.

Berger, Joseph. "Video Conferences Give Immigrants a Link to the Families They Left Behind." *New York Times*, late edition. Jan. 8, 2005: B1. Explains how a New York area bank has set up video conferencing between the United States and Colombia to keep Colombian Americans linked with family back home.

Chaney, Elsa M. "Colombian Outpost in New York City." In *Awakening Minorities: Continuity and Change*, 2nd ed., edited by John R. Howard. New

Brunswick, NJ: Transaction Books, 1983, pp. 67–74. Investigates the initial growing immigrant wave of Colombians coming to New York during the early 1980s.

Ordonez, Franco. "Colombians Press for Protected Status: Proposed Legislation Renews Hope for Many Seeking to Stay in U.S." *Boston Globe,* Sept. 14, 2004: B4. Discusses how hundreds of undocumented Colombian workers in the Boston area could receive temporary protection by being granted asylum.

World Wide Web

"Colombia: In the Crossfire." http://www.migrationinformation.org/Profiles/display.cfm?ID=344. Contains an extensive discussion of the history of Colombian migration. Includes statistical table of patterns and an examination of legal, economic, and cultural complications that have arisen due to Colombian migration, especially to the United States. Includes links to relevant articles on this topic.

"Colombian Americans." http://www.everyculture.com/multi/Bu-Dr/Colombian-Americans.html. Contains a comprehensive overview of Colombian Americans in terms of immigration, history, and culture. Also includes a relevant source bibliography for further research.

"Colombian Immigrants in the United States." http://www.latinamericanstudies.org/colombian-immigrants.htm. Provides a detailed graph of migration from Colombia to the United States and other nations between 1996 and 1999.

"Colombian Migration to South Florida: A Most Unwelcome Reception." http://lacc.fiu.edu/research_publications/working_papers/WPS_009.pdf. Florida International University's Michael W. Collier analyzes the economic, political, and cultural transformations occurring in South Florida since the waves of Colombian immigrants in 1990s.

"U.S. Citizenship and Immigration Services—Humanitarian." http://www.uscis.gov/portal/site/uscis/menuitem.eb1d4c2a3e5b9ac89243c6a7543f6d1a/?vgnextoid=194b901bf9873210VgnVCM100000082ca60aRCRD&vgnextchannel=194b901bf9873210VgnVCM100000082ca60aRCRD. Contains definitions of terms for incoming immigrants who seek asylum or Temporary Protection Status. Includes links to current immigration statistics and relevant articles.

Multimedia Source

"Colombian Immigrants." http://www.npr.org/templates/story/story.php?storyId=1054298. July 1999 National Public Radio podcast profiles the growing Colombian immigrant population in South Florida who are seeking asylum in the United States.

88. Homies Unidos Chapter Formed in Los Angeles (1998)

With the assistance of former rival gang members, Magdaleno Rose-Avila created the first chapter of Homies Unidos (Homies United) in El Salvador in 1996. Two years later, he assisted Alex Sanchez and Hector Pineda in establishing a branch in the Pico Union area of Los Angeles, a largely Latino enclave. The 12-year civil war in El Salvador, which began in 1980, sent hundreds of thousands of refugees to the United States seeking asylum and work opportunities. Parents left behind children to carve out a place in the United States. However, this served only to break down traditional family structures and force many youth who had remained behind in El Salvador to turn to the rapidly forming street gangs as familial surrogates. By the end of the conflict, those young Salvadorans who had gone to the United States with family and who had criminal records were sent back to El Salvador where they were absorbed into existing gangs, making them stronger and more visible. Homies Unidos sought to break the cycle of gang recruitment by offering advice and advocacy to gang members and their victims. The organization, made up of many former gang members, sought to negotiate with gang leaders while encouraging others to abandon a life of drugs and violence. Like the chapter in El Salvador, the Los Angeles-based branch that was started in 1998 is dedicated to giving educational and occupational alternatives to young men and women as a way out of and away from the violent gang culture. Under the direction of Alex Sanchez, Homies Unidos in Los Angeles has worked extensively as a community organization to reach gang members and foster a sense of collectivity within the Latino community.

TERM PAPER SUGGESTIONS

1. Because gang members live fast and dangerously and do not believe they will live beyond their mid-twenties, they readily participate in drugs, criminal activities, violence, and unprotected sexual patterns. Identify how Homies Unidos attempts to connect with gang members

and provide them with a sense of responsibility and a vision for a longer, more productive life.

2. Discuss why Alex Sanchez, Executive Director of Homies Unidos in Los Angeles, was arrested in June 2009. Argue whether his arrest was unjustified and cite evidence from the federal indictment against him as well as public letters and statements that have addressed the arrest of Sanchez.

3. Research the history and evolution of one of the most powerful transnational gang organizations: Mara Salvatrucha or MS-13. This was a gang established by young Salvadoran immigrants living in Los Angeles who had been displaced by the civil war in El Salvador in the 1980s. Discuss its membership, organization, and culture as well as how this organization negotiates with gang-peace advocacy organizations such as Homies Unidos and others.

ALTERNATIVE TERM PAPER SUGGESTIONS

1. Assume the role of Executive Director for the Los Angeles Chapter of Homies Unidos Alex Sanchez, and prepare a series of podcasts addressing your role in the organization and your response to your legal indictments. Structure the messages based on Sanchez's actual words as well as what important figures have stated about him and his work with Homies Unidos.

2. As a member of the Los Angeles Police Department, you have been called before a legal subcommittee to address not only the growing gang culture in the Los Angeles area but the effectiveness of outreach groups such as Homies Unidos and their leaders. Design a PowerPoint presentation that addresses concerns over gang life and anti-gang organizations and conclude with significant resolutions.

SUGGESTED SOURCES

Primary Sources

"Homies Unidos." http://homiesunidos.org/. Official Web site of the organization includes blogs, information for getting involved with the group, and significant programs and resources.

"Peer Education with Gang Members: Protecting Life and Health." http://www.pathfind.org/pf/pubs/focus/Project%20Highlights/homies.html.

Outlines the philosophy and criteria for Homies Unidos as articulated by its founder Magdaleno Rose-Avila.

Secondary Sources

"Anti-Gang Leader Arrested in Crackdown in Los Angeles." *Xinhua News Agency,* June 24, 2009. Covers the arrest of Los Angeles Chapter leader Alex Sanchez for racketeering offenses and conspiracy to murder.

Hayden, Tom. *Street Wars: Gangs and the Future of Violence.* New York: New Press, 2006. Documents U.S. gang violence since the 1980s but focuses on its prevention and the community organizations, like Homies Unidos, who intervene in gang culture.

Montes, Joseph. "Gang, Community Members Must Talk, Says Group Founder." *Knight Ridder Tribune Business News,* June 18, 2006: 1. Presents Homies Unidos founder Magdaleno Rose-Avila and his discussion at a Tacoma, Washington, middle school regarding gang violence and alternatives.

Rodriguez, Luis J. *Always Running: La Vida Loca: Gang Days in LA.* New York: Touchstone, 1993. Memoir documents life as a gang member written by a renowned former Los Angeles gang member-turned-gang-prevention advocate.

World Wide Web

"Harassing Homies: LAPD Campaigns against a Church-based Gang-Peace Project." http://www.streetgangs.com/people/asanchez.html. Profiles the arrest of Alex Sanchez in 2000 over immigration issues and suggests that Sanchez is being targeted by law enforcement despite his pivotal position as a gang negotiator.

"Homies Unidos Board Throws Full Support behind Alex Sanchez." http://blogs.laweekly.com/ladaily/crime/homies-unidos-board-throws-ful/. *LA Weekly* blogger Patrick Range McDonald provides an in-depth discussion of Sanchez's arrest.

"Por Vida." http://www.lacitybeat.com/cms/story/detail/?id=382&IssueNum=23. Sueng Hwa Hong's article examines the history of Homies Unidos and its formation in the United States.

Multimedia Sources

"Magdaleno Rose-Avila and Homies Unidos." http://proxied.changemakers.net/studio/avila/avila.cfm. Includes an overview of the Homies Unidos founder's international activist career and provides an audioclip on his life and work.

Sin Nombre. Universal City, CA: Universal Pictures, 2009. DVD. 96 minutes. Fictional account of a man and his daughter who venture from Honduras to New Jersey and, along the way, encounter a young Mexican gang member. Alex Sanchez, the Executive Director of the Los Angeles chapter of Homies Unidos uses the film to promote what his organization does. Web site containing details of the film and trailers as well as more detail on Sanchez's life: http://www.filminfocus.com/article/homies_unidos____will_never_be_defeated.

89. California Proposition 227 (1998)

In June 1998, California voters passed Proposition 227: English Language in Public Schools Initiative Statute with more than 60 percent of the vote. The initiative, nicknamed "English for our Children" by supporters, was written and sponsored by Silicon Valley software engineer Ron Unz who argued that bilingual education was failing to teach students English. Proposition 227 requires California's public school teachers to instruct students in English, the exception being a one-year bilingual class for Limited English Proficient (LEP) students. The initiative also permitted parental waivers to allow further bilingual education, which would later prove instrumental against legal challenges to Proposition 227 in the courts. Additionally, Proposition 227 required California to provide $50 million annually for the "community-based English tutoring" of adult English-language learners. Advocates for Proposition 227 argued that the nearly 25 percent of California's student population held LEP status and that bilingual education was both expensive and ineffective, with students leaving the public school system with a poor grasp of the English language. In contrast, the initiative's opponents contended that forcing LEP students into English-only classrooms would merely reduce student comprehension in all subjects; some also argued that the initiative held racist undertones by privileging English in an age of increasing internationalism. Since its passage, several court cases have been filed against the initiative's provisions, but none has been successful. Several studies have also been conducted on Proposition 227's impact. Some argue that Proposition 227 has been a great success while others cite that most test-score improvements can be traced to other factors, such as content changes in the student aptitude tests themselves. The provisions of Proposition 227 remain in effect today, dividing educators and citizens on the role bilingual education should play in California.

TERM PAPER SUGGESTIONS

1. Ron Unz, author of Proposition 227, has stated that the Ninth Street School Boycott of February 1996, where parents pulled their children out of school to protest bilingual education, inspired him to write the initiative. Research this boycott and analyze its connection to Proposition 227.

2. Describe the impact of Proposition 227 on California's bilingual education. How did the initiative alter bilingual classrooms? What exceptions were made to provide additional bilingual education?

3. Several court cases (for example, *Valeria G. v. Wilson, Doe v. Los Angeles Unified School District,* and *Quiroz v. State Board of Education*) were filed against the constitutionality of Proposition 227. Study one of these cases and discuss the arguments made against Proposition 227. Why did the courts find for Proposition 227 in all of these cases?

4. Compare Proposition 187 with Proposition 227. What similarities and differences can be found in their provisions for education? Examine why Proposition 187 was found to be unconstitutional while Proposition 227 was not.

5. After its passage into law, several studies analyzed the success of Proposition 227. Examine these studies then take a position on the impact of Proposition 227 on a specific area of education, such as test scores or school attendance. From your research, do you believe Proposition 227's provisions have helped or hindered LEP students?

6. Discuss the impact of Proposition 227 on other states in the United States. How has the initiative influenced bilingual education or calls for English-only education in other states? What states have implemented similar statutes?

ALTERNATIVE TERM PAPER SUGGESTIONS

1. Imagine you are a lawyer contesting or defending one of the many court cases filed against Proposition 227. Write a brief discussing the legal arguments you will use to prove the initiative is (un)constitutional.

2. Design a PowerPoint presentation discussing pro and con positions of Proposition 227. Be sure to include data from the several studies on Proposition 227's impact on LEP students, their test scores, and their school attendance.

SUGGESTED SOURCES

Primary Source

"Proposition 227: English Language in Public Schools." http://primary98. sos.ca.gov/VoterGuide/Propositions/227.htm. Contains the proposition along with the original arguments in favor and against the initiative.

Secondary Sources

American Institutes for Research and WestEd. *Effects of the Implementation of Proposition 227 on the Education of English Learners, K–12: Findings from a Five-Year Evaluation.* Sacramento: California Department of Education, 2006. http://www.air.org/news/documents/227Report.pdf. Offers chapters on the legal and political background of Proposition 227, along with its impact, the perspectives of educators, and the implementation barriers still present.

Del Valle, Sandra. *Language Rights and the Law in the United States: Finding Our Voices.* Bristol, UK: Multilingual Matters, 2003. Subchapter on bilingual education focuses on Proposition 227, particularly the impetus for the initiative and the legal cases that followed.

Gándara, Patricia. "Learning English in California: Guideposts for the Nation." In *Latinos: Remaking America*, edited by Marcelo Suarez-Orozco and Mariela Páez. Berkeley: University of California Press, 2008, pp. 339–359. Chapter covers the impact of Proposition 227 on bilingual education and its teaching workforce.

Johnson, Kevin, and George A. Martínez. "Discrimination by Proxy: The Case of Proposition 227 and the Ban on Bilingual Education." *UC Davis Law Review* (Summer 2001): 1227–1276. Article by two well-known legal experts argues that Proposition 227 violates the Fourteenth Amendment to the U.S. Constitution.

Valencia, Richard. *Chicano Students and the Courts: The Mexican American Legal Struggle for Educational Equality.* New York: NYU Press, 2008. Valencia's chapter on bilingual education ends with a discussion of Proposition 227 and its impact.

World Wide Web

"English for the Children." http://www.onenation.org/. The official website for Proposition 227 supporters offers a pro stance on the initiative as well as links to articles on the proposition's success.

Escobedo, Deborah. "Propositions 187 and 227: Latino Immigrant Rights to Education." http://www.abanet.org/irr/hr/summer99/escobedo.html. Escobedo's article for the American Bar Association discusses the ways in which these two initiatives have changed public schooling for Latino immigrants in California.

Krashen, Stephen. "Proposition 227 and Skyrocketing Test Scores: An Urban Legend from California." http://www.sdkrashen.com/articles/prop227/all.html. University of Southern California Professor Emeritus Stephen Krashen's article argues that the change in the test itself, not Proposition 227, accounts for higher student test scores.

Sifuentes, Edward. "Proposition 227: 10 Years Later. English-only Education Continues to Spark Debate." http://www.nctimes.com/news/local/sdcounty/article_ec5de000-1999-580b-86a1-40ba1d26934f.html. Article discusses the continued debate over Proposition 227.

Multimedia Source

Lost in Translation: Latinos, School and Society. Learning Matters/PBS Home Video, 1998. DVD. 56 minutes. Discusses the impact of Proposition 227 on school performance and attendance of Latinos.

90. Cuban Five Arrested and Convicted (September 12, 1998)

The Cuban Five were five Cuban and Cuban American intelligence officers who were convicted of espionage, conspiracy to commit murder, and other illegal activities in the United States. They were Gerardo Hernández, Antonio Guerrero, Rámon Labañino, Fernando González, and René González. The Cuban Five were part of a Cuban spy network that observed and infiltrated several Cuban American organizations. Reportedly, the Cuban Five took jobs as laborers at the Key West Naval Air Station and sent the Cuban government top-secret information regarding detailed descriptions of the base's layout as well as the mobilization of military jets and personnel. However, the group's central crime had been the infiltration of Cuban American exile groups such as the Brothers to the Rescue organization, who made unauthorized flights over Cuba to drop political pamphlets. Because of the information the Cuban Five provided, two aircraft from the Brothers to the Rescue organization were shot down by the Cuban military after consistently entering Cuban airspace. As a result, four civilians on board the craft perished. All five men were arrested in Miami, Florida, on September 12, 1998, by Federal Bureau of Investigation (FBI) agents and were charged by the U.S. government on 25 different counts. The trial, which began in November 2000, went on for many months. In June 2001, the group was convicted of all counts by a U.S. federal court in Miami. The Cuban Five received different sentences and were placed in separate prisons throughout the country. Gerardo Hernández received a double life sentence, Antonio Guerrero and Rámon Labañino were each given a life sentence, while Fernando González received 19 years and René González was given 15 years. They are regarded as political prisoners by the Cuban government, which insists that the Cuban Five were attempting to block anti-Castro groups who wish to commit acts of terrorism against Cuba. Since the incarceration of the Cuban Five, many advocacy groups and prominent individuals have spoken out against the sentencing and have lobbied on behalf of the group. The trial is the only judicial proceeding to be condemned by the United Nations Human Rights Commission. Additionally, Amnesty International and eight different Nobel laureates have condemned the sentences.

TERM PAPER SUGGESTIONS

1. Explain why Gerardo Hernández was charged with the death of the five civilians shot down over Cuba after they had violated Cuban airspace. Decide whether the charge is justified and provide detailed evidence to support your position.

2. Many claim that the U.S. government's defense against the Cuban Five was questionable and unjust. Review the case and write an argumentative essay that discusses whether this claim is true.

3. Decide whether groups such as the Cuban Five have the legal right to defend Cuba, as they have claimed, from anti-Castro "terrorist" organizations in the United States such as Alpha 66, Brothers to the Rescue, Cuban American National Foundation, and F4 Commandos. What arguments has the Cuban government made regarding

their sovereignty and their right to defend themselves against invasion and conspiracy from the United States?

4. Based on the dramatic differences between each of the sentences received by the Cuban Five members, discuss to what extent each member was involved in curtailing plots against the Cuban government. What were their roles that eventually led in their arrest?

ALTERNATIVE TERM PAPER SUGGESTIONS

1. In June 2009, the U.S. Supreme Court chose not to hear the case of the Cuban Five. As a lawyer, create a PowerPoint presentation for the Court either defending or denying the rights of the Cuban Five had the case been taken. Review the arguments from both sides and determine which is most legal in your opinion.

2. With a small group of students, design a WebQuest on the Cuban Five with links to relevant information. In this WebQuest, present conclusions about the group's significance in terms of legal issues and human rights.

SUGGESTED SOURCES

Primary Source

"The Case: Cuban Five Message to the American People after They Received Their Sentences." http://www.thecuban5.org/thecase3.html. Contains an appeal to the U.S. public written by the members of the Cuban Five on January 17, 2001.

Secondary Sources

Dávalos Fernández, Rudolfo. *United States vs. the Cuban Five: A Judicial Coverup.* Havana, Cuba: Editorial Capitán San Luis, 2006. Provides comprehensive dissection of the court case that is well researched and argues that the U.S. court unjustly sentenced the men.

Lawrence, Matt, and Thomas Van Hare. *Betrayal: Clinton, Castro, and the Cuban Five.* Bloomington, IN: iUniverse, 2009. The writers, advocates of the Brothers to the Rescue organization, argue against the innocence of the Cuban Five members.

Morejon, Nancy, and Alice Walker, eds. *Letters of Love and Hope: The Story of the Cuban Five.* New York: Ocean Press, 2005. Features an anthology of letters and essays about the Cuban Five by friends, advocates, and relatives.

World Wide Web

"Brothers to the Rescue Background and Information." http://www.hermanos.org/ Background%20and%20Information.htm. Includes an overview of the organization's beginning and their purpose to liberate Cuba from Castro.

"The Cuban Five." http://www.thecuban5.org/. The site is of an advocate group that provides detailed information regarding the Cuban Five case, pending appeals, biographical information on the five members, and links to media coverage.

"The Popular Education Project to Free the Cuban Five." http://www.freethe cuban5.com/. An advocacy group lobbies on behalf of the Cuban Five and educates the public regarding the case. Includes links to case updates, media coverage, and documentaries.

Urbina, Ian. "Judge Reduces Sentence for One of the Cuban Five." *New York Times,* Oct. 13, 2009. http://www.nytimes.com/2009/10/14/us/14five. html. Details a Miami judge's decision to lessen the life sentence given to Antonio Guerrero from 262 months to 240 months.

Wides-Munoz, Laura. "Supreme Court: No Re-Trial for Cuban Five Convicted of Spying." *The Huffington Post,* June 15, 2009. http://www. huffingtonpost.com/2009/06/15/supreme-court-says-no-re_n_215592. html. Outlines the reasons for the U.S. Supreme Court passing on the Cuban Five legal case.

Multimedia Sources

"Cuban 5 Appeal to Supreme Court for New Trial." http://www.democracy now.org/2009/2/6/cuban_5_appeal_to_supreme_court. Contains the February 6, 2009, interview with the Cuban Five's lawyer, Thomas Goldstein. Site includes audio and visual presentations of the interview.

"National Committee to Free the Cuban Five." http://www.freethefive.org/. Includes events and audio and video links to important interviews and relevant articles, all of which focus on the release of the incarcerated Cuban Five members.

91. Vieques Island Dispute (April 1999)

The small island municipality of Vieques off the eastern coast of mainland Puerto Rico had been used for decades as a U.S. military training station; however, long-standing disputes with residents and Puerto Rican organizations have insisted that operations be suspended and the military leave the island. Between 1940 and 1950, the U.S. Navy purchased land used for sugar cane production and transformed it into outposts. The western third of the island, which was around 8,000 acres, stored munitions, while the eastern third of the island, roughly 14,000 acres, was used for military exercises and training. This included ship-to-shore gunfire, air-to-ground bombings, and amphibious landing maneuvers by Marines. Residents occupied the central strip of the island. Until 1999, these tactics occurred 180 days out of the year. Widespread protesting escalated in the late 1970s when the military ceased operations on the nearby island municipality of Culebra after extensive opposition from the residents there and increased operations on Vieques. Central to the residents' concerns have been the following: environmental impact on local fishing economy, ecological damage to the island, health risks from chemicals used during exercises, extensive noise from artillery and bombs, safety risks for locals, and disregard from the U.S. Navy. In April 1999, a local resident was killed and four others were injured when a bomb strayed from a target. Prior to this, countless residents have been killed or injured from unexploded bombs scattered across the island. The 1999 incident fueled widespread condemnation from Puerto Rico and local community organizations such as the Vieques Fishermen's Association and the Crusade for the Rescue of Vieques. Marches and sit-ins continued into May 1999. In 2003, the United States ceased military operations on the island.

TERM PAPER SUGGESTIONS

1. In response to the outcry in April 1999, U.S. President Bill Clinton and Puerto Rican Governor Pedro Rosello created the Clinton-Rosello Plan, which would go into effect on January 31, 2000. Explain what this plan involved and what the response was from the Puerto Rican community.

2. Compare the role of various activists and organizations involved in protests and uprisings on the island municipalities of Culebra and Vieques since the 1970s. What was the result of their efforts? How did the issues on these islands underscore Puerto Rican resistance to U.S. occupation for all of Puerto Rico?

3. Highlight the economic and environmental impact the long-term presence of the U.S. naval operations had on the island of Vieques.

4. The George W. Bush administration decided that military operations would end on Vieques in 2003. Articulate the political climate of the Puerto Rican Governor's administration at the time that led to this decision and include the reactions from other U.S.-based groups.

ALTERNATIVE TERM PAPER SUGGESTIONS

1. As a representative of the people of Vieques, Puerto Rico, prepare a report that you will deliver to the U.S. Congress demanding the immediate suspension of military exercises and withdrawal of the U.S. Navy. Highlight the economic and environmental devastation the naval presence has caused to illustrate your protest.

2. Create a detailed and interactive map showing the U.S. naval presence and residential occupation of Vieques. Also include key fishing areas, agricultural tracts, and tourist locations affected by the naval operations.

SUGGESTED SOURCES

Primary Sources

Murray, Charles. *The Vieques Island Training Range Controversy.* Newport, RI: United States Naval War College, 2001. Includes official investigation by the National Security Decision Making Department into the military exercises on the island.

U.S. House Committee on Armed Services. *Naval Training Activities on the Island of Vieques, Puerto Rico: A Report of the Panel to Review the Status of Navy Training Activities on the Island of Vieques.* 96th Cong. 2nd Sess. Washington, DC: GPO, 1981. Provides detailed discussion and investigation into the presence of the U.S. Navy on the island and the various impacts it has had during occupation.

Secondary Sources

Ayala, César. "From Sugar Plantations to Military Bases: The U.S. Navy's Expropriations of Vieques, Puerto Rico, 1940–1945." *Centro: Journal of the Center for Puerto Rican Studies* 13, no. 1 (Spring 2001): 22–44. Examines how the military offset the economic infrastructure of Vieques by replacing the sugar industry during World War II and using the land for military purposes.

Baretto, Amílcar Antonio. *Vieques, the Navy, and Puerto Rican Politics.* Gainesville: University Press of Florida, 2002. Focuses on the overall design of military presence on the island and the difficulty this creates politically for the residents.

McCafferey, Katherine T. *Military Power and Popular Protest: The U.S. Navy in Vieques, Puerto Rico.* New Brunswick, NJ: Rutgers University Press, 2002. Provides a close examination of the long-standing antagonistic relationship between residents and the U.S. Navy.

Murillo, Mario A. *Islands of Resistance: Vieques, Puerto Rico, and U.S. Policy.* New York: Seven Stories Press, 2001. Closely examines the lack of clemency given to a number of pro-independence incarcerated activists and the death of a Puerto Rican during U.S. naval exercises on Vieques.

Wilcox, Joyce. "Vieques, Puerto Rico: An Island under Seige." *American Journal of Public Health* 91, no. 5 (May 2001): 695–699. Documents the health hazards for island residents resulting from U.S. naval bombing exercises.

World Wide Web

"Hispanics Blast Clinton as Climax of Island Dispute Draws Near." http://www.puertorico-herald.org/issues/vol3n49/HispanicsBlastClinton-en.html. Covers the negative response from the Puerto Rican community regarding President Bill Clinton's anticipated decision to resume military exercises on Vieques in 1999.

"The Importance of Vieques Island for Military Readiness." http://www.heritage.org/research/nationalsecurity/bg1411.cfm. Argues why the island is strategic for the U.S. military and questions the George W. Bush administration's plan to end military operations there.

"Vieques: The Expropriations of the U.S. Navy in the 1940s." http://www.sscnet.ucla.edu/soc/faculty/ayala/vieques/. Provides maps, historical overview, bibliography, relevant links, and PowerPoint presentations concerning the U.S. naval presence on the island.

"Vieques, Puerto Rico Naval Training Range: Background and Issues for Congress." http://www.history.navy.mil/library/online/vieques.htm. Presents U.S. government's positions on the function of Vieques Island and examines George W. Bush administration's decision to end military exercises there in 2003.

"Voice for Independence: In the Spirit of Valor and Sacrifice." http://www.peacehost.net/WhiteStar/Voices/. Includes a report on Carlos Zenón's involvement as president of the Vieques Fishermen's Association in the protests and hearings concerning U.S. naval presence on the island.

Also includes a report on the public resistance of Ismael Guadalupe, president of the Crusade for the Rescue of Vieques.

Multimedia Sources

The Battle of Vieques. New York: Cinema Guild, 2006. DVD. 40 minutes. Examines the impact of the U.S. Navy and its bombing exercises through interviews with residents and community leaders.

Vieques: Worth Every Bit of Struggle. New York: Filmakers Library, 2005. DVD. 55 minutes. Uses interviews with residents and military officials to investigate the controversial presence of the U.S. Navy on the Puerto Rican municipality.

92. Immigration and Naturalization Service Seizure of Elián González (April 22, 2000)

In November 1999, Elián González, age 6, and his mother boarded a small boat in Cuba headed for Miami. The boat's defective engine prevented their crossing, and Elián's mother, Elizabet, and 10 others drowned. The Coast Guard rescued Elián and two survivors on November 26, 1999 (Thanksgiving Day). After a brief hospitalization, Elián was placed in the custody of Lazaro González, his paternal great-uncle and closest U.S. relative, who argued that Elián should be granted U.S. refugee status, as Elián would have been eligible had his mother survived the voyage. In Cuba, Elián's father argued for his son's return, contending that international law gave him custody. The legal battle for Elián soon became a media frenzy, with Cuban leader Fidel Castro personally calling for Elián's return and with Cuban Americans protesting for Elián's right to stay. On March 21, 2000, a U.S. federal judge dismissed the asylum petition filed by Lazaro González on Elián's behalf. Thereafter, Attorney General Janet Reno set an April 13, 2000, deadline for Elián's repatriation to Cuba. In protest, civic leaders and Cuban American residents, including Miami Mayor Alex Pelelas, publicly refused to cooperate with Reno. Although the 11th Circuit Court of Appeals ruled that Elián must remain in the United States for appeal hearings, Reno decided to remove Elián from his Miami relatives' home. On April 22, 2000, over 100 Immigration and Naturalization

Service (INS) personnel surrounded the house and removed Elián by force. That day, he was reunited with his father on a U.S. military base to await the appeal trial. The 11th U.S. Circuit Court of Appeals ruled on June 1, 2000 that Elián was too young to petition for asylum and ordered Elián's return to Cuba. On June 28, 2000, the Supreme Court declined to hear the appeal, and Elián and his father returned to Cuba that day. Ultimately, Elián González became a symbol for Cuban Americans of their own exile from Castro's Communist rule, and the case called attention to the status of Cuban American concerns nationwide.

TERM PAPER SUGGESTIONS

1. Investigate the INS seizure of Elián González. What legal grounds did Attorney General Janet Reno cite? What resistance did Reno encounter from Elián's family, Miami officials, and the Cuban American community? Was his removal from the home legal?

2. Analyze how and why Elián González became a symbol for Cuban Americans of U.S.-Cuban relations and their own immigration. How did the case impact U.S. relations with Cuba and the federal government's relations with Cuban Americans?

3. Examine the international custody and immigration laws surrounding the Elián González case. Do you agree with the decision to return Elián to Cuba or do you believe he had the right to seek asylum? In your paper, be sure to discuss the U.S. asylum policies reserved for Cubans, such as the 1995 U.S.-Cuban Immigration Accord and the 1966 Cuban Adjustment Act. Be sure to examine why these policies do not apply to other immigrant groups, such as Haitians.

4. Discuss the media frenzy surrounding Elián González and his status as a Cuban refugee. How did he become a representation for Cuban Americans of their exiled status? What did he symbolize for Fidel Castro, who took a vested interest in his return?

5. Explain the unique status of Cuban Americans in the United States. What role did Castro's rise to power play in their immigration? How do their immigration, economic, and socio-political patterns differ from those of other Latino immigrant groups?

6. Many election specialists argue that the decision to deport Elián Gonzales may have cost Vice President Al Gore the 2000 presidential election. Examine the impact that the case had on Florida's

Cuban American voters. How did they respond politically to González's repatriation? Given the role Florida played in the general election, do you agree with political analysts that the INS seizure and return of González gave George W. Bush the presidency?

ALTERNATIVE TERM PAPER SUGGESTIONS

1. Design an interactive timeline of the Elián González case. Be sure to feature key players and court decisions pertinent to the events, as well as photos and video clips from the INS seizure.

2. Assume the role of an attorney and prepare a legal brief explaining why Elián González should or should not be granted asylum in the United States. In your brief, be sure to research and cite relevant law, such as U.S. Cuban amnesty policies and international parental custody laws.

SUGGESTED SOURCES

Primary Sources

"Elián." *60 Minutes*. Oct. 2, 2005. DVD. 13 minutes. Bob Simon interviews Elián González, then 11 and living in Cuba, about his experience.

"Elián González: The Boy from the Sea." 2000. http://www.vkblaw.com/Elián/ Eliánindex.htm. Contains links to government statements, court decisions and appeals, and photos and news links surrounding the case.

"González v. Reno." http://caselaw.lp.findlaw.com/cgi-bin/getcase.pl?court=11th& navby=docket&no=0011424opn. Features the 11th Circuit Court of Appeals' ruling on the case.

Secondary Sources

Bardach, Ann Louise. *Cuba Confidential: Love and Vengeance in Miami and Havana*. New York: Random House, 2002. Focuses on Elián González as a symbol of Cuban-U.S. relations. Features interviews with Castro and González's family.

Guerra, Cesar. *Elián: Shame or Sham?* Bloomington: iUniverse, 2002. Cuban expatriate Guerra questions the national and international legality of González's Miami seizure and repatriation.

Morley, Jefferson. "U.S.-Cuban Migration Policy." *The Washington Post.com*. July 27, 2007. http://www.washingtonpost.com/wp-dyn/content/article/ 2007/07/27/AR2007072701493.html. Morley explains how U.S. immigration policy differs for Cubans.

Reisman, Marcia M. "Where to Decide the 'Best Interests' of Elián González: The Law of Abduction and International Custody Disputes." *The University of Miami Inter-American Law Review* 31, no. 2 (Spring–Summer 2000): 323–355. Discusses the Hague Convention and U.S. abduction laws related to González's case.

World Wide Web

"Elián González Case." http://www.latinamericanstudies.org/Elián.htm. Contains photos and links to over two dozen videos featuring the 1999 to 2000 news coverage.

Online Newshour. "The Elián González Case." http://www.pbs.org/newshour/bb/law/Elián/index.html. Provides links of this television program's coverage of the events.

Multimedia Sources

Cobiella, Kelly. "Elián González Now a Communist." *CBS News,* July 17, 2008. 2:22 minutes. http://www.cbsnews.com/video/watch/?id=4185 830n&tag=related;photovideo. News video recounts the saga of Elián González's arrival in the United States and return to Cuba, along with his current induction into Cuba's young communist party.

A Family in Crisis: The Elián González Story. 2000. DVD. 90 minutes. Includes Alma Award-nominated dramatization of the events surrounding González's experience.

"Saving Elián." *Frontline,* Feb. 6, 2001. DVD. 60 minutes. Television documentary reviews the events surrounding Elián González's case.

93. American Airlines Flight 587 Crashes (November 12, 2001)

Nearly two months after the September 11th terrorist attacks, American Airlines Flight 587 took off from the John F. Kennedy airport in New York on the morning of November 12, 2001, only to crash just moments later in the borough of Queens, New York. Since this was a regularly scheduled flight between New York and the Dominican Republic, there were about 251 passengers on board, 90 percent of whom were Dominicans or Dominican Americans, along with nine crew members. Everyone on the plane died in the crash, including five people who were on the ground. At first, terrorism was suspected because the crash had been so close to the September 11th attacks. Furthermore, in May 2002, convicted terrorist Mohammed Jacarah, who had links with al-Qaeda and a Southeast Asian militant Islamic organization called Jemaah Islamiyah, confessed that terrorist suspect Abderraouf Jdey had succeeded in destroying American Airlines Flight 587 with a shoe bomb. Two years later, al-Qaeda released a list of 18 attacks they claimed to be responsible for, Flight 587 being among them. Nevertheless, after a detailed investigation into the crash and the replaying of the flight data and cockpit voice recorders, it was decided that the crash was a manual error on the part of the crew rather than a terrorist plot. Flight 587 had taken off nearly two minutes after a Japan Airlines Boeing 747 on the same runway, and because the American Airlines plane had been caught in the preceding aircraft's powerful wake, it was unable to stabilize itself properly. The crew members had aggressively worked the rudders too much, which took a toll on the plane's body. Flight 587 was an important plane route for Dominican Americans who would travel back and forth between the United States and the island, so the death of so many Dominicans was felt particularly in the Dominican neighborhood of Washington Heights in Manhattan. This crash was considered one of the worst in U.S. aviation history. On the fifth anniversary of the crash of American Airlines Flight 587, a memorial was dedicated near the crash site, and six months later, a ceremony was held at Woodland Cemetery in the Bronx to bury the unidentified remains of the crash victims.

TERM PAPER SUGGESTIONS

1. Why were there so many conflicting accounts as to how American Airlines Flight 587 was destroyed? Examine the theories involved and assess which ones seem more plausible than others.

2. Because the crash of Flight 587 occurred so soon after the September 11th attacks, many throughout the greater New York metropolitan area were convinced this was a new terrorist attack. Describe how the city responded as though the Flight 587 had been caused by terrorism. What actions were taken and how did residents, particularly within the Dominican American community, react to the crash?

3. The death of a large number of Dominican Americans on Flight 587 recalled for many Latinos the Latino victims in the World Trade

Center. Discuss how these two disasters were connected in terms of a loss in the Latino community. How did these events define what role Latinos played in discussions of September 11th and the tragedy's impact on American society?

ALTERNATIVE TERM PAPER SUGGESTIONS

1. Create an iMovie that reports on the crash of Flight 587 and focuses on the lives that were lost and the family members who mourned the event. Emphasize how this was a regular flight taken at one time or another by most Dominican Americans living in the New York area.

2. As a member of the Dominican American community, write a eulogy that commemorates not only the victims of the crash and their family members, but also the role that back and forth migration plays for Dominican Americans. Underscore how this community is part of both worlds in the United States and the Dominican Republic.

SUGGESTED SOURCES

Primary Sources

"Flight 587: Final Passenger List." http://www.guardian.co.uk/world/2001/nov/15/airbuscrash.usa. Offers the complete list of those who perished on Flight 587, with additional links to articles concerning this event.

"Island Republic Mourns Lost Sons and Daughters." http://www.guardian.co.uk/world/2001/nov/13/airbuscrash.usa4. Profiles Dominican family members who were lost on Flight 587.

"Shocked Relatives Gather at Dominican Airport." http://archives.cnn.com/2001/WORLD/americas/11/12/dominican.families/index.html. Includes a brief article on family members' reactions to the crash and contains links to interviews and footage of the crash and of waiting relatives in the Dominican Republic.

Secondary Sources

"Hector Algarobba." http://www.guardian.co.uk/world/2002/sep/11/september112002.september1161. Brief essay underscores the need to remember the children of the plane crash victims, written by a son who lost his parents on Flight 587.

Lee, Trymaine. "Only 4 Coffins, But 265 Victims Are Mourned at Mass in the Bronx." *New York Times,* May 7, 2007. http://www.nytimes.com/

2007/05/07/nyregion/07remains.html?_r=1. Covers the memorial service to bury the unidentified remains of crash victims.

Wald, Matthew L. "For Air Crash Detectives, Seeing Isn't Believing." *New York Times,* June 23, 2002. http://www.nytimes.com/2002/06/23/weekinreview/23WALD.html. Discusses the extensive eyewitness accounts of Flight 587's crash and analyzes the conflicts between these reports.

World Wide Web

"Canadian Report Causes 587 Stir." http://www.rockawave.com/news/2004/0903/Front_page/033.html. Explores the connection that al-Qaeda operative Abderraouf Jdey may have had in the destruction of Flight 587.

"FDNY Responds: Flight 587 Crashes in the Rockaways." http://www.nyc.gov/html/fdny/html/incidents/flight587/index.html. Provides details from the New York Fire Department's role in the plane crash and includes maps and photographs of the crash site.

"Flight 587 Memorial Dedicated in Rockaways." http://www.wnyc.org/news/articles/68947. Brief article discussing the memorial that was dedicated to the crash victims in 2006.

"Flight 587 Memorial Project." http://www.nyc.gov/html/fund/html/projects/flight_587_memorial.shtml. Details New York City Mayor Michael Bloomberg's dedication of a memorial designed by Dominican artist Freddy Rodriguez with links to the memorial's image.

"Pilot Error Blamed for Flight 587 Crash." http://www.iasa.com.au/folders/Safety_Issues/RiskManagement/A300previous.html. Includes two separate articles, one by Leslie Miller (*Associated Press*) and the other by Sara Kehualani Goo *(Washington Post)*, that examine the pilots' blame in the crash.

"*U.S. Read's* Flight 587 Preliminary Report." http://www.usread.com/flight587/Prelim_Report/default.html. A 2004 investigation report examines key parts of evidence concerning the Flight 587 crash.

"Why Did American Airlines 587 Crash?" http://www.danielpipes.org/2053/why-did-american-airlines-587-crash/. Daniel Pipes from *FrontPage Magazine.com* considers the conflicting reports regarding the crash. Provides links to further resources regarding this event.

Multimedia Sources

"Animations and Videos from Public Hearing." http://www.ntsb.gov/events/2001/AA587/anim_587.htm. Contains actual footage of Flight 587 in the air shortly after take-off and a simulation of the plane's loss of control with crew conversation.

Engineering Disasters. New York: Arts and Entertainment Networks, 2006. 5 DVDs. Disc 5. 50 minutes. Disc 5 includes an investigative report on the crash of Flight 587.

94. Jimmy Carter Visits Cuba (May 2002)

Among increasing accusations by the George W. Bush administration that Cuba was producing chemical and biological weapons and selling them to terrorist organizations, former President Jimmy Carter accepted a general invitation made by Cuban leader Fidel Castro for anyone to visit Cuba and see that such accusations were false. Carter's historic six-day trip to Cuba between May 12 and 17, 2002, marked the first occasion a sitting or former U.S. president has stepped foot on the island nation since Calvin Coolidge's brief visit in 1928. During his trip, Carter met with Castro as well as senior Cuban leaders and government officials. He also visited scientific research facilities to dispel rumors that Cuba was involved in generating weapons of mass destruction, much to the White House's embarrassment. At the University of Havana, Carter delivered a speech in Spanish criticizing the Cuban nation for its violation of civil rights and democratic principles for all Cuban citizens; however, he balanced his speech by emphasizing the progress Cuba has made in advancing AIDS research and in broad educational opportunities given to Cubans. His meeting with several outspoken political dissidents drew worldwide media attention and established a road toward open dialogue among various political factions in the republic. At the close of his trip, Carter underscored that since the Cuban Revolution, the United States and Cuban have grown more and more polarized as neighbors, and he had hoped that this visit would renew relations between the nations in the near future.

TERM PAPER SUGGESTIONS

1. Analyze what Carter had set out to accomplish initially by visiting Cuba. What message was he trying to convey not only to Cubans, but to the United States and the rest of the Americas by meeting with Fidel Castro? State whether you maintain that he jeopardized U.S. diplomacy by acting as a private citizen, as he has been accused of in the past, or whether you believe Carter has redefined the role of the post-presidency.

2. Although Carter was given open access to institutions, public figures, and facilities, explain how Cubans received him. What were they expecting from this visit? How did the Cuban American community react to Carter's visit with Fidel Castro?

3. What transpired during Carter's significant meeting with political dissidents such as Oswaldo Paya or Oscar Espinosa? What messages were exchanged by the men and what impact did this have not only on Cuban government officials but the general citizenry of Cuba?

4. Carter served as president between 1977 and 1981. Research what Carter's policy toward Cuba had been during his tenure as president. Compare how his administration took an alternative approach to Cuba versus other presidential administrations before and after. How did Carter's policies regarding Cuba change or confirm his tone and declarations during his May 2002 visit?

ALTERNATIVE TERM PAPER SUGGESTIONS

1. When Jimmy Carter publicly contradicted the Bush administration's accusation that Cuba was generating and selling weapons of mass destruction to suspected terrorist organizations, the White House was embarrassed. As a member of the Bush staff, create a series of press releases that responds to Carter's critique. Focus not only on this particular incident during Carter's trip but also on other reports of Carter's activity while visiting Cuba. Use actual press releases and speeches made by White House officials to inform your project, but create your own statements so that you can expand on the Bush policy on U.S.-Cuban relations and the White House's attitude toward Carter's diplomatic role there.

2. Design a WebQuest with links to import features of the historic Carter visit to Cuba. Present conclusions about what made this visit significant and emphasize whether you maintain that the trip was a success or simply a soft gesture on behalf of a former U.S. president.

SUGGESTED SOURCES

Primary Sources

"Carter's Speech to Cubans." http://news.bbc.co.uk/2/hi/americas/1988566. stm. Delivered from the University of Havana, this speech calls for human rights initiatives in Cuba and for the United States to lift the long-standing trade embargo against Cuba.

"Former U.S. President Jimmy Carter Visits Cuba." http://english.people.com. cn/200205/13/eng20020513_95546.shtml. Brief overview of Carter's visit and his mission.

"Jimmy Carter Visit to Cuba, May 12-17, 2002." http://www.latinamerican studies.org/carter-cuba.htm. An extensive archive of primary newspaper articles detailing Carter's visit to the island and his activities there. Also includes a large number of photographs of Carter meeting with important figures including Castro and speaking at various locales.

Ramonet, Ignacio, and Fidel Castro. *My Life: A Spoken Autobiography.* New York: Scribner, 2006. Chapter 20 details Castro's recollection of Carter's 2002 visit to Cuba.

Secondary Sources

Gaillard, Frye. *Prophet from the Plains: Jimmy Carter and His Legacy.* Athens: University of Georgia Press, 2007. Provides a detailed account of Carter's life work as a politician and human rights activist. Chapter 8 includes a large section devoted to his 2002 trip to Cuba.

Williams, Mike. "Carter's Cuba Speech Gives Dissidents Hope Georgian Provoked Dialogue among Islanders." *Atlanta Journal-Constitution,* Jan. 5, 2003: B1. Explores the ramifications of Carter's visit with political activists in Cuba and the former president's public advocacy of human rights in Cuba.

World Wide Web

"Carter Center Announces Dates for Historic Trip to Cuba." http://www.carter center.org/news/documents/doc436.html. Covers Carter's proposed trip and intention for visiting Cuba and underscores Carter's continued commitment to global human rights.

"Carter Challenges Bush Administration on Cuba Bioterror." http://www1. voanews.com/english/news/a-13-a-2002-05-13-21-Carter-66282527. html?moddate=2002-05-13. Focuses on Carter's dismissal of the Bush administration's accusation that Cuba has been producing weapons of mass destruction and selling them to terrorist organizations.

"Carter Criticizes Cuba, Call U.S. to Lift Embargo." http://www.common dreams.org/headlines02/0515-05.htm. Includes exerpts from Carter's famous speech delivered in Spanish at the University of Havana during his visit and provides contextual discussion.

Multimedia Sources

"Carter's Cuba Tour." http://www.npr.org/search/index.php?searchinput=
carter%27s+visit+to+cuba. Includes a series of audio news clips from
National Public Radio following Carter's trip to Cuba.

"Free Speech Radio Lineup: Carter Goes to Cuba." http://www.archive.org/
details/fsrn_20020514. The first audio story examines Carter's visit to
Cuba and what social, cultural, and political implications it had on
issues of human rights and U.S.-Cuban relations.

95. NBC Purchases Telemundo (2002)

On April 12, 2002, NBC Universal, a subsidiary of General Electric,
purchased Telemundo from Sony and Liberty Media for a record $2.7
billion. At the time, this was the largest price paid to date for a Spanish-
language network. Telemundo began as a single television station in
Puerto Rico in 1954 and was subsequently acquired, along with other
local stations, by Reliance Communications in 1987. Reliance formed
these various stations into an international media conglomerate called
Telemundo Group, Inc., before selling the corporation to Liberty
Media and Sony in 1988. Although the network ranks a distant second
to Univision, the world's leading Spanish-language network, Telemundo
is said to reach nearly 90 percent of Spanish-speaking households and
to offer far more original programming than Univision, which, in contrast, tends to buy shows from existing networks in Mexico, Argentina,
and Venezuela. Additionally, several of Telemundo's *telenovelas* (Spanish-
language soap operas) feature U.S. settings rather than Latin American
ones. Since the NBC purchase in 2002, Telemundo also has the distinction of being the only Spanish-language network to offer closed cap-
tioning in English, a result of the network's attempts to interest both
bilingual and second-generation Latino audiences. Along with the purchase, NBC obtained the highest-rated television station in Puerto Rico
and several local stations in large Hispanic markets, such as KVEA in
Los Angeles, California, and KXTX in Dallas, Texas. Initially, when
NBC announced the deal in October 2001, there was some concern
that the purchase would violate the Federal Communications Commis-
sions' (FCC) ownership limits, which prevent a single entity from owning more than two stations in certain markets. However, the purchase
was approved by the FCC and completed by April the next year. At the

time of the purchase, 13 percent of the U.S. population was Hispanic, offering NBC around 35 million potential viewers. The purchase reflects the growing importance of Latinos in the media marketplace.

TERM PAPER SUGGESTIONS

1. In interviews, many NBC spokespersons commented on the growing role of Latinos in the media marketplace, an element that made Telemundo a most desirable acquisition. Explain why Latino audiences are so coveted in the 21st century. In your argument, you might want to address population growth, regional demographics, and other factors that make owning and operating a Spanish-language network so desirable for media conglomerates such as NBC.

2. In 1988, Telemundo began an advertising campaign calling itself "Lo Mejor de los dos Mundos" ("the best of both worlds"), a phrase meant to reference Telemundo's commitment to a bilingual Latino audience. Another campaign that shortly followed this one advertised statements such as "Ketchup + Salsa = Telemundo." Investigate some of the features of Telemundo's Web sites and network television shows. What features of both are meant to appeal to this bilingual audience?

3. A central argument regarding the NBC purchase of Telemundo was whether the purchase gave NBC a duopoly (a type of oligopoly where only two producers control the entire market) of Spanish-language media outlets in New York, Los Angeles, Dallas, and Miami. Others informally argued that NBC's control would limit the amount of local news coverage in favor of a centralized system, and NBC did indeed condense several stations in these regions. Write an essay arguing for or against central ownership of television stations such as Telemundo and Univision by corporate entities such as NBC.

4. A considerable portion of Spanish-language television is devoted to airing *telenovelas*. One of the most famous of Telemundo's was *Yo Soy Betty, La Fea*, a show remade by ABC for American English-speaking audiences as *Ugly Betty*. Watch an episode of both *Yo Soy Betty, La Fea* and *Ugly Betty* or any other American soap opera and a Telemundo telenovela (full episodes are available on YouTube.com as well as ABC and Telemundo's main Web sites). Discuss the major similarities and differences between these shows. Why do you think

so much of Telemundo's and Univision's programming is centered on these dramas?

ALTERNATIVE TERM PAPER SUGGESTIONS

1. Assume you are an executive for NBC in 2001. Write a letter to the management of General Electric explaining why the company should or should not purchase Telemundo for $2.7 billion. Consider what programs and features Telemundo has to offer and what obstacles General Electric might face, both from the FCC and from competing networks, to completing the purchase.
2. Create a chart detailing the history of Telemundo. Be sure to note the changes that new ownership and management has generated, and, where possible, the market share that Telemundo achieved as your timeline progresses.

SUGGESTED SOURCES

Primary Source

Federal Communications Commission. "FCC 02-113: FCC Grants Transfer of Telemundo Communications' TV Stations." April 10, 2002. http://www.fcc.gov/Bureaus/MB/Orders/2002/fcc02113r.txt. This is the legal document that allowed NBC to purchase Telemundo.

Secondary Sources

Bielby, Denise D., and C. Lee Harington. *Global TV: Exporting Television and Culture in the World Market*. Albany: NYU Press, 2008. The chapter, "Discourses of Distribution," offers a discussion of the implications of the NBC purchase of Telemundo on its global programming. Another chapter, "The (Continued) Relevance of Genre," focuses on the limits of cross-cultural programming.

Cambridge, Vibert C. *Immigration, Diversity, and Broadcasting in the United States, 1990–2001*. Athens: Ohio University Press, 2004. Cambridge's fifth chapter provides a detailed overview of the role Telemundo plays in the U.S. cable television market.

Constantakis-Valdés, Patricia, and Horace Newcomb, "Telemundo." In *Encyclopedia of Television*, 2nd ed., edited by Horace Newcomb. Chicago: Museum of Broadcast Communications, 2004, pp. 2290–2292. Offers a comprehensive history of the network from origins to present.

Davila, Arlene. *Latinos, Inc.: The Marketing and Making of a People.* Berkeley: University of California Press, 2001. Although Davila's book predates the NBC purchase of Telemundo, its fifth chapter offers an in-depth comparison of Telemundo's and Univision's programming.

Einstein, Mara. *Media Diversity: Economics, Ownership and the FCC.* Mahwah, NJ.: Lawrence Erlbaum Associates, 2004. Einstein's first chapter focuses on NBC's purchase of Telemundo and the legal implications of the transaction, particularly with regard to accusations that the purchase resulted in an illegal duopoly.

Subervi-Vélez, Federico A., et al. "Mass communication and Hispanics." In *The Handbook of Hispanic Cultures in the United States,* Vol. 4, edited by Nicolás Kanellos, Felix M. Padilla, and Claudio Esteva Fabregat. Houston, TX: Arte Público Press, 1994, pp. 304–326. Article predates the NBC purchase but offers a unique and inclusive comparison of mainstream American media's practices with those of Telemundo and Univision.

World Wide Web

Furman, Phyllis. "With Telemundo, NBC Habla Español." *New York Daily News Online,* Oct. 12, 2001. http://www.nydailynews.com/archives/money/2001/10/12/2001-10-12_with_telemundo__nbc_habla_es.html. Coverage includes interviews with both NBC and Telemundo leadership about the deal.

Shore, Elena. "Attention NBC Telemundo: Latinos Need Local News Too." *New American Media,* November 1, 2006. http://news.newamericamedia. org/news/view_article.html?article_id=1d7944d313122e7ca7f9262bc4dcdb61. Shore's article focuses on the reduction in local news coverage offered by Telemundo as a result of the merger.

Telemundo's MSN Web site. http://msnlatino.telemundo.com/.This Web site, like its English MSNBC.com counterpart, offers streaming video for an array of Telemundo's music videos, sports, and television shows. Direct links to Telemundo's regional news stations can also be found here.

Telemundo International's Main Web site. http://www.tepuy.com/.Features Telemundo's International News Division, with English and Spanish content.

White, Elizabeth. "It's a Deal: NBC Buys Telemundo." *Media Life,* Oct. 12, 2001. http://www.medialifemagazine.com/news2001/oct01/oct08/5_fri/news1friday.html. White's article focuses on the financial aspects of the buyout.

Multimedia Source

Siegel, Robert. "NBC-Telemundo." *All Things Considered*, Oct. 12, 2001. http://www.npr.org/templates/story/story.php?storyId=1131341. 4:18 minutes. Radio program details why Telemundo is an important purchase for NBC.

96. U.S.-Mexico Border Trafficking Tunnel Discovered (January 24, 2006)

While creating tunnels underneath the U.S.-Mexico border has been a growing phenomenon among drug cartels since the 1990s, the discovery of the largest and most sophisticatedly constructed tunnel elevated the practice of tunneling to a new level. On January 24, 2006, Mexican authorities uncovered a tunnel system that ran nine stories into the sandstone earth. Two tons of marijuana was discovered in the opening of a Tijuana, Mexico, warehouse along with a 2,400 ft. passage that terminated in a huge warehouse in Otay Mesa, California, just outside of San Diego near the border. Likewise, U.S. agencies including the Immigration and Customs Enforcement, Drug Enforcement Agency, and the Border Patrol uncovered 200 pounds of marijuana on the U.S. side. Although no one was arrested at the time of discovery for having any connection with the engineering or use of the trafficking tunnel, authorities suspected that the notorious Arellano-Felix drug cartel in Tijuana was responsible. Aside from the tunnel's length, the craftsmanship of the passage and the fact that no one had detected its construction concerned border enforcement agencies. The discovery of elevator mechanisms, concrete support systems, lighting, ventilation, and groundwater drainage networks in the Otay Mesa tunnel compromised the U.S.-Mexico border aboveground technological advancements provided by the Secure Fence Act passed in October later the same year. Drug cartels that have created a $25 billion industry have the ability to invest millions of dollars into establishing sophisticated tunnels, which has worried border authorities because they have been unable to keep up with this new, 21st-century method of trafficking contraband.

TERM PAPER SUGGESTIONS

1. Discuss how U.S. and Mexican law enforcement agencies have responded to the construction specifically of trans-border trafficking

tunnels since the early 1990s. How do trans-border collaboration policies operate and what difficulties arise in attempting to curtail trafficking over the border?

2. Critics of the Secure Fence Act of 2006 have argued that a good portion of border reinforcement or construction mandated under the act really is not a fence or wall at all. Rather, it is something called "vehicle fencing" and "virtual fencing." Explain what this type of fencing is and whether it has been effective in carrying out the mission of the U.S. Border Patrol. Include in your analysis a discussion of tunneling technology and how authorities are attempting to address this tactic.

3. Explain the various crude and complex methods used by cartels to traffic drugs and people across the U.S.-Mexico border. Assess the effectiveness of the cartels' endeavors despite efforts from U.S. and Mexican border agencies to curtail the flow of contraband over the last several decades. Identify locations of tunnels and sites of border breaching to underscore the widespread tactics employed by cartels.

4. While the U.S. government has authored expensive border securing policies such as Operation Gatekeeper in the mid-1990s and the Secure Fence Act of 2006, explain what approach Mexican drug and border enforcement agencies have taken to combat drug cartels and curb the flow of drug and human trafficking across the U.S.-Mexico border. How is the situation different on the Mexican side of the border? What challenges have authorities faced there? Be sure to identify specific programs and policies that have been adopted and implemented.

ALTERNATIVE TERM PAPER SUGGESTIONS

1. Develop an interactive map with hyperlinks that illustrates the phases of Operation Gatekeeper and the Secure Fence Act along the U.S.-Mexico border. Provide relevant information, such as images, statistics, and links to pertinent articles and sites. Include in this map the sophisticated trafficking tunnels that have come into vogue among drug cartels since the start of the 21st century.

2. As a representative for the U.S. Department of Homeland Security, write a well-researched and compelling report that is to be presented before a congressional subcommittee in which you detail the discovery of several highly sophisticated and technological tunnel systems since the start of

the 21st century. In your report, discuss counter measures that have been taken; however, propose that new research must be undertaken to address the growing phenomenon of border trafficking tunnels.

SUGGESTED SOURCES

Primary Sources

Bohn, Kevin. "Feds Smoke Out Largest Drug Tunnel Yet." *CNN.com*, January 26, 2006. http://www.cnn.com/2006/US/01/26/mexico.tunnel/index. html. Includes a general overview of the discovery.

"Inside Mexico's Drug Tunnels." http://www.time.com/time/photogallery/ 0,29307,1895418,00.html. *Time* magazine's collection of trafficking tunnel photographs, including the largest one discovered in January 2006.

Secondary Sources

Serrano, Richard A. "High-tech Border Fence Is Slow Going." *Los Angeles Times*, February 22, 2010. http://articles.latimes.com/2010/feb/22/ nation/la-na-border-fence22-2010feb22. Reports the delays and set-backs facing the technological overhaul of U.S.-Mexico border security since the Secure Fence Act of 2006.

Stier, Ken. "Underground Threat: Tunnels Pose Trouble from Mexico to Middle East." *Time*, May 2, 2009. http://www.time.com/time/nation/article/ 0,8599,1895430,00.html. Discusses the 21st-century subterranean threat tunneling under borders is creating in terms of security.

Tucker, Robert E., et al. "Protecting Secure Facilities from Underground Intrusion Using Seismic/Acoustic Sensor Arrays." *Engineer* (May–August 2009): 72–76. http://www.wood.army.mil/ENGRMAG/PDFs%20for%20 May-Aug%2009/Tucker-Rowan.pdf. Comprehensive technology study of methods being developed to detect underground construction.

U.S. Dept. of Homeland Security. "Progress in Addressing Secure Border Initiative Operational Requirements and Constructing the Southwest Border Fence." http://www.dhs.gov/xoig/assets/mgmtrpts/OIG_09-56_Apr09. pdf. Extensively details the U.S. government's needs and approach to technologically securing the border as of April 15, 2009.

World Wide Web

"Authorities Find Mexico-U.S. Tunnel with Lighting, Ventilation and Elevator." http://www.ticklethewire.com/2009/12/03/authorities-find-mexico-u-s-tunnel-with-lighting-ventilation-and-elevator/. Summary of the Otay Mesa tunnel discovery focuses on the technical sophistication of the tunnel's construction.

Pamfret, John. "Tunnel Found on Mexican Border." *Washington Post*, January 27, 2006. http://www.washingtonpost.com/wp-dyn/content/article/ 2006/01/26/AR2006012601963.html. Discusses the discovery of the border trafficking tunnel in the context of other similar, yet smaller and less successful, tunnels discovered since the 1990s.

"Soldiers Find Tunnel under US-Mexico Border." http://www.brisbanetimes. com.au/world/soldiers-find-tunnel-under-usmexico-border-20091029-hlgd. html. Highlights an October 2009 discovery by Mexican soldiers of an incomplete tunnel from Tijuana to San Diego.

"Tunnel along U.S.-Mexico Border Discovered." http://www.officer.com/web/ online/Homeland-Defense-and-Terror-News/Tunnel-Along-US-Mexico- Border-Discovered/8$40921. Presents a brief summary of the event and highlights the investigation.

"Up Against the Wall." http://www.govexec.com/archdoc/1096/1096s1.htm. Katherine McIntire Peters' in-depth coverage details how Operation Gatekeeper has changed the role of several U.S. Border Patrol agents she interviewed.

Multimedia Sources

Soto, Onell R., and Leslie Berestein. "Two Tons of Pot Found inside Mexico U.S. Border Tunnel." *San Diego Union-Tribune*, January 26, 2006. http://archives.signonsandiego.com/uniontrib/20060126/news_7n26 tunnel.html Outlines the event and incorporates interviews with U.S. and Mexican law enforcement agencies. Provides link to video footage, photographs, and maps.

"The Wall." http://thewalldocumentary.com/. Includes extensive video clips and previews of the documentary on the Secure Fence Act created by Ricardo Martinez. Also provides comprehensive background information on the Secure Fence Act and plans for its implementation, media reception, and screening information.

97. "A Day without Immigrants" (The Great American Boycott) National Marches (May 1, 2006)

On May 1, 2006, in over 50 cities across the United States, millions of protestors took to the streets to denounce restrictive U.S. immigration policies and to draw attention to the contributions of an estimated 11 million illegal immigrants working in the United States. Several groups, including the Mexican American Political Association and the Coalition for Humane Immigrant Rights of Los Angeles (CHIRLA), organized what was called the Great American Boycott, better known as "A Day without Immigrants." At the center of these national marches, which were orchestrated to coincide with International Workers' Day, was a recently passed House of Representatives bill, H.R. 4437: The Border Protection, Antiterrorism, and Illegal Immigration Control Act of 2005. The bill, sponsored by Rep. James Sensenbrenner of Wisconsin, called for many provisions that seemed targeted at the Latino community, including the erection of 700 miles of fence line between the United States and Mexico, a reduction in the number of green cards offered annually by the U.S. government, and increased penalties for employing or housing illegal workers. Although the bill never passed in the Senate and was thus never enacted into law, H.R. 4437 fueled the boycott, and demonstrators took to the streets to protest the bill in most major U.S. cities, including Washington, D.C.; Los Angeles; Chicago; New York City; San Francisco; Las Vegas; Atlanta; Denver; Phoenix; and New Orleans. Alongside these nationwide rallies, participants were asked not to attend work or school for the day and to avoiding buying or selling U.S. goods and services of any kind. The goal was to demonstrate the vast and interconnected role that legal and illegal immigrants, particularly those from Latin American countries, play in supporting the U.S. economy. As a result of worker boycotts, several businesses, notably Goya Foods, Tyson Foods, and Cargill Meat Solutions, suspended operations for the day. All told, the Great American Boycott was one of the largest protests in U.S. history and has influenced similar protests, such as the "Day without Gays" boycott of December 10, 2008.

TERM PAPER SUGGESTIONS

1. Examine some of the opinions and views of some of the strike's organizers. Along with attending the rallies instead of work, why did they argue that participants should neither attend schools nor purchase items as a part of the boycott?

2. Supporters and opponents of the strike disagreed on whether the boycott was successful strategy to demonstrate the role that immigrants play in the U.S. economy. Take a position on the effectiveness of this boycott and support your position with specific examples.

3. Examine the HR 4437, the House of Representative's bill that fueled the boycott. What provisions in the bill angered activists? In your

opinion, do elements of the bill seem targeted toward Latino immigrants in particular?

4. Compare rallies and the press coverage given to them in two or more U.S. cities across the country. How did the events differ, for example, in Los Angeles and in New York City? How did the press coverage of the event differ depending on the region?

5. Explain the role that unions played in organizing the publicity for this boycott. What key players made an impact? What funding support did they contribute to the boycott?

6. Research the statements of support or disagreement made by various governors, mayors, and other elected officials in the regions where major rallies were held. How do their statements compare? What suggestions did they have for the strike's participants?

ALTERNATIVE TERM PAPER SUGGESTIONS

1. Create a PowerPoint presentation on the history of International Workers' Day. How does "A Day without Immigrants" compare with other boycotts and political activities that have taken place on this date throughout world history?

2. Write a letter to your Representative in the Senate or the House of Representatives explaining your views on H.R. 4437 and the boycott.

SELECTED SOURCES

Primary Sources

"H.R. 4437 [109th]: Border Protection, Antiterrorism, and Illegal Immigration Control Act of 2005." http://www.govtrack.us/congress/billtext. xpd?bill=h109-4437. This is the full text of the H.R. 4437 bill, as presented to the Senate.

Ouellette, Jeannine. *A Day without Immigrants: Rallying behind America's Newcomers.* Mankato, MN: Compass Point Books, 2008. Ouellette's book is geared toward junior high school students but offers personal testimonies of the marchers, a timeline of events, and images from the marches.

Secondary Sources

Allen, Zita. "Labor's Role: A Day without Immigrants." *New York Amsterdam News*, (May 4, 2006): 1+. http://findarticles.com/p/news-articles/

new-york-amsterdam-news/mi_8153/is_20060504/labors-role-immi-grants/ai_n50592428/Article focuses on the organization drives, funding, and security provided by labor unions before and during the march.

Joyner, Ashley Tusan. "We the People." *New York Amsterdam News* (May 4, 2006): 1+. Offers an overview and interviews with demonstrators in the New York City rally.

Pulido, Laura. "A Day without Immigrants: The Racial and Class Politics of Immigrant Exclusion." *Antipode* 39, no. 1 (Jan. 2007): 1–7. Pulido's article links the Great American Boycott to historical and present-day anti-immigration practices and policies, particularly those geared toward people of color.

Robinson, William. "'Aqui estamos y no nos vamos!' Global Capital and Immigrant Rights." In *Contemporary Readings in Social Problems*, edited by Anna Leon-Guerrero and Kristine M. Zentgraf. Thousand Oaks, CA: Pine Forge Press, 2008, pp. 132–141. Robinson discusses the links between the boycott, migrant workers, and global capitalism.

World Wide Web

Glaister, Dan, and Ewen MacAskill. "U.S. Counts the Cost of a Day without Immigrants." *The Guardian*, May 5, 2006. http://www.guardian.co.uk/world/2006/may/02/usa.topstories3. Offers a comprehensive overview of the rallies along with a frequently asked questions and answers section about the boycott.

Hamilton, Amy. "A Day without Immigrants: Making a Statement." *Time*, May 1, 2006. http://www.time.com/time/nation/article/0,8599,1189899,00.html. Hamilton's report covers many of the basic features of the strike and its impact on the U.S. economy.

"U.S. Immigrants Stage Boycott Day." *BBC News*. http://news.bbc.co.uk/2/hi/americas/4961734.stm. BBC's coverage of the events includes links to charts regarding U.S. immigration and several story links in a section called "U.S. Immigration Debate."

Ydstie, John, and Tejvir Singh. "Some Legal Immigrants Left Out of the Debate." NPR.org, May 2, 2009. http://www.npr.org/templates/story/story.php?storyId=5376038&ps=rs. Discusses the boycott's emphasis on illegal immigration at the expense of legal immigrants. Has links to the radio program featuring this interview as well as other articles centered on the boycott.

Multimedia Sources

A Day without a Mexican. Xenon Films, 2004. 100 minutes. This fictional story was the original inspiration for the national march. The DVD also includes the director's 1998 short film in its special features.

"A Day without Immigrants Music Video." http://www.youtube.com/watch?
  v=kWbyi8Oty2Q. Contains a quality compilation of news broadcasts
  and live marches across the United States.

Kahn, Carrie. "Impact Varies on 'A Day without Immigrants.'" *Morning Edition,* May 2, 2006. 4:22 minutes. http://www.npr.org/templates/player/
  mediaPlayer.html?action=1&t=1&islist=false&id=5376023&m=
  5376024. Covers the events with an emphasis on the perspectives of
  the boycott's participants and detractors.

"Whose America?" *NBC News.* 7:38 minutes. http://www.msnbc.msn.com/id/
  21134540/vp/12581934#12581934. Provides streaming video from
  NBC Nightly News' coverage of the boycott.

98. Secure Fence Act (October 26, 2006)

Widespread concern about unsecured U.S. border checkpoints and
increasing levels of illegal immigration prompted lengthy debates in the
U.S. Congress in the first decade of the 21st century and called for
innovative and realistic solutions. Both Democratic and Republican
Congressional members attempted to strike a balance between enforcing laws while maintaining the integrity of human rights and civil liberties. Despite past efforts to secure the border, illegal crossings have
continued, including drug, human, and arsenal trafficking. Therefore,
in 2006, several leading Republican members of Congress, including
Rep. Pete King of New York and Sen. Bill Frist of Tennessee, authored
a bill that would reinforce the U.S.-Mexico border from the Pacific
Ocean to the Gulf of Mexico by erecting a 700-mile series of physical
and virtual fences that would employ the latest ground and aerial surveillance technology. U.S. President George W. Bush signed this legislation on October 26, 2006, insisting that it would be an effective and
comprehensive response to curtailing illegal border crossings. To expe-
dite the process, the Act mandated that the U.S. Department of Homeland Security would assume operational control of the U.S.-Mexico land
and marine borders, increase border checkpoints and agents, and vastly
increase the U.S. Border Patrol's budget to $10.4 billion. In spite of these
efforts, the U.S. government has encountered opposition from a number
of agencies such as human rights organizations, environmental groups,
neighborhood associations, and business and city officials. Although the
U.S. Department of Homeland Security maintains the Secure Fence Act
has been effective, others have called the act too expensive and an unreal-
istic response to the issue of border security and immigration.

TERM PAPER SUGGESTIONS

1. The Secure Fence Act was a response to illegal immigration through the U.S.-Mexico border. However, this act stirred a great deal of controversy, particularly with U.S. homeowners along the U.S. border. Discuss the broad nature of this controversy and the political, cultural, and environmental impact it had in U.S towns and cities.

2. Critics of the Secure Fence Act have argued that a good portion of the border reinforcing or construction mandated under the act really is not a fence or wall at all. Rather, it is something called "vehicle fencing." Explain what this type of fencing is and whether it has been effective in carrying out the mission of the U.S. Border Patrol.

3. Enacted shortly before the mid-term U.S. Congressional election in 2006, the Secure Fence Act was a response to the complicated illegal immigration issue in U.S. politics. Argue whether the act was simply an impractical and political response to growing concern over the immigration issue impasse in Congress or whether the act was an appropriate and realistic response to concerns of illegal immigration and securing of U.S. borders.

4. Compare the differences between Operation Gatekeeper, which began during the Clinton administration in 1994, and the Secure Fence Act. Determine the success and failures of Operation Gatekeeper and why the Secure Fence Act was established to address border security and illegal immigration.

ALTERNATIVE TERM PAPER SUGGESTIONS

1. Develop an interactive map with hyperlinks that illustrate and highlight the construction of the border wall as mandated under the Secure Fence Act of 2006. Include charts and descriptions to enhance this project.

2. Most Mexican political leaders were strongly opposed to President Bush's signing of the Secure Fence Act in 2006. Take the role of a member of Mexico's Congress, and create a series of podcasts underscoring the climate of political opposition by Mexican leaders.

SUGGESTED SOURCES

Primary Sources

"Bush Signs Mexico Fence into Law." http://news.bbc.co.uk/2/hi/americas/ 6088084.stm. Presents the details of the act and the reaction by groups within the United States and Mexico.

"H.R. 6061." http://www.biologicaldiversity.org/swcbd/PROGRAMS/blbw/ secure-fence-act.pdf. Contains the actual congressional document of the Secure Fence Act.

"Library of Congress: Thomas." http://thomas.loc.gov/cgi-bin/bdquery/ z?d109:h6061: Archives the language of the bill and congressional members who wrote it. Includes links to relevant legislative information.

Secondary Sources

"Border Fence? Bring It On, West Texas City Says." http://www.chron.com/ disp/story.mpl/special/immigration/5877438.html. Focuses on the City of Del Rio, Texas, and the city council's unanimous decision to sell 70 acres of its border land to the U.S. Department of Homeland Security for $1.2 million.

"Border Security: Barriers along the U.S. International Border." http:// bibdaily.com/pdfs/CRS_border_fence_june2007.pdf. Lengthy report commissioned by the U.S. Congress suggests the walls erected under the Secure Fence Act are not curtailing the flow of illegal immigration coming in from Mexico.

Wood, Daniel B. "Where U.S.-Mexico Border Fence Is Tall, Border Crossings Fall." *Christian Science Monitor*, April 1, 2008. http://www.csmonitor. com/USA/2008/0401/p01s05-usgn.html?page=2. Investigates the impact the new border methods have on illegal immigration as a result of the Secure Fence Act mandates.

World Wide Web

"2006 Secure Fence Act." http://library.uwb.edu/guides/USimmigration/ 2006_secure_fence_act.html. Summarizes the act and contains several useful links for further research on this piece of legislation.

"No Border Wall." http://www.notexasborderwall.com/. Grassroots organization provides a critique of the Border Fence Act and the political, economic, and environmental repercussions of its implementation.

"Fact Sheet: The Secure Fence Act of 2006." http://georgewbush-whitehouse.
archives.gov/news/releases/2006/10/20061026-1.html. Provides official
White House report on the Bush administration's comprehensive plan
to enact a progressive policy toward illegal immigration across the
U.S.-Mexico border.

"The Hard Truth: U.S./Mexican Border Fence Project Incomplete." http://
bkl1.wordpress.com/2009/01/26/us-mexican-border-fence-project-
incomplete/. Analyzes the type of fencing construction taking place
under the Secure Fence Act and explores the policy's shortcomings.

"Our Border, Our Future." http://www.texasbordercoalition.org/index.php?
option=com_content&task=view&id=25&Itemid=41. The Texas Border Coalition's comprehensive plan to re-secure the border and reform
past congressional acts that have attempted to address the issue of U.S.
border security but have failed, in the Coalition's opinion.

Multimedia Sources

"Secure Fence Act Signing." http://www.c-spanvideo.org/program/195124-1.
Covers U.S. President George W. Bush's signing the act in 2006.

"The Wall." http://thewalldocumentary.com/. Includes extensive video clips
and previews of the documentary on the Secure Fence Act created by
Ricardo Martinez. Also provides comprehensive background information on the Secure Fence Act and plans for its implementation, media
reception, and screening information.

99. Postville Raid (May 12, 2008)

On May 12, 2008, nearly 1,000 Immigration and Customs Enforcement
(ICE) officers surrounded Agriprocessors, Inc., a kosher meatpacking
plant in Postville, Iowa, generating one of the largest immigration raids
in U.S. history. That day, nearly 700 of Agriprocessors' workers were
arrested, and 389 were detained for U.S. immigration law violations and
identity theft (for using stolen social security numbers on the I-9
employment forms). Later that summer, two of Agriprocessors' supervi-
sors were also charged with fraud and aggravated identity theft for aiding
and abetting the corporation's hiring of undocumented workers. Concerns were also raised about the age of undocumented workers employed
at the plant, and later interviews revealed that some workers were in their
early teens. The arrests had a tremendous impact on Postville's Latino
community, who comprised 99 percent of those detained for illegal

immigration, with 75 percent of detainees coming from Guatemala and 24 percent from Mexico. Detainees were taken to the National Cattle Congress, a local fairground site, in Waterloo, Iowa, where 300 trials were held over the next four days; in almost all of those 300 trials, the defendants agreed to a guilty plea agreement, and concerns were raised about whether such speedy trials allowed for appropriate due process. The raid also had a significant impact on Postville, a town of fewer than 2,500 residents, many of whom were employed by Agriprocessors. A significant portion of the town's population was arrested, detained, and deported. Eventually, the deportation of such a large portion of Postville's population led to school closures and, in November 2008, the closing of the Agriprocessors' plant when the corporation filed for bankruptcy. Although larger ICE searches have followed, the Postville Raid is notable for its impact on a small-town rural Latino community and for applying identity theft law against undocumented workers for the first time.

TERM PAPER SUGGESTIONS

1. Examine the raid on Agriprocessors and its impact on Postville. How did the raid, detention, and deportation of the plant's workers change the town? What was the raid's effect on the area's Latino communities? What similar ICE operations have occurred in the United States since this 2008 raid?

2. Review the U.S.'s Illegal Immigration Reform and Immigrant Responsibility Act of 1996. How does this act provide the legal basis for the raid? What provisions in the act allow ICE to detain and deport plant workers? What impact does this law have on Latino families with small children, born in the United States or born elsewhere?

3. One of the large debates surrounding the raid involved the use of statutes against aggravated identity theft, for using falsified social security numbers on employment forms. Examine Agriprocessors' hiring practices that led to this raid and analyze the corporation's role in these identity theft cases. In this case, should charges of identity theft have been used against workers or the corporation or both parties?

4. Critics have debated whether raids such as Postville are effective in providing a deterrent to illegal immigration and undocumented

employment or whether raids such as these are ineffective, destructive, and costly. Research both sides of this issue and take a position.

ALTERNATIVE TERM PAPER SUGGESTIONS

1. Create an iMovie account of the Postville Raid using video footage, photos, and interviews with key participants. Be sure to discuss the raid and its impact on Postville and Latino communities in similar areas.

2. Research the emerging populations of Latinos working and living in the Midwest, particularly in meat packing towns such as Postville, and prepare a PowerPoint presentation on this topic. Be sure to discuss the reasons why Latinos are moving to these regions and the socioeconomic and cultural transformations taking place as a result.

SUGGESTED SOURCES

Primary Sources

Camayd-Freixas, Erik. "Interpreting after the Largest ICE Raid in U.S. History." In *Behind Bars: Latino/as and Prison in the United States*, edited by Suzanne Oboler. New York: Macmillan, 2009, pp. 159–174. Camayd-Freixas' personal account of his two weeks in Postville serving as an interpreter for ICE detainees recounts the human rights' violations he witnessed and the problems with the ICE deportation procedures.

Duara, Nigel, William Petroski, and Grant Schulte. "Claims of ID Fraud Lead to Largest Raid in State History." *Des Moines Register*, May 12, 2008. http://www.desmoinesregister.com/apps/pbcs.dll/article?AID=/20080512/ NEWS/80512012/1001. Local coverage features interviews with residents, ICE officials, as well as photos and maps of the raid.

Hsu, Spenser S. "Immigration Raid Jars a Small Town." *The Washington Post*, May 18, 2008. http://www.washingtonpost.com/wp-dyn/content/article/ 2008/05/17/AR2008051702474.html. Coverage includes interviews with Iowa's congressional representatives, Postville local leaders, as well as facts and photos of the raid.

Secondary Sources

Camayd-Freixas, Erik. "The Day Democracy Died: The Postville Raid and the Criminalization of Migrants." http://www.clintonfranciscans.com/

Camayd-Freixas%20-%20New%20Essay%20(2).pdf. Analyzes U.S. immigration policies and their relationship to the ICE raid in Postville.

Grey, Mark, Michael Devlin, and Aaron Goldsmith. *Postville: USA: Surviving Diversity in Small-Town America*. Boston: Gemmanmedia, 2009. Discusses Postville's Latino population and the raid's socioeconomic and cultural consequences for Postville.

Martinez, Virginia, Jazmin Garcia, and Jasmine Vasquez. "A Community under Siege: The Impact of Anti-Immigrant Hysteria on Latinos." *DePaul Journal for Social Justice* 2, no. 1 (Fall 2008): 101–141. Contends that failed immigration reform policies have led to increased hostility toward Latinos and increased racial profiling of both legal-status and undocumented Latinos.

Moyers, Peter R. "Butchering Statutes: The Postville Raid and the Misinterpretation of Federal Criminal Law." *Seattle University Law Review* 32 (2008–2009): 651–674. Argues that the ICE misused legal statutes on aggravated identity theft and judicial removal in their legal cases against undocumented Agriprocessors' workers.

Sioban, Albiol., R. Linus Chan, and Sarah J. Diaz. "Re-Interpreting Postville: A Legal Pespective." *DePaul Journal for Social Justice* 2, no. 1 (Fall 2008): 31–64. Examines the constitutionality and human rights violations of the raid, ICE detention centers, and the legal proceedings that followed.

World Wide Web

"297 Convicted and Sentenced following ICE Worksite Operation in Iowa." *U.S. Immigration and Customs Enforcement*, May 15, 2008. http://www.ice.gov/pi/news/newsreleases/articles/080515waterloo.htm. ICE's report about the raid contains facts and statistics about the charges brought against Agriprocessors and its workers.

Artz, Georgeanne M., Rebecca Jackson, and Peter F. Orazem. "Is It a Jungle Out There?: Meat Packing, Immigrants and Rural Communities." http://econ2.econ.iastate.edu/research/webpapers/paper_12966_08024.pdf. Examines the growing role played by Latino labor in Midwest meatpacking plants and the socioeconomic impact of Latino migration to small rural towns.

Murguía, Janet. "The Implications of Immigration Enforcement on America's Children." *National Council of La Raza*, May 20, 2008. http://www.nclr.org/content/publications/download/52035. Contains transcript of Murguía's speech on behalf of National Council of La Raza regarding INS raids such as Agriprocessors and its impact on infants and young children.

Preston, Julia. "Immigrant Speedy Trials after Raid Become Issue." *The New York Times*, August 8, 2008. http://www.nytimes.com/2008/08/09/us/09immig.html?em. Discusses the controversy surrounding the 300 ICE trials held in just 4 days.

Schulte, Grant, Jennifer Jacobs, and Jared Strong. "Town of 2,273 Wonders: What Happens to Us Now?" *Des Moines Register*, May 14, 2008. http://www.desmoinesregister.com/apps/pbcs.dll/article?AID=/20080514/NEWS/805140371/-1/SPORTS09. Interviews residents about the raid and its consequences for Postville.

Multimedia Sources

"abUSed: The Postville Raid." 2009. http://abusedthepostvilleraid.com/. Contains photos and streaming video to two documentaries about the raid and its aftermath.

Belay, Tim. "Immigration Raid Leaves Mark on Iowa Town." National Public Radio, June 9, 2008. 4:30 minutes. http://www.npr.org/templates/player/mediaPlayer.html?action=1&t=1&islist=false&id=91327136&m=91328901. Radio program offers details about the raid and interviews residents of Postville.

"Immigration Raid Scars Iowa Town." National Public Radio, May 18, 2009. 10:04 minutes. http://www.npr.org/templates/player/mediaPlayer.html?action=1&t=1&islist=false&id=104240854&m=104240847. Radio interview with Postville minister Gary Catterson discusses the impact on Postville's economy and community one year later.

"In the Shadows of the Raid." http://streetdogmedia.wordpress.com/. Provides links to trailers, interviews, and information about the full-length feature documentary about the Agriprocessors workers deported to Guatemala after the ICE raid.

"In the Shadow of the Raid." CBC Radio. 9:01 minutes. http://www.cbc.ca/dispatches/thisseason/index.html. Radio interview with Greg Brosnan discusses his film about the May 12, 2008, raid.

100. Sonia Sotomayor Becomes the First Latina U.S. Supreme Court Justice (2009)

On May 26, 2009, Sonia Maria Sotomayor made history when President Barrack Obama nominated her to replace retiring Justice David

Souter on the United States Supreme Court. Prior to her nomination, Sotomayor, a graduate of Princeton University and Yale Law School, had a distinguished and varied career in the U.S. legal system, serving as an assistant district attorney in New York, a private practice lawyer, a commercial litigation attorney, a U.S. District Court of Appeals Judge, and a U.S Court of Appeals Justice for the Second District. Similar to her rise in the U.S. justice system, Sotomayor's early life is often considered a rags-to-riches example of the American Dream in action. Born in 1954 to Puerto Rican parents with limited English skills, Sotomayor was raised in housing projects in The Bronx, New York. When Sotomayor was eight, she was diagnosed with diabetes; at age nine, her father died, leaving her mother to raise Sotomayor and her younger brother alone. Yet, Sotomayor's dedication to her education led to a full scholarship to Princeton, where she majored in history and graduated summa cum laude before entering Yale Law School in 1976. Throughout law school and in her formidable career thereafter, Sotomayor has been an active voice for increased Latino presence in the U.S. judicial system and has written about the need for a greater Latino presence in law schools, courtrooms, and the judiciary. These remarks, particularly her claims that "a wise Latina" could offer a perspective on the law unavailable to a European American justice, became a source of controversy during her Senate confirmation hearings. On August 6, 2009, the Senate confirmed Sotomayor, 69–31, making her the first Latina U.S. Supreme Court Justice in U.S. history, as well as only the third woman and the third person of color ever to serve on the Supreme Court.

TERM PAPER SUGGESTIONS

1. Examine Justice Sonia Sotomayor's qualifications for the U.S. Supreme Court. What types of judicial and legal positions has she held in her career? What publications has she written? How have her varied roles within the U.S. judicial system made her uniquely qualified among jurists for the U.S. Supreme Court?

2. Explain the significance of Sotomayor's confirmation as the first Latina on the U.S. Supreme Court. How has Sotomayor served as a role model and mentor for Latinos in the U.S. legal system prior to her confirmation? How does her presence on the highest court impact Latinos and women of color?

3. Law scholars often refer to Sotomayor's judicial philosophy as legal realism (as opposed to legal formalism). Define and describe Sotomayor's judicial philosophy using key rulings Sotomayor made prior to becoming a Supreme Court justice. What, if any, connections exist between her judicial decisions and her experiences as a Latina?

4. Examine Sotomayor's controversial 2001 speech about the need for a "wise Latina" in the U.S. judicial system (see following primary source for link). Why was this statement such a controversial one during her confirmation hearings? What public statements has Sotomayor made to explain and defend this comment? Do you agree with Sotomayor's arguments on Latina court representation?

ALTERNATIVE TERM PAPER SUGGESTIONS

1. Create a Webography for Justice Sonia Sotomayor. In your Webography, include her childhood, education, and varied positions in the U.S. judicial system. Be sure also to include links to her most famous rulings and her legal scholarship.

2. Design an interactive timeline detailing the significant role Latinos have played in U.S law. In your timeline, include summaries and links to important Latino court cases, Latino law organizations (such as The Mexican American Legal Defense and Educational Fund (MALDEF) and The League of United Latin American Citizens (LULAC)), and Latino citizens who, along with Sotomayor, have demonstrated the vital presence of Latinos in the U.S. legal system.

SUGGESTED SOURCES

Primary Sources

"Judge Sonia Sotomayor Confirmation Process." http://www.c-span.org/Supreme-Court-Sotomayor-Senate-Confirmation-Hearings.aspx. Includes streaming video footage of Sotomayor's Senate confirmation hearings.

Sotomayor, Sonia. "A Latina Judge's Voice." *Berkeley La Raza Law Journal* 13, no. 1 (Spring 2002): 87–93. http://berkeley.edu/news/media/releases/2009/05/26_sotomayor.shtml. Contains Sotomayor's 2001 speech on the importance of a "wise Latina" voice in the U.S. justice system.

Secondary Sources

Bishop, Eric. "The Sonia Sotomayor Case File: A Pundit's Primer." *Esquire*, May 27, 2009. http://www.esquire.com/the-side/feature/sonia-sotomayor-judicial-philosophy-052709. Reviews six of Sotomayor's most important appellate court rulings.

Johnson, Kevin R. "On the Appointment of a Latina/o to the Supreme Court." *Harvard Latino Law Review* 5 (Spring 2002): 1–16. Focuses on the reasons a Latina/o Supreme Court justice would benefit the United States and its lawmaking.

Moreira-Smith, Zorayda, "The Right Thing to Do, The Right Time to Do It, and the Right Place: A Latina/o United States Supreme Court Justice." May 2009. http://www.chci.org/doclib/2009817129391502-Lawand InternationalAffairswhitepages.pdf?trail=201015194350. Moreira-Smith's White Page for the Congressional Hispanic Caucus Institute argues that a Latina/o judge on the court would contribute a much-needed Hispanic perspective, much the way Thurgood Marshall's appointment was for African Americans.

"Raising the Bar: Latino and Latina Presence in the Judiciary and the Struggle for Representation." *Berkeley La Raza Law Journal*. 13, no. 1 (Spring 2002). Symposium issue offers 16 articles on the role of Latinos in the U.S. courts, including one written by Sonia Sotomayor.

World Wide Web

Balz, Dan. "Republicans Walk Fine Line Questioning Sotomayor." *The Washington Post.*, July 14, 2009. http://www.washingtonpost.com/wp-dyn/content/article/2009/07/13/AR2009071303215.html?sid=ST2009071202351. Discusses this issue of race in Sotomayor's confirmation process.

Bazelon, Emily. "The Place of Women on the Court." *NewYorkTimes.com*, July 7, 2009. http://www.nytimes.com/2009/07/12/magazine/12ginsburg-t.html. Interview with Supreme Court Justice Ruth Bader Ginsburg discusses Sotomayor's confirmation and the role women justices play in the U.S. legal system.

Dorf, Michael C. "What Is Sonia Sotomayor's Judicial Philosophy?" *FindLaw.Com*, June 3, 2009. http://writ.news.findlaw.com/dorf/20090603.html. Defines and explains Sotomayor's "legal realist" approach to the law.

Nicholas, Peter, and James Oliphant. "Two Sides to Sonia Sotomayor." *Los Angeles Times.Com*, May 31, 2009. http://articles.latimes.com/2009/may/31/nation/na-sotomayor-profile31. Discusses Sotomayor's law school and early work experiences with racial discrimination.

Nichols, John. "The Nation: The New Justice." National Public Radio, Aug. 7, 2009. http://www.npr.org/templates/story/story.php?storyId= 111648669. Examines Sotomayor's confirmation and its historic connections to those of Thurgood Marshall and Sandra Day O'Connor.

"Sonia Sotomayor Topics Page." http://topics.nytimes.com/top/reference/times topics/people/s/sonia_sotomayor/index.html. Provides links to articles about Sonia Sotomayor originally published in the *New York Times*.

The White House Office of the Press Secretary. "Justice Sonia Sotomayor," May 26, 2009. http://www.whitehouse.gov/the_press_office/Background-on-Judge-Sonia-Sotomayor/. Contains the White House's official press release on Sotomayor.

Multimedia Sources

"President Obama Comments on Sotomayor Confirmation." 3:03 minutes. http://www.youtube.com/watch?v=B8erBibSsfI&feature=related. Features President Barrack Obama's press conference following Sotomayor's confirmation.

"Sotomayor on 'Wise Latina' Comment." 0:58 minutes. http://www.youtube.com/watch?v=7ZAds-jEMxY. Sotomayor explains the phrase that became a controversial topic in her confirmation process.

"Sotomayor Refuses to Renounce 'Wise Latina' Word." 2:44 minutes. http://www.youtube.com/watch?v=I-zg0FduCRE. Associated Press' television coverage features Sotomayor's defense of her 2001 speech.

"Sotomayor Sworn in as Supreme Court Justice." *The Washington Post*. http://www.washingtonpost.com/wp-dyn/content/gallery/2009/07/13/GA2009071301 792.html?sid=ST2009071202351. Photo gallery contains over 50 photos of Sotomayor throughout the nomination and confirmation process.

"Swearing in Justice Sonia Sotomayor." 2:39 minutes. http://www.youtube.com/watch?v=032K9yzRevA&NR=1. Contains CSPN's August 8, 2009, coverage of Sotomayor's oath of office.

"Testimony of Rep. Velazquez at Judge Sotomayor's Confirmation Hearings." 7:03 minutes. http://www.youtube.com/watch?v=kOpjuR39Xis. Features July 16, 2009, testimony of Congresswoman Nydia Velazquez, who chairs the Congressional Hispanic Caucus.

Index

About the Authors

MICHAEL P. MORENO, Ph.D., is Associate Professor of English and Ethnic Studies at Green River Community College in Auburn, Washington. A contributor to a number of literary collections, journals, and reference texts, his areas of scholarship include Latino/a literature, ethnic studies, and spatial theory.

KRISTIN C. BRUNNEMER, Ph.D., is Associate Professor of English and Film at Pierce College in Lakewood, Washington. The author of several articles, her areas of interest include film and visual culture, comparative minority discourses, contemporary fiction, and popular culture.